NOT DUMB, NOT BLONDE

DOLLY IN CONVERSATION

NOT DUMB, NOT BLONDE

DOLLY IN CONVERSATION

EDITED BY
RANDY L. SCHMIDT

OMNIBUS PRESS

London / New York / Paris / Sydney / Copenhagen / Berlin / Madrid / Tokyo

In loving memory
Margie L. Berry
(1919–1994)

Gentle as the sweet magnolia
Strong as steel, her faith and pride
She's an everlasting shoulder
She's the leaning post of life

CONTENTS

Part III • City of Schemes

Part IV • Toast of Dollywood

Part V • Steel Magnolia

Part VI • CEO of Dreams

INTRODUCTION

In 2016, Dolly Parton turned seventy years old. At an age by which many artists have long been retired, she shows no signs of slowing down. In fact, Dolly is still one of the busiest entertainers in show business. Having first gained recognition as a singer-songwriter, she became country music's most honored female performer of all time, as well as a celebrated actress, bestselling author, Broadway composer, and humanitarian. Today, Dolly is a living legend, a national treasure, and still every bit the superstar that she was at any pinnacle in her illustrious career.

As a businesswoman, Dolly manages a multimillion-dollar empire reaching far beyond her musical roots. There's Dollywood, the popular theme park near her hometown in the Great Smoky Mountains, as well as the Splash Country water park, DreamMore Resort, and several restaurant chains, including the Dixie Stampede and Lumberjack Adventure. But Dolly's favorite of her many endeavors is the Imagination Library, a program providing free books to children all over the world.

NBC-TV's telecast of *Dolly Parton's Coat of Many Colors* on December 10, 2015, brought Dolly's childhood story to the small screen in a very big way. It captured the attention of 15.9 million viewers, making it the most-watched film on broadcast or cable television in nearly seven years. The film was such a success that a sequel, *Dolly Parton's Christmas of Many Colors: Circle of Love*, was ordered and began filming during the summer of 2016. Dolly made a cameo appearing as the trashy town trollop she says inspired her gaudy look.

Instead of relaxing and taking time off during her "golden years," Dolly is full steam ahead into her next ventures. She announced in March 2016 that she would embark upon her biggest North American concert tour in more than twenty-five years. Before it's over, the acoustic-style Pure & Simple tour will play more than sixty dates around the United States and Canada and usher in the release of *Pure & Simple*, her forty-third studio album. At the end of May, Dolly's tour paused just long enough for her and husband Carl Dean to celebrate their golden anniversary with a private vow renewal ceremony. With her datebook bursting at the seams, retirement is nowhere in Dolly's vocabulary. "Why would I ever do that?" she exclaimed in an August 2016 interview for *Digital Spy*. "That word doesn't register with me. I cannot possibly imagine retiring. What would I retire to? [...] I'm going to be productive, positive and work as long as I can."

"*Nobody* knows Dolly like Dolly." By 1978, the country queen had crossed over to become a sensation in the pop music world when she sat with *Star* magazine's John Latta to take verbal inventory of her new status as international superstar. "I'm still the same person," she said, "but I'm happier now and I feel even more confident that I can accomplish the things I've dreamed of doing. . . . I've always planned to achieve total musical freedom for myself, and that's where I'm headed."

Dolly Parton had left *The Porter Wagoner Show* in 1974 after seven years of recording sessions, television tapings, and touring alongside Wagoner, who'd been her duet partner, mentor, and Svengali. "What I've always wanted [is] to be a singing star with my *own* show," she told journalist Dave Hickey in *Country Music* magazine that same year. Hickey noticed a sparkle in her voice. "When Dolly says *star* it's like you've never heard the word before," he observed. "The idea has so much force for her, and its meaning is so obviously clear. . . . When she uses the word *star*, you know that, to her, it isn't just a fantasy or a vague term denoting success. It's what she's going to be . . . *will* be . . . is."

Dolly and Wagoner maintained an amicable business relationship for the next two years, but the two severed ties completely in 1976. That's when she broke free and began to put into place an extensive revamp of her image and music, one that would reach broad and new audiences, far beyond the field of country music. Backlash from some unhappy country fans led Dolly to repeatedly have to explain her makeover. "I'm not leavin' country music," she'd say, "I'm takin' it with me!"

It was a time of musical, physical, and spiritual metamorphosis for Dolly, who was a self-proclaimed butterfly in spirit. "Butterflies remind me of myself," she told the press, explaining why she'd chosen them as her insignia. "They don't bother anybody, they just go about their business, gentle but determined." In 1975, a gentle Dolly had been easily upset by cruel and humiliating jokes about her voluptuous figure. "It embarrasses me and it hurts my feelings," she said. But by 1977, a determined Dolly emerged. A new Dolly. One that seemed almost at ease bantering with Johnny Carson when he inquired about her "zaftig" on *The Tonight Show*:

Carson: What would they call that where you grew up in Tennessee?

Dolly: I can't say!

Carson: Healthy?

Dolly: Healthy, I guess . . . bosomy. Well, I've always been pretty well blessed. People are always askin' if they're real and this and that.

Carson: Oh, I would *never* . . . I would *never*, you see!

Dolly: No, you don't have to ask.

Carson: I would *never*.

Dolly: I'll tell you what . . . these are *mine*.

Carson: I have certain guidelines on my show . . . but I would give about a year's pay to peek under there!

"It used to kind of embarrass me because I didn't know quite how to take it," she told biographer Alanna Nash, "but anymore I just kinda play along with it myself, and come up with some funny things. There's no way to hide it, you know. That's something you're gonna have to accept."

With this newfound, carefree confidence, an image was born . . . a character . . . a façade . . . a persona. Even Dolly has compared herself to a cartoon. "I look one way and am another," she told Cliff Jahr in *Ladies' Home Journal* (an article that appears within this book). "It makes for a good combination. I always think of 'her,' the Dolly image, like a ventriloquist does his dummy. I have fun with it. I think, what will I do with *her* this year to surprise people? What'll *she* wear? What'll *she* say?"

Harry Wasserman, a writer for *High Times*, shared his comical take (or was he serious?) on the "Dolly" image in the August 1977 issue:

> Dolly Parton is a Deep South truck driver's dream. Her snapshot is taped to his windshield and her songs are on his radio. She's his daughter, her little-girl voice singing of her dirt-poor childhood in the mountains of Tennessee. She's his mother, her voluminous breasts overflowing with the milk of human kindness. She's his wife, singing songs of everlasting devotion to her one and only man. She's his mistress and his whore, all dolled up in a cascading platinum wig, flirtatious false eyelashes and come-hither painted lips, waiting breathlessly for a wild night on the town. But most of all she's his truck. When he tools down the highway and pops his clutch he's dreaming of Dolly's big rig, her chassis, her headlights and her chrome. Her voice can purr softer than his engine or blare as honkie as his horn.

It's no wonder that the image became such a burden for Dolly at times that she considered abandoning it altogether for a different guise. "I might throw the wigs away tomorrow, next month, next year," she told *Star*. "Maybe never. If I feel the need to, I might do something drastic when I'm ready to shock the people again. . . . It's unfair to keep a person bound to an image. It's time to look inside the hour-and-a-half-glass figure and the hair, to look at the music and the talent. I deliberately chose this appearance so that the image could sell the talent, and the talent would sell the image. But the talent was always more important and should take over now."

It's safe to say that Dolly never threw out her wigs. In fact, when she's asked how many wigs she owns now, the answer is always the same: "Oh, I have at least 365 . . . one for each day of the year!" Instead of shedding the image, or even toning it down some, Dolly embraced it and nurtured it until it became a full-fledged character. "A character never grows old," she told Alanna Nash. "A character lives forever, just like Mae West, like Zsa Zsa Gabor. Liberace. I guess I *am* a character only because I'm just totally what I am. I'm not afraid to be that and say what I want to, and just do what I want to."

Not only did she keep the wigs, Dolly has worked meticulously and tirelessly to hone and refine just about every aspect of her character and public image. In fact, her strict control over visual image is rivaled only by her strict control over how she's portrayed in the media. Since the late 1970s, Dolly has been a favorite cover girl for women's interest magazines, country music weeklies, and, of course, the tabloids. She even refers to herself the "queen of the tabloids," and has joked that she once considered suing them for printing lies about her in the *middle* of the magazine instead of on the cover. "Let's put it this way," she told journalist Joel McNally in 1994, "I'd just as soon never be in [the tabloids], but I am in 'em, and it doesn't bother me. Like I say, I kinda like bein' the queen of pretty much anything. But I am one of those white trash kind of people. I'm fun to write about. So I leave myself kinda open for that particular kind of reader."

To follow the course of Dolly's evolution in the press is to witness a slow and steady development of media manipulation, all masterminded by her and her associates. In some of her earliest conversations with the press, Dolly came across as a bit naïve and unsophisticated. Before Porter Wagoner, she was reserved and serious when answering questions for reporters, seldom elaborating or making jokes. Following Wagoner's lead, Dolly grew more comfortable with the interview process.

Once on her own, Dolly was more talkative than ever. Her self-awareness and self-deprecation came into play, and she quickly became a more detailed and dynamic storyteller. But there was also an air of mystery about her. And she wanted to keep it that way. "I guess I *am* mysterious, because there are so many things that I don't tell," she said to Alanna Nash. "But I don't want to. I mean, I'm sure everybody has lots of things that they do that they don't want people to know they do, or things they feel that they wouldn't want to say for fear somebody'd think they're perverted or crazy or somethin'. But you still feel 'em just the same."

This baffled and confused many of the writers assigned to follow Dolly around and somehow get to the bottom of the mystery. Following a four-hour interview in Hollywood, journalist Martha Hume said, "I'm not sure I know much more about Dolly Parton than I did before I met her. Such an air of fantasy surrounds this shimmery-voiced singer that I still find myself wondering whether Dolly herself is a fantasy." But as Dolly unabashedly told Hume, "Nobody could ever know all of me. I don't. I'm even fascinatin' to myself. I'm mysterious to myself because I often do things that I wouldn't have thought the day before I would do. But that's good—I don't get bored with myself. . . . I just have my own rooms in my mind where I don't want nobody else to go. . . . I go there to find peace of mind even in a crowd. Most people want to tell it all. I don't want to tell it all 'cause if you know it all, then I wouldn't be fascinatin' at all to you. There would be no mystery about me. All those crazy stories that you hear—that my husband don't really exist, that that's just a cover for an unnatural relationship with somebody else—that's just because I don't share my private life. There's just so much you should share."

Noel Coppage of *Stereo Review* instructed his readers to learn to read between the lines if they wanted to get any insight into Dolly's "carefully controlled interviews." He went on to explain: "She can seem to answer a question without really answering and end up with God on her side and the interviewer backing off." Others agreed: "The woman could charm the pants off a barnyard hog!" exclaimed Michael Musto of the *Village Voice*. "But go into unwanted territory and she'll smilingly brush you off and invite you to get in touch with her again, anytime! (Or try to.)"

By the end of the 1970s, Dolly had joined forces with manager Sandy Gallin and the image factory was working overtime, almost to the point of oversaturation. "I think you *can* overdo it, especially somebody as weird as me and, you know, outrageous and all," she told radio personality Chuck Brinkman in 1977. "You've seen me once, you've seen me. I'm like Brylcreem . . . a little dab'll do ya! But I don't like to be overexposed. I think exposure is good, I just think you have to choose the things you do as far as publicity . . . your articles, your cover stories of magazines, and TV. And I think my management is real smart. At the time that people are just about to get sick of me, they take me off the market for a little while. So I leave that up to them."

It didn't take long for the press to notice a pattern emerging in Dolly's interviews. The anecdotes and wisecracks that garnered the most laughs from audiences or reporters were frequently retold and often-times embellished to make for an even grander story the next go-round. She told the same stories so many times that a number of journalists became aggravated when their "exclusive" with Dolly turned out to read just like that of a colleague's. "She's got like 20 lines that she just keeps trotting out every so often, and it's very calculated," Dave Hirshey of the *New York Daily News* explained in 1978. "Occasionally she'll slip and give you something different, but rarely. Like Rodney Dangerfield has 100 rehearsed bits. She even has a rehearsed giggle. Everything is recycled. But she didn't give me the same anecdotes that she gave *The New York Times*. She knows the market."

With this phenomenon came the birth of the Dollyism. Dollyisms are clever and cutesy one-liners or witty phrases and quotes that Dolly has practiced and perfected for more than four decades now. Topics range from her career, diet tips, and love life, to makeup, wigs, and her famous womanly assets. Dollyisms have been the basis for numerous articles, a commonly used social media hashtag, and even entire books, namely *The Quotable Dolly* and *Pocket Dolly Wisdom*. Here are a few:

- "It costs a lot of money to look this cheap!"
- "I'm not offended by all the dumb blonde jokes because I know I'm not dumb. And I'm not blonde either."
- "I count my blessings far more than I count my money."
- "If I see something sagging, dragging, or bagging, I'm going to have it sucked, tucked, or plucked."
- "The way I see it, if you want the rainbow, you gotta put up with the rain."

- "I'm not running for president because we've had enough boobs in the White House."
- "I was the first woman to burn my bra. It took the fire department four days to put it out!"
- "Don't get so busy making a living that you forget to make a life."
- "I look just like the girl next door . . . if you happen to live next door to an amusement park."
- "Now people are always asking me, 'What do you want people to say about you one hundred years from now?' I always say I want them to say, 'Dang, don't she still look good for her age.'"

Dolly used her Dollyisms sparingly in the early years. They were simply fun ornamentations to her conversations with the press. Over time, though, they grew to become the foundations for many conversations with her, and in recent years (with a few rare exceptions), most of Dolly's interviews have been "Best Of" collections of Dollyisms. Employing these go-to phrases seems to have made it easier for Dolly to control her interviews, especially when it comes to tough questions. A well-placed Dollyism has been known to divert a conversation and sometimes get her out of a jam. In fact, interviewers can be so delightfully distracted that they're unaware of a sidestep.

Dolly: My Life and Other Unfinished Business, the autobiography, was published in 1994 to much acclaim and spent more than two months of the *New York Times* bestseller list. Writing it took more than three years, but Dolly was never fully invested in the project, admitting she only did it for the money. "How can you write your own story when you ain't lived it?" she said on a 1998 episode of *CMT Showcase*. "But it's there. Just like all this other cheap stuff. I did it for money! Are you happy now? [. . .] I've almost, in many ways, regretted that I wrote this book, to be honest. I've never said that before, but it's almost like once people know that much about [me], I'd rather tell it and live it and show it, and do it like we do in interviews and have people really hear it come from me."

Dolly on Dolly: Interviews and Encounters with Dolly Parton collects and presents some of her most important interviews from the past five decades. Selections appear in chronological order and are arranged into six sections: part I opens with a new transcription of an extraordinarily rare 1967 *Music City News* interview, then covers the Porter Wagoner years; part II includes material from Dolly's crossover period (1977–1979) and features landmark interviews for *Rolling Stone* and *Playboy*; part III includes the 1980 *Rolling Stone* cover story and embraces Dolly's work in the films *9 to 5* and *The Best Little Whorehouse in Texas*; part IV contains material from the mid- to late-1980s, including an interview conducted by pop artist Andy Warhol, as well as coverage of the launch of her Dollywood theme park; part V begins with a piece on the making of the film *Steel Magnolias* and continues through the end of the 1990s; and part VI incorporates varied pieces from 2002 through 2015.

With rare exception, I have chosen to keep these articles and interviews complete, intact, and uninterrupted. Interview transcriptions new to this volume were personally transcribed with only minor editing for clarity. It was also important for me to see that Dolly's voice was kept alive on the printed page, so I have made no attempt to "clean up" or correct any of her grammar gaffes. In my opinion, those touches are an integral part of her spoken charm. In an effort to more smoothly adapt spoken word into print, I have omitted excessive uses of "um" and "uh," repeated words, and similarly unnecessary utterings by Dolly and those who interviewed her. More substantial omissions are indicated with ellipses in brackets, while ellipses without brackets indicate hesitations or pauses. Intentional stylized capitalization, creative wordplay, and other trendy literary devices used by various authors remain intact. Simple misspellings (especially names of well-known individuals, titles of films and songs, etc.) have been silently corrected, while other editor's notes within a piece are indicated with brackets. The brief "Dolly Diamonds" excerpts presented in-between entries have been selected from interesting and important pieces not included here in their entirety.

I would like to take this opportunity to acknowledge a number of individuals who provided support at various stages throughout this project. Thanks to Amy Aboumoussa, Laura Adam, Mark Bego, Cindy Breeding, Chuck Brinkman, Walter Briski, Jr., Amie Cleaver, Peter Dawe,

Bill DeMain, Ralph Emery, Diana Falheim, Bonnie Franz, Doyle Gilliam, Kyle Grainger, Allan Hall, Landon Harless, Sam Irvin, Richard Tyler Jordan, Andrew Justice, Jeremy Kinser, Gary Lane, Larry Lane, Harry Langdon, Beverly Lee, Mark McCarty, Chris Middleton, Michael Musto, Patric Parkey, Stella Parton, Bobby Rivers, Tom Santopietro, Dennis Shears, Joe Skelly, Barry Tamburin, J. Randy Taraborelli, Chris Tassin, Annelle Tubb, Chuck Weiss, Solomon Willis, and Chip Yeomans. An extra special thanks to Gregory Kulhanjian for generously supplying a number of articles and interviews for my consideration, but most of all for his encouragement and expertise. Additionally, Mr. Kulhanjian wishes to acknowledge the late Ileane Balakirsky for her friendship and invaluable contribution to his personal collection.

My appreciation also goes out to the following libraries, institutions, and organizations, and especially the librarians and representatives who offered such valuable assistance: Academy of Motion Picture Arts and Sciences, Margaret Herrick Library; The Country Music Hall of Fame and Museum (Becky Miley); Dolly Parton Productions (Ted Miller); The Dollywood Foundation (David Dotson); Middle Tennessee State University, Center for Popular Music—Everett Corbin Collection (Martin Fisher, Rachel K. Morris); Nashville Public Library, Special Collections Division; Sevier County Public Library System; Sony Pictures Television (Ed Zimmerman); Tennessee Archive of Moving Image and Sound; University of North Texas—Willis Library; and Vanderbilt University, Special Collections—Jack Hurst Collection (Kathy Smith). Additionally, I extend thanks to the various online communities of Dolly fans who have been so generous and supportive.

For their continued encouragement of my passion for exploration, research, and writing, I wish to recognize my family. First, thanks to my parents for that Dolly Parton doll when I was three, and to my sister for trading her record player for my horse when I was eight. And to those who've endured the past two years living in our very own Dollywoodland: Jaime, my patient and reassuring husband, who spent many late nights reading aloud to me for this project, and daughters Camryn and Kaylee, who've let me talk and talk and talk about everything Dolly. I also wish to acknowledge my Grandma Margie, to whose memory this book is dedicated. Not only did she introduce me to Dolly's music, she instilled in me a love of *all* music from a very young age. I can hardly remember a time she wasn't humming, singing, whistling, or yodeling around the house. To her I say, "Here I come a-writin' at ya!"

Finally, my utmost thanks to Dolly Parton. As silly as it sounds, I cannot recall a time in my life without her. One of my earliest memories is of standing in front of Grandma Margie's giant Zenith TV and witnessing an angelic creature descending on a swing from the heavens. She stepped down and walked directly toward me. Flashing a warmhearted smile, she began to sing "Love Is Like a Butterfly." I was mesmerized by the giant wigs, the glitzy clothing, that curvaceous figure . . . everything. But above all this, I was captivated by her storytelling. Dolly sang in such a conversational and intimate manner that I was convinced that she was singing only to me.

PART I
Blonde Ambition

"I had this something that kept pushing me forward, even when I was so scared I wished I could die. It was something I had to do, not because somebody else had told me I had to, but because I had told myself I did. It was just a need to see and be seen, I guess. It certainly wasn't to be rich. I didn't know what rich was."

—To Jack Hurst, *Chicago Tribune*,
January 31, 1976

INTERVIEW: *MUSIC CITY NEWS*

Everett Corbin | June 7, 1967 | Interview Tape

Dolly Parton's first interview with a major country music publication was conducted by Everett Corbin for *Music City News* during the summer of 1967. Corbin, who served as editor of *MCN* at the time, visited with twenty-one-year-old Dolly in the living room of her pre-fame Nashville residence at the Glengarry Heights Apartments. The up-and-comer was rather reserved during this conversation. Almost timid. There are hints of her sense of humor, which would erupt in forthcoming interviews, but here she remained polite and precise with her answers.

The headline atop the September issue of *Music City News* declared DOLLY PARTON No 'DUMB BLONDE'. Corbin's feature appeared prominently on the publication's front page. "Hers is a success story of almost unbelievable proportions," he wrote, "[and she] is quickly making her mark upon the Country music scene as singer supreme and songwriter extraordinary. . . . A winning combination—beauty and talent—is beginning to pay dividends for Monument recording artist Dolly Parton, 'the Girl with a Song in Her Heart.'"

What follows is a transcription from Corbin's forty-five-minute tape recording that served as the basis for his *MCN* cover story. He also recorded Dolly's answers to several supplemental questions at the end of the tape. Those remarks have been worked into the interview according to chronology and/or theme. —Ed.

Everett Corbin: This tape was made June 7, 1967, at Glengarry Apartments on Murfreesboro Road and we're interviewing Dolly Parton, Monument recording artist. Dolly, I suppose to write this story easy it'd help me if we just go back to the beginning and we'll let you tell

us about your background and where you were born and take us up to the present time.

Dolly Parton: OK, that'll be fine. I was born . . . We'll start with when I was born, OK? I was born on January the nineteenth, in 1946 in Sevier County. It's Sevierville, Tennessee, a little town between Knoxville and Gatlinburg. You might shorten it by sayin' "the foothills of the Great Smoky Mountains." But if you wanna know the names of some hollers and some ridges and knobs where I lived, I was born at Pittman Center on Pittman Center Road. Then, when I was about five years old, we lived in a place called Boogertown. It really wasn't the name of it, but that was what everybody called it. Then we moved to a place called Locust Ridge and I lived there for several years. We owned the whole big farm. We just farmed and that's all we did. I used to work in the field and all this bit . . . hoe corn and set tobacco and all that.

Well, now this first town where you say you were born, was it a community or a town?

It was really what I guess you'd call a community, but it was called Pittman Center Road, but the town, the little community, was called Pittman Center. But where I lived, you might say, up til I moved out . . . I live on Birds Creek now, my folks do. But it was called Locust Ridge.

Are all these places that you name in the same general vicinity?

Yeah, just a few miles between each one.

Now, the town that you claim now as home is what?

Well, it's Sevierville, Sevier County, but it's called Birds Creek.

And all these communities are in the county?

Yeah. The Caton's Chapel community and all that.

When did you start singin'?

I'm twenty-one years old now. I started singin' . . . Mama said I was squallin' when I was born. I'm still squallin' . . . But I started singin' in church. My grandfather was a preacher. I started singin' in church when I was, oh . . . it was as far back as I can remember. I would imagine [I was] five or six years old. I started singin' on a television and radio show in Knoxville at the age of ten and it was called *The Cas Walker Show*. We had a radio show in the daytime from 11:30, I think, until 1:00, and then we had a TV program on Monday, Wednesday, and Thursday nights. I think they started on Saturday night after I left. I sang on there during school vacations, in the summer, on holidays, and Christmas vacation.

What about your background?

There are twelve children in our family, as well as my mother and daddy. My daddy's name is Robert Lee Parton and my mother's name is Avie Lee. My daddy is forty-five and my mother is forty-three, if you're interested in that. My mother is a housewife. My father is a construction worker. He works with a company that travels some. But he really don't travel that far away from home that he has to stay away from home that much, but sometimes he'll have to go two hundred or three hundred miles from home for maybe a couple of months. But usually he works around within a one-hundred-mile radius. So that's about all that. So anything else you want to ask?

Were there really any bad hardships?

Oh, yes. There was twelve children in our family. Up until I was about eleven or twelve years old, we just farmed. We all had to work in the field and we all had a job to do. When you're just farmin' and that's the only income you have, and you have twelve children, well, then you don't have really have too much. In fact, we didn't have anything. We had to walk about two miles to school and all that. That was the first four of us children. Then the last eight, the last seven and eight, had it better than the first four of us did. But we had a real hard time.

There were four children before you?

No, there were three children before me. The first four and five of us had it real bad, you know. We had it rougher than the rest. But then we moved out to what we called over in the holler. That's where we lived. We owned the whole thing and we just farmed. I went to a one-room school until I was in the fifth grade. Or fourth grade. First through eighth grades it was Locust Ridge School. We had a teacher that taught first through the eighth. There were really about twelve students in the whole school. That was just farm families that lived here and there. We had to walk to school and the teacher would come there and teach us. He couldn't have got paid much. I don't think he had more than a high school education. But you know how it is. That's the only school we had to go to. That's the only way that we could have any education. But then we moved out and when I was in fifth I started going to a big public school. We still had it rough, though. [*Laughs*] We're *still* havin' it rough! Not as rough as we used to. When I graduated from high school, which was in '64, I came to Nashville. I graduated on Friday night and hurried to get to Nashville, so I came down on Saturday mornin'. That was the first of June and I've been here three years. About two weeks after I came to Nashville I went down on Music Row to get my contract or an audition. I tried two or three places and they all were filled up with girl singers and the whole business. So then I heard that Fred Foster might be interested in me. He's the president of Monument Records.

Right. Well, now can you tell me how did you happen to develop the interest or the desire, or maybe in some cases the nerve, to try for a recording contract?

[*Laughs*] Well, now I'd always loved to sing. I don't know. And I'd been writin' songs, too. I started writin' when I was seven or eight years old. I was writin' a little poetry and little things. The first song that I ever wrote—a real song that you might classify as bein' fair—was when I was eight years old. But I've always had the urge to be in the music business. It's just a talent that was a long background of music in our family. My mother and all my mother's people sang and played instruments, and some of my daddy's people, too. But I knew that I wanted to be in the music business and be a star. [*Laughs*] You might put it that way. But I really didn't have to pick up the nerve because, see, I started when I was ten years old and you might say I got professional during that time. Or whatever you'd call it. I really wasn't bashful at all. I always had a big mouth. And so I just made up my mind that's what I wanted to do and anything I ever made up my mind I wanted to do I usually did it. So I came here to Nashville to get a contract. I didn't come to get a job or anything, I just came to record.

What did you want most in your mind? To record your songs?

Well, mostly. I came to get a recording contract as well as a writin' contract. And I did. With the same company.

Your first attempt with Monument, did it succeed?

Now, I guess I did jump the guns just a little bit. Before, while I was still in high school, when I was fifteen years old, I came to Nashville then. See, I had tried. I had come down occasionally. When I was twelve or thirteen years old, I did the Grand Ole Opry on a Friday night. They call it the Friday Night Opry. I did that and I got three encores, which was good. They said it was real good, you know, for a young girl and all that. I recorded a record for Mercury when I was fifteen and was still in school and couldn't travel. I couldn't leave school. Daddy and Mama were rather strict. They didn't want me out runnin' around at that age. You couldn't blame 'em. I recorded a record for Mercury and it didn't do anything. It was called "It May Not Kill Me" and then on the back side of it was . . . Oh, I don't remember what the back side was of that song. But I did that and nothin' happened all during high school. I really didn't try because I wasn't able to leave school. [*Released in 1962, Dolly's promotional single for Mercury was actually titled "It's Sure Gonna Hurt," and the flipside featured a tune called "The Love You Gave" by Robert Riley and Marie Jones. —Ed.*]

Was that the only recording there?

That's not really the first. The first recording I ever had was one I really don't even talk about because it was on a very small label when I was eleven or twelve years old. I did a record a long time ago. But I guess you would say the first record that I recorded to try to do anything with and to try to work with it and to go out on the road or promote it was with Monument Records. It was called "I Wasted My Tears" and the back side was "What Do You Think About Lovin'?" which I cowrote with my uncle Bill Owens. The back side I cowrote with Bill Owens and another uncle, Robert Owens.

Do you recall what date this was? What time?

It would have been in '64. That's when I graduated and I came down. It would have been in the winter of '64, close to '65, so after that I was doin' pop. I really came to do country because I always sung country. That's what I was and what I wanted to be. My voice is pitched real high and people thought it sounded childish. They thought it sounded young—too young—so they thought I might have a better chance in rock 'n' roll since you really didn't have to sing any certain way [*Laughs*] to be rock 'n' roll. So they recorded me pop. Anything you wanna ask me, just go ahead. I was just kinda buttin' in.

So they recorded you pop at Monument?

They recorded me pop for two years, up until now. Up until the last year. See, I'd been writin' all this time, too, gettin' all my songs gathered up, gettin' a pretty good bunch of songs to have somethin' to work with.

How many records did you have up until then?

I recorded five records for Monument before I got to do the country record that I had wanted to do all along. I wrote a song with my uncle Bill Owens called "Put It Off Until Tomorrow," which was a top ten song. We won a BMI award off that song, and I think it got to number four nationwide. I sung with Bill Phillips on it. It was recorded on Decca by Bill Phillips and I got to sing some harmony on it.

How did this happen with you being on Decca?

Well, I really wasn't signed to Decca. The way that it happened . . . See, we hadn't had any songs recorded before. Maybe a couple. And Bill Phillips was on a fairly good label and all that. I had done the demonstration tape on it with another man and they wanted to copy that arrangement as close as they could. They liked the way it had been done and asked Mr. Foster—Fred—if I could sing on it. He was real nice about it and said yes because we were getting a song recorded and he was tryin' to help me every way he could. But I wasn't tied up with Decca. I did more of a harmony part. I was more noticeable than they had intended because my voice is so odd. You can tell who I am, even if I'm singin' in a group. My name wasn't on the record as a singer, just as writin' the song. Then all the disk jockeys were calling from everywhere wantin' to know who the girl singer was on "Put It Off Until Tomorrow." We got so much publicity off of that and we had somethin' to fight with since I wanted to do country music. So we had a little discussion with Fred Foster. Saying "we," I mean my uncle Bill Owens and I. We've always worked together. He's always acted as my personal manager, you might say. We told him that I wanted to do country music, that's what I felt, that's what I wanted to do, and I had a better future in country music because I'd never had a pop hit. I had a song out called "Happy, Happy Birthday, Baby." That was the best thing I'd had and it wasn't even considered a hit at all. Then I did an answer to "Put It Off Until Tomorrow." Fred agreed that I could do country because he had begun to see that I would have a better future in that. We had written a song, an answer to "Put It Off Until Tomorrow," and I did that, and it was backed up with a song that Bill Owens and I had written called "The Little Things." After that came "Dumb Blonde," which was the biggest record I've ever had of myself. It was a top ten record. It did *real* well for me.

Who wrote "Dumb Blonde"?

We didn't write "Dumb Blonde." Curly Putman of Tree Music—who wrote "Green, Green Grass of Home" and "My Elusive Dreams," the new song that's out now—he wrote "Dumb Blonde." We went pickin' material and wanted somethin' that would be different and gimmicky that would get me on the road—somethin' different—and we thought that suited me. [*Laughs*] I *am* a dumb blonde! No, but . . . Then came my new record that is just out. It's called "Something Fishy." And that brings us up to where we are now. It's doin' *real* well. In fact, it's been out two and a half weeks, almost three weeks, and it has done real well. It came onto the charts in *Billboard* this week. That brings me up to date, as far as recording goes. I've written lots of songs.

Yeah, you wrote "Something Fishy."

Yeah. Yes, I did. I wrote "Something Fishy" myself.

I believe a few weeks ago I heard you on WENO [Radio in Nashville] and I don't know if you were talking to Don Howser or who.

Yeah, it was Don Howser. Yes, it was. Yeah, I wrote "Something Fishy" and I've written a song recorded by Hank Williams Jr. that's out now called "I'm in No Condition to Try to Love Again." Or "I'm in No Condition" is the title of it. I wrote that myself. And then I cowrote with Bill Owens the song that's just been out with Skeeter Davis that's called "Fuel to a Flame." That did pretty well. I think it got to number eight. Then we wrote "Put It Off Until Tomorrow" and then we wrote the song that was a follow-up to "Put It Off" by Bill Phillips just after that. It was called "You're Known by the Company You Keep." That I cowrote with Bill. Then I had a song recorded recently by Jan Howard called "Your Ole Handy Man" that I wrote. We've had several small songs that didn't do anything and then some that did. We have Kitty Wells's next release, too. The name of it is "More Love than Sense." That about brings it up to where we are. So you can ask me anything you want to.

OK, now speaking of your songwriting career, would you give an estimate for how many songs you may have written?

Oh, mercy. Since I've been writin', I guess I've written four hundred or five hundred songs. I wouldn't say I've had that many *good* ones, but I've written that many . . . cowrote and wrote by myself.

Are you as strong as a songwriter as you are a singer? How do you feel about the two?

You mean would I make a choice between the two?

What preference do you have?

Well, I really couldn't make a choice because I have to write and I have to sing and I'd rather do both. I don't really care to sing my own songs but I do *like* to sing 'em because I think I can put more of the kind of feelin' I want in it, rather than a song that someone else has written for me. But I wouldn't say that all the time, 'cause I get tired of singin' my own songs. [*Laughs*]

First publicity photo, Goldband Records, 1959.
Author Collection

Monument Records and Moeller Talent
headshot, 1967.
Author Collection

DEAN, MR.&MRS.CARL

Newlyweds Carl and Dolly Dean pictured in the
Radnor Church of Christ directory, Nashville, 1967.
Courtesy Annelle Tubb

DOLLY PARTON AND HER GUITAR

Photographed for *Music City News*
in her Nashville apartment,
June 1967.
Courtesy MTSU Special Collections

DOLLY READS COPY OF 'MUSIC CITY NEWS'

APRIL 1968/50¢

couniry

Dolly Parton
Hank Williams, Jr.
Marty Robbins
Minnie Pearl

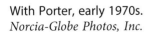

With Porter Wagoner on the cover
of *Country* magazine, 1969.
Author Collection

With Porter, early 1970s.
Norcia-Globe Photos, Inc.

On her own, 1974. *RCA Records*

In concert at the Bottom Line in New York City, May 1977. *Globe Photos, Inc.*

Striking a playful pose with journalist Lawrence Grobel during the *Playboy* photo sessions, 1978.
Courtesy Larry Grobel / Used by permission of Harry Langdon

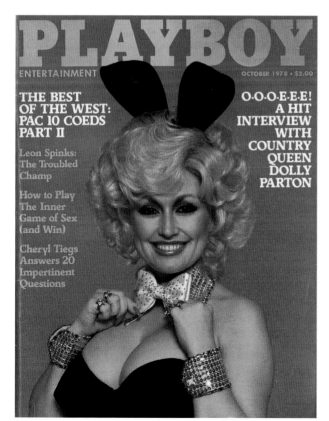

Playboy magazine, 1978.
Author Collection

Joined on stage by Linda Ronstadt and Emmylou Harris during a concert at the Universal Amphitheatre in Los Angeles, September 24, 1979.
Nancy Barr-Globe Photos, Inc.

For Academy Consideration
Best Song
"Nine To Five"
Written and Performed by **Dolly Parton**
Produced by Gregg Perry

With *9 to 5* costars Lily Tomlin and Jane
Fonda at the film's Los Angeles premiere,
December 12, 1980.
Ralph Dominguez-Globe Photos, Inc.

Trade ad touting "9 to 5" for the "Best
Original Song" Oscar®.
Author Collection

On the town with *Whorehouse* costar Burt Reynolds, 1981.
Ralph Dominguez-Globe Photos, Inc.

Interview magazine photo session, 1984. *Herb Ritts-Globe Photos, Inc.*

What type songs do you prefer?

I like ballads. Real strong, pitiful, sad, cryin' ballads.

Do you have any favorite songwriters?

Yeah, I do, but I don't never like to say who I like. But I have several. And I have several singers that I like more than others, but I don't really like to say who.

Why don't you tell me about your current plans.

Well, since I had "Dumb Blonde" and "Something Fishy," I've never really worked the road too much. Now I've got lots of things lined up. In fact, I'm booked almost through this month and the next month, and I have dates on out through the summer. I'll be booked almost all summer, so things are real busy now. I have a new album out, I didn't mention. It's not out but it will be. It's called *Hello, I'm Dolly* and it's featuring "Dumb Blonde" and "Something Fishy."

This will be out before September?

Yeah, it should be out by the end of this month.

So we can say that?

So yeah, it'll be out by then, I'm sure.

Twelve songs?

Yeah. And all these songs that are in the album, my uncle and I wrote. I wrote a couple by myself that are in the album and then the rest of 'em we cowrote together. There's twelve songs that we've written. So I guess that takes care of the album.

How about your home life or family life? You care to mention anything?

No, I don't care to. They don't usually like for me to me to mention it. Fred and them don't really like for me to mention it or to emphasize it *real* big, but I got married a year ago, the thirtieth of last month, on Memorial Day last year. My husband's name is Carl Dean. He and his father are in the asphalt paving business here in town. You might classify that as a contractor or whatever. But anyway, we don't have any children as yet and don't have any on the way, but we plan to have some children. We'll probably start our family or start tryin' to have a family next summer because I need to do all this booking and everything now. I'm just getting started. But I'd like to have at least four children. I'd like to have six if we can afford it and if things go well . . . if everybody's healthy and I got the energy to take care of 'em! [*Laughs*] I'll know after the first one! But there are twelve children in my family. I was from a family a twelve. There's six girls and six boys and I have a sister and two brothers older than me and I have eight children younger than me.

Are there any in the music business?

Well, not really. Some of 'em sing, but they never really had the ambition to really make it in the music business. I have two sisters that sing real well. In fact, I guess you'd say they're the only ones that really sing. My older sister writes some. She never really did anything with it, but she writes some poetry and some songs. Sometimes I work on her material for her. But I have two sisters that sing together. The three of us used to sing together in church and on the local radio stations some when I was home, but they don't really have any ambition to really get in the music business. And I wouldn't try to encourage 'em to if that's not what they want 'cause it's a hard life. [*Laughs*]

Is it a hard life now?

Well, it's not a hard life. I mean it's hard work. And if you enjoy it, that's fine. That's what I mean. I wouldn't encourage anybody that really didn't have their heart set on it, because I'd feel responsible if things didn't go right.

How many days do you stay on the road now or anticipate staying on the road?

I didn't book that much off "Dumb Blonde." I just started. When "Dumb Blonde" was out I'd average about six to eight bookings a month, but now I would probably do about twenty days. Probably.

Who is your booking agent?

I book through One-Niters, Incorporated, which is run by Dub Allbritten, Brenda Lee's manager. That's who I book with, too. I write for Combine Publishing Company, which is run by Bob Beckham, and he really does a good job for us. That's through Monument Records, owned by Monument, and I record for Monument Records. And Bob—well, I don't know if he'd want me to mention that or not, so I won't go into that, but—he used to be a singer, too. He still is. In fact, I think he's gonna record again, too. He had a couple of big pop records "Just as Much as Ever" and a pop version of "Crazy Arms" for Decca. But you might not want to mention that because I don't know how he feels about that, but anyway, he runs the company and does a real good job. He works real hard on our behalf. That's about all I'll say about him.

At what rate, do you know if your songs are being placed or recorded?

Well, I can say this. Up until "Put It Off Until Tomorrow," we really didn't have hardly any songs recorded. Then we had one big hit. "Put It Off" was our first big hit, and then we've had at least two or three songs placed a week.

Do you have artists waiting for songs?

Yes, we have artists coming to ask for songs, and if we find out who's recordin', then we take 'em songs. The publishing company always checks to see who is in town and who's recordin'. We pick out songs that we think would fit certain artists and then we take 'em and leave 'em there. If they like 'em, fine, if they don't . . . But lots of times certain artists will come to listen to our material.

Do you have a lot of requests for tailor-made songs?

Yes, I do. Lots of times a lot of people ask us to write a song for 'em or a certain artist is recordin' and we try to write a song for 'em or see if we've got anything that'd fit 'em. We do that all the time.

It seems from the information you're giving me, that you're as active as a songwriter as a singer. This is something sort of new for girls. They haven't been as prominent as men, have they?

No, I don't think they have. In fact, I guess you might say I'd been doin' better in my writin'—up until "Dumb Blonde" —than I had been singin'. I had several songs recorded. I still write a lot to keep up songs for myself to record and other artists, too, so it really takes up all your time. I wouldn't rather be a songwriter than a singer and I wouldn't rather be a singer than songwriter. I have to do both because that's what I feel.

What kind of contract do you have with Monument Records?

I'm signin' a new contract with Monument now for three years. I had a three-year contract that expires in September, and I'm signin' up for three more years. I'll sign with the writin', too, in September, for three more years. So that covers all that with Monument.

Have you played any of the big radio shows like the Opry or Wheeling or Shreveport or any of those?

No, I haven't. Like I said, I played the Opry once and I'm scheduled to be on the Opry this month or next with "Something Fishy." I really could have done it before, but I just never did because I didn't really care to be on the Opry unless I had a record out so that people would know who I was. I really never thought that much about it until I did have a record. I always wanted to be on the Opry, but I always wanted to have some *reason* to be on it. I've done some TV shows. I've done *The Bill Anderson Show* that's shown on Saturday evenings in most places, and I did *The Wilburn Brothers Show* two weeks ago. That's really about all I've done. I have been doin' a lot of local TV work here. I'm not doin' that much anymore. With the bookings I have, and recording, and tryin' to keep up with my writin', and tryin' to keep the house decent enough to live in, the apartment, I really don't have that much time to do anything. At any rate, that covers about all that. So if there's anything else . . .

In addition to this increased activity on the road now, what are your plans?

I really don't have any plans other than bookin' and recordin' and writin'. That'll take up all my time. And doin' what I have to do here.

I know a lot of country music people recently have made some country music type films.

Oh yeah. Well, I think I am supposed to do some of those. I could have done some of those before, too, but it goes back to what I said about the Opry. I really didn't care to do anything like that until I had something that people would know me from. I think they're making a new movie here in town that someone had mentioned to me here the other day that they wanted me to be in it. I've had offers lots of times to do some acting, but I don't care to act.

You don't care about dramatic acting?

No. I told 'em I would do a part where I could sing and maybe just have a few lines, but I'm too common to try to act. I really don't care to 'cause of all the writin' and my family to take care of, and singin', and bookin' and recordin' I really don't have any desire to get involved in anything I'm not that interested in. But I will be doin' some singin' parts in some movies and stuff. That's really all I care to do.

How are you presented on the road? What kind of band do you have with you?

Like I told you before, I hadn't really been doin' all that much bookin'. Since I came here I'd do occasional bookings or go out with somebody, but really I never did do that much bookin'. Up until now, I've always had a lead guitar player that we would go on the road and he would play on my songs and lead the other band. Usually we played with the band that was already there. I'd just book as "take one musician." Now I just started a new band. I got a band together. They're all my relatives on my mama's side. They all sing and play somethin'. But the name of the band will be called the Kinfolk. Dolly Parton and the Kinfolk.

So how many will be in the band?

There'll be three in the band. I play on stage. I really don't play that much in clubs or anything because I like to do little routines and all. But I'll have drums. Dwight Puckett will be on drums, Louis Owens on bass, and Bill Owens on lead guitar. Later on we'll pick up a steel player. It's so hard to find anybody who can play a steel, or one that plays all that well that's not already booked with somebody. Most of the good steel players are booked.

Do you play straight guitar?

I play straight guitar. I play other instruments but I really haven't done anything. I'm gonna try to work up a little routine. I play piano and I can use tambourine and play banjo a little. Just very little. But I've always played guitar. That's the only thing that I can do a really good job at. I really can't do that hot at that! So that's about it. That covers that part.

Speaking about playing musical instruments, do you practice much or does it come naturally or what?

Well, I really don't play that well. I've always played guitar. I've always fooled around on the guitar, but I started playin' on the shows when I started singin' in Knoxville when I was ten years old. I've been playin' guitar enough to know everything I played—just straight chords—since I was eight. I'm really not a master on guitar. I just play my own songs and I don't play any lead. I can play a little folk, but I really don't practice guitar. I just write so much and sing so much I just use it all the time anyway.

Speaking about folk music, do you have any other types of music that you're interested in besides country?

Oh, I love folk music and sacred songs.

Do you have any plans to record any sacred songs?

I certainly hope so. I've written several sacred songs, but I hope to do a sacred album just as soon as I can 'cause that's always been something I really look forward to. Just as soon as I can do that, I hope to. We were talking about it not long ago that I might get my two sisters that I used to sing with and let them sing with me on it. Just somethin' different because we always used to sing together in church and everything. I enjoy country and ballads and all that stuff.

It'd be nice to do like Tennessee Ernie Ford. He went back to Bristol and made a hometown album.

He did, yes. That's a good idea! Well, I know he's done several, but I don't really recall when he did that. I think it would be a good idea and I would enjoy it and they would, too. It would be something for the family to always have. I hope to do a folk album, too, just as soon as I can. I do a lot of folk music—country folk, you might call it—and then I write an awful lot of that, too. That seems to be my specialty. I write a lot of poetry and some stories. I never did anything with 'em, but I still get 'em out of my system.

Do you have any plans of publishing them?

Well, someday I hope to publish some kind of little volume of my poetry and some short stories. I like to write little children's stories, so maybe I can have it published for my children. Just somethin' to keep for them. I doubt that I'll ever try to have anything done with them 'cause it's just somethin' I like to do. I guess you might say it's a hobby.

Speaking about children's songs, some of the older country artists used to record a lot of children's songs. I believe that one artist was on M-G-M [Records] and I can't recall his name right now. Do you know many of the older artists? I think Carson Jay Robison or somebody he was affiliated with at M-G-M used to record a lot of children's songs.

I really don't know who you're talkin' about but I really haven't heard that many. Burl Ives does a lot of children's songs and all that. Just albums. But I'm really not too familiar with people.

I remember now . . . Tex Ritter had a number of children's albums out, but none of the current country artists I know of have recorded anything of that nature.

That would be a good idea. I might do that, too. Don't be surprised if you see one comin' out!

I think it'd be not only rewarding but lucrative, too.

Yeah, I love to do things like that.

It looks like it'd be an open field for country artists.

Yeah, that's a good idea. I might do an album on that. I've never really ever brought it up. Like I said, if nothin' else, I'd like to put down the things like that just to keep for my own children and for grandchildren and all that.

I'm sure there'd be a big market for it and there probably is a void there. I would think so.

I've really never heard anybody talk about it. I guess it would be a good idea. So maybe. Don't be surprised if you see one comin' out . . .

We'll be lookin' for it.

Dolly Parton . . . *Dumb Blonde Sings Childish*. [*Laughs*] I like some of all types of music, but my favorite songs are sacred and country and folk. And I like *some* pop. I like songs like "My Cup Runneth Over" and "Yesterday" and things like that. I really don't care to be in rock 'n' roll field. I wouldn't mind at all havin' a good song that would go pop but I just want to stay basically country because that's what I feel. 'Cause if that's what you are, that's all you can feel, really. . . . I did a song that I wrote, and I love to write sacred- or spiritual-flavored songs and I have a song that I just recorded while I was doin' the album they pulled for a single. It's called "Everything Is Beautiful (In Its Own Way)" and it might be the next release. It'll have a real country song on back of it, but it's not pop, it's kinda folky/sacred/country/pop. [*Laughs*] Real different. It's about life, the way it is, and all the things that are really beautiful that people don't stop to see that God has made that way. These're the kind of songs I like. It could be a pop record, but yet it's country lyrics. I just put down what I feel, and however it turns out, then that's the way I record it. I don't think anybody would dislike that because if that's what you feel, I think that's what you should do. I feel country, but songs like this come from the heart and I just do 'em like the way they feel that they should be done.

Do you have any favorite hobbies?

Everybody always asks me what my hobbies are. I really don't have any special ones or anything outstanding other than I fish. I like to fish. And

I write the short stories that I was talkin' about before. And I write some poetry. And I do just a few things occasionally but nothin' that I'm really hung up on. So you might say my hobbies are fishin' and writin' 'cause I really don't have time for a real strict hobby by the time I do everything else. So that's about the extent of my hobbies, too.

Have you gotten any reports of any pop action on any of the two recent records?

Well, I heard . . . I had several people say that they were playin' "Something Fishy" on some pop stations, but it's a country record—really country—with steel guitar and the whole thing, but that's what I mean. You never know what's gonna go pop. You might record "Possum up a Gum Stump" and it'd be a big pop record. And then again, you might try for the pop and it wouldn't play at all. You just never can tell. But I'd like to record something that could go either way, but I still want to be country, basically country. I'll never record a record with both sides pop flavored. There'll always be a real country song on one side and no farther out than maybe a Sandy Posey type thing.

Do you try to balance your songs with both ballads and novelties?

I try to. That depends on what I do. It really wouldn't have to be a novelty to be uptempo but I think most record companies try to record one ballad and one uptempo. That's what I have done so far. So I imagine that's what I'll be doin'. Really, there's no set rules on that, I don't think. Depends on what you want played. But at any time it seems like they'll let you have a slow song and uptempo. They'll usually play the uptempo quicker than they will the ballad. You just never can tell. I mean, if people knew what was gonna sell and what was gonna go on, they'd never have to worry if this was a good song to record and all this.

Now, since this story will come out in September and your record has just come out, would you have anything right after this that you might think would be released?

Well, I don't know that there would be one released that soon. But that's what . . . Let's see . . . This is June . . . July, August, September . . . Four months. Yeah. I imagine I will have. And maybe it would be that . . .

Do you have anything ready to go?

Yes, I have several things ready to go. The song I was tellin' you about, "Everything Is Beautiful (In Its Own Way)" is a beautiful song. It's somethin' different and it's a clean idea. It's somethin' people need. People seem to forget about God and ever'thing when all this stuff is goin' on in the world and they don't really think to look around at the things that really mean anything. So I think it would be a good song to put out now. But I really don't know for sure if that will be it or not, but I can let you know by then.

May I ask you how you get your ideas?

Well, now that depends. A lot of people write about their own experiences. I wrote some about my own experiences, but not really that much because I write a lot of sad songs and I just write about things I've seen happen or things that have been in the family or things I've read. And in a general conversation with somebody, I might just get some good ideas. I just write. I don't know where I get my ideas. I don't really go out to look for any, they just seem to come natural.

What length of time would you say that it takes to write a good song?

That would depend. Some of my very best songs I've written within thirty minutes' time. And then some songs it takes me [longer]. Really, I can't really say that I've ever taken more than an hour on a song. Usually I can write a song—especially an uptempo song—in just a few minutes. Especially if I have the idea and everything in my mind. Now, I can write a song in fifteen minutes and complete it. But then I start sayin' it back over and everything and I'll hear a lot of things I don't think would be good in there. So I go back and change lines and change ideas.

Do you put things on tape right away?

No, I don't. Now I do sometimes, but usually I'll just write. I'll write the chords or the words, but usually, after I sing a song a couple of times, I'll remember how it goes.

Can you read music?

No, I can't. But I write all my tunes and my words and everything. Now I can read a little music, but not enough to brag about. Not enough to really work with. It depends on the song and what I'm tryin' to write. If it's somethin' real deep or somethin' that I want to write about and get a lot of good ideas in, then sometimes it will take me longer. It won't take me that long if I will just sit and write it, but sometimes I'll be writin' a song and I'll be cookin' or I'll be doin' this or that and I'll just be thinkin' while I'm doin' it and I just write when I think of a good line. I just think before I write it down. Sometimes—I think most everybody does—I dream of songs. I dream of writin' songs. Sometimes I can remember 'em the next mornin' and then sometimes I can't. Usually I get a lot of good ideas in the night. I guess it's 'cause it's so quiet. I'll get up and write 'em down and maybe finish them the next morning. And then maybe I'll just stay up and write 'em. It depends on how knocked-out I am! [*Laughs*] So my ideas just come from different places. I get inspired from different things. So that's about the extent of that.

MISS DOLLY PARTON: BLONDE BOMBSHELL OF GREAT SMOKIES

Jack Hurst | September 27, 1970 | *The Tennessean*

Dolly's first full-length album, *Hello, I'm Dolly*, released on Monument Records in July 1967, quickly captured the attention of national press. *Billboard* referred to "Something Fishy" as "more clever material penned by Ms. Parton and performed to perfection. This one should fast top her 'Dumb Blonde' hit and establish her as one of the label's consistent top sellers."

It is likely that Dolly's two hit singles captured the attention of country star Porter Wagoner. The long-legged crooner was in the market for a new girl singer to replace Pretty Miss Norma Jean on his popular syndicated television show and invited Dolly to join *The Porter Wagoner Show*. She made her debut on September 5, 1967, before an audience of more than forty-five million people.

Surprisingly, Dolly was not well received by many of Porter's faithful viewers in the beginning. Norma Jean was widely beloved by fans, so Dolly politely endured chants of "Norma Jean! Norma Jean!" from the crowd during her first few shows. "I couldn't *begin to imagine* how hard it was *really* going to be," she said in a 1971 press release. "It just froze me because I was stepping into big, big shoes. Norma had been with the show for seven years, and I knew everybody would just naturally resent me for trying to, well, replace her. Even the band, until they got to know me, 'cause she had just left, and I had to step in right away. . . . Oh, I can never make it plain to anyone what torture it was the first few times on that show, knowin' that everybody was wanting to see and hear someone else. It was like murder!"

Having attracted the attention of executives at RCA Victor, Dolly soon left Fred Foster and Monument Records to join Porter on his longtime label. In January 1968, the new

Parton-Wagoner team released *Just Between You and Me*, the first of what would be more than a dozen duet albums. The album made the *Billboard* Top 10 Country Albums Chart and won them the Country Music Association award for Vocal Group of the Year, as well as the *Music City News* award for Duet of the Year.

"We used to sing a lot on the bus and Porter got the idea for the duets," Dolly told Ralph Emery in 1971. "It was so rough on me at the beginning . . . I guess Porter just got tired of watchin' me suffer and trying to get recognized. [The duets were] to give me a chance to show what I could do where people would listen without bein' prejudiced."

Released later in 1968 was Dolly's first solo single for RCA, "Just Because I'm a Woman," which was also the title of her first solo album for the label. By the time of this 1970 cover feature for *Showcase*, a supplement to the Sunday edition of the *Tennessean*, her version of Jimmy Rodgers's "Mule Skinner Blues (Blue Yodel No. 8)" had peaked at Number 3 on the *Billboard* country charts. "Miss Dolly Parton . . . is more to the *Porter Wagoner Show* than just a country music Marilyn Monroe," the *Showcase* cover stated. "She's a prolific little balladeer who says her writing is a mechanism for escape."

It's evident here that Dolly was steadily accumulating solo accolades and accomplishments in the country music world, but her dependence on Wagoner is certainly obvious, too. Dolly's loyalty to Wagoner seems to have been at its fiercest here, as evidenced by a phone call made on her behalf to writer Jack Hurst after the conclusion of the interview. She wanted to be sure Hurst understood that any success she'd achieved was all due to Porter Wagoner. —Ed.

My voice was real different—not that it's good, because a lot of people just cannot STAND to hear me sing. Anybody with a real different voice, a lot of people don't like to hear sing, but people who do like them usually like them especially well. —Dolly Parton

On the wall behind the desk at which her uncle sat, her picture—a large and engaging color photograph framed in gold—beamed down on all who might enter Owepar Music.

Her hair hung in perfect golden ringlets beside her face, and she was smiling in the wacky way she does when people tell her she is beautiful, grinning as if it is maybe the most hugely funny lie she has heard all week.

"Dolly'll be in in just a minute," the uncle, Louie Owens, said rather nervously to the prospective interviewer. "She's talkin' to somebody about a song and won't be but a second."

On the wall opposite the picture, facing the desk at which Louie Owens fidgeted, hung several framed Broadcast Music Inc. award citations to Owepar for songs Dolly had written or co-written. Over there also hung the latest recording popularity charts distributed by Billboard and Record World.

"She's doin' pretty good right now," her uncle said. "'Muleskinner Blues' is No. 1 in Record World and No. 3 in Billboard. And 'Daddy Was An Old-Time Preacher Man' is No. 8 in Billboard."

In the minute or so he had forecast, his niece walked into her office in a glittering black jumpsuit dotted with regularly-spaced, diamond-shaped, white patterns the size of once-folded dollar bills. The blonde hair hung long today, not done up high in ringlets, and she extended her hand in the frank, happy shake folks use back home in the hills.

"Hi, I'm proud to meet you."

She sat down in the chair, crossed her legs and then clasped her hands across her waist to wait for the first question.

Not long after it came, however, she kicked off the gold shoes and pulled her feet up into the chair with her, holding her knees in both arms.

By that time, she was well into remembering who Dolly Rebecca Parton used to be.

The Bombshell

Dolly Parton, who at her present age of 24 years is the blonde bombshell of The Porter Wagoner Show, was born the fourth of a dozen children of a farmer-turned-construction worker in Sevier County, Tenn.

"Mama and Daddy were married pretty early in life—she was 15 and he was 17," she said. She sighed and then smiled that wacky smile. "So they done . . . pretty well."

Her first memories seem to be of a farm of several hundred acres "'way back in the Smoky Mountains at a place that was called Webb's

Mountain then." The family moved there when she was three and stayed—raising crops and animals "mainly just for our own survival, rather than to sell"—for about five years.

"I graduated from Sevier County High School in 1964, but up until then I went to elementary school just wherever we would move to, because we used to move quite a bit after we left the big farm," she recalled.

After having moved around the county for a couple of years, the Partons finally settled in tiny Caton's Chapel community when Dolly was around 10. Her parents still live there today.

Religion and Fun

At Webb's Mountain and Caton's Chapel and the other small communities in which Dolly grew up, religion was both a solemn duty and a looked-forward-to recreation.

Particularly was this true of the Partons. Dolly Parton's grandfather was a minister, the Rev. Mr. Owens, an old-time preacher man.

In the words one of his daughters and one of his granddaughters would use someday, the Rev. Mr. Owens "preached hell so hot that you could feel the heat." In the song about him which currently is among the top ten country songs in the nation, Dolly Parton and Mrs. Dorothy Hope tried to convey the spirit of the way it was in that fundamentalist church in the hills.

"There's a verse in the song where it says, 'Sister Leona would get up to testify,'" Miss Dolly said, "and I actually did have an Aunt Leona and she actually would get up in the service to testify.

"I was brought up in the Church of God, which is the church where they shout and sing and everything, which I love," she continued in a more subdued way. "I always loved to sing in church. When you get to singing those old gospel songs and get that good spiritual feeling —well, there's just nothing else like it."

Before long, however, Dolly Parton was singing something besides hymns, and she was singing so well that one of her mother's brothers, Bill Owens, decided to get her on the radio in Knoxville.

By the time she was in high school, she was writing some of the songs she sang, and some were uncommonly good for a girl her age. Growing up in small farm communities in the mountains, where the work was hard and time often passed slowly, Dolly Parton became fascinated with the transmigration that was possible with a guitar, a piece of paper and a stub of pencil.

"When I'm writing," she said curled up in that easy chair in her Music Row office, "I can be anywhere and anything that I want to be. If I'm writing about a dog or a cat—whatever I'm writing about, I am that thing. And I'm the kind of person that even the ugliest duckling is pretty to me, some way or another."

One wonders what her classmates at Sevier County High thought of her then as they saw her on the Knoxville television station, singing on a program sponsored by grocery king Cas Walker.

"Live and In-Person"

Last spring, as "live and in-person" recordings at such places as Carnegie Hall became the vogue for country singers, Miss Dolly gathered up an RCA engineering crew, stage boss Porter Wagoner and Wagoner's Wagonmasters. She took them with her one evening to do her own "live" album. But rather than Carnegie Hall, she took them to Sevier County High School.

The day before the performance that evening—a day called "Dolly Parton Day" in Sevierville—the blonde bombshell announced she was donating her part of the proceeds of that night's show to set up a scholarship fund for deserving students at the high school. She promised to return for benefit shows whenever they were needed to maintain the fund.

Dolly Parton Day, 1970, was a roaring success.

It must have made the honoree recall a certain Saturday morning six years before, the morning following her graduation night, when a less-assured Dolly Rebecca—accompanied only by her suitcase—took a long look at Sevierville from a different vantage point.

It was from the high window of a Greyhound bus getting into gear for the run to Nashville.

Memorable Walk

The uncle who had gotten her on the *Cas Walker Show* in Knoxville, Bill Owens, had moved to Nashville with his wife and young son three weeks before his niece graduated from high school.

"So I was to stay with them until I could get something going and find myself a place of my own," Dolly remembers.

When she arrived at the Owens' apartment in the State Fairgrounds area of South Nashville, Dolly Parton had some clothes to wash because she had left for Nashville in such a hurry.

So, taking her dirty clothes in her arms, she walked to a nearby laundromat on her first afternoon in Nashville. It turned out to be memorable in more ways than one.

Her long yellow locks shook as she giggled, remembering it.

"I got me a big RC Cola and while my clothes were washing I just went out walkin' down the sidewalk to see Nashville," she said.

"I was just walkin' down the street and this boy came by in this white '59 or '60 Chevrolet. He went down first and he flirted and, of course, being fresh from the country, well, up where I come from everybody was friendly to everybody because everybody was friends, and I didn't know that you just couldn't do that anywhere."

The young man in the Chevrolet shouted at her, and she smiled and waved.

"'Cause I was just so proud to be here,' you know," she said, laughing.

"I guess kind of in the back of my mind I was maybe flirtin' a little, too," she admitted, "but mainly I was just bein' friendly because I'd always been the kind of person who would speak back and smile."

In a few minutes, the Chevrolet was passing her for the second time as she strolled along the street, and she was thinking perhaps she should not appear so friendly. The car slowed again and the young man hung his head out the window.

"Hey, you're gonna get sunburned out walking around like that," he yelled.

"I don't reckon it'll hurt anything," Dolly replied.

He stopped the car and got out to talk.

"Where you from?" he asked.

"I told him I was from Knoxville because I didn't figure he'd know where Sevierville was," she said. "He still kids me about saying I was from Knoxville. He says I said it kind of highfalutin' or somethin', but I didn't."

He tried to get her to go out with him, but she would not at first.

"I didn't know him," she said. "I didn't know anything about him."

She was to babysit with her uncle's son while his wife worked her shift as a waitress at the Shoney's Big Boy restaurant on Harding Road. She told her sudden suitor that he could come over to her uncle's house the next afternoon, while she baby-sat.

"He came over and we sat out in the yard and talked," she said. "But I still wouldn't go on a date with him for several days. When I finally did, the first place he took me the first night we went out was to his parents' house, and that made me feel a lot better about him."

Almost exactly two years after she had met him on her first day in Nashville, Dolly Parton was married to Carl Dean, now 28, a partner in his father's small but busy asphalt paving company in Woodbine.

Hungry Years

The two intervening years were busy ones for the little hill-country blonde. They were often also hungry ones, she recalls.

"I stayed about six months with Uncle Bill, and then I got me an apartment of my own," she said. "I couldn't afford a car or a telephone, and—" she laughed—"'bout the only time I ever ate was when I went out on a date, and I didn't go out on that many dates."

She stopped laughing pretty quickly and looked down at her hands in her lap.

"Well, actually, that was about the way it was, even though I was trying to make a joke out of it," she said. "Lots of times, my refrigerator was just about empty, except for mustard or turnip greens—things you always keep."

Her activities did not pay her very much, but she had gotten consistently busier as time went by. She began recording demonstration records for songwriters to pitch to successful recording stars.

She was on a "draw," writing songs for Combine Music for a weekly salary. She began making her own recordings for Monument Records, where executive producer Fred Foster took a keen interest in her ability. He found her a song called "Dumb Blonde."

"'Dumb Blonde' was written by Curly Putnam, who wrote 'Green, Green Grass of Home' and a lot of other great songs," Dolly said. "Fred thought the song would be good for me because it was up-tempo, for one thing, and it didn't really take a lot of singing.

"He figured it would make people forget about whether my voice was any good or not and just listen to the song." Foster must have been correct. "Dumb Blonde" was her first really successful recording. She was working on Eddie Hill's show on WLAC-TV—being paid out of Hill's pocket rather than by the station because the Hill show was already over its budget.

"I was working and making a little money, but not very much considering all the things I was having to do with it and trying to send a little money home when I could," she said.

Unexpected Call

One afternoon she received an unexpected telephone call from a country singer she had never met in her journeys up and down Music Row: Porter Wagoner, a slim Missourian who long has made fame and fortune selling country music fans patent medicine and heartbreak-and-honkytonk music.

Wagoner asked her if she could come by his office and talk business. Of course, she said she would be there as quickly as she could.

"I didn't know Porter, except for watchin' his TV show every week there at home with the family—which every country family that can possibly pick it up does," she said.

She supposed Wagoner wanted to see her about one of her songs.

"I had songs out all over town trying to get them recorded, and Porter and Norma Jean—the girl singer with his show—had a couple of them. Somebody at Combine had told me Norma Jean liked one of them especially well.

"I figured they were callin' me over there to tell me they were taking one of the songs, or maybe wanted to get me to make some changes in one of them, or something."

That was not what Wagoner wanted. He told her that Norma Jean was getting married and leaving the Wagoner show to move back to Oklahoma, and Dolly Parton was under consideration for the job.

That First Afternoon

One recent night at WSM-TV, where he and Dolly and the Wagonmasters were videotaping two more of their weekly shows, Porter Wagoner grinned as he remembered that first afternoon Miss Dolly visited his office.

"You tell him about . . . many hymns?" he asked Dolly, nodding toward the reporter.

She blushed and shook her head.

"No," she said. "He asked the questions and I just answered them."

Porter grinned wider.

"We were talking about how she would fit into the show, you know," he began, "and I asked her if she would mind wearing fairly conservative clothes because of the family type of show we try to do. Well, she said that was fine with her, and then I asked her if she knew many hymns.

"Well, she thought a minute, and then she said, 'Minnie Hemms? No, I don't believe I know her.' We'd been talking about dresses and she thought Minnie Hemms was a seamstress."

The very embarrassed Miss Dolly brought a hand up to her face, hung her head and smiled with a red face.

"Then I caught it," she said, "and I laughed and then started telling him all the hymns I knew, trying to cover it up if I could. I didn't want him to think I was ignorant—at least not the first time he ever saw me."

"Nobody's Fool"

Miss Dolly is about as dumb as that dumb blonde she sings of—a young lady who, according to the lyrics, "ain't nobody's fool."

She writes nearly all of her own recordings, many of Wagoner's, and most of their duets. Thus, it is much more than her beauty that makes Miss Dolly valuable to the Porter Wagoner Show, the longest-running and most successful of Nashville syndicated country music television shows.

After four years on that show, Miss Dolly is moving toward a place among the female superstars of the business—women like Loretta Lynn and Tammy Wynette. Her current recording of "Muleskinner Blues," which is not unlikely to become a classic, was her first No. 1 song in the trade magazine charts. It is safe to bet there will be more.

Miss Dolly, meanwhile, wears her hair either incredibly high or incredibly long, and sometimes is seen in clothes that are at the very least gaudy—like a pink jumpsuit she wore on the Grand Ole Opry stage at last year's Disc Jockey Convention. With high, gauzy pink collars that looked like wings, the suit made Miss Dolly look like an extremely well-developed moth.

Her off-the-cuff comments also are sometimes a little surprising; witness a recent Grammy presentation dinner in which she came to the rostrum with Wagoner to present an award and acknowledged the warm applause by making a familiar pitch for a sponsor of the Wagoner TV show:

"Buy Cardui brand tablets, ladies!"

But she seems to take herself remarkably unseriously, particularly for a country girl who has come so far so fast.

Not long before the reporter left that interview that day, she seemed to touch on the reasons for that.

"Awful Lucky"

"I was tellin' Porter the other day that I'm awful lucky to have got here and got into the business before the competition got as tough as it is now. There's always been competition in the business, but when I started six years ago it hadn't really started to get hot yet, the way it is now."

She seems to think of her success not so much as something she achieved herself but more as a gift from a lot of people . . . such people as her uncle Bill and Fred Foster, who really believed in her.

The reporter was home a half-hour after the interview, playing back the tape, when one of those Owepar uncles, Louie Owens, called back.

"Uh, Dolly left me a note here to call you," he said.

"Okay."

"She wanted me to—well, here's what the note says," Owens said. "'Ask him to please be sure and put in that any success I've achieved in the last few years I owe to Porter Wagoner, who is a fine man and everything he appears to be.'"

All right. Whatever she says.

Even if Porter does like to tell that story about Minnie Hemms.

PORTER WAGONER AND DOLLY PARTON

Gene Guerrero | May 1971 | *The Great Speckled Bird*

The *Great Speckled Bird* was a New Left counterculture underground newspaper published by the Atlanta (GA) Cooperative News Project from 1968 to 1976. The *Bird* was profiled on *60 Minutes* in 1971, with Mike Wallace calling it "the *Wall Street Journal* of the underground press," and thirty years later, *Atlanta* magazine recalled the publication as "one of the most fascinating and most forgotten artifacts of Atlanta culture."

In 1970, Gene Guerrero, country and bluegrass music writer for the *Bird*, favorably reviewed *My Blue Ridge Mountain Boy*, Dolly's fourth solo studio album. "Dolly is a great singer," he wrote. "Her voice is a crystal clear soprano. She has a distinctive delivery, placing her emphasis on surprising syllables, cutting off short on one word and allowing her voice to drop off gradually on another. In the finest country tradition, she conveys intense emotion without using her voice as an emotional gimmick."

Guerrero was especially taken with "Evening Shade," a song about a very oppressive orphanage where the kids revolted. "That theme appealed to us," recalls Guerrero. "Then, out of the blue, I received a nice letter from Dolly thanking me for the review. I contacted her office in Nashville and asked if we could come up and do an interview. We were amateur journalists and did not bring a photographer with us. When we got there, Dolly asked us to include Porter. Both were all dressed up in their stage clothes for the photographer we failed to bring. Later, at least twice, when they came to Atlanta for shows, Dolly and Porter acknowledged us from the stage, and even had us on their bus."

It should be noted that the interviews were originally published as a two-part feature spread across the May 17 and May 24 issues of the *Bird*. Although Dolly's interview appears here in its entirety, Wagoner's has been omitted since it was mostly unrelated to Dolly and their partnership. —Ed.

Porter Wagoner and Dolly Parton are country music superstars. Porter's been on the Grand Ole Opry for years and as much as anyone else has been responsible for the continuance and growth of good "hard" country music, turning out hit after hit over the years. Dolly, in her mid-twenties, has skyrocketed to the top in the last few years with hits like "Something Fishy," "Just Because I'm a Woman," and "Joshua." In 1967 Dolly joined the Porter Wagoner Show and together she and Porter have developed perhaps the best duet in country music today.

But Porter and Dolly reject the superstar label—not in words but in the way they relate to people. If you've ever seen them in person or even on TV you'll know what I mean. They are warm, friendly people.

I was apprehensive as we walked up to the little house on music row in Nashville that serves as their office, afraid that Porter and Dolly would turn out to be as phony as some of the rock superstars I've met. They're for real, two of the nicest people you'll find anywhere. When they talk about their music they talk about the people who listen more than they talk about themselves.

The most exciting part of the interview was afterwards. Dolly sang us a beautiful song she and Porter had written, then we listened to tapes of new material. A demo tape of a rock and roll song Dolly wrote. She sang on the tape although she doesn't have any plans to record rock herself. It was a good song.

Listening to her sing rock I thought of Aretha Franklin. Both have the same powerful voices and the same incredible range. Porter played tapes from an album he's producing with Buck Trent, his lead guitarist and banjo player. Buck plays material he and Porter have written. It will be a great album—simple, exciting, beautiful country rock, some of the best I've ever heard.

The afternoon with them was a genuine natural high. They're fine people who turn out great country music and are continuing to grow. They understand the strength of country music and their thoughts printed below add to our understanding. Part Two of the interviews will appear in next week's Bird.

–gene guerrero

BIRD: *Many of your songs seem to come out of your own background. Can you tell us a little bit about how you grew up in East Tennessee?*

DOLLY: I was from a family of 12 children and we grew up on a farm. The song "In the Good Old Days" told it just about like it was. We were a poor family but we stayed together—we all had to work the fields together. We had a little church that my grandfather built, who is the man I wrote the song about—"Daddy Was an Old Time Preacher Man." And it was a little Church of God and we used to go and and I'd take my guitar and sing in church and we had the tambourines and it was kind of like a colored church, everybody singin' and shoutin', very spiritual and all of that. I enjoyed it. That's the only thing I ever knew and it's really the only kind of church I really enjoy now.

We lived in a place called Mountain View when I was just a child, or we called it Locust Ridge, or over in the holler—we had three names for it. We lived there until I was 8 years old, then we moved out. We still lived on a farm, but it was out closer to civilization. Before that I used to go to a little one room school—first thru the eighth—the grades all in one room.

BIRD: *I understand that you've written a song called "Coat of Many Colors." Could you tell us about that song?*

DOLLY: The song about the coat of many colors is a real touching thing to me. My mama used to read us all the Bible stories. I know the Bible pretty well, and I especially loved the stories. I had never had my picture made in school, because they just didn't have a man to come around to a small school like we had then, and I never had seen a picture of myself. But one day, after we had moved out of the holler, they were havin' pictures made at the school. People used to send us things, like relatives who had children, they'd send clothes and rags and things and mama would make quilt tops out of the rags. This particular time though, she made me a coat to have my picture made, plus I needed one anyway. I didn't have a blouse under it, it was just a little jacket-like coat. So I wore it to school and the kids started making fun of my coat. Well, I was proud of it, and like I say in the song, mama had told me the story about Joseph and the coat of many colors from the Bible.

I thought it was the grandest thing I'd ever owned in my life. So they started laughing about it, said I didn't have on a blouse. Course, being a child I said I did cause I was embarrassed. When they made the picture I was crying, but I was smiling cause I wanted my picture made so bad. I still have the picture and about a year and a half ago I wrote a song about it, when it didn't bother me so much anymore. And if I write about things that bother me then they don't bother me anymore. That's really why I wrote it.

BIRD: *I guess it's sort of obvious in your songs that growing up in a church and singing gospel music really had an impact on your music overall.*

DOLLY: Well, I think it is. In our church everybody done just exactly what they felt like doin'—your spirit was free and you were just free to do whatever you wanted to do, if you wanted to shout—of course, I never done much shoutin' but I done an awful lot of singin'. I think it just naturally shows the soul and the feeling when you do grow up like that. If I do have any soul, that's where it would have come from—the church.

BIRD: *Also in the mountains there is the traditional kind of bluegrass and high-pitched mountain music. How were those things mixed together, how did they all combine to produce what you put out now?*

DOLLY: I wasn't really that familiar with any other music besides gospel music then because we didn't have a radio and we didn't have a television until I was almost grown. So all the singin' I heard was all the singin' we done in church and then all my mama's people sung and played some kind of instrument—then we used to all get together and everybody sang till way down in the morning.

BIRD: *What kind of instruments did they play?*

DOLLY: Well, several of them played the guitar, and I had one cousin who played the mandolin, and my grandpa, the preacher, he played the fiddle and he played the guitar too. Then I played the guitar and we had an old piano too, with all the ivory gone off of it—it was just junky instruments, but we got a pretty good sound out of it.

BIRD: *How did you get into country music itself? I know you were on the radio for a while.*

DOLLY: I started writing songs before I could even write. I started makin' songs before I even started to school and my mother used to write 'em down for me. They weren't really gospel songs, some of 'em were and some of 'em weren't. When I was ten years old I had an uncle named Bill Owens that took me to Knoxville. This man [*Cas Walker —Ed.*] had a supermarket that sponsored a TV show on Monday, Wednesday and Thursday nights. So I worked in the summer months from the time I was ten years old till I graduated from high school in '64 when I turned 18. And I worked Christmas vacations and any holidays and I got paid a little bit of money for it. That's where my radio work started.

BIRD: *Tell us about coming to Nashville? How did you come?*

DOLLY: Just as fast as I could. Of course for years I had planned to come to Nashville but I wanted to finish school because my Daddy was strict and old-fashioned and I wouldn't have been allowed to leave home anyway unless I'd run away and I didn't want to leave that way. I wanted to stay until I could leave on my own. So I graduated in '64 from high school and the next morning I already had my things packed, for months really, the things that I was going to take other than the clothes I was wearing. I rode the bus down here. Of course I had an uncle that had just moved down, Bill Owens. He had already moved down and got a place, him and his wife, and they had a little boy. So I came on down to their house. His wife went to work at Shoney's, and he was working on the road with Carl & Pearl Butler and I kept their little boy for my board.

Few months later I got on Monument Records. It was the first contract that I had after I came here. They put me on salary for writing. I made $50 a week. Then I moved out and got my own apartment. I lived by myself until I got married.

BIRD: *In one interview I saw, you talked about the difficulty of remaining a country artist, and how people were trying to get you to become a pop artist.*

DOLLY: I have a real strange voice. A lot of people it just irritates them to death, 'cause it's piercing. I can understand it, cause there's been a lot of people I don't like to hear sing. My voice is real unusual. I sound a lot like a child, I guess. They thought people wouldn't buy me unless I was covered up with music. They wanted to drown out my voice to keep from hurting my feelings, getting embarrassed when I heard the record. I'm sure they believed in me but they thought that was the best thing to do. So I recorded a type of music that I never had been familiar with.

Of course I like music in general. Now I can I feel like I can sing it, and I do a lot of demos. I do a lot of rock songs that I write, and folk songs, different types. But at that particular time I wanted to do country because that's what I was and it showed just like it was. It was just country words, and country sound with a rock beat.

BIRD: *You're writing some rock songs?*

DOLLY: I've written a lot of rock songs—hard rock and then some—I don't know how to define the category. Then I've wrote some pretty songs that could be easy listening stuff. I just write what I feel.

I love all kinds of music. I just flip my radio from one station to another. If I hear a country song I don't like, I flip to a rock station. Cause I just like music. It don't make any difference to me. I listen to WVOL, which is strictly a colored station, a lot of times. And another thing—I like to keep up with what's going on, in order to write about what's going on.

BIRD: *Has soul music had an influence on country music and vice versa?*

DOLLY: Well, I think so. Because I think that soul music or colored music, whatever you want to call it—I think that's the colored people's earthiness. I mean that's what they feel in their soul. The country people are just a little more earthy and just don't have as much feeling actually. I would define soul music and country music closer than anything else, cause they're both realism, expression without gimmicks and things.

BIRD: *How do you write songs? Do you have a particular way?*

DOLLY: I don't write music and I can't read a note of music. I just do it all by ear. Then sometimes I get words and I'll put a melody to it. A lot of writers have a pattern they write by. But it don't have to be quiet for me to write if something hits me. I could sit down in the middle of a room where they're playing and everything and I can just plunk it out and just write it down and I can write anywhere. I can write in church for one thing—it's not very proper, but I mean I think of things and I get ideas from everything.

BIRD: *You work out the music yourself, then record it, and somebody else puts it down?*

DOLLY: Yeah. I just write the words and remember the melody, then the man that does our copyrights writes the music for me. I don't even know what he's wrote—I just take for granted that it's right.

BIRD: *Many of your songs talk about women, like "Just Because I'm a Woman," and what I think is your best, "Don't Let It Trouble Your Mind." What are you trying to say about women in your songs? Many of our readers are interested in Women's Liberation.*

DOLLY: I don't know all the details of the women's liberation thing—I believe enough in God and the Bible to know that a man should rule his household *but* I also believe enough in people and believe enough in the way life goes. Just like up home, people thought if a woman had ever made a mistake in her life that she was nothing. A man could go out every week and have any woman he wanted. When he got ready to marry though, he had to have somebody untouched and all this. That just always bothered me. Because I don't understand why that's fair. I know it'll always be that way cause the woman can't do anything. The man can do anything—as far as morals.

BIRD: *Do you really think it'll always be that way?*

DOLLY: I think it will with certain people, certain parts of the country. Now I know there are people that are broad-minded enough that it don't make any difference to them. As far as I'm concerned, it wouldn't to me if I was a man. I wouldn't expect something I'm not myself. It just kinda always got to me—even my own brothers and my own family. If a woman made a mistake—or whether it was a mistake or not, even if she meant to do it—whatever she had done she was just tagged. And she was probably a better person than they were—inside and the way she thought about things. But I just kinda like to express what I think about it and know that women all feel that way.

BIRD: *How 'bout in the music industry? Has getting in as a writer and a singer been any problem for you as a woman?*

DOLLY: Well, I don't pride myself on being all that smart, but I think I got good common sense. It's something born in me and something I was brought up with, and when I come to Nashville people accepted me pretty well. And I could get in to talk with people easier because I was a girl and at that time they probably thought I was just a dumb country girl that wouldn't know what was going on and wouldn't suspect anything. But I did. Because I was aware of things, because I had been all my life. I have an understanding of life and people. I can just about read what people think.

But now I have a lot of things told on me against my morals which are not true. I'm no angel, but if I'd done half the things I've been accused of I wouldn't be sitting here, I'd be wore out somewhere—I'd be dead. I have a lot of things I like to talk about. Some of my very best friends are men because women—I like women cause I am one, my mother was one—but like if I have something to say, I don't know that many women that would understand what I'm talking about businesswise or understand my ideas. So I might want to go somewhere and eat supper with a man friend. But I don't very often. Cause if they see you with somebody—it has to be bad. A woman just don't go out with a married man unless there's something going on. It kinda irks me really to think that people are so narrow minded.

Country music is exactly that way. It tells of life the way it is.

The exciting thing about Porter and Dolly's music is that it continues to grow—as their new albums indicate. Porter's latest is *Simple as I Am*. It has a really clever Red Lane/Dottie West song, "Funky Grass Band," which is the story of a raunchy band from Hazard, Kentucky. All the incidents in the tale are based on actual experiences of various bands, like the time the driver pulled the bus over next to the side of the mountain so when Bill Monroe stepped out to take a leak he went halfway down. Another fine song is "That's How I Learned to Love Good Old Country Music," full of memory-pulling references to things like listening to the radio in Del Rio, Texas.

Dolly's most recent release is *Joshua.* Besides "Joshua," one of the best upbeat country songs of late, the album includes "You Can't Reach Me Anymore," another great song about women:

I once looked up to you, while you were looking down,
It used to tear me up when you would tear me down.
Love that once lived in my heart, it don't live there anymore,
And you can't reach me anymore.

The one I listen to most is *Two of a Kind,* the latest duo album. It shows the beauty of their voices together in "Oh the Pain of Loving You." Near the first of the song there's a series of high notes that are chilling—the harmony is so good. The song itself was written by Porter and Dolly together and shows how well they understand people and human relationships.

Another song, like the interview below, illustrates how they're trying to reach out with their music. It's "Curse of the Wild Weed Flower," about heroin, written by Louis Owens and Dolly.

I know all this sounds like p.r. hype but I won't apologize for it. If Porter and Dolly come to Atlanta, or to your town, don't miss their show. You'll see.

–gene guerrero

Bird: *"Evening Shade" describes an orphanage where a matron mistreats the kids until one girl burns the place down. I understand there's an orphanage in Sevier County where you're from and I wondered how the matrons at that home felt about the song?*

Dolly: Well, I really didn't have any reason to write the song. It's just something I made up in my mind, which I do lots of times. I've got a wild imagination. Even the title—I just mostly wanted to write something different from what people would think it would be just by looking at the title, so I just called the home "Evening Shade"—but I never knew of a place called that. Now I did have a lot of friends that lived at the orphanage in Sevierville and I used to go up. But they were, as far as I know, good to them there. It was just a wild story.

After I got into the story I realized that I would write it about a home, a juvenile home, where I had heard that they were mean to them. But then after that I just got to thinking what I would have done if I had been there and she had whipped me cause I peed in the bed. Cause I had in the story about this child that wet the bed. But I just put that part in there because it was just back home. But it didn't really have any bearing on anything except my mind.

Bird: *What's responsible for the growing popularity of country music?*

Dolly: I think mostly people nowadays have tried just about everything, they've been everywhere. They've been beatniks, on dope, all this. They've lived in a world of fairy tales for a good while and I think people are just beginning to be more earthy and get down to where the simple things in life are. People just now want more realism than fantasy.

Bird: *Where do you think country music itself is going? On the one hand there's a growing popularity of the hard country sound and then on the other hand country rock seems to be very influential.*

Dolly: I really don't know what it will come to. Everybody'll eventually get to where, at some time or other in the not-too-distant future, there'll just be music. Then we could record a rock song or they could record a hard country and nobody would identify you with just any particular thing. I think there'll always be, though, the real hard country artist, cause that's the salt of the earth. I believe in progress but I don't believe in getting out of your field if it's going to ruin your career. I think every song should be treated as an individual. I don't think you can take just every song and say, "We're going to have a steel guitar and a fiddle and this and that." I think certain songs talk to certain instruments. I don't define music as too much pop or country or rock or such—I just define it as music.

Bird: *Tell us about working with Porter. I feel like that's really important—I get a sense that y'all add a lot to each other's music.*

Dolly: I think it's important to my career because if it hadn't been for him I may have still been struggling along and trying to get in the business. But he was good enough and saw far enough to where he thought I had something going, that I could be worked into something. I enjoy doing the duets. I think it's a good contrast in our voices. And it's good for both of us. That way you've got three artists really, him, me, and the two. And we've always got something in the charts.

Porter is a great great person to work with. Of course it's not always smooth sailing because we're both so much alike and I have my own ideas about things and it's just natural for him to think I don't really know what's going on and I feel like I do and sometimes we have conflict over that and get into heated arguments but that's just part of it—at least I'm smart enough to know he's the boss and he's been at it longer than me, but still I have to present my ideas and if I have to I'll argue about them. But all around it's great—a great relationship and Porter is a great person—cause he's so much like me. We are so much alike in a lot of ways—we like the same things, we both respect the business the same, that's all we both ever wanted. It really gets on my nerves to see somebody abuse the business and not treat it right.

Bird: *I'm not sure what you mean by abuse but it seems to me that one abuse is that some artists tend to get away from the people. That's one thing you and Porter have maintained—a closeness—even though you've been successful commercially.*

Dolly: Well, I think that's cause we're both so country and were brought up with the same kind of people that we're playing to. I understand them and he understands them. I know how they think cause all my people are just the same way.

But I was talking about abusing the business like artists who only want to do what's good for them. If they can get on a network show and if it's just for them and they're going to make money, they don't care if it's good for the business, if it's good for country music, they don't care how it's presented, just as long as it's good for them and they're going to make a bunch of money, and they're going to be a star whether it's country music or not. I think that's abusing the business. And like getting drunk on stage, and insulting the fans and the disk jockeys and all this. There's a place for everything and that shore ain't the place.

Bird: *It's really remarkable how you all are able to communicate with the audience, like even on the TV show.*

Dolly: Well, it's just sincerity and being honest with people. When I, and Porter's the same way, when I'm singing a song, I'm looking at the people and not the camera. And I'm looking at them like I want them to look at me and say, "Well, she means what she's saying; I don't like that song, or I don't like to hear her sing, but you can tell she's serious about it." The way I do it, I always do everything like I'm doing it for my family. Like I'm singing just to my folks, and people can sense that. They know if you mean it or not. Even myself, I can spot somebody unreal a mile away. I can see somebody walking across the yard and if they're a smart aleck I can just feel it, but that's because of the common knowledge that I was brought up with.

Bird: *Why do you think you have that understanding? Does it have anything to do with things like being picked on about the coat when you were a kid? I feel that people understand more when they've been on the receiving end.*

Dolly: Well, I think that's got at least 50% to do with it, and I think being born with the gift of understanding. Because it's like I've always been able to talk with people that had a problem. They know and could sense that I did understand, even if I didn't know what they were talking about, if I had never experienced it myself. There's nothing that shocks me—I don't care how dirty, how bad, how clean, how good or anything, I can just understand it and know that there's reasons for all things and accept it that way. And I think being brought up hard and poor like we was, and understanding each other like we did and knowing all my people. There's so many people in my family. There's thirteen in my Daddy's family and nine in Mama's and then all these cousins. There's bound to be a personality of every kind in the family and problems of every kind in the family. Well I seen all that, I understood it and knew that person personally and knew that they were a good person basically no matter what they done. So I think that's got a lot to do with it, the way I was brought up.

Bird: *Do you feel like, with all the attention that country music's getting, that there's a danger that people will abuse it more?*

Dolly: I think so. Like different people trying to get into country music that really don't care anything about it. They just want to be in it for the money cause that's where the money is. I think that's bad. That's another way of abusing it. You've got to be serious about it in order to do well for a long time. You might have some hit records but when people find out what you are you ain't going to be around for too long.

Bird: *It seems that "Joshua" was a little different song musically. How do you see your music going in the future?*

Dolly: Well, I don't really have any plans for it to go any certain direction. I just think every song I write is an individual and I think the music on it will be fitting for that. Wherever it goes, I'll be proud naturally—the bigger it is the better you like it—but I don't really have any plans of it going any directions other than just country. If it does go, it'll be great as long as it's country oriented.

SAY HELLO TO THE REAL MISS DOLLY

Jerry Bailey | October 20, 1974 | *The Tennessean*

The duo of Dolly Parton and Porter Wagoner was tremendously successful. They produced fourteen Top 10 hits together, but the two artists were constantly at odds. Wagoner sought to confine and control Dolly, but she was determined to break free. In 1974, bolstered by the successes of songs like "Coat of Many Colors," "My Tennessee Mountain Home," and the Number 1 country hit "Jolene," Dolly stopped touring with Wagoner's show, left the cast of his television show, and set into motion a plan for their professional separation.

"I worked with Porter Wagoner on his show for seven years," Dolly told the *Los Angeles Times* in 2008. "I don't mean this in a bad way, so don't play it up that way—but he very much was a male chauvinist pig. Certainly a male chauvinist. He was in charge, and it was his show, but he was also very strong-willed. That's why we fought like crazy, because I wouldn't put up with a bunch of stuff. Out of respect for him, I knew he was the boss, and I would go along to where I felt this was reasonable for me. But once it passed points where it was like, your way or my way, and this is just to control, to prove to you that I can do it, then I would just pitch a damn fit. I wouldn't care if it killed me. I would just say what I thought."

Included on the popular *Jolene* album was Dolly's farewell song of gratitude to Wagoner, "I Will Always Love You," a song that would soon become her signature tune. She explained the story behind the song to Bill DeMain of *The Performing Songwriter* in 1996: "He wouldn't listen to nothing at that time because he was so angry and so spiteful and so mean about the whole thing that he wouldn't allow me a conversation to try to explain why I was doing what I was doing. I thought, 'Well, the only way I'm going to be able to express it is to write it.' Everybody can understand a song. There were so many things I wanted to say, there was so much emotion, feeling and heartache on his part and my part. Once I started it, the song seemed to pour out." —Ed.

"People are always kidding me about my figure. I have too much up here. It's always been that way, and people have always just used me as a punching bag or a guinea pig or something. People think if you've got anything at the top, you couldn't come by it naturally—that you have to have it hand-made." —Dolly Parton

She was standing there in the hallway, autographing pictures of herself.

The photographic image which said, "With Love, Dolly Parton" across its left shoulder didn't exactly look like her, but either she didn't agree or didn't mind. It hardly seemed possible the face in the picture could ever blush. She went right on signing until the stack was finished.

Judging from Dolly's appearance, one might have thought she was on the way to a concert or television taping, rather than just another interview. There were mounds of blonde hair—some real, some not. A white western jacket and matching pants. The face that draws stares, and, of course, the figure that feeds the imagination like a candy shop.

It's all been said before.

Prior to opening the door to her office, she told the secretary to hold her telephone calls for a while. Embarrassed, she giggled, "Don't I sound like a big executive?"

After switching seats a couple of times, she settled down in the big reclining chair behind her desk. It didn't seem to be where she wanted to sit, but was a matter of technical necessity since the only plug in the room for a tape recorder was behind the desk.

––––––––––––

There were so many things to talk about. The relationship with Porter Wagoner, the new band, new bus, new booking agent, new directions, new freedom. Then there were old jokes, old gossip, old habits and the good old childhood days in the Smoky Mountains. Maybe a few surprises, too.

Most of it hasn't been said before.

Since Dolly ended her seven-year partnership with Porter Wagoner, the man with wagon wheels on his coat, a lot of people have been wondering what's going to become of her. After all, Porter had a mighty big hand in making her what she is today. That's what she used to say.

Why did they split? Only Porter and Dolly know for sure. The reason given was Dolly wasn't getting the recognition she deserves while riding Porter's wagon. There were smiles and hugs and words like, "We've worked for this day," but to skeptics it all sounded too smooth and sudden. Whether it was so peaceful is a story that probably will never be told. Dolly said she didn't want to talk about it. However, she did say she is happy to have her freedom.

"I've always pretty well done things my own way as far as my personality is concerned," she said. "But now I want to do things more my way than I have in the past. I was proud to be a part of the Porter Wagoner organization, but this gives me a chance to prove myself and carry on in my own way. This gives me a chance to do some things that I wouldn't have felt were fair for me to suggest in his show just because I felt they would be better for me."

Porter and Dolly still have adjoining offices on 18th Avenue South. They still are friends—even business partners in a sense—but only when it feels right. "The work we do now together is just the work we choose to do," she explained. Sort of like Loretta Lynn and Conway Twitty or Barbara Mandrell and David Houston. In country music, a duet album is a synonym for bonus money, so Porter and Dolly continue to cut them.

During the last year, perhaps her greatest concern has been problems with her voice. She has had to curtail interviews with disc jockeys and reporters, and even hold off on autographs at times because she can't afford to talk to the fans.

"I've had nodes on my vocal chords for the past year," she said, "and I've had to give them a rest. I've done that four times in the year and been out of work for several weeks at a time. They say that if I don't cut back, I'll have a serious problem. It hit me at a bad time, trying to get started and re-organize. Starting the first of the year, I'm going to have to work quite a bit less."

———————————

Dolly Parton's new band is largely a family affair. Her brother, Randy Parton, fronts the group and plays bass. Two cousins, Dwight Puckett and

Sidney Spiva, play drums and steel guitar. The only non-family member is Bill Rehrig, whom Miss Parton said she has "adopted" into the band. Her road manager is an uncle, Lewis [*sic*] Owens, who has helped her career since the earliest days.

"I didn't use my kin folks because they were kinfolks," she said in a soft, but defensive voice. Nobody had attacked. "I used them because I thought they were the best I could find." In the cases of brother Randy and cousin Dwight, she even went to their concerts and stood in the audience to see if their unaffected stage styles were what she wanted. Being very family oriented, she said she was glad she could find suitable kinfolks, but maintained that if difficulties arise, kinship will be ignored.

Dolly Parton likes to use the time traveling between shows for writing new songs. She said she composed 17 new tunes while rolling down the highway last month in her new bus. During the four months after the split with Wagoner, while preoccupied with building her own show, not one song found its way onto paper. She said she wanted to keep her mind clear until the business matters were settled.

Songwriting means a lot to this 28-year-old entertainer. She once said she started writing songs before she could even write songs—before she ever went to school, when she couldn't write or read or spell. Music has always been near the center of her life, and generally it's been her music, not created by anyone else or patterned after another style. "My writing is more personal to me than anything," she said, "and to think that somebody would really take the time to listen . . . 'cause I'm saying a lot more in my songs than a lot of people may know. Even the simplest of my songs, I've got really deep feelings inside of them."

It is perhaps easily understandable that some of Dolly Parton's most ardent fans have tended to exercise their eyes at the expense of their ears. It is as if the fact that she is a genuine country singer with a unique style and repertoire is only a secondary feature. But to play down the importance of music to Dolly Parton would be to not understand Dolly Parton. She may not have worked especially hard to quash the myth that beautiful blondes and brains do not run together, but a few minutes' conversation with her would be enough to convince any skeptic that she has a good head on her shoulders, a vivid imagination, and a great dedication to succeed as a musician.

The quality of her writing, and the fact that she loves to have an audience listen carefully to each word may bring her to the attention of a new group of listeners. The "underground" country fans, the younger set, love a singer capable of putting life into lyrics. While Dolly was with Porter, she might as well have been the cornerstone of the Nashville establishment.

Few self-respecting Waylon Jennings fans would dare get caught with one of her albums in their rack. Not that they didn't sneak a listen. Porter and Dolly simply worked for a different audience. But with Dolly's show of independence and the contemporary sound of her records (which are largely produced by Wagoner) there just might be a match in the making.

"You've got plenty of reason to think that," she agreed. "In fact, that's all I hear lately. People keep asking me if I'm aware of how popular I'm becoming in those areas. I'm tickled to death because I wasn't expecting it. But like I said before, I'll always be me. I won't be no different than I have always been. I will work the college circuit. I may throw them a few songs to please them on those particular shows because I don't want them to think I don't care whether I work them or not. But to me, it'll just mean more people are aware of what I can do—my writing."

"I'm real inside," she said. "What I wear on the outside, well, that's got nothing to do with the way I am. I'm a totally different person from the way I look. I really am. If I was as real on the outside as I am on the inside, I would look like a blank wall.

"The reason I like my hair and pretty clothes is it's something I never had as a kid," she said. "I had to look and live like the hippies are look-ing and living now. As children, we had to wear britches with the hind end out of them and patches all over. The faded denim and stringy hair and scrubbed faces. It was fine, but we had no choice. So then, I auto-matically thought when I get grown up, I'm going to have pretty clothes and pretty jewelry and pretty make-up and pretty hair-dos. I wanted to know what it feels like.

"So now, the young people have gone back to what I have already been through, and that's what the connection is. That still laces us together. I've been there. I know what it feels like to live down to earth—to be earth people. I still am inside."

Although Dolly's musical success has had a dramatic financial effect on her life, most clearly illustrated in her appearance, any change has been self-imposed. The mere thought of anyone suggesting that she conform to someone else's tastes was enough to set her off on the afternoon of this interview, a few days before the Country Music Association award show.

She leaned back in her chair, propped her feet on the desk and spoke her piece.

"I ain't gonna never change unless I want to," she asserted stubbornly. She may have been trying to sound tough, but the hint of a smile in her face told you she wouldn't scare a kid on Halloween night. "I don't try to follow no styles," she continued. "I told you this before and I'll tell anybody else. I ain't in style, but I like to think I've got my own style.

"A while ago, I was talking to some people with the CMA (Country Music Association). I won't mention who, but on the show—I'm going to be on the awards show—they mentioned that I should wear less hair. They said, 'Has anybody approached you with the fact that you should wear less hair?' I said, 'No, and if they do, I'll say I'll not wear less hair because if I can't be comfortable, I'm not going to be on the show. I'm not selling nothing but my talent, and I'm wearing what I please.' That's the way I feel.

"I mean it," she said, gathering a second wind. "I thought, 'What do they want me there for. Are they trying to make me into something different than what the CMA stands for?'

"People know that I wear a lot of hair. They already know I wear make-up. My country music fans have already accepted that fact. It's the people who don't know no different that are trying to change me all the time. But they aren't gonna change me." She was smiling openly now, but this was not a time to smile back. Miss Dolly wasn't finished.

"It's just like people are talking and said, 'Well, have you heard any . . .'" She paused, then gathered courage. "I maybe shouldn't mention this, but I don't reckon it'll hurt nothing to be honest," she reasoned. "I won't say who it was. They said, 'Have you heard any controversy about the people who've been nominated for the awards?' They said, 'All kinds of people are mad because Olivia Newton-John and Mac Davis are nominated.' They said, 'Have you heard anything?'

"I said, 'No, I don't even know who's nominated. I know that I am because they told me at the office. And I know that Olivia Newton-John is because I heard it on the Ralph Emery Show.' I said, 'It doesn't make any difference to me because all the country people are trying to go pop and all the pop people are trying to go country. So whoever wins, I figure it's equal.'

"I told them I would like to win the award some day, but whether I do or not won't make me work any less hard. Because if I was working for an award, I would have quit long ago. I think it would be wonderful to win. I'm proud to be country. And I figure the CMA should know what they're doing. If they don't, I can't change them."

She stopped herself again, probably wondering how all this was going to sound in print. The Country Music Association, an organization within the industry with the stated aim of promoting country music, might not take too kindly to her airing her complaints so publicly.

"I maybe shouldn't be telling all this," she began slowly. "Please don't make it sound hard like I was really fussing. All I am saying is every year I've been on the CMA awards show, even when I was just presenting, they have always asked me to wear less hair and make-up. Then I would be like everybody else and I don't want to be like everybody else. I'm not doing anything to be different. I just don't follow people's trends. I've got to do what I want to do and wear my make-up and hair like I want to."

Dolly Parton's reasons for wearing such generous amounts of hair go beyond mere stubbornness. She may look quite tall with the four-inch heels on her feet and golden swirls on her head, but in truth, she's far from being a skyscraper. "I'm little. I'm only five feet tall," she confessed. "I've always had a complex about being short, so I like my hair high.

"I wear wigs for the convenience of it, but my own hair is blonde and long, and when I fix my own hair, I fix it the same way. I wear wigs just because I don't like to sit for long under a hairdrier and I don't like to spend all day primping. A lot of people think, from the way I look, I spend hours and hours getting ready, but I can completely be dressed in 30 minutes."

———————

Talking at such length about her looks perhaps was wearing Dolly's defenses thin. Her feet still were nonchalantly propped on the desk, but she no longer seemed quite so authoritative. Maybe it was frustration and the need to vent her emotions that pushed her on. Whatever the reason, she was talking freely, pausing only to blush with embarrassment or giggle girlishly at her confessions.

Her eyes sparkled and she broke into laughter as she thought of telling off those persons who dwell on the outer Dolly Parton. Still giggling, she added, "For years, when people would talk about my dimples, I would say it's nothing but the sink holes in my make-up."

"I can laugh at myself because I'm not a pretty person," she explained. "I mean I don't have all that natural beauty. But I'm like every other woman. I like to look as good as I can with what I've got to work with. I love to play in my make-up and I love hair-dos and clothes.

"But you know, people are always kidding me about my figure. I have too much up here. It's always been that way, and people have always just used me as a punching bag or a guinea pig or something. People think if you've got anything at the top you couldn't come by it naturally—that you have to have it hand-made. You know?

"It runs in our family, and it's not that big a deal. It used to embarrass me and hurt my feelings when people would say, 'Yeah, I know, she went to so-and-so and had plastic surgery.' I'm serious. But I didn't go nowhere and have plastic surgery. It really bothered me for a long time. See, for years, since I was 13 years old, I've been over-grown. Really."

"Just once . . . well, twice . . . I wore a real low-neck dress," she confessed. "It embarrassed me to death. I sat and pulled at it, you know. I only wore it because other people talked me into doing it. I was so uncomfortable. I would rather wear a turtle neck than something low-neck any day."

"Oh, yeah, I know about the gossip," she said without resolution. "People have had me and Porter married and me and Charley Pride married, and then me running with everybody in the business. For one thing, it's not true, because I'm a better person than that. And for another thing, if I was gonna run with anybody, I wouldn't dare run with anybody in the music business because it's like a family. I mean, that would be like running with your kinfolks or somebody.

"Everybody would know it. If you had any self-respect, you wouldn't do it. Like I said, I don't do it anyway." She grew tired of the subject and concluded, "It don't make no difference anyway. I don't want to come out sounding self-righteous, but people are going to say and think what they please anyway. It don't bother me so much anymore."

A few minutes later she was in the yard before her office, posing for pictures. She was clearly self-conscious, nervously posing her leg, trying different positions for her hands. Giggling all the while.

An unseen admirer in a building across the street let go a long, low wolf whistle. Dolly pretended he wasn't there.

DOLLY DIAMOND

On Ambition

"Yes, I'm ambitious. But I hope I'm not hard. I don't want anything at anyone else's expense. If I ever get to the point where I really go off on an ego trip, I hope there's someone there to put me down."

—To Bob Greene, *Chicago Sun-Times*, February 2, 1976

DOLLY DIAMOND

On Growing Old

"I have no fear of gettin' old. Gettin' old don't mean you can't be creative. I picture myself as an old woman still bein' very useful and writin' things for people to enjoy. I imagine my whole life full of songs and poems and stories about real things and genuine people. Dolly Parton's a Mountain Gal, true and simple."

—To Kevin Kelly, *Boston Globe*, July 3, 1977

PART II
Elusive Butterfly

"I wanted to take my music into some areas where I'd never taken it before. I've had a large following in the contemporary field for a number of years but I'd just never really gone on their territory. But that doesn't mean to say I won't still be doing country shows because I will. I love the public but I have no fear of them. I don't want to offend [country fans] because I love them most of all. I'm doing this because I enjoy it. I'm not gonna stand still for nobody."

—To Monty Smith, *New Musical Express*,
June 4, 1977

INTERVIEW: DOLLY PARTON

Chet Flippo | August 25, 1977 | *Rolling Stone*

Dolly's solo endeavors received rapid and widespread recognition. She brought home the prestigious CMA Female Vocalist of the Year award two years in a row (1975 and 1976), but Dolly's sights were set far beyond Nashville. When she signed with the high-powered West Coast management firm of Katz, Gallin, and Cleary, Dolly set off on a path to completely restructure her professional life. Determined to increase her visibility and push her music in a more mainstream pop direction, she personally masterminded an ambitious crossover campaign, overseen by new manager Sandy Gallin.

The first order of business was to disband the Traveling Family Band and assemble a more professional ensemble adept in more diverse musical styles. She called the new band Gypsy Fever. Dolly's detractors warned that she might alienate and ultimately lose her country music fan base, but she was unyielding. "Y'know, I love the public, but I have no fear of [country fans] because I love them most of all," she told *New Musical Express* in 1977. "I'm doing this because I enjoy it. I'm not gonna stand still for nobody."

Chet Flippo started writing for *Rolling Stone* magazine while still working toward a master's degree in journalism from the University of Texas. He became the publication's New York bureau chief in 1974, and graduated to senior editor in 1977 when the magazine relocated from San Francisco. "[Dolly] was bound and determined to break out of the country-music ghetto and find a national audience and carry her music and her message to the world at large," he later recalled. "'Crossover,' it was called at the time. Part of the campaign involved revamping her media image. That's why she was happy when I called her people to see about an interview. . . . She was perched at a crucial crossroads in her career, and that was why I had been able to convince the magazine's editors that the time was right for the rock bible yclept *Rolling Stone* to do a major take on a five-foot-tall, bewigged, rhinestoned country singer."

Dolly was on a six-week tour with Mac Davis when Flippo joined her for several days in Connecticut and New York. According to Flippo, the two enjoyed one another's company and the interview process. "She was surprised and grateful to find that I actually knew her music quite well, all the way back, and knew what all she had been through," he said. "I was happy to find an interview subject—whose music I loved—who lived up to her work. You would be surprised to discover how seldom that happens in pop and rock and country and jazz. But Dolly fit the bill, all across the board. I knew, as I seldom know with an artist, that she could accomplish whatever she wanted to accomplish. It was only a matter of will." —Ed.

What would you get if you crossed Mae West with Norman Vincent Peale?

What a grand feeling it is to be heading out of town in a fast, sky blue rent-a-Mustang with a cold six-pack on the floor, the June sun streaming down, the radio turned up loud and Dolly Parton sitting beside me. She's singing along with Jimmy Clanton's oldie "Just a Dream" and it occurs to me that a certain amount of fantasizing is impossible to avoid. *Let's see . . . we'll find a nice little meadow beside a stream for our picnic and as the day gets hotter we'll want to go for a cool dip in the clear, inviting waters and since neither of us brought a swimsuit. . . .* A battered Chevy pulls up alongside and two pimply teenagers do triple takes at Dolly with her cascading blond wig and tight-fitting shirt. I don't even have to lip-read to get the message: "Hey, what a great-looking chick! She's so *fine*. Lookit the creep with her."

And I realize I'm ten miles out of town and instead of clear streams, all I'm passing is liquor stores.

"Gee, Dolly, maybe I shoulda made reservations somewhere or somethin', I dunno."

"What about this graveyard?" she asks.

"You serious?"

"Yeah, I love cemeteries, they're so quiet. You know, people are dying to get into 'em. Really, I write in cemeteries a lot; nobody bothers you there."

I turn off into the Middlefield, Connecticut, cemetery and slowly cruise through. But the caretaker is slashing his way around the tombstones with a 100-decibel ride-a-mower. Clearly, this is not the spot for a quiet picnic.

I break into a slight sweat; adolescent memories. It is not at all cool to take the best-looking girl in school out for a summer picnic and then have to deposit her in a parking lot somewhere behind a Grand Union supermarket. Talk about a last date. *Please, God, find me a patch of grass somewhere.*

Finally, God leads me to a brook, a shade tree and a reasonable facsimile of a meadow. Dolly spreads a yellow blanket and we get down to serious business: the making of big, sloppy bologna and tomato sandwiches and the opening of wine.

Dolly stretches her arms out. "Oh, I just love it outdoors. You can just feel God all around you."

You certainly can, I reply.

A loaf of Wonder Bread, a jug of Italian Swiss Colony and Dolly Parton beside me in the wilderness. Ah, that paradise should come so early in my young life.

"Ooh, you got cherries for dessert," Dolly says. "Urn, good. I ain't had a cherry in a long time." She looks at me mischievously. "I don't think I ever had a cherry. If I did, it got shoved so far back I was usin' it for a tail-light!"

I must have looked shocked.

"I'm just kiddin'," she winks as she throws a cherry seed at me.

I have heard singers called many things, from four-letter words to 27-letter words, but I have never heard one called a "purifier". I always presumed that word applied only to such items as smog devices, our Lord Jesus Christ and Tareyton charcoal filter tips. But came one recent Friday morning when my own purifying sleep was disturbed by a phone call. I dispatched my helpmate to deal with it, but couldn't help overhearing her end of the conversation, which was mostly astonished gasps.

"What was all that about?" I asked. It was, I was told, an editor of a certain women's magazine and she was just calling to inform us that Dolly Parton had "purified" New York's Bottom Line the night before.

"What'd she do, take an ax to the place?"

"No, her music purified the audience. She's a *purifier*."

Well, damn me. I have known Dolly Parton for some time and known her as someone who writes a hell of a good country song and sings with an achingly sweet soprano and looks like what heaven should be populated with. But I also know her as a good ol' girl you can kid around with and not have to be too careful of what you do or say. Hardly someone, though, to get all mistyeyed or mystical over or go sobbing about in nightclubs. Further callers throughout the day, however, report similar quasi-religious experiences and cleansings of the soul. What is going on?

Butch Rutter has been purified. He gets backstage to see Dolly after her show at London's Rainbow Theatre even before Chita Rivera because Butch is a . . . very special case. Thus far, he is the only known human being on this planet to have his entire back tattooed with a full-color depiction of a Dolly Parton album cover, topped with her autograph and an inscription of love across his shoulder blades. He shows up in full cowboy regalia, accompanied by fellow members of his Alamo Club, a London group of Dolly Parton lovers. They are carrying, besides an air of puppylike devotion, a lovingly crafted brass plaque of Dolly's entire body in accurate profile. They have come in committee to formally ask Dolly to be official queen of the Alamo. Butch gets a regal kiss for that and then he drops his shirt to exhibit the Parton chef-d'oeuvre: a well-done copy of her *Love Is like a Butterfly* album cover. He had the tattoo started in 1976, and when Dolly played Wembley he got her autograph above the butterfly. He spent 12 hours under the needle. He did it because he loves her.

"You didn't get infected from tattooin' over my ink, did ya?" Dolly asks. "Hmm, that turned out real good, didn't it". She winks as he pulls up his shirt and makes to leave. "Well, at least you're gonna have *one* woman with you forever."

Butch laughs. "I've 'ad a fallin' out or two wi' me wife over this."

"Is that for real?" one of her band asks. "Oh yeah," says Dolly. "When I saw him last year he was still all scabbed over". She shrugs and giggles and gets ready to receive Chita. Butch Rutter recedes into the dim regions of Parton acolytes. I am suddenly reminded of a scene in New York

City. It was after the second night of Dolly's purification rites at the Bottom Line and she was hosting an early-morning champagne party at Windows on the World, atop the 110-story World Trade Center. There was a long line of fans and celebrities waiting to shake her jeweled hand and be photographed standing next to that famous body. One of those celebrities was Mick Jagger. Dolly put a hammerlock on him and the second the strobes went off he looked for all the world like a 12-year-old schoolboy blushing and gawking the first time a truly beautiful woman hugs him. Mick Jagger may be beyond *purification* but he clearly experienced *something*.

Back on the yellow blanket in the Connecticut countryside, Dolly and I are swapping tales of childhood indiscretions. I do not feel in the least purified and do not mind it a darn bit.

A pre-adolescent boy ambles through the sun-dappled field, a fishing pole on his shoulder. He halts in his tracks and gives Dolly a long, questioning glance and then moves slowly on toward his fishing hole. Sweet dreams, Jack. Dolly is oblivious, just grooving on being outside and escaping the Holiday Inn and forgetting for a while the week's booking as opening act for Mac Davis at the Oakdale Musical Theatre in Wallingford, Connecticut. Dolly and Mac will be followed there by Rock Hudson starring in *Camelot*.

As the young fisherman disappears, with one final glance over his shoulder, I take a moment to look at Dolly. She was not always as I see her before me; not always an angelic, creamy-skinned, honey-wigged, golden-throated, flashing-eyed, jewel-encrusted, lush-bodied, feisty enchantress of a songwriter and singer. Back there in Sevierville, Tennessee, she was thought at one time a rather unexceptional, born plain child. The fourth of Lee and Avie Lee Parton's 12 children, she was born in the Parton cabin January 19th, 1946. She matured *early* and by ten ran the family during her mother's illnesses. She had already recorded her first single, "Puppy Love," (she rode a Greyhound bus to Lake Charles, Louisiana, to record it, where an uncle had arranged studio time) and had started appearing on regional TV and radio shows. Her vocal style was set then: a shimmering, childlike trill, influenced mainly by church music and by the Elizabethan ballads her mother sang.

She was also ambitious and knew even then—and still knows—just what she wanted and just how to go about getting it, even to taking an unprecedented step for a country-music singer: last year she totally shut down her career to retool for a wider audience. She got a new band, a new management firm, a new booking agency. She changed everything but her mind. And her music.

And . . . and all of a sudden she looks away from the leafy oak she's been studying and finds me studying her. "I and I," she says, invoking an earlier discussion of Rastafarian grammar, "had better get I-selves back."

Back last fall, Dolly Parton was about as hot a country property as there was. Everybody from Patti Smith to Linda Ronstadt and Emmylou Harris was singing her songs. She had already started her independence movement in 1973, when she left the *Porter Wagoner Show* after six years. She and Porter, the lean, lanky, pompadoured epitome of flash and glitter in country music, were as famous a C&W duo as George and Tammy and Conway and Loretta. But Dolly had wider horizons in mind. Then last year came the shift toward pop audiences.

In September I went to talk to her about that. She was not, as the common misconception had it, leaving country music. "This is a new freedom for me," she said. "Just total self-expression and daring to be brave, just to really see music the way that I totally feel it. I just had to make a total break in order to see this thing through and it was *time*. I am 30 years old. I mean, if you let so many years go by, then you miss out on your chance and I think that I am in my season now. I have a lot of big dreams and, before, I had a lot of people who couldn't dream as big as me. I wouldn't allow myself to, I didn't understand what it was to dream, so I just wanted to dream free. . . ."

And what, I asked, would she do if she should fail? She looked up from where she was lying on the floor and trained those baby blues on me: "Well, I'm a brave little soldier." I felt a twinge of purification.

A song that she wrote then became her declaration of independence and I hear it constantly invoked by women who discern more sense in it than in feminist tracts or *Fear of Flying*. It's called "Light of a Clear Blue Morning" and it is a very revealing and moving song.

Driving back to the Holiday Inn in Connecticut, I ask her about that song. "That just told how I was feeling at the time, feeling like a captured eagle, and an eagle is born to fly, and now that I have won my freedom, like an eagle I am eager for the sky. And that is exactly how I felt. I just had to let the people know how I felt and that kind of eased my pain some. Can I have an ice cream cone?" We are, in fact, passing a drive-in, since I have gotten lost, so I wheel in and get her a double dip, to the envy of the other louts loitering in the parking lot.

I ask her about that purification business in New York and the converts she made there. She looks puzzled. "I wouldn't know what *purifying* is, but it's a nice compliment. City people, I think they get caught up with a southern, a country person who has a contentment and a peacefulness. I am certainly *not pure*, but I guess that depends on how you look at things."

We finally regain the Holiday Inn and retire to her $16-a-night single that overlooks the parking lot and the setting sun. Dolly kicks off her five-inch, rhinestone-studded heels and curls her legs up. On the dresser is a supply of the liquid protein she's been dieting with to get back to fighting weight of 110 pounds on her five-foot frame.

In person, she is stunning. I have seen people spontaneously break into applause when she enters a room. I tactfully suggest that she was probably the foxiest schoolgirl in Tennessee history and that, as a result, she may have had a tough time in school.

I get a smile of irony with her reply. "Well, I tell you, it was kinda rough for me because I was the most popular girl in school in the *wrong* way. *Everybody* talked about Dolly but I didn't have as many friends as I should have had. My best friends were boys because they understood me and weren't tryin' to find fault. But, you know, I never dated the boys in school. I seemed so much older. I only had a couple of dates with boys from school and I felt like their *mother* or somethin'. I had a lotta stories told on me, a lotta lies, just because I looked the way I did. I always was big in the boobs, small in the waist and big in the butt. I just grew up that way and I had that *foxy* personality, too.

"I mean, I was *real* outgoin', real friendly, I think it was scary to people. But I never felt I belonged. Never belonged in my whole life, even as a little kid. I was just *different* and so I never really found my place till I moved to Nashville and got in the music business. That was my *real* place, so I fit in. I was born restless, I really was. I guess I was born with gypsy fever. Now, there is nothin' I like better than goin' home to have a few weeks off, do as I please, go in the yard half-naked, without makeup and without havin' my hair done, or play with the dogs or romp around with the cows. But when I am ready to go, there is nothin' I like better than to pack it up and head it on out. I just couldn't stay, and in my later years when I am writing books and poems mostly I think I will travel around and do that: I really wouldn't want to stay at home all the time; that would be a *bore*."

When Dolly lit out for Nashville the day after she was graduated from high school in 1964, she hit town with little more than a cardboard suitcase full of songs. It didn't take her long to start selling those songs, to get a recording contract with Monument and then to switch to RCA when Porter Wagoner, impressed by her television appearances, tapped her to replace singer Norma Jean on his show.

The first thing she did when she hit town, though, was her laundry. In the Wishy Washy laundromat she met a man named Carl Dean.

She married him two years later. He is now an asphalt contractor and, so Parton mythology has it, has never seen her perform and their marriage is a very private thing and he is the stabilizing influence in her gypsy life. I teasingly ask her if he really exists.

"You know he does," she half-explodes before she laughs at the absurdity of the question. "And the stories are wrong—he has seen me perform. And he liked it. So there."

For a person who looks the way she does, it comes as a surprise when she claims that few men in the music business have ever seriously tried to put moves on her. She attributes that, naturally, to her fiercely independent nature. She does, however, write ingenuously sensuous songs. One of the more explicit ones is "He Would Know". One line is "I would love to love you but he would know."

"That is true," she says. "You couldn't be human, especially in this business, and not run across people now and then that *really* move you. And you have to be really strong to avoid temptation and even if you don't avoid it you have to be smart enough to know how much of it you can take. So, when it's more than I can stand, I just get my pencil and guitar out and I start writin': 'In my mind I make love to you often/But *only* in my mind can it be so/Because there is someone home who is counting on me/And if I *did*, I'm sure that he would know'. That's not sayin' I ain't made mistakes and won't make mistakes but if I can just write it and say this is a song about our situation, I hope you can better understand how I feel about it and why it can't be."

Another song Dolly wrote, the beautifully crafted "Bargain Store," was banned by some country stations and that still rankles her.

"I just thought," she says, "well, why don't a person compare your body and your mind and your heart to objects, like an old broken heart sittin' on a shelf and some plans and dreams as if they were things you could see". She starts singing: "'My life is likened to a bargain store/And I might have just what you're lookin' for/If you don't mind the fact that all the merchandise is used/ But with a little mendin' it can be as good as new'. That means that I have been in love before and kicked around and banged around and had my head and my heart broke, my cherry stole, but I can grow *another* one if that's what you want." She laughs a loud, exuberant laugh.

"When I said the bargain store is open, come inside, I just meant my life is open, come into my life, so I wasn't even thinkin' of it as a dirty thing. I just felt at that time I had been probably kicked around some. Not by my husband—he is the best person that ever lived. But you know, me and Porter, we just kind of said things, hurt each other's feelings and, you know, trampled around on territory that was real sensitive, cut each other about songs. It's just—I felt black and blue and I just wanted to heal back up and mend myself back together and get on with my life."

Another of her better songs is haunting and Gothic and describes fears she herself might have: "Where Beauty Lives in Memory" is the story of a beautiful woman, a Cinderella whose heart and mind are stolen by a prince who leaves her. She waits before her mirror for 40 years until he returns and then she drops dead.

"I knew a woman who was beautiful and she was married to this man and she was crazy about him but he would do bad things to her and he got to tellin' people she was crazy. She almost grieved herself to death and now she is like a child, she still talks about him, she has kind of gone back in time. She still thinks she is as young and pretty as she ever was. It just touched me so deep and I could just imagine that happening to *me*."

[. . .]

Common courtesy and a sense of fair play prevent me from asking Dolly Parton what her remarkable measurements might be but they don't stop me from evoking stripper Blaze Starr's song and how Blaze's 38DD got her out of the mountains and that Dolly's own configuration certainly hasn't hurt her career and what does she think about that song and, while I'm at it, did she ever think about being a stripper?

She is somewhat taken aback and pauses to collect her thoughts. For today's session in her motel room, she's wearing a taut black jumpsuit and a hot pink shawl with a matching orchid in her hair. There is a pizza left over from last night and we are just contemplating warming it up a slice at a time on the bottom of her steam iron when Blaze Starr comes to mind.

"That [38DD] is a unique idea," she finally says. "Bette Midler should record it, she could get away with it. I don't think people would accept that from me. I have never been the one to play up that sort of thing about myself. It's always been the public and the press. I have really tried to not promote nothing but my talent, and the way I look is the way I *like* to look. I'm just an extremist and so I like to dress the part—if I have extreme parts of my body, then I might as well have extreme hair-dos or have extreme clothes to match the boobs and the hairdo. And, my personality is really extreme. I do just as I please, I always have and always will. I try to live my own life; I don't try to live somebody else's life, and I don't like people tryin' to live my life. Now there, how do you like that? Buddy, I *mean* that."

It would be an understatement to observe that, through her song-writing and especially her image, Parton is very secure in her femininity. She espouses a very personal kind of femaleness which, despite her fierce independence, is in many ways very traditional. She carries no soapbox, delivers no rhetoric—though she's not hesitant to speak her mind. And she enjoys being a girl.

"I think that women have it made, if they know how to go about it," she says. "A woman don't have to work, *really*, if she don't want to and if she is smart enough to make a man a good wife he's gonna take care of her. I know that I couldn't be a stay-at-home woman, just raise kids and keep the house, that's not in me, but I'm just sayin' that women by nature *do* have it easier because they were made to be a man's helpmate, so to speak. Just to be a companion. But—if a woman is smart enough and she has a desire and an ambition to do something else, that's fine too. I would prefer to be a woman because a man has to get out and work because that is just the law of the land. And a woman doesn't have to unless she wants to."

But how did her own exaggerated feminine image come about? Wasn't she more of a tomboy as a child?

"Yeah, I was mean as a snake. I'm still a tomboy, a lot more than you might think. But I always loved to be feminine, I always liked frilly things and perfume. I used to use Merthiolate for lipstick and there wasn't nothin' daddy could do to get *that* off."

On her lips? Surely that hurt. "It was worth the pain. I was 15 when teased hair came out and I *loved* that and I loved makeup. I always wore tight clothes. When I walked down the hall, everybody was a-lookin' to see how tight my skirt was that day or how tight my sweater was. I never did like to go around half-naked but a lotta people said I might as well be naked, as tight as my clothes were. But even as a little bitty kid, if my mamma made me wear somethin' that was loose on me, I used to just *cry*. I wanted my clothes to fit me. Even though they was rags, I wanted them to fit close to me.

"When people started changin' their hair styles, I wasn't ready to quit—I just kept makin' it bigger and bigger. I just thought, well, somebody is noticin' it and I'm enjoyin' it. I liked it and still do. I teased my own hair for years and years and it's real damagin' to your hair so about three years ago I started wearin' wigs because it's convenient. But people come to expect that of me and I come to expect it of myself, the flashy clothes and jewelry and all the gaudy appearance. I guess I did invent that part of me. I was always fascinated with fairytale images. Half of a show is the lighting and the shine and the sparkle. Stars are supposed to shine and maybe I just want to be a *star*."

Surely, though, she might become trapped in the carefully sculpted Dolly Parton image?

"No. If I wanted to get out of it—you know how stubborn I am—if I get ready to quit it will be of my own choice and I'll quit it in a minute. I love my audiences but I don't fear the public. I do what makes me happy first and hope that I can make them happy with it. So my music will stand on its own and in a while everybody will see what it is I am tryin' to do."

About her breasts Dolly drops a line on me with her usual smile and a wink. "There are going to be those who will say, 'I know that they're false; I knew her when' and there will be some who say, 'I know they're real'. I say: 'Let 'em guess'."

She's smiling hugely but those big eyes are flashing. So I get back to Blaze Starr for a minute. In the mountains in the South, the traditional and only ways for a woman to escape poverty were either to marry or to run off and become something like a stripper.

She giggles at that, very childlike. "*Okay*, I thought about bein' a stripper. But I decided that I really better not. I didn't want to get married. All I had ever known was housework and kids and workin' in the fields. But I didn't want to be domestic, I wanted to be *free*. I had my songs to sing, I had an ambition and it *burned* inside me. It was something I knew would take me out of the mountains. I knew I could see worlds beyond the Smoky Mountains."

Dolly's first country hit was a song called "Dumb Blonde" (one of the few songs she's recorded that she didn't write or cowrite) but she is light-years away from being that. Even though she hated school and is not a heavy reader (though she can—and does—quote easily from the Bible), she is clearly well endowed with street smarts. She also, I discover, was born with a natural gift for intense positive thinking and that, coupled with her burning ambition, makes her a fearsome force.

I discover this in a late-night session in her motel room in Connecticut. We are eating Big Macs and washing them down with Budweisers and I make some remark about setting goals. That sets her off on a 45-minute discussion on achieving and how to do it.

"I'm always sure of the goals I set for myself," she says, reaching out for some more french fries, "but I like for them to be flexible because I may get midways and get a big brainstorm. Then I can change. I just set new goals. There will *never* be a top for me—other than the *one* I am famous for." I try unsuccessfully to avoid glancing at her chest while she laughs at me.

"I mean there is no top and no bottom to my career because once I accomplish the things I decide I'm going to, then I want to get into other things. I am a list maker. I like to write my goals and plans down and keep them in a secret place where people can't see them. You'd be *amazed* that even *year*s ago the things I'd written down on my list, that I just mark 'em off as they come true and I think, boy, if *that* ain't proof that positive thinkin' is a marvelous thing. I mean if there is something I *really* want, why, I write it down on a piece of paper and I look at the list and I *concentrate* real hard on it, try to visualize it happening, and I just go through all the motions as if it's already been done."

And, I ask, a bit cynically, does it work?

She jumps forward in her chair, excited. "Yes! It *does*! If I get sick, I think myself well. That's why I never did worry when my throat was botherin' me. I tell you, it is strange the way it works."

I get us out two more Buds and ask her if she possesses any . . . *special* mental powers or something.

"No more than anybody else, if they develop and exercise it. I was born with that gift and that great faith and it wasn't until about two years ago that I discovered that there were books written about positive think-ing. But, you see, I had practiced that all my life, *that's* what got me out of the mountains. Even as a little child, I daydreamed *so* strongly that I just saw these things happen and sure enough, they would, so it was just a matter of growing up to meet that. We can be whatever we want to be, the Bible says that, that *all* things are possible to those that *believe*. It don't say *some* things are possible, it says *all* things are possible and it says that if you have faith even as a grain of mustard seed then you shall move mountains and that nothing shall be impossible unto you."

Well, I say, beginning to believe, would you please write down on one of your lists that you want me to become a rich and famous writer?

She smiles a Madonna's smile. "I *could* think you into that, but you have to help me some. That is within *everybody*. People just neglect what they got to work with. *But*—I ain't *near* where I'm goin'. My dreams are far too big to stop now 'cause I ain't the greatest at what I do, but I become greater because I *believe*. What I lack in talent I make up for in ambition and faith and determination and positive thinking."

Thursday afternoon, I call on Dolly in room 347 and find her, as usual, curled up before the picture window. Today she's reading—a book on fasting. I barely get settled opposite her when she throws the book down. "Have you had supper yet?" she asks. "Well, let's go down to the restaurant. I am sick and *tired* of fastin'. I want some food."

She draws three autograph seekers in the restaurant, and lowers her voice as they walk away: "Just goin' out to eat is the hardest thing now. Just about the time you get somethin' chewed up real good, just when you got it good in your teeth and everything, they come up for an autograph and you got mashed potatoes on your thumb. I never go anywhere without bein' recognized. But—" this with a philosophical shrug—"that's part of success." She polishes off her stuffed shrimp and starts in on the strawberry pie.

We had talked earlier about her religious upbringing and I bring up one of her songs that is closest to being pure gospel, "The Seeker."

"I tell you, that's a song I love. I do believe, I know there is a God and He is still the best friend I got in the world. I talk to Him often, but I'm one of the world's sinners. I think I'm a vanilla sinner—too bad to be good and too good to be bad. Because it wouldn't be *all* that hard to be good but I just don't know that I *want* to be. I think I won't have no fun if I'm *too* good. But I had some friends that had just been renewed and they were real happy about it and so religion was real heavy on my mind. I just could not decide whether I wanted to be a Christian or not.

"So I was out in the kitchen a-cookin' and I started thinkin' about how serious that was, so—I am a seeker, a poor sinful creature, there is none weaker than I am, I am a seeker and you are a teacher. So I was just thinkin', 'Lord, you're gonna have to hit me with a bolt of lightning because I ain't gonna do it on my own.' So I wrote that out of a heavy heart. Because I am certainly not a Christian. I will try *some* of *anything*, I mean I will."

She would make a great singing evangelist, I say—a singing Kathryn Kuhlman.

She looks at me very seriously. "Are you jokin'? I often wonder what my calling really was because I often thought I was born for a purpose other than just to be a country singer. My mamma always predicted that someday I would lead a lot of people to the Lord. She said, 'I don't care where you go or what you do in this world, you are one of God's children and someday you are going to do a great work for the Lord'. "Dolly laughs shakily. "So, maybe I *will*. Someday".

We leave the Holiday Inn for the Oakdale Theatre a good two hours before her curtain time—or ramp time in this case. The Oakdale is what is commonly called a hardtop tent. It's a dome that's open all the way around and the inside slopes down to a revolving stage, a feature Dolly is not fond of. "I got to put my band in the pit and I just stand out there like a sore thumb. And I never did like to go around in circles."

Just before she gets on her bus, a cluster of young girls runs up for autographs. She gives them a dozen red roses she's carrying and the next morning comes a letter from a mother, a letter that's almost dripping with tears of appreciation. "I just love kids," Dolly says on the bus. "But I don't really need one of my own. I've written a lot of children's stories, though. I never show them to anybody—not till I get ready to publish 'em. I've got trunkfuls of things I've written. I've been writin' poetry since I was in grammar school. When I was a teenager I wrote a lot of *real* hot and heavy love stories, I was just so horny myself."

Well, I say, she should write a book. Her life story might be interesting and . . .

"I'm *already* doin' that," she says, turning in her seat to train on me the butterfly-encrusted Christian Dior shades that Porter Wagoner gave her. "I'm gonna call the whole thing *Blossom*, 'cause I used to be called Blossom when I was little, which I think will be a great movie and the whole thing—you know, to blossom into this and blossom into somethin' else."

We ride along in silence for a while. This is the least ostentatious and most decorous musician's bus I've ever seen. Country singers' buses are more often closer to being re-creations of Tijuana whorehouses or

explosions in a Sears furniture department. Dolly's is very understated—
the bus does not even carry her name. All that makes it distinct from any
GMC bus is the destination window or whatever those things are that say
"Des Moines" or "Salt Lake City". Hers says "Coach of Many Colors," a
play on her favorite song. "I just don't like to advertise myself," she says
of that. Which is consistent with her inconsistencies. Flamboyant while
within the public eye proper, she values solitude (because of oglers she
does not go swimming and seldom goes shopping).

Her musicians and backup singers are orderly, too; what one would
call well-mannered men and women in their 20s. They are sitting in the
lounge area of the bus listening to a Lou Rawls tape. They unanimously
praise Dolly as the finest person in the world to work for. Still, she has
considerable turnover as she looks for musicians who are both com-
petent and compatible. The latter is just as important. There was the
time she took the band out for dinner after her London show. I was at
a table with Dolly and Gregg Perry, her piano player. Perry does not
drink and one of the other musicians started razzing him about that.
No one said anything, but Dolly's expression changed. When I caught
up with her in Connecticut, the offender was no longer with her. "I'm
gonna have to make changes musically. I love everybody in my group,
but I don't have the right group yet. I'm willing to sacrifice to get the
right group. I cannot let friendship or nothin' enter into it. But it's not
a matter of whether they can pick or not; it's a matter that it's not the
right combination."

She gets up and heads for the back of the bus to put on her makeup
and get dressed for the show. It's an unstated thing that she prefers staying on the bus until showtime. Nor does she stick around for the Mac
Davis show, nor does she stay for an Oakdale custom: the "Reception
Line". At the end of the evening the performers are expected to stand
like horses in a stall and shake hands with the public. No autographs,
just genteel handholding and murmuring of compliments.

"It's a typical Mac Davis audience," she would say later. "But I
wouldn't continue this, wouldn't let this be my career. This whole year has
been an exception to all rules for me because of needing the money to run
an organization. But after this fall I'll be working more to contemporary

and country audiences. This is not my type of audience and I say it's good for me because they all remember seeing me. Whether or not they come back is beside the point."

She's certainly right about the crowd. With all the white shoes and burgundy sport coats and gowns it looks more like the clubhouse of a race track. Latecomers linger outside to chat while Dolly gamely tries to get some feeling out of the crowd. She is partially successful and would later joke that "it's too bad we can't pipe marijuana smoke into the place; maybe they'd giggle durin' 'Me and Little Andy.'"

The latter is one of her Gothic children's tales, about a little girl and her dog who run away from a wayward mother and drunken father and show up at the narrator's house to escape the bitter cold. During their sleep, "the angels take them both to heaven."

That's a common thread in many of her songs: unhappy kids dying off left and right and going on to glory. Dolly did not have a happy childhood and she seems destined to continually rewrite it.

Standing at the back of the Oakdale, listening to two geriatric cases rambling on about Mac Davis during "Little Andy," I remember her talking about that song. "I *love* that. Pitiful, though, ain't it? When child molesting and child abuse was in the news, it bothered me a lot and I just got that idea to write a nursery rhyme. Story of a little kid, kinda switchin' back and forth. You know how a little kid will do if it's mind is scattered—it knows the real hurt but it's still child enough to go like, 'Ain't you got no gingerbread, gitty-up trotty horse goin' to the mill, and London Bridge is fallin' down and Daddy's drunk again in town.' I just cry ever' time one of those things is in the news. That is a sad song but even long before that I was writin' sad songs like 'Jeannie's Afraid of the Dark' [Dolly herself will not go to sleep without a light on], 'Silver Sandals,' 'I Wish that Milena Had Wings'. Milena would run and play every day in the meadow, she would chase butterflies and she would say with a smile, I wish I could fly that-a-way. And she always wanted wings so she could fly like a bird, so on her birthday she died—the song didn't say she died, it just said the angels came for her and they gave her wings. Usually, if you notice, all my sad songs have happy endings. They go to a better place where they're real happy."

That's straight out of her fundamentalist upbringing, of course. She grew up in the House of Prayer, a Church of God in Sevierville where her grandfather, Jake Owens, was the preacher. "Oh," she had told me, "I remember the hellfire and brimstone he used to preach and how I used to be *real* scared of that and I think that inspired me or *depressed* me into writin' all these sad, mournful songs. You kind of grew up in a horrid atmosphere about fear of religion. We thought God was a *monster* in the sky." But then, I remember, in the next breath she had a bright smile as she recalled how she would sit in the last pew in church and the boys would come and scratch at the window, trying to get her to go outside. "Sometimes I would go to church just to see who would walk me home."

Just listening to her talk, I reflect, has become pure delight, especially when she's so open. It's almost like she's 31 going on 12, a remarkable combination of childlike innocence and joy and adult bravery and determination. How extraordinary to encounter a gifted performer who is exactly what she seems; nothing more and nothing less; one whose vulnerability is her strength and vice versa. I have never, I realize, looked at her before with city eyes. In the South, she had seemed to me a good buddy, one whose talents I took for granted. Seeing her working her ass off before an indifferent audience that demanded to be convinced, I start studying the crowd and picking out those who are willing to listen and are telling their neighbors, "Well, isn't she corny but charming" and those who by God came to see Mac Davis and anything before Mac Davis is an irritation that will be endured with scant patience.

She finishes "Me and Little Andy"—which *is* corny—and gets moderate applause. From behind me, I can hear oohs and ahhs as Mac Davis arrives at the dressing room. Dolly, a tiny figure on the revolving stage, with a pink spotlight silhouetting the tight red pants outfit under her flowing, spangled chiffon, pauses to introduce her most autobiographical song: "This means more to me than any song I wrote."

With that, she begins her haunting "Coat of Many Colors" [. . .] She is clearly singing from the heart, her voice constantly on the edge of breaking and I remember what she had told me about the episode that led her to write that song.

"That was a very sad and cutting memory that I long kept deep within myself. I remembered all the pain of it and the mockery. How the kids had tried to take my little coat off and I was just sprouting . . . boobs, you know, and I didn't have a blouse on under it because I had done *well* just to have a little jacket to wear. So when the kids kept sayin' I didn't have a shirt on under it, I said I *did* because I was embarrassed. So they broke the buttons off my coat. They locked me in the coat closet that day and held the door closed and it was black dark in there and I just went into a screaming fit. I remembered all that and I was ashamed to even mention it and for *years* I held it in my mind."

When she hits the last note she looks up defiantly and I find that I am glad it is still dark in this hardtop tent, for I seem to have drops of water coursing down both cheeks. Damn you, Dolly, I silently swear. You finally got to *me*, too. Purification, indeed. I'll tell you off about this. But of course I never do.

DOLLY DIAMOND

On Her Appeal

"My crossover was something planned by *me*. I always wanted to appeal to everybody. I just wanted to be everything I could. When I came to the decision that I wanted to do all this, I knew it could be done overnight, which it pretty much was. I *love* country music. It's my first love. It's what I actually do best. But it was confining. You can only go so far in a circle, as you know. I felt like I had done everything I could within country music. But I certainly didn't leave country music behind—that's very much part of me. My show is very much country and always will be, probably. But I wanted people in other areas that didn't like country music to accept my music, and to keep my country fans, too. . . . What I'm trying to do with my albums is that you know it's me singing, and no matter what style of material I do, it still reeks with Dolly. You can call it whatever. There's no point in calling it anything. I'd like you to call it *good*, if it is."

—To Michael Musto, *Soho Weekly News*, August 17, 1978

DOLLY DIAMOND

On Her Look

"I don't know if I could ever look normal," she mused. "It's like Groucho without his cigar. Hitler without his moustache. People take me more seriously now."

—To Michael Musto, *Soho Weekly News*, August 17, 1978

PLAYBOY INTERVIEW: DOLLY PARTON: A CANDID CONVERSATION WITH THE CURVACEOUS QUEEN OF COUNTRY MUSIC

Lawrence Grobel | October 1978 | *Playboy*

The publication of Chet Flippo's *Rolling Stone* interview was expertly timed to coincide with the release of Dolly's "Here You Come Again," which became her first million-seller. In true crossover fashion, the single topped the country charts for five consecutive weeks and also went to Number 3 on the pop charts. Suggestions that Dolly's country music followers might abandon her if she went *too* pop were negated when she was named Entertainer of the Year for 1978 by the Country Music Association. "I had this dress made in case I won and about five minutes ago I was hopin' I wouldn't win because I busted the front out of it," she said during her acceptance speech. "My daddy said that's what I got for puttin' fifty-pound-a-mud in a five-pound bag!"

During this period, Dolly made many television appearances, including a memorable and frisky chat with Johnny Carson on *The Tonight Show*, and a high-profile interview on *The Barbara Walters Special*. She also graced the covers of many national periodicals, including the popular *Life* and *People* magazines. Although Annie Leibovitz photographed Dolly with a virtually unknown (and nearly naked) "Mr. Universe" Arnold Schwarzenegger for the August 25, 1977, issue of *Rolling Stone*, that week's prominent cover spot went to the cast of *Star Wars*. Still, the exposure was all part of an intensely focused strategy—a well-oiled publicity machine—to raise the public's awareness of Dolly Parton, her image, and her music.

There is some truth to the long-running joke declaring, "I read *Playboy* for the articles." By 1978, a large number of the magazine's readership *did* buy the magazine for the articles—and more specifically their distinguished series of conversations known as the Playboy Interview. Hugh Hefner's periodical perfected the format and its interviews achieved a distinction for classy and comprehensive journalism rivaling that of its reputation for nude pictorials of women. "Playboy has made an art of the form," explained Peter P. Jacobi in his book for writers, *The Magazine Article: How to Think It, Plan It, Write It*. "Its interviews are almost psychoanalytical autobiographies in quotes."

Barry Golson, who edited the interviews from 1975 to 1989, once explained *Playboy*'s unique approach to Jacobi saying, "The interview isn't an article *about* someone. To an extent, it is *by* that person. The interviewer has to prod and challenge and draw out, but ultimately the subject of the interview must have enough to say—and the ability to say it well." When *Playboy* netted Dolly Parton for their interview series, it was Golson who called upon Lawrence Grobel for the job. Grobel was known for his painstaking and systematic investigations, researching his subjects for weeks and sometimes even months before actually meeting with them. His desire was to be fully aware of his subjects, so he made it a point to see their films, read their books, and go to their concerts.

Grobel's first meeting with Dolly came in Los Angeles in March 1978. "Even though she's not very tall, with her high heels and high hair and that hourglass figure she had, she seemed larger-than-life," he recalled to this editor in 2016. "I had to catch my breath. Though I have met many celebrities over the years, very few had this effect on me. But she seemed so open and friendly, so genuine, that she put me at ease—which is really my job when I meet someone I'm about to interview in-depth."

Joining Dolly's entourage on tour in Virginia two months later, Grobel recorded their conversations on the tour bus between cities and in motel rooms after shows. A friendship blossomed during their time together, which made for a more candid and intimate interview. "I had the benefit of time," Grobel explained. "When you get to know someone over a period of days, weeks, even months, you can't help but get along. . . . Those days though are mostly over, as celebrities don't feel the need to sit for such extensive interviews now that they can get their message across through social media."

Although she was photographed for *Playboy* in Los Angeles by glamour photographer Harry Langdon, Dolly wasn't sure she was ready to be their cover girl. "If I approve the picture, I'm gonna be on the cover," she told the press. "If I don't, I'll still have the article in the magazine. I have to see how fat I look, I guess." She eventually approved several of Langdon's photographs and agreed on the now-famous cover image. "I wasn't naked," she later explained. "All you saw was me in my bunny suit, with my boobs sticking out a little. I wouldn't do a layout. I'm not that brave, nor do I look that good!"

As the publication date neared, Dolly asked Grobel if she could read the completed interview. He wasn't comfortable with that, but agreed to show her the galleys. Dolly asked for only one change, which concerned something she'd said about Elton John. "Maybe I shouldn't call names," she said during the interview, but she requested Grobel to put an *an* before Elton John's name as to not be so specific. After reviewing the galleys, Dolly was delighted to share the news of her upcoming appearance in *Playboy*. "[It's] the wildest thing I guess I've ever done in the line of publicity," she said in a press conference, but clarified, "it's only because there's a real lengthy article in there that I'm quite proud of." Lengthy it was, spreading across seventeen of the magazine's pages.

Dolly has remained proud of the *Playboy* interview and still cites it as one of her most honest and open discussions ever. "I said a lot in that interview," she recalled in 1997 to *Paper* magazine. "That was the first time I really opened up to the press." It's been said that circulation doubled for Dolly's issue of *Playboy*, and nearly forty years after its publication, that cover still generates more attention from her fans and followers than any of the hundreds of periodical covers she's graced. In fact, it was such a big seller that the magazine's editors have approached her on several occasions over the years to do another cover photo shoot. "They just recently wanted me to do another cover," she told *AdWeek* in 2014. "I said, please don't ask me, and I didn't do it again because of all the programs I do for children now and the Imagination Library."

Would she ever pose nude? In her 1994 autobiography *Dolly: My Life and Other Unfinished Business*, Dolly stated that she would pose nude for *Penthouse* magazine. "On my hundredth birthday," she clarified. "Everybody is going to be sorry." But "No," she recently told Chicago's US 99 radio station. "I have been asked, back in the day, but that was so totally not me. I would never do that. But that was a good article they ran in [*Playboy*], and it was just a fun thing to do. That was just another way I was trying to market myself, at that time, to kinda get in the mainstream and take it right to the edge, but not do the whole dirty deal." —Ed.

Two days before the Palomino club in Los Angeles sponsored its first Dolly Parton Look-Alike Contest, Dolly Parton was wondering whether or not she should attend. She'd been to some others in different parts of the country and she'd been mostly disappointed. In Los Angeles, however, it might be different. But she knew if she attended, she would also enter.

And she was wondering if there was any chance she might lose. "Wouldn't that be hysterical?" she said. "But I doubt if I would. I mean, I look too much _like_ her."

The contest was on a Wednesday night. Dolly was rehearsing for a TV special and wasn't sure if she'd be through in time to run over with a friend to the North Hollywood club. On Thursday, she'd been invited to her friend Emmylou Harris' house. Emmylou said there were some people she wanted Dolly to meet. Although her schedule was as tight as her clothes, Dolly accepted without hesitation.

There was much talk in Los Angeles about the top-secret album Dolly and Emmylou and Linda Ronstadt were working on. They'd been meeting and recording in full-day sessions that had been closed to the press. But there had been managerial problems as well as scheduling conflicts and the album was still an on/off project.

Ronstadt and Harris had wanted to meet Parton after having recorded some of her songs. When the three met, they hit it off immediately and have become friends. Parton was concerned that Harris and Ronstadt might put her down for the way she looks—for her gaudy rhinestone outfits, the blonde teased wigs, the five-inch heels, the heavy make-up. She was afraid that Johnny Carson and Barbara Walters would put her down for the same thing. But they didn't—and few others have. People apparently see beyond the ostentatious appearance. "I don't think it takes people long to know I'm not ignorant," she says.

But Parton felt that without her props, it would have taken her longer to attract a broad audience, so, not one for waiting, she did what she could to promote herself. In so doing, she became the exaggeration that Bette Midler is trying to be and that Mae West was. Parton _is_ the incarnation of West in certain ways: She doesn't show much, but she hints at a lot; she pokes fun at herself and makes a fortune at the jokes; she knows what she wants and she won't let anything interfere with her becoming as big a star as she can possibly become.

Parton has come a long way from her Tennessee mountain home; she was born in a Locust Ridge "holler" in Sevier County in the Smoky Mountain foothills on January 19, 1946. The fourth of 12 children, she was the first in her family to finish high school, the first to become famous.

"I never had a doubt I would make it," she reasons, "because refusing to think I <u>couldn't</u> make it is the reason I <u>could</u>."

For Parton, making it meant getting out of the backwoods and into the limelight. Her rise was rapid: She began writing songs at seven, recording them and singing on the Cas Walker radio and television show at ten, making her first appearance at the Grand Ole Opry at 12.

The day after she graduated from high school, she left with her uncle, Bill Owens, for Nashville to become a star. That same day she met, and within two years married, an asphalt worker named Carl Dean. Dean is a publicity-shy, earthy man who is as independent as Dolly and the two seem to have a solid, often at-a-distance relationship. She's on the road most of the year and he's at home working their land.

When country singer Norma Jean, who sang with Porter Wagoner on the road and on his syndicated TV show, decided to quit and get married in 1967, Wagoner asked Dolly if she'd like to join his show. Overnight, her salary rose from next to nothing to $60,000 a year and, at 21, she had achieved one of her goals: a broad and popular audience.

Although she and Wagoner became hugely successful and their duo albums sold well, she became restless and made a decision to go out on the road with members of her family. It proved to be almost disastrous. She and her Travelin' Family Band went from state fair to rodeo to high school gymnasium amateurishly managed and poorly booked. Making her most painful decision to date, she told her family it wasn't working out and took time off to put together a more professional band. She also hired a Los Angeles–based manager and public-relations firm, who saw enormous potential in this energetic and prolific woman.

By then, she was ready to "cross over" into the pop/rock world. Her albums were popular in Japan, France, Australia and England (where she was twice named Female Vocalist of the Year) and she coproduced her own album, "New Harvest." She followed that with her "new sound": "Here You Come Again," which recently went platinum, more than quadrupled the sales of many of her earlier albums.

With 20th Century-Fox offering her a three-movie deal, publishers bidding for the novel she's writing, her autobiography in the works, TV network executives trying to line her up for specials and record albums starting to sell in the millions, PLAYBOY *decided to send freelance writer Lawrence Grobel to talk with Dolly and see how it all happened and how it has affected her.*

Grobel, who previously interviewed Henry Winkler and Barbra Streisand for PLAYBOY, *began the interview in Los Angeles and then joined Dolly at the beginning of her six-month nationwide road tour. His report:*

"I've met busy people before, but in Dolly's case, her scheduling is extreme. Her energy matches her ambition, which is limitless. If she's not writing or recording her own songs, she's recording with Linda and Emmylou, rehearsing with her band, taping a TV show, throwing a wedding for her younger sister, giving a concert for ABC-radio executives in Las Vegas or touring.

"I managed to pin her down for five hours in an apartment she rents in Los Angeles. The first thing I noticed was how sparse it was; nothing plush or comfortable, no indication that a star lived there, obviously a place used for little more than sleeping. The only bit of eccentricity was a small, low, round trampoline, which she said she used after giving up on jumping rope, 'for a couple of good reasons.'

"Dolly wasn't born with a voice like Streisand's, but what she has is an enormously infectious personality. To meet her is to immediately like her. Although she appears larger than life, she is actually a compact woman—dazzling in appearance; but if you took away the wig and the Frederick's of Hollywood five-inch heels, she'd stand just five feet tall. Of course, her height isn't the first thing one notices upon meeting her. As she herself kids onstage, 'I know that you-all brought your binoculars to see me; but what you didn't realize is you don't need binoculars.'

"The next time I saw Dolly was in Winchester, Virginia, where she was scheduled to appear at the Apple Blossom Festival. By then, it was as if we were old and trusting friends and I soon discovered that she was the least hung-up celebrity I've ever been with. She was open, honest and only rarely asked to go off the record; and even then, it was on matters such as being unsatisfied with a particular dress designer or not wanting to dwell too much on godly topics. When it came to her personal life, her dreams, her ambitions, she never hesitated.

"One little girl who had written to Dolly came to visit her after a show. Dolly was in a nightdress and greeted the child as her father took Polaroid pictures. But the picture I'll always remember was of the father telling his wife to take a shot of him behind Dolly. He had this crazy gleam in his eyes, his tongue popped out of his mouth and I was sure he was going to cop a feel. But he restrained himself, as most people do around her. Because she is so open and unparanoid, she manages to tame the wildest instincts of men.

"Our last night together stretched out until morning. We talked from ten P.M. until five A.M., exchanging stories and not in the least bit tired. By the time we hugged goodbye, I was saddened that we were talked out. Our talk is what follows . . . though it does take a while to get over Dolly's appearance."

PLAYBOY: Hello, Dolly.

PARTON: Hi. I'll save you the trouble of askin': Why do I choose to look so outrageous?

PLAYBOY: Is that the first question interviewers usually ask you?

PARTON: That's what we usually end up talkin' about.

PLAYBOY: Actually, that was going to be our *second* question. We were going to start with the PLAYBOY cover. It's pretty eye-catching. Was it fun?

PARTON: I was afraid at first, when we talked about it. I didn't want to be naked or something on the front of a magazine unless everybody knew it was a joke. I mean, I wouldn't want to be naked even then. It might not offend *me*, but I was afraid maybe a lot of my country fans and some of the people who love me who are of a religious nature might not understand.

People will make jokes and things, not because of my beauty but just because of that physical thing that's built around my boobs. I didn't know if I wanted to be put in a category of where I was flaunting something I had never flaunted before. Then I thought, It isn't something I should be ashamed of. PLAYBOY's a real classy magazine. And I mean, who *else* but Dolly Parton should be on the cover of PLAYBOY? If you wanted an outrageous person to be an outrageous magazine cover, who else? I just hope people will take it in the spirit in which I did it—you know, something cute and off-the-wall for me.

PLAYBOY: OK. Now, why *do* you choose to look so outrageous?

PARTON: People have thought I'd be a lot farther along in this business if I dressed more stylish and didn't wear all this gaudy getup. Record companies have tried to change me. I just refused. If I am going to look like this, I must have had a reason. It's this: If I can't make it on my talent, then I don't want to do it. I *have* to look the way I choose to look, and this is what I've chose. It makes me different a little bit, and ain't that what we all want to do: be a little different?

It's fun for me. It's like a little kid playing with her paints and colors. I like to sit and tease my hair. If there's something new on the market in make-up, I like to try it. You've got to have a gimmick. You've got to have something that will catch the eye and hold the attention of the public. But the funny thing is, no matter how much I try new stuff, I wind up looking just the same.

PLAYBOY: Do you think you'll become a fashion trend setter? Isn't there already a Dolly Parton look?

PARTON: [*Laughing*] Can you imagine anybody wanting to look this way for *real*? When people first get to know me, they say, "Why do you wear all of this?" Then, after a week of knowing me, they totally understand. They know it's just a bunch of baloney. But why not? Life's boring enough, it makes you try to spice it up. I guess I just throw on a little too much spice.

PLAYBOY: Why are there so many Dolly Parton look-alike contests?

PARTON: Because they're fun. Who would be better to impersonate than Dolly Parton? All you gotta do is get a big blonde wig, make-up, and if you're pretty well proportioned . . . or you can even fake it. The best parts of Dolly Parton look-alike contests are guys dressed up like girls. It's so *easy* to do me.

PLAYBOY: Have you ever met any of the winners?

PARTON: I sure have. They were the biggest bunch of pigs I ever saw, most of them. I thought to myself, Is that how people think I look? I thought, Oh, Lord, some of them were in worse shape than I even thought I was. I've only seen two that would even be classified as a human being.

PLAYBOY: So you don't think they've ever been able to imitate the real, sexy you?

PARTON: Listen, I never thought of myself as being a sex symbol. It never crossed my mind that anybody might think I was sexy.

PLAYBOY: But surely, after all the media exposure you've received, you have to be conscious of what people say and think about you.

PARTON: I didn't say what *you*-all thought. I said that it never once crossed *my* mind, even now. I still can't get it through my head that people think I'm supposed to be sexy or somethin'. I don't want that responsibility. I don't want to have to keep up an image like that. I don't want to have to be like a beautiful woman, like a Raquel Welch— which is no trouble, I never would anyway. I'm just sayin' I wouldn't want people to look at me and if I gained ten pounds, they'd say, "Oh, God, she's ruined her looks." I'm made up of many things. I'm very complex. I have much more depth than just my looks, which to me are not all that hot, anyway. I've always looked a certain way and had an image. I like the big hairdo, the gaudy clothes. There's not much sexy about that. Men are not usually turned on by artificial looks and I've always been like that.

PLAYBOY: If that's true, why do you suppose there's such a huge cosmetic industry in this country?

PARTON: I'm talking about *my* kind—the big wigs, the total artificial look. I don't try to dress in style or to be really classy. I've got my work to do and I *like* to look good, but I don't try to keep an image other than just this gimmick appearance that I have. If I was trying to really impress men or be totally sexy, then I would dress differently.

PLAYBOY: How would you look?

PARTON: I would wear low-cut things. Try to keep my weight down. Try to really work on my body. I would find a new, softer, sexier hair style—it would be my own hair, some way. But why bother? I'm already married and *he* don't mind how I look. He likes me gaudy or ungaudy.

PLAYBOY: When were you first attracted to gaudiness?

PARTON: I was always fascinated with make-up. We didn't have any when I grew up. We weren't allowed to wear it. But we used to have this medicine, what you call Merthiolate, that's what I would put on my lips as a little kid. I'd paint my lips and there was nothin' Daddy could do. He couldn't rub it off. He would say, "Get that lipstick off you!" And I'd say, "It won't come off, it's my natural coloring, Daddy." Then he'd say, "Bull." When we wanted eyebrows, we'd get burned matches and make little eyebrows. When I was a sophomore in high school, the teased hair came into style and I started doing that, and ever since, I've done it. And I wore my skirts so tight I could hardly wiggle in them. I liked tight sweaters. I just like tight clothes, I always did.

I just like to feel things next to me, I guess. Even before I had a figure, I liked my clothes snug and tight. People would always kid me in school about my little butt and my little blue jeans or whatever. Momma, she always understood stuff like that. She'd say, "Don't get them so tight you can't move in them, where they cut your wind off." But she'd seam them up and if they weren't quite tight enough, I'd say, "Won't you fix them a little right in here?" And she would. See, she was a daughter of a preacher and when she was a child, they wouldn't let *her* wear any make-up. They all had long hair then and she wanted her hair cut. The very day that her and Daddy got married, she cut her hair off and she kept it short ever since. She said, "I swore then that when I had kids, I would not make 'em do things that they were uneasy with."

PLAYBOY: What did your father think of your tight clothes?

PARTON: Daddy didn't like us to wear real tight clothes back at the start. He was more strict with us, he just didn't understand how to be a father. A father of girls, especially. He just didn't want us to date. He trusted us, but he didn't trust the guys we was goin' with.

PLAYBOY: You must have looked more mature than a lot of your class-mates when you were a girl.

PARTON: Well, I looked more mature, I *was* more mature. I used my mind in different ways. I developed my mind by writing and thinking deep and planning and dreaming. I *thought* serious. I looked as old as the teachers. When I was in high school, I looked like I was 25 years old.

PLAYBOY: Was the fact that you were physically more developed than the other girls a problem for you? Were you teased much?

PARTON: It was always a problem, to a degree. But I had a real open personality. I don't think I was teased openly; it was more what people were sayin' behind my back: "No, they're not real, she's got Kleenex in there."

PLAYBOY: Did that bother you?

PARTON: It was kind of embarrassing, but it must not have bothered me too much. I'm a real obvious person; all the things you see are obvi-ous. But my body is not really as extreme as people make it out to be. I am just a small, tiny, little person, five feet tall, with a small frame. I have plenty, but it's not like what people say: "Oh, gosh, she must be 45 inches." I'm not nowhere near it, you know.

PLAYBOY: Why have you always refused to disclose your measure-ments?

PARTON: There's just no point. I'm not sayin' it's not *there.* A lot of people claim, "I remember when you wasn't that big." And I say, "Yeah, but you remember when I wasn't this fat, too." I'm not *that* well endowed. I'm not as *huge* as people make me out as being. I really ain't. I mean, if you look real *good* . . . I've got plenty, but I know a lot of people that are so big it's unhealthy, it hurts their back. I am so extreme, if I didn't have some, I would sure have made some. But from the time I was just a young girl, they've been there.

Some book said I had my bust lifted at Vanderbilt Hospital. Well, I never even been doctored at Vanderbilt Hospital. People will always talk and make jokes about my bosoms. When somebody says that this doctor claims he did it, I always say that plastic surgeons are all alike, they're always making mountains out of molehills. But, no, I didn't go to Vanderbilt Hospital. And if I had had something done, it would be a very private thing to me and it would be one of my secrets. But a lot of people that know me would know the difference. We won't say which-a-way *that* goes. So we will just leave the people wondering. But why dwell on that? Why don't they look underneath the breasts, at the heart?

PLAYBOY: All right. How would you describe yourself to someone who had never seen or heard you?

PARTON: Well, I would start by saying that I pride myself on being a fair and honest person. I am free and open enough to be able to try new things. I'm outrageous. I feel like I have a lot of depth that only the people closest to me really see. I'm compulsive and very ambitious. I'm playful. I'm joyful. I'm mischievous. Serious when I mean to be serious. I can be strong when I need to be and weak when I want to be. I can tell you where to put it if I don't like where you got it. I'm not a very moody person. I don't fall into great states of depression. Very sentimental and highly emotional. I'm a baby when it comes to bein' a baby. I like to be spoiled and petted. I get touched real easy. I'm curious, I have to know everything that goes on. I'm not a brilliant person, but I have a lot of guts. I just don't have a fear of life. I love life, so why should I fear somethin' I love? And why should I not reach out to the things that I know I can touch? I'm strong-willed. I can think like a workingman because I know what a workingman goes through. I'm a person you could sit down with even if you were a total stranger and tell me the thing you thought was the most horrible thing and I would understand it. And I wouldn't tell. I'm a good friend. I'm loyal and devoted to the things that I believe in. . . . I'm full of shit!

PLAYBOY: That's quite a description. Now, how would you assess your talent?

PARTON: I like to be appreciated as a writer and, if not a great singer, at least a stylist and an original, creative person.

PLAYBOY: You don't feel you're that good a singer?

PARTON: I don't think so. My manager just hates me to say that, because he says it's not true. I don't have a great voice. I have a *different* voice and I can do things with it that a lot of people can't. But it's so delicate in other ways, there's no way I can do some of the things other singers can.

I just love to sing. It is joyful, it's something I can scream, it's a release for me. I used to have a lot of vibrato in my voice. It could almost be real irritating to a lot of people's ears. It was a natural thing for me, but some people say, "You sound like you been eating billy goat." Bah, bah. I guess I overdone it, so I tried to learn at takin' some of the vibrato out. I would like to improve my voice to be able to hit better notes. My notes are not always true. But my heart is always true. And the emotion I put in is always true.

PLAYBOY: Do you listen to yourself often?

PARTON: No, never. Unless I'm in the studio tryin' to decide what goes in the album. I'm not necessarily a fan of my own. I'm not one of my favorite singers.

PLAYBOY: Is it true that your husband doesn't like your singing?

PARTON: He didn't used to, but he's become a real big fan of mine now. I played this new album, *Heartbreaker*, and he really liked it.

PLAYBOY: Does that mean a lot to you?

PARTON: It means more than anybody could ever know.

PLAYBOY: You and Carl have been married 12 years and no one's ever seen a picture of the two of you together. Why the mystery?

PARTON: He just don't have *any* desire to be in show business. He don't want to have his picture in the paper. He don't want to go out to the supermarket and have people say, "That's Dolly Parton's husband." There's been a lot of distorted press about how I only see him six weeks a year, which is not true. It's true that last year I was only at home about six weeks, but he joined me on the road a lot.

PLAYBOY: Is he as shy and bashful as the press makes him out to be?

PARTON: No. He's just the funniest, wittiest guy in the world. He's really bright. He's not backward at all. I just really wish that people would let him be. He's a home-lovin' person. He works outside, he's got his tractor and his grader, he keeps our farm in order. He wouldn't have to work no more, because I'm making good money now, but he gets up every morning at daylight. If he ain't workin' on our place, he'll take a few jobs, like grading somebody's driveway or cleaning off somebody's property, to pick up a couple of hundred bucks. He likes his own money to horse-trade with.

PLAYBOY: Do people say anything to him about Dolly Parton's husband grading their driveway?

PARTON: Oh, sure; he don't give a shit. He don't go up and say, "Hey, I'm Dolly Parton's husband, can I grade your drive?" If somebody knows it, he don't make a big thing of it; he'll play it down, he'll say, "Well, I ain't in show business, I got to work, now what can I do for you?" Or he'll say, "Hell, *she* ain't makin' no money." He's a man with a lot of pride; even though my money is his money, his money is mine.

PLAYBOY: What is it about him that attracted you?

PARTON: His honesty. His decency. His earthiness. I like the way he loves me. His understanding of me and the things I do. The way he lets me be free. And lets me be me. He don't try to choke me and demand anything from me.

PLAYBOY: Does he ever give you advice about your career?

PARTON: He never interferes with me businesswise. That's why I hire managers. Carl and I only talk about our own things. We talk about what we're gonna do with the house, the farm. Or he wants me to see a truck he's rebuilt. He's like my little boy. But he's like my daddy, like a brother. And I'm all those things to him. I call Carl Daddy.

PLAYBOY: What does Carl call you?

PARTON: When he's talking to other people, he says "the old lady" or "she." Or "crazy woman." He never says Dolly, never. And if he does, it hurts my feelin's so bad—ain't that crazy? If I say Carl, he won't even react. He hates me to call him Carl. He'll say, "Call me son of a bitch, call me anythin', but don't call me Carl." That's what everybody calls him, so it's not personal enough.

PLAYBOY: Is he a jealous person?

PARTON: Not a bit.

PLAYBOY: Are you?

PARTON: I'm not, either.

PLAYBOY: Would it matter if he were seeing someone else while you were away?

PARTON: He's not.

PLAYBOY: If he were, would you want to know?

PARTON: No, I wouldn't want to know and he wouldn't want to tell me. But if he did, it wouldn't be like the end of the world for me. I would just say it was as much my fault as his. I would probably cry and pout for a day for the attention of it, and then it would be over. To me, life is life and people is people. You cannot control every emotion that you have.

PLAYBOY: How would he feel if you had an affair?

PARTON: The same way. He wouldn't want to know. I think I would keep it from him. He would be more apt to tell than me. He knows I ain't goin' nowhere. No matter who I met or what kind of an affair I might ever have, ain't nobody in this world could take Carl's place. There ain't no way in this world I'd ever lose this man.

PLAYBOY: Someone on the road as much as you are could sleep around a lot—

PARTON: How do you know I don't?

PLAYBOY: Because you speak so freely and guiltlessly about your relationship with Carl. You'd have to really be a good actress to cover up a lot of affairs.

PARTON: Oh, I *am*. I guess men think they can get away with it or somethin'. That all depends on the person. I just feel what's fair for the goose is fair for the gander. Whether I do or whether I don't is my concern. If I was ever weak enough to do something like that, it would never involve him, he would never know it, he would never feel any effects from it. Those are very personal questions and I'm a very private person, but I'm just like you—you don't always tell everything, do you? Let's put it this way: If I wanted to do it, I would; if I should do it, it would affect nobody but me and the person involved. Maybe it would be somethin' that would even make me be a happier person.

PLAYBOY: But couldn't it also lead to complications in your life?

PARTON: Well, kiss me, we'll see.

PLAYBOY: This is what's known as an awkward pause.

PARTON: There are a few people that I have been attracted to real strong, but I avoid that. There is no way in heaven's name that I could ever leave Carl, so why should I put myself and another person through that kind of torment?

PLAYBOY: It sounds like marriage at a distance can be healthy.

PARTON: It is. We're so used to the lifestyle, if I'm home two or three weeks, I want to get to work and he wants to get back to work, so he's just as anxious to see me go as I am to leave. It probably don't make much sense, but it makes sense to us.

PLAYBOY: When you are home, do you entertain much?

PARTON: When I'm home, we don't like people at the house other than our family and our own friends. We don't want fans comin' in our yard. And there's no artist in the business that is any more devoted and loves their fans more than me. I've always tried to belong to the public when I'm out there, and I've always tried to be honest enough with them to say, "I don't want you to come up to the house unless you've been invited, because I may be up there half-naked." I shouldn't have said that; they'll probably be comin' up to take pictures now. That's why we bought a piece of property where we could have the privacy to get out in the yard in shorts or looking tacky.

PLAYBOY: How tacky?

PARTON: Tacky-tacky . . . no make-up, looking like anybody.

PLAYBOY: Is privacy a problem?

PARTON: We do have fans that jump the fence. That's not a very polite thing to do, but I don't get bent out of shape over it. I just figure if it's that important to somebody, least you can do is try to be nice.

PLAYBOY: When you're performing, are your fans rowdy?

PARTON: It is getting so now the crowds are getting wilder and there are a lot of younger people and a lot of pushing and shoving. Some people get overexcited. They can run over a kid and bust his brains out or something without meaning to. It is kind of frightening. But they are the most devoted fans, standing there, rain or snow, freezing to death. It is amazing.

PLAYBOY: Are audiences different in different parts of the country?

PARTON: It's pretty much the same in every part of the country, except Texas. Texas audiences are the loudest and most responsive. They are just fun-lovin' people *all* the time. Texans are in a world of their own. It's a great place for music.

PLAYBOY: What about fan mail? Do you ever get any letters that might be considered strange?

PARTON: I used to get letters from a man who was in a mental institution. He was a big fan but just distorted. It was more perverted than anything else. I kept those. I get a lot of mail from prisoners and usually they are very nice letters. Sometimes they get a little horny.

PLAYBOY: Have you had any difficulties getting your fans to accept your new image? Are there diehard country-music buffs who can't accept your crossing over into the pop/rock field?

PARTON: We had some of that when I started, when I first got the bigger band and started doin' more rocky things. Some people hollered, "Do your country, we don't need your rock 'n' roll." I don't *do* rock 'n' roll. I knew what I was tryin' to do and I didn't have time to try to explain it to them.

I have not changed because of success, and I never will. The only thing success does to you, like Barbra Streisand said in *her Playboy Interview*, it just don't allow you to be alone anymore. Everybody is tryin' to get to you. It just gets to the point where people demand so much from you you just can't give it and you have to take all kinds of hurts and insults. It bothers you. Of all things, for somebody to say that I've changed, that just burns me up.

PLAYBOY: But your music *has* changed to some degree. Didn't you say that your *Here You Come Again* album is slicker than you wanted it to sound?

PARTON: Well, you see, that was the first thing that I did after I made the change and it was not exactly what I had in mind. But it proved to be the smartest thing. I knew *Here You Come Again* would be a hit song, but I don't know if I should be identified with it, because it's so smooth and pop-sounding. That's such a good song a monkey could have made it a hit. Well, you're looking at a million-dollar monkey.

PLAYBOY: Do you feel that in order to reach a larger audience you have to sweeten or smooth out your sound?

PARTON: Yeah, here and there. I was kind of afraid that people would think, Boy, this is too drastic. I just didn't want the country people to think that I totally left them. That was *such* a polished pop sound! But it was the biggest country record I ever had, as well.

PLAYBOY: Are you close to most of your band members?

PARTON: I'm close to all the people in my band. I'm not above them just because I am the star. They are not sidemen to me. We are all musicians making a living for each other. The way we travel, I couldn't work with a bunch of loonies, a bunch of squirrels. I don't mind drugs, I don't mind drinkin' in my group as long as it don't interfere with my show. We're together 24 hours a day, but that one hour onstage is mine. That's what I pay for. I don't care what you do after the show, I don't care what you do until four or five hours before the show. As long as everybody is straight, so if I want communication when we're onstage, I have it.

PLAYBOY: And you feel you're close to that now?

PARTON: My group is pretty clean. See, I live with the band. I travel with 'em, I don't like to separate myself from my group. In summertime, we take our barbecue grill and travel by bus. We only fly when we have to. Rather than stopping at a truck stop or a restaurant, we get a volleyball net out, we stop along the side of the road and have a picnic. I cook, there's another girl in my group, we have a real good time. We have water fights, cake fights, food fights . . . like brats. It's like a family. When the day comes when I can't enjoy it or there's no fun doin' it, there's lots of things that I can find joy in, and I would.

PLAYBOY: You once toured with members of your own family. What happened to your Travelin' Family Band?

PARTON: There was a lot of hurt caused by some press. They made it sound like I had fired my family. I did not fire my family. I had brothers and sisters and cousins in my group and I was really havin' to go through things I shouldn't have—poor lighting, poor sound, poor management, poor everything. I just decided I was goin' to quit for a few days, just stop everything and do some thinkin'. Because I won't let somethin' run me to a psychiatrist or to a doctor; I can take care of my own things, me and the Lord can talk it over. I was brought up religious and even if I'm not a fanatic, I have a communication with God, which helps me like a psychiatrist might help somebody else.

PLAYBOY: Were either of your parents musically talented?

PARTON: All of my momma's people were singers, writers, musicians. And a lot of my daddy's people were really involved in music. But it was just around home and in church; nobody had ever done anything as far as making any money with it. I was the first one that ever became popular doin' it, but there's a lot of 'em a lot more talented than me. I just had this grit and all these dreams and plans.

PLAYBOY: Do you resemble your mother?

PARTON: I look like her and my daddy, too. Daddy's people are fair and blond and blue-eyed. My momma's people have a lot of Indian blood, so they're dark, with high cheekbones and real dark hair. I have Momma's features: Momma's smile, dimples; but I have Daddy's nose. I got Daddy's pride and determination and I got Momma's personality. My momma's people and my daddy's people grew up as good friends, that's how they met, so there's a lot of marriages between the Partons and the Owenses. In the mountains, there's not that many people, so most people are related on one side or the other, and then they marry in, which makes you all kinfolks. I have double first cousins, first second cousins, stuff like that.

PLAYBOY: What is a double first cousin?

PARTON: Let me see if I can explain it. My mother's mother's sister married my daddy's brother. So their kids are my first—second?—cousins. It sounds like I'm my own grandpa, don't it? Anyway, you can figure it out later. However it is, we got some double first cousins and first second cousins. That kind of thing. Who can tell about mountain people?

PLAYBOY: Did you go to school with all your relatives?

PARTON: We lived in the mountains and there were very few people lived where we did, way back in the holler; our closest neighbors were a long ways off. We walked a long way to school, a one-room school that had the first through the eighth grade. Only like 10 or 15 people in the whole school and one teacher. The grades were in rows: There might be two kids in the first grade, three in the second, one in the third . . . and so the teacher would just take a chair and sit in the aisle and the other kids had to study. I was the first one in our family that went to high school. My daddy didn't particularly want me to go to school, my momma didn't care. In the mountains, schoolin' is not that important.

PLAYBOY: How did you know it *was* important?

PARTON: I wanted to finish high school just so I could say I did, because I knew I'd learn things there that I would probably need to know, because I had already decided I was going out into the world. I was the most popular girl in school but in the wrong way. I wore tight clothes and told dirty jokes.

I never failed a subject, but I was never a good student. I never studied, I just used my own common sense to get by. I wanted to take band so I could bring my grades up. I didn't want to play horn or anything I had to really learn, so I asked if I could play the drums. I never did learn to read a note of music. I got like 98 in band, which brought up my other grades at the end of the semester. But I didn't play well. I didn't know what I was doin'.

PLAYBOY: Did you like school?

PARTON: I hated it. Even to this day, when I see a school bus, it's just depressing to me. I think, Those poor little kids having to sit there in the summer days, staring out the window. It's hot and sweaty in the schoolroom. It reminds me of every feelin' and every emotion that I had in school. I'd hate to have to make my own kids go to school. I know that sounds terrible. A lot of people will say, "What a dumb person." I hated school every day I went, but it was better than stayin' home every day. Momma was sick a lot; we had some real hard times.

PLAYBOY: What were those hard times like?

PARTON: Momma had kids all the time—she had one on her and one in her. She was always pregnant, and the time she wasn't pregnant, she was just really rundown sick, and back then, you didn't have doctors that much. Momma took spinal meningitis once. The doctor said there was no way she could live, only one person in a thousand did live, and if she did live, she'd be crippled up. He told Daddy and my grandma she wouldn't live through the night. So they had church that night and they prayed all night. They packed Momma in ice, her fever was way past where it would do brain damage, and the next mornin', when the doctor came in, Momma was sittin' up in bed, kickin' her foot—Momma always kicked her foot, like I do, it's a rhythm thing. The doctor came in and she said, "I've been healed." And he said, "You sure have been healed, there's been a miracle happened here." They never could explain it. The only thing it did to Momma, it left her deaf in one ear, which just made her talk louder.

PLAYBOY: How old were you at that time?

PARTON: Eleven, twelve.

PLAYBOY: Were there other illnesses at home?

PARTON: One time, Momma had a miscarriage. It was really scary. We were all little. She started having this miscarriage . . . and she would always read the Bible; she'd be in bed and sing sacred songs—that was real depressing. We always knew when Momma was bad sick, she would do that. It was during school, my first year. The way we got to school was we walked to this green barn. The man who owned that property had some bulls and they were mean. We had to walk along the fence row to get to school, and if the bulls would start out for us, we'd just roll under the fence. Anyway, Momma was at home with the two younger kids, they were just, like, two and three years old. Momma knew she was gonna die if somebody didn't do somethin' for her. So she told my little brother and sister what they had to do: "Now, you get your stick and go to the schoolhouse and get the kids, because Momma's sick. You take the stick and walk along the fence and if the bulls start after you, just roll under the fence or just hit 'em with the stick." Here was these little kids, it was really sad. It was a long way, even for us. And these two little kids must have took forever. We were in the middle of class and these two little kids . . . it was just so sad, there's a lot of things that almost make you cry. My little brother stuttered a lot and he couldn't talk good. The other kid couldn't even talk at all yet. But my older sister, Willadeene, knew what was up when she saw them there. She jumped up and grabbed the rest of us and said, "Let's go, Momma's sick." So we just all ran home. My two older brothers had to run and find somebody to help us. At the time, we had some neighbors that didn't like us. We'd had a feud—it was kinda like the Hatfields and the McCoys. But they were good that time; it was just God's will, I guess.

PLAYBOY: What was the feud about?

PARTON: These people that lived near us, they had big kids and they were just mean. In the country, you're just born mean. They would whip us every day as we walked to school, hit us with rocks. Daddy made us another path through the woods where we could go to school and avoid 'em. They got to where they would meet us on the trail and still beat us up. Well, Daddy just got tired of it. He just went to the people and told them, "I'm gonna kill somebody if your kids don't stop beatin' my kids up." It started from that and then it got all the older people involved. My daddy and brothers got in a fight with these people and Daddy whupped about five grown people in that one family. So it was a real bad thing, we couldn't go by their house—they had dogs and they'd let them loose on us if we had to walk that way. But when Momma was near dyin', we just had nowhere else to go, which goes to show you there is good in everybody. These two women came and they ran out to the main road, which was a long, long way, and they had to track Daddy down. Daddy was workin' at a sawmill somewhere.

PLAYBOY: And then what happened?

PARTON: There was only two funeral homes in Sevierville, which was the nearest town to us. The funeral home that we didn't even belong to, they come to get Momma. It was just a bloody mess. We didn't have sheets on our beds; Momma would always just sew up rags. I remember seeing these people coming in these white jackets and this stretcher with these snow-white sheets, and you could see it a mile away. We just ran behind the house, cryin' and prayin' that Momma wouldn't die.

PLAYBOY: Did you understand death then?

PARTON: We understood that it was final. When Momma had spinal meningitis, she was pregnant and all the effects went to the baby she was carrying. When it was born, it only lived nine hours. It was the first time I'd ever seen my daddy cry.

We always looked forward to the babies born. A lot of people thought we were crazy. Even our relatives. I remember when my little brother died, I heard somebody say at the funeral home, and it stuck with me forever, "It's a blessing the little thing died." As if we didn't need any more kids. I thought, What a cruel thing to say, because we waited for each baby. It was like a joy. And there were so many of us Momma would say, "Now, this one's gonna be yours." And we kinda took care of it; it was like a new baby doll. With Momma being at the hospital and Daddy having to be with her a lot, we were by ourselves and it was just a real hard, depressed time.

PLAYBOY: What kind of man is your father?

PARTON: Daddy never had an education, but he is the smartest man I ever knew. There was never a time when Daddy didn't know what to do. My daddy used to make moonshine when he and Momma were first married. He got out of it because Momma didn't like it, but that's just the way of life in the country. That's revenue money. If somebody's gonna drink it, somebody's got to sell it.

PLAYBOY: Did you ever drink it?

PARTON: No, I never did drink moonshine. I tasted it. It tasted terrible. It's not a really good drink. I mean, you'd have to want it real bad to drink that stuff.

PLAYBOY: Did your parents discipline you a lot?

PARTON: Momma was so lenient, she just practically grew up with us. He was strict, he kept us in line. If he was mad, he whipped us with his belt. He didn't beat us, but he'd whip us hard. We'd have to go get a switch and they were pretty good-sized ones. I don't remember ever getting whupped with a board; I remember getting whupped with a stick of stove wood once.

PLAYBOY: Did you have a lot of childhood fantasies?

PARTON: We didn't have television and we didn't have radio. We didn't have electricity. Every now and then, if we could afford a battery—we had a battery radio—we'd listen to *The Grand Ole Opry* and *The Lone Ranger* maybe once or twice a week.

But we'd see catalogs—the wishbook, Momma called it. Made you wish you had things you didn't have. I wanted fancy clothes, I wanted jewelry, I wanted to be pretty.

We related to the Bible a lot, lots of stories we played out were from the Bible. We were Disciples and we would paint on our feet these sandals, and then we found these staffs and we just roamed those hills as shepherds. We played out Jacob and Joseph and the coat of many colors. I wrote a song once . . . my favorite story was the coat of many colors.

So that was kind of a fantasy we lived in. We didn't have books to read, except at school, and we tried not to read those.

PLAYBOY: Did you see magazines or newspapers at all?

PARTON: We'd hear about war stories and about famous people, movie stars. Sometimes my aunt in Knoxville would bring newspapers up, which we used for toilet paper. But before we used it, we'd look at the pictures. And we'd hear about people who would get rich and you'd have all the food you wanted to eat and fancy clothes and houses. In our minds, there was so many of us, anybody that had a clean house was rich.

PLAYBOY: When did you first use a flush toilet?

PARTON: My aunt in Knoxville had a toilet in the bathroom and we were *so* fascinated. We were afraid to use it. I just thought it was goin' to suck us right down. She also had the first television we ever saw.

PLAYBOY: What about bathing?

PARTON: Funny, I was just thinkin' how nobody has ever asked me about how we bathed or how we . . . you know, because we didn't have. . . .

PLAYBOY: Toilets and facilities?

PARTON: Yes. We made our own soap and in the summertime, we'd go to the river. That was like a big bath. And we'd all go in swimming and we'd wash our hair, wash each other's hair. Soap was just flowin' down the river and we were so dirty we left a ring around the Little Pigeon River.

PLAYBOY: What did you do in the winter?

PARTON: In the wintertime, we just had a pan of water and we'd wash *down* as far as possible, and we'd wash *up* as far as possible. Then, when somebody'd clear the room, we'd wash *possible*.

PLAYBOY: How often did you bathe in the winter?

PARTON: I had to take a bath every night to be clean, 'cause the kids peed on me every night and we all slept three or four in a bed. As soon as I'd go to bed, the kids would wet on me. That was the only warm thing we knew in the wintertime. That was our most pleasure—to get peed on. If you could just not fan the cover. If you kept the air out from under the cover, the pee didn't get so cold. When you started fanning that cover, then it got bad, cold. Lord, it was as cold in the room where we slept as it was outside. We'd bundle up to go to bed.

PLAYBOY: When you bathed in the river, was it in the nude?

PARTON: We were real modest as kids. The boys would go swimmin' naked and the girls, sometimes we would, but we didn't go naked swimmin' together. As soon as you started sproutin' at all, you put on a shirt and you didn't take it off. I never did see Momma and Daddy naked. I'm glad I didn't.

PLAYBOY: Did your parents teach you the facts of life or did you learn them in school?

PARTON: It's somethin' I learned in the *barn*. [*Laughs*] I probably shouldn't say this, but it's just the truth: We were always just findin' out things on our own. We had uncles and cousins that were maybe two or three years older than us that knew a lot of stuff. When they would come to visit us, they'd teach us all kinds of meanness or tell us about this or that. And soon as we got a chance, we'd try it.

PLAYBOY: Are we talking about sexual things?

PARTON: Now, what were *you* talkin' about?

PLAYBOY: Just making sure.

PARTON: We were real curious. A lot of people won't admit it, but I just always had an open mind about sex. We all did. It was not a vulgar thing. We didn't know what we were doin', we just knew we weren't supposed to let Momma and Daddy know it. You never imagine your parents ever—

PLAYBOY: With 12 kids, they obviously did.

PARTON: Yeah. A lot of people say, "Well, how in the world could you live in a house with 12 kids and never hear things?" I don't know how they did it or where, but we never did know nothin' about it. But they *must* have done it.

PLAYBOY: So your mother never explained where all you kids came from?

PARTON: Momma always told us early that God was responsible for people havin' babies. I don't even know how I learned it. I learned real early. I think I probably knew it before Momma did. [*Laughs*] She learned when she was about 15 and I don't think she knew what was goin' on until she done had four kids. I was just so open-minded that I found out. If somebody wouldn't tell me, I'd ask the first person I thought I could ask.

PLAYBOY: What were the kinds of things you were asking? Where it comes from? Does it feel good? Does it hurt?

PARTON: Yeah. We just never did have a bunch of hang-ups. Momma never said, "Oh, don't do this, you'll go to hell." She didn't say *do* it, either. She didn't *say*. Daddy would have probably blistered our rear ends if he'd caught us foolin' around. We would just play doctor and nurse, just explore and experiment.

PLAYBOY: What about those guys who used to beat you all up—your neighbors—did they ever sexually abuse any of you?

PARTON: No. That's why they beat us up—because we wouldn't do anything. [*Laughs*] We didn't want to do it with them. I mean, we *were* choosy! But we never got sexually jumped or anything by them.

PLAYBOY: What was your first sexual experience like?

PARTON: I always loved sex. I never had a bad experience with it. I was just very emotional. I felt that I could show my emotion just like I show my emotion with words. If I felt I wanted to share an emotion, then I did. To me, sex was not dirty. It was somethin' very intimate and very real. I don't ever remember bein' afraid of it. I wasn't afraid the first time I tried it.

PLAYBOY: How old were you the first time?

PARTON: Now, I can't tell you that, because that would probably be real perverted. As little kids, we were *always* experimenting.

PLAYBOY: Well, you seem to have had a healthy childhood. Did you share your dreams of being a star with your parents?

PARTON: Yeah. I started writing songs before I went to school. Momma always wrote down stuff that I'd make up. I just had a gift of writing. I'd hear my people talk about relatives bein' killed and I would make up all these heartbreakin' songs about it. They'd forget they'd talked about it and they couldn't imagine where I would come up with all these ideas. I just knew how to put it into story form. And Momma would write them down.

PLAYBOY: When did you start singing on the radio?

PARTON: I had an uncle that told me there was this radio show in Knoxville and that sometime he might take me down there and I might get to be on it. I wanted to do that. So, when I was ten years old, I sung on the radio. And they all liked me real good, so they wanted me to work in the summer months. They said they'd pay me $20 a week. My aunt in Knoxville said she would take me up to the radio stations and the TV shows if Momma and Daddy would let me stay, and she did. I worked there in the summers until I was 18. I went from $20 a week to $60 when I left.

PLAYBOY: What kinds of songs were you singing?

PARTON: I sung country music, some songs I wrote. I was singing by myself and playing the guitar. But I guess it was because I was a little kid they were sayin' people liked it. I wasn't that good.

PLAYBOY: Were any of your songs recorded then?

PARTON: I made my first record when I was around 11.

PLAYBOY: And when did you make your first appearance at the Opry?

PARTON: I was just a kid, 12 or 13. My uncle told the man at *The Grand Ole Opry* that I wanted to be on. The man said, "You can't be on *The Grand Ole Opry*, you are not in the union." And I said, "What is a union?" I didn't know if it was a costume or a room to practice or what. I kept tellin' everybody. I said I'll just sing one song. Most of the artists at the Opry at that time had two spots. Nobody would let me sing and I walked up to Jimmy C. Newman, who was goin' to sing next, and told him I wanted to be on. He told Johnny Cash that I was goin' to sing. And so Johnny Cash brought me out and I sung and I just tore the house down. I had to sing it over and over and over. I thought I was a star. That was my first time.

PLAYBOY: How did you feel?

PARTON: I was kind of scared, but I was excited, because I knew Daddy and Momma were listenin' on the radio. I didn't grasp all what it meant, but I knew I had to be on *The Grand Ole Opry*, that is all there was.

PLAYBOY: Were you always encouraged to be whatever you wanted to be?

PARTON: Where I came from, people *never* dreamed of venturing out. They just lived and died there. Grew up with families and a few of them went to Detroit and Ohio to work in the graveyards and the car factories. But I'm talkin' about venturing out into areas that we didn't understand. To me, a little kid coming from where I did and having that ambition and sayin' I wanted to be a star, people would say, "Well, it's good to daydream, but don't get carried away." People would say you can't do this or you can't become this. Well, if you don't think you will do it, nobody else will think it.

I've got more confidence than I do talent, I think. I think confidence is the main achiever of success, I really do. Just believin' you can do it. You can imagine it to the point where it can become reality. When I made my change to do what I'm doin' now to appeal to a broader audience, people said, "You can't do that, because you are goin' to wreck your whole career; you are goin' to lose your country fans and you're not goin' to win the others, and then you're goin' to have nothin'. You just better *think* about that, girl." That didn't matter to me, because I knew I had to do it and I knew I *could* do it.

PLAYBOY: What other kinds of things could you do as an entertainer?

PARTON: I don't think there's anything I can't do. Under the right conditions, I could just about do anything. Even a Broadway play, if it was a mountain musical where I didn't have to be a Streisand-type singer or have a beautiful trained voice. If it was somethin' written just for me, I think I could do anything. Most people don't have that kind of confidence in themselves.

PLAYBOY: Have you seen many Broadway plays?

PARTON: I've never seen a Broadway play . . . I've never been to an opera . . . I've never seen a live stage performance. I guess I'm not very classy.

PLAYBOY: But you *have* been to the movies and you may be doing three films.

PARTON: I never wanted to be in the movies. I have never done any acting at all, never thought I'd be particularly good at it. But the people at 20th Century-Fox really feel like I can be, or that I am, a natural actress. When they approached me, all I said was, "I don't know if I can or can't, but if you think I can and you want to take that chance, I'll take it with you." It's as simple as that. Can you imagine me bein' an actress? But a lot of people are interested. Sandy Gallin, my manager, is making a hellacious deal, but no one knows if I can do it at all.

PLAYBOY: Are you planning on taking any acting lessons?

PARTON: No. They're just goin' to find a script where I can play my true personality, rather than tryin' to play like some girl from Australia. It's goin' to have to be Dolly Parton without bein' Dolly Parton. I'm goin' to write my own story, but it's not time yet. There's so much to my life that I can write a series of things, if I want. I can take a subject and make a full-length movie, if I want to do that.

PLAYBOY: Have you any properties in mind?

PARTON: No. I've been asked to do the Mae West story. I don't know that much about Mae West. A lot of people have often compared me to her . . . not our looks or not just the way we seem to be built or anything, but our attitudes, you know. We were both creative and we knew what we wanted and we pretty much rolled into the things we did. And they say she pretty much wrote everything she'd done. I've never seen her. Also, somebody felt I should do the Marilyn Monroe story. I don't think I want to play somebody else. I think I'm a character myself—for me to try to play somebody else's character would not be as wise as for me to create one of my own.

PLAYBOY: Do you have any directors you might go to?

PARTON: To be honest, I never thought about bein' in the movies enough to get that far along with that. I'm not really that involved in who does what. I don't really know who the directors or producers are. They say that if you've got the right director, that anybody can act. It's all kind of new, this movie thing. I've met a few people, but I can't remember their names.

PLAYBOY: How about screenwriters, say someone like Neil Simon?

PARTON: That is who I wish would write somethin' for me. I saw *The Goodbye Girl* and that's the type of thing that I see myself in. It's got depth, it's a comedy, it's got love . . . it just reminded me of the way I would react under the same conditions. You know, crazy and stupid, tryin' to make the best out of a bad situation. I'm even goin' to call my manager; it's probably farfetched. . . . Neil Simon may not even have an interest in me, period. But I can see myself doin' the type of things he writes.

PLAYBOY: What about Woody Allen?

PARTON: I love Woody Allen. I think he's sexy. He is so cute that he is sexy. I go with the depth and that turns me on sexually.

PLAYBOY: Would you like to be in a Woody Allen movie?

PARTON: Yes, if he'd be in it with me. I loved *Annie Hall* and I loved *The Goodbye Girl,* and for the same reasons, because they were both very realistic—funny, serious, even the bad times were good. Maybe we'll team Woody and Neil up and they can do somethin' *really* great.

PLAYBOY: Do you have any favorite movies?

PARTON: My favorite movie of all times is *Doctor Zhivago*. I've always liked movies with lots of production in them, especially things that were true, like *The Ten Commandments*.

PLAYBOY: Have you ever seen a porno movie?

PARTON: Yes, I have. Once, this secretary that worked in one of our offices, her husband had a print of a real awful one. I'd never seen anything up until that time. I always wanted to, but I didn't want anybody to know I was doin' it. She brought it to work and she brought the projector. When everybody left for lunch, she said, "Why don't we all watch?" Because none of us had ever seen one. We got to watchin' that thing and we got so embarrassed with each other. It, of course, moved you, but it was real embarrassing. And it got real gross, too.

Another time, I saw one in a public place. My girlfriend and me went to New York. This was a long time ago, I was about 21, and I wasn't that recognized. We had always wanted to see a *real* one. We thought it would be somethin' dirty enough to enjoy. We tried to sneak in when nobody would see. There is somethin' real shameful about goin' there, but we dared each other to do it, so we went. It had an awful smell in that theater.

PLAYBOY: Where was it?

PARTON: I don't know; it was down in one of them slum areas. We just got a cab, it was a Friday night, and this terrible thing happened. We sat at the very back, in case there were some maniacs in there. It was mostly men, a couple of women alone, no couples. Me and my girlfriend was sittin' in the back, so we were goin' to make a quick exit if we needed to, and then this movie came on. It looked OK for a few minutes, and all of a sudden, it got into the most gross things. I didn't know how to react and she didn't, either. We were embarrassed in front of each other, we didn't know whether to look or not. We were so curious we couldn't keep from lookin'. I didn't know how to react with her. If I had Carl there or somethin', we might have got down to business. So we ran out and we started runnin', so nobody would know where we came from. At that time, we didn't know that prostitutes ran in pairs in New York City for protection. And there is no way in the world that you can catch a cab on a Friday night in New York City. We didn't know that.

All of a sudden, these men started approachin' us on the street. They thought we were up for sale. You can imagine how ridiculous I looked. I would look like a streetwalker if you didn't know this was an image. I would look like a total whore, I suppose. I'm sure we looked just like what they thought we were. But I had a gun. I never traveled without a gun, still don't. I always carry a gun.

PLAYBOY: What kind?

PARTON: A .38 pistol. I have a permit for it in Nashville. I just carry it for protection. I feel safer when I've got it. I just don't like the idea of knowin' I'm totally helpless. I'm always scared in a big city and New York was totally foreign to us. Anyhow, these men would approach us and I'd say we're from out of town. We didn't understand why they were after us. I said we were waitin' on a cab and weren't interested, but thanks for the compliment. [*Laughing*]

I was doin' all the talkin', because my girlfriend always knew I'd get us out of any situation, and she started laughin' at me. That made me mad, because I was *so* scared! This one man came at me and he was really pullin' at me, he was tryin' to handle me, just maul me, the whole works. I told him, "Just get away and don't bother me anymore." He kept sayin', "Oh, come on, honey, I know you want it." He was offerin' us money and I said, "Look, I don't know what it is, we are *not* interested, we are *not* on the make, we are tryin' to get home, don't you understand that?" There I was, with my big Southern accent and my big wig. He just thought if he bargained long enough that I'd give in. He kept pullin' at me and I was getting furious and I was cussin' him, and I don't cuss that much. I was sayin', "You son of a bitch, you dirty bastard!" Just things like that is not like me at all, but I was *terrified*, and I was mad, too, because I can't stand people who pull at me unless I want to be pulled at. And my girlfriend was against the wall, dyin' laughing. We could have both been raped or killed, but she was gettin' such a kick, because she'd never seen this side of me before. I got furious at her and I told her, I said, "Boy, you just better stop laughing or I'm gonna beat the shit out of *you*, too!" And I got my gun out of my pocketbook. I told the man, "If you put your hands on me one more time, I swear to God that I will shoot you." And I *would* have. I wouldn't have shot him in the stomach or nothin', I would have shot his feet off or shot at the ground. My girlfriend was just hollerin', laughin' and, boy, I told her when we got rid of him, "If you ever do that to me again, I swear to you I may not whup your ass, but I'll be caught dead tryin'." [*Laughing*] She never did quit laughin', she just thought that was the funniest thing she'd ever seen. We headed out to a porno movie and it wound up bein' a comedy.

PLAYBOY: Was that your first time in New York?

PARTON: It was, and for years I thought I hated New York City for that very reason. Since then, it has become one of my very favorite cities; I go back all the time, there's great people there. It's just that then I didn't understand them and they *sure* didn't understand me.

PLAYBOY: Now that you've had your say about New York, let's try Los Angeles. You've been spending a lot of time out there lately. Do you like it there?

PARTON: It's beautiful and it's exciting. I really enjoy it for a week. After that, I go L.A. crazy. I just got to get out of there, it's so crazy and wild, especially the places I have to be and the people I have to be around when I'm out there; most of them are so spaced out or just involved in all sorts of weird things, even the people you work with, especially show people. I just have to get away from them. I get homesick. The country in me says, "What in the world are you doin' walkin' on concrete when you could be rollin' in the grass?"

PLAYBOY: Let's get to the country in you. Do you get insulted when people put down country music?

PARTON: Terribly insulted. Saying somethin' about country music is like saying somethin' about a brother or sister or my momma and daddy. Because it has made me a livin', it is somethin' I love and appreciate. I know what it stands for, I know what it is. It is a music to be respected.

PLAYBOY: What is it about country music that attracts people?

PARTON: It's the simplicity of it, it is everyday stories about everyday people. It deals with human emotions, human relationships; it is love and heartbreak and fun things and honky-tonk . . . the way that the truck drivers and the average middle-class American lives. Then, too, country music through television and radio started getting broader. When country started gettin' on TV, people realized that we are not just hillbillies and hicks, toe jam and bare feet—we only go barefooted 'cause we want to, not 'cause we can't do no better. To me, it's the greatest music because it does deal with life, with people, and it deals with simple sounds. If it is done right, it is the best music there is.

PLAYBOY: What would you say is the difference between country singing and pop or rock singing?

PARTON: There is a certain quality, a certain purity in country voices. They sound plainer, countrier, more blunt. They don't do a lot of screams and squalls.

PLAYBOY: Are you more prolific as a songwriter than most?

PARTON: Yes. It's just a natural gift. I like to write and I write all the time. I've written less in the last year and a half, but even at that, I've written more than most writers do. It's just so easy. I've got hundreds and hundreds of songs, thousands, actually. I've had a few hundred published and recorded. The good thing about it is this: I've been writin' all these years, if I never wrote another song, I've got it made. People are goin' back now and gettin' songs of mine and recordin' them, things I did on albums years ago. Of course, I still will write. It's like most people will sit down and smoke a pipe, I just sit down and pick up a piece of paper. . . .

PLAYBOY: Do you write in longhand?

PARTON: Yeah, I scribble; nobody can read it but me, hardly. I write on torn paper, Kleenex boxes, napkins. I wrote "Coat of Many Colors" on the bus. It's my most famous song. I was with Porter and he had some clothes cleaned and I took the tickets off of his cleanin' bags and wrote the song on them. After the song became a hit, he had the tickets framed.

PLAYBOY: What's the biggest song that you've had recorded?

PARTON: *Jolene* was the biggest hit I've had. It was also recorded by Olivia Newton-John. I also had a song called *I Will Always Love You*, which Linda Ronstadt recorded. I've had tons of songs and albums recorded by other people. But I've yet to have that big, smash, 1,000,000-selling song of my own. I've had lots of number-one songs, but when you get involved in how much they sell, it's rare to get a 1,000,000 seller.

PLAYBOY: Is most of what you write autobiographical?

PARTON: Everything I write is not about me. You have to be able to relate to the things you write about, but you don't have to live them personally.

PLAYBOY: One of your songs, *Bargain Store*, in which you compare your body to used merchandise, was banned by some radio stations. Were you surprised?

PARTON: I was in total shock, 'cause I never meant nothin' dirty in that song. In *It's All Wrong, but It's All Right*, I really *did*. I meant for it to be what it was. You know, what people call makin' love to somebody you're not married to. With lyrics like, "Hello, are you free tonight?/I like your looks, I love your smile;/could I use you for a while?" Just how plain can I be? But I thought the times would laugh at that. But there was some question about it. Even in this day and time, when you can say everything, country music is a little bit more delicate and I respect that.

PLAYBOY: What do you feel when you're performing your songs onstage?

PARTON: I just get *real* excited onstage, because I love to sing and per-form. It takes me about three hours to come down. Your openin' tune is usually the one you get off on if you're goin' to get off. Sometimes I get so excited over a certain moment onstage, I could just swear that it's the same thing as sex. . . . Music is the closest thing to it to me.

PLAYBOY: Do you have any ideas about how you might change the kinds of shows you perform now?

PARTON: I would want to be more bizarre as time goes on. I would like to have a screen behind me onstage when I do the songs and tell the stories of the mountains.

I'm havin' some people even now begin to film things from the mountains, like the tobacca-spittin' contest, the greased-hog contest and the horse-turd-throwin' contest that they have in Kentucky every year. That's a real occasion, the Annual Kentucky Horse Turd Throwin' Contest. Can you imagine gettin' crowned Horse Turd Queen of the day? They probably make a crown out of horse turds. I'm not tryin' to be dirty, I swear that's what they call it. An audience would love to see that, because they've never seen it. I'd like to have that onstage, narrate the happenings, and then have the music. I just have a lot of crazy, wild ideas and some of these days I'm gonna get them all together and hope somebody don't steal them. And if you do, you're a sorry son of a bitch!

PLAYBOY: Where do you see your career at the moment?

PARTON: Most people say in this business the life span of a career is five years from the time you really get hot to the time you start getting colder, like an Elton John. Maybe I shouldn't call names. That's just what I heard, that you don't expect to really be the hottest except for maybe five years, and with a TV show, it's usually a three-to-five-year thing, and then you cool off, people have seen what you do. I think maybe I am right now starting in my first year of from one to five. That's what I'd like to think.

PLAYBOY: Since we're on the subject of names, let's get your opinion of some of your contemporaries. We'll start with the woman you think is the true queen of country music, Kitty Wells.

PARTON: She was the first extremely popular female country singer. She was like a pioneer for all the rest of us. She sold all kinds of records to soldiers and jukeboxes and honky-tonks. She is such a natural, pure and authentic singer. She sings from the heart and she don't worry about what the noise is goin' to sound like.

PLAYBOY: Johnny Cash?

PARTON: Johnny is dramatic. I don't think Johnny is a good singer, but I think he is one of those people that is so believable that people can relate to it. He's got a way of deliverin'; you just know that it had to happen if Johnny said so.

PLAYBOY: Loretta Lynn?

PARTON: Sings with a lot of human emotion and country emotion, a lot of purity and honesty in her voice. Similar to Johnny Cash's—not the greatest voice I've ever heard, but it's believable.

PLAYBOY: Her sister, Crystal Gayle?

PARTON: A beautiful voice. Crystal clear, if you'll pardon the expression.

PLAYBOY: Tanya Tucker?

PARTON: If she ever gets with the right producer and the right label and gets the right manager, I think she can really be great, especially as a rock-'n'-roll singer. Her voice is so powerful, like a Janis Joplin or a Linda Ronstadt. . . . She could really be a huge artist, because she is great on the stage.

PLAYBOY: Janis Joplin?

PARTON: Her voice was like mine, you either liked it or you didn't. I never particularly cared for it. It was different. But I do appreciate what she left behind in the world of music.

PLAYBOY: Linda Ronstadt?

PARTON: She is one of the greatest female voices I ever heard.

PLAYBOY: Emmylou Harris?

PARTON: I love Emmy's voice, it's so delicate and so pure.

PLAYBOY: What's happening with the album the three of you are doing? The release date keeps being postponed. Is it finished?

PARTON: We've done several tracks, but we haven't decided whether or not to do more acoustic things or do some rock things. Any time you get three people, with three different labels and three different managers, there's always complications. But it's somethin' we've always wanted to do. We have talked about it for years. We are friends; there's a mutual respect and admiration among the three of us. If it was a matter of business, it would have been a rush release. We want it to be free and happy, a labor of love. There is a possibility it will never reach the market. I personally feel it would be a shame and a waste of talent if business and personal problems prevented it from being released.

PLAYBOY: How did you get to know Linda and Emmylou?

PARTON: Through my music. They were fans of mine. I had heard that they wanted to meet me, and so we made it a point to do that, and then we became friends. I met Emmy first, when she came to Nashville. She had recorded *Coat of Many Colors*. When I came back to L.A., she invited me to her house. Linda was invited over to supper that night and that's how we met.

PLAYBOY: Did you ever meet Elvis?

PARTON: No, I never did. But I always felt that we were kin. I feel like I know exactly how he was. Every time he'd come in town, even if I was home, I just wouldn't go, somethin' always kept me from goin'. There were other people I liked to hear sing better, but there was nobody that I ever related to more.

PLAYBOY: What was it about him you related to?

PARTON: He was very loving, very emotional, very sensitive, very giving, very humble, thankful, grateful. I always felt that he was totally in awe of his own success and he didn't quite understand why he had been so chosen and why he was such an idol. How he felt about God and religion was always somethin' I related to a lot, because I know he was brought up with his mother in the Assembly of God. It was a real free-spirited, shoutin' church. I watched and heard how he reacted to Gospel music and how he loved that the best of all and how he almost seemed to feel he had a callin' to do somethin' different and maybe more spiritual than what he actually was doin', but you know, he never got a chance to try. He touched people's lives in a lot of ways. He was the sex symbol of the world and when he started gainin' weight and gettin' fat, he lost a lot of his glamor to a lot of people. I always thought his manager was brilliant, as well. They built that mystery up about him. When he started losin' his glamor and doin' those concerts, he became more ordinary. That's when they started publishing all the things about him. Then people realized that he was not a god of any sort, but he was just an extraordinary human bein'. I think if he hadn't died when he did, within the next five years he wouldn't have been a hero at all, because he was talked about too much . . . seen too much. That's how cruel the public can be.

PLAYBOY: Do you think that there will be another Elvis, or someone of his stature, to come along?

PARTON: I don't think it will be soon, I don't think it will be anythin' you and me will ever see.

PLAYBOY: What about a female Elvis?

PARTON: That is possible. I think there is due a person, a female, which there has never been. A person of that type, with that great magnetism and that great mysterious thing, that great love, that charisma and magic to draw people to her, that can help people in many ways just through her music. Yes, I think that a female is due, I do. And your next question: Do I think it is me?

PLAYBOY: You're the one smiling.

PARTON: Well, let me say, I would never be an Elvis, and I would never want to be Elvis. But I would like to be a person truly loved enough to be able to have that much of an impact on people as far as bein' able to guide them or help them or let them see that you're caring.

PLAYBOY: Your mother has said that she always expected you to lead people to the Lord. Do you think that someday that might happen—besides just singing, you might start preaching?

PARTON: Yes, I think that is definitely possible. My mother and many people have always said that they saw the love of God in me. I expect that someday, in some way, before I die I'll have done some good for God, who I think has done all the good in me that's ever been done. I think that people for years have passed God right up, looked right past Him, thinkin' that He was some great monster in the sky and that you had to live with these horrible guilt feelin's and you had to crawl under a bed if you'd done somethin' wrong. I have a totally different concept of God. I'm God-fearin', but I'm not afraid of God. The way I look at God is, I think He means somethin' different to everybody. We are all God's children, if we just clear a way for Him to work through us. You don't have to be standin' in a church house to reach people to change their lives to do good. I don't want to get so involved in this that people think, Oh, another country-music fanatic, because I'm not a fanatic, never was. If I need to make a decision or somethin', I just talk out loud to God. I joke with God. He don't ever say nothin' back.

PLAYBOY: Do you go to church?

PARTON: No, not anymore. Carl and I are probably afraid we'll become total Christians and then we'll . . . I don't know. I always want to go home when they're havin' a revival, though. Someday, when I can have some time off, I want to go back to the house and stay home for a couple of months, spend the summer, work the fields and go to the orchards, can apples and peaches—do stuff like I used to. And if they're havin' a revival, I'll go. I'll get up and sing, too.

PLAYBOY: You first became nationally prominent as part of a team with Porter Wagoner. Tell us about your relationship with him.

PARTON: Porter has been one of the greatest and most popular country artists of all times. I can never take the credit away from Porter for givin' me a big break. I learned a lot from him. He inspired me and I inspired him. We were good for each other in many ways and just a disaster for each other in a lot of ways. I'll always love him in my own way.

PLAYBOY: In what ways did your working together become a disaster?

PARTON: We just got to where we argued and quarreled about personal things. Things we had no business quarreling and arguing about. It was beginning to tarnish a really good relationship. We didn't get along very well, but no more his fault than mine. We were just a lot alike. Both ambitious. I wanted to do things my way and he wanted to do things his way.

PLAYBOY: He has said that for two years he devoted 95 percent of his time to you and then he didn't hear from you for a year. He sounds bitter.

PARTON: I'm sure he is bitter at this particular point. He is so strong-headed and bullheaded, he won't accept things sometimes the way they are. I won't, either, sometimes. We're kind of involved in some legal things. I'm tryin' to buy my part of the catalog back, where I'll have all my songs back together. Someday I hope we can be friends. We are not enemies. We just don't ever see each other.

PLAYBOY: How much money was Porter paying you?

PARTON: The years I was with Porter, I worked for $300 a night, which is another reason I needed to get out on my own; I needed to make more money.

PLAYBOY: That was how much a year?

PARTON: Sixty thousand dollars a year. I started from no money at all and that sounded like a *lot* of money to me. And it was. But why should I work for hundreds and thousands when I can work for hundreds *of* thousands?

PLAYBOY: How much a night did you make when you worked on your own, after leaving Porter?

PARTON: When I went out on my own, I was working for $2500, then it got up to $3000, and now I have no idea. It is way up in the thousands.

PLAYBOY: Is it around $30,000?

PARTON: I don't know exactly how much I make; I would say anywhere from $15,000 up a night now. I know I got $30,000 for some shows I've done recently. And I was offered $50,000 to do a special show, but for some reason, I didn't do it. That's the most I've been offered at this point, I think.

PLAYBOY: How many businesses do you own?

PARTON: Quite a few. I own three publishing companies. I'm startin' a production company. I own quite a bit of property. I have the Dolly doll, for which we own the company. We have program books, colorin' books, souvenir things of that type. I have lots of investments, lots of tax shelters. I've got some good smart business people now. I have some really wild dreams and plans. I really love to hear crazy ideas. I'm goin' to have a line of wigs. I think that would be a perfect business for me.

PLAYBOY: We've been meaning to ask about your wigs. Are they real hair or synthetic?

PARTON: Synthetic. They never lose their curl.

PLAYBOY: Loretta Lynn has said that while most singers aren't particular in the dressing room, you always go behind a little curtain to dress. She says nobody has ever seen you without a wig on.

PARTON: Loretta has seen my own hair. I think she forgot or just wanted to make a bigger thing than it was. Maybe she just didn't recognize it as bein' my own hair. My own hair is blonde. I keep it blonde. I'll eventually wear my own hair again, once I become so successful that people know you can become successful by lookin' and bein' any way you want to if you've got enough ambition and talent. A lot of people have approached me in a way that sounded like I was supposed to dress and undress in front of other people. I happen to be a very modest person and I just won't dress in front of people. I don't know why they would want to look, anyway. Out of curiosity, I guess. What other people do does not bother me at all. I only wish that what I do wouldn't bother them.

PLAYBOY: Let's wind this up by asking you some random questions. If you could go back in time and be someone else for a while, who would you like to be?

PARTON: That's not a random question, that's a *great* question! I've never thought about that in my life. . . . I think, maybe, Will Rogers. He reminds me of my own people and of myself.

PLAYBOY: What if you could invite any five people from history to a dinner party—whom would you choose?

PARTON: Will Rogers would be my main guest. Beethoven. Bob Hope. Strother Martin. Festus, from *Gunsmoke.*

PLAYBOY: What would you serve them?

PARTON: Fried potatoes and green beans, country-style creamed corn, corn bread and biscuits, pinto beans and turnip greens, meat loaf. I'd probably make up a vanilla pudding. I'd have to fix Beethoven a chef's salad. I don't think he'd want all that grease.

PLAYBOY: What's your favorite food?

PARTON: Potatoes. I'm a starch freak. I'm a junk-food person, too. I like pizza, potato chips, Fritos. My main weakness is overeating. Now it's beginning to dawn on me that I have a weight problem and I have to learn to control it some way. I am getting approached for so many things, for movies, for the PLAYBOY cover. So I'm on a diet.

PLAYBOY: Weren't you once on a liquid-protein diet, which lately has been proved to be dangerous?

PARTON: I did that and I lost 23 pounds. Fat persons don't care if they die tryin' to get it off. [*Laughs*]

PLAYBOY: Are you attracted to thin or to muscular men?

PARTON: I've always been more attracted to real slender men. My husband is skinny as a rail, and tall. They say that you usually will be attracted to the opposite of yourself.

PLAYBOY: Is it hard to design clothes for you?

PARTON: It's not hard, 'cause all you got to do is make up the gaudiest thing you can make. Just pile as much stuff that don't belong on it as you can and I'll like it.

PLAYBOY: How many rooms of clothing do you have?

PARTON: I've got clothes in the closets of every room in my house—23 rooms. One whole wing of my house is filled with costumes and casual clothes.

PLAYBOY: And you sometimes shop at Frederick's of Hollywood?

PARTON: I buy my shoes there; it's the only place I can find shoes high enough and sexy enough to suit me. I buy thousands of dollars of shoes every year. I can't wear their clothes, because I can't buy clothes off a rack.

PLAYBOY: Do you support the Equal Rights Amendment?

PARTON: Equal rights? I love everybody. . . .

PLAYBOY: We mean equal rights for women.

PARTON: I can't keep up with it.

PLAYBOY: Do you read any books on the women's movement?

PARTON: Never have. I know so little about it they'd probably be ashamed that I was a woman. Everybody should be free: If you don't want to stay home, get out and do somethin'; if you want to stay home, stay home and be happy.

PLAYBOY: Do you have favorite books or authors?

PARTON: I don't read that much. I probably should be ashamed to say that. I read mostly articles and things I'm interested in. I always liked Agatha Christie, but I never did read all that many of her things. I like books like *The Magic of Believing*. Positive-thinking books, self-improvement books. Long before I knew there were books about that stuff, that was my philosophy of life.

PLAYBOY: What about politics?

PARTON: I hate to say this and people probably think I'm real dumb to do it, but I am so involved in my work and my music I don't even know what's goin' on in the world. I don't even know who the Vice-President is. Well, I *do* know . . . but as far as gettin' politically involved, it's like bein' denominations. If you're a Democrat, the Republicans hate you; if you're a member of one church, then the other ones hate you. Every denomination thinks they're the only ones gettin' to heaven and they feel sorry for the other denominations. I think we can all get there if we work right.

PLAYBOY: Moving right along . . . has sex changed for you over the years?

PARTON: Sex? Yes, it gets better. The reason it gets better is because you get more mature, you're more relaxed, you experience more things until you become more comfortable with them, and then you feel also comfortable to experience new things, totally new and different things. It takes you a while to trust somebody enough to be able to tell your fantasies.

PLAYBOY: How strong are your fantasies?

PARTON: Pretty strong. But I think all creative people and highly emotional people have strong fantasies.

PLAYBOY: What are some of yours?

PARTON: I'm not tellin' you all that stuff. . . . Get over here and I'll show you. [*Laughs*] Are you perverted?

PLAYBOY: Why? Are you sexually aggressive?

PARTON: I'm very aggressive. I don't mind bein' the aggressor if it comes to somethin' I need or want.

PLAYBOY: Do you like dangerous sex?

PARTON: Nothin' better than sex when you think you have to sneak it.

PLAYBOY: Now for the big question: Do you sleep in the nude?

PARTON: It has just been the last couple of years that I've really started sleepin' naked. Sometimes I sleep naked with Carl and sometimes I don't. If I'm up writin' and I have on a robe, I'll write until I fall asleep and crawl into bed. If we go to bed together, I usually go naked. But I have to have a cover on me, summer or winter. I can't stand just a sheet.

PLAYBOY: How would someone who had written something get a song to you?

PARTON: Do you mean to tell me that we've spent all these days and hours and went through all this horseshit just so you could pitch me a song?

PLAYBOY: You're a funny lady. Is it true you used to flirt with local disc jockeys when you'd appear in various towns?

PARTON: Either my life is a total flirt or I'm not a flirt. I just go in with open arms and open heart. I'm just using my personality. But the only ones I ever flirted with were the ones I was attracted to. Can't say I never flirted with one, but I never flirted with one to get my record played.

PLAYBOY: And what about all the erotica you used to write as a teenager? You claimed you were very horny.

PARTON: All teenagers are horny, some just keep it hid better than others. I'm writin' a story even now; it's pretty hot and heavy. It's got a lot of sex and love and violence and religion, all the human elements.

PLAYBOY: Will you shock a lot of people?

PARTON: Yeah; that's why I ain't puttin' them out today or the day after tomorrow. When I decide to publish some of my books, I'm goin' to write in the front that those who think they might be offended, don't read them. Then, if you are offended, don't blame me, because now I'm not just a singer but also a writer; and as a writer, I have to have freedom of total expression.

PLAYBOY: Would you use a pseudonym?

PARTON: I want to do everythin' under my own name, 'cause when I go down in history, I want to go down good and solid.

PLAYBOY: They could put that on your tombstone: Good and solid.

PARTON: I don't want a tombstone. I want to live forever. They say a dreamer lives forever. . . . I want to be more than just an ordinary star. I want to be a famous writer, a famous singer, a famous entertainer; I want to be a movie writer; I want to do music movies, do children's stories; I want to be somebody important in time; I want to be somebody that left somethin' good behind for somebody else to enjoy.

Everybody wants to be successful at whatever their inner dream is. I'm not near with what I want to do, with what I want to accomplish. When I feel like I have accomplished the things that I want to accomplish, then maybe I will personally think of myself as a superstar. I want to be somebody that extremely shines. A star shines, of course, but I want to be really radiant.

DOLLY DIAMOND

On Backlash from Country Fans

"Today somebody brought a paper up to me and it said 'GOODBYE DOLLY WE DON'T WANT YOU NOW.' It's just like if you're black, they wanna call you nigger. If you're country they wanna call you hillbilly. And if you try, they call you son of a bitch. So what're you supposed to do? But it won't stop me. I'll go to my grave doin' everything I can to make the world a better place and myself a better person."

–To Colin Irwin, *Melody Maker*, November 11, 1978

DOLLY PARTON: THE SEXY SUPERSTAR OF COUNTRY POP

Laura Cunningham | January 1979 | *Cosmopolitan*

With a media frenzy surrounding her appearance on the cover of *Playboy*, Dolly's limelight shone brighter than ever. Although she had reservations about gracing the cover of such a "wild" magazine and worried that some among her conservative country following might take offense, the overwhelming response to the cover—and especially the interview—was encouraging and positive.

It seemed that the only person *not* in love with Dolly Parton was Porter Wagoner. Her former boss and partner was interviewed in October 1978, shortly after Dolly's *Playboy* hit the stands, and their long-simmering feud came to a boil in a cover story for the *Tennessean* bearing the headline, Porter's Bitter Remarks Turn Dolly's Happiest Hour Sour. "Dolly wants to do everything that is possible for her to do," Wagoner told the reporter, "but she lives in a fairy land. . . . I don't believe a country girl singer would do things in the manner she's done them. Like the *Playboy* thing. Do you think Kitty Wells would do that?"

Dolly didn't respond to Wagoner's criticism for many years, but finally detailed their dispute to Kevin Sessums of *Vanity Fair* in 1991: "I thought, *Well, I guess not*. I don't think *Playboy* would want Kitty Wells on the cover. But it was that kind of mentality: Kitty Wells wouldn't do that, Loretta Lynn wouldn't do that. Well, I'm not Loretta Lynn. I'm not Kitty Wells."

Wagoner insisted in his interview that he was not bitter about the duo's breakup but went on to say that their parting wasn't Dolly's choice, but his. "No, no, no, she couldn't stay," he told the *Tennessean*. "I let her go. Dolly didn't quit me. I gave her notice in Tulsa, Oklahoma, that she needed to get her own band together because I wasn't going to travel and have'a girl that I had to fight with on the road with us. I'm not bitter because Dolly left my show in any sense. I was just disappointed to find out she's not made of what I thought she was. . . . To me, Dolly Parton is the kind of person I would never trust with anything of mine. I mean, her family, her own blood, she would turn her back on to help herself. I'm not that kind of person. I don't care about talkin' about it 'cause most people would think I'm bitter at Dolly. I'm not bitter at her at all."

When asked about the feud and Porter's remarks to the press, Dolly told *Melody Maker's* Colin Irwin she had no comment. "I won't put myself on his level. I will say that it was unfair and untrue and that's all I'll say. . . . It kills you when somebody tells things that just aren't true. It just killed my daddy, it was just so bitter and untrue. But I really don't care to discuss it if you wouldn't mind. I could say a lot of things, but I'm a more considerate person on that level. I don't think I have to slander people to be accepted."

For *Cosmopolitan*, Laura Cunningham hit the road with Dolly and her entourage and penned this fascinating "day in the life" profile of the star at her first of many zeniths. The ins and outs of touring were explored, with every aspect detailed: the band, the bus, the motels, the fans, the makeup, the wigs, the costumes, the diets, and, of course, the dreams. Spoiler alert: What makes this piece extra special is that Dolly's reclusive husband, Carl Dean, came out of hiding long enough to make a rare appearance in this feature, and Cunningham was on hand for his thirty-sixth birthday celebration at a Howard Johnson in Albany, New York.

It should be noted that, like a handful of journalists before and since, Cunningham attempted to capture Dolly's distinctive dialect and country twang, as evidenced in the stylized spellings found here. For example: *rul* = real, *mah* = my, *yer* = your, *wus* = was, and so on. Apparently, these stabs at phonetically sounding out Dolly's speech patterns irritated her. When writer Gerri Hirshey (whose work appears elsewhere in this collection) showed her a piece by a writer in Green Bay who quoted Dolly as saying "Ah" for "I," Dolly became livid and exclaimed, "She tried to make me sound like a country bumpkin!"—Ed.

You know about her six-inch wigs, slinky glitter getups, and truly <u>amazin'</u> figure. But there's more—yes, <u>more</u>—to this prodigiously talented lady than meets the bedazzled eye . . .

Dolly is the one with the breasts, the high blond wig, and the six-year-old-child's soprano. That's how she fits into the hierarchy of the Four Sisters of Country Music: Loretta is the sad one, with sucked-in cheeks. Tammy is the soft one, who's suffered through all those divorces. Crystal's the young, cool one, in control of her life. And then there's Dolly—pouter-pigeon chest, cotton-candy hair, and the baby voice that begs:

"Jo-lene, Jo-lene, Jo-lene,
Please don't take my man . . ."

Not since Marilyn Monroe has a blonde defused her blatant sexuality with such obvious vulnerability. Like Marilyn, Dolly is adored by women and children as well as by men, a fact that needs explaining if you've seen only her photo. For, truly, doesn't she look, in her skintight, sequined jump suit, like someone women would resent? And yet, it ain't so, it ain't so . . .

Why ain't it so?

To discover the real woman encased in the impossible body and behind the lacquered image, I track down Dolly Parton and her touring band, Gypsy Fever, to a Howard Johnson's motel near Albany, New York. By a fortunate coincidence, my car radio bleats a Dolly Parton favorite:

"My life is [likened] a bargain store,
And I may have just what you're looking for,
If you don't mind the fact that all the merchandise is used . . ."

The song ends with Dolly's invitation: "The bargain store is open, come inside." "The Bargain Store" was banned in some parts of the Bible Belt.

Ringin' in my ears, too, is the love song of Dolly Parton's public-relations lady: "I cried. The first time I heard her sing that song about li'l Andy, I just cried. And I heard people sing before. But *no one* has moved me like Dolly."

Dolly has moved her PR lady not only with her singing, but with her downright goodness. "I would never say a curse word in front of Dolly. I mean, she is Little Mary Sunshine!"

Also drumming in the echo chamber of my brain—the intriguing phenomenon known in music circles as the "*New* Dolly." Dolly Parton has recently become the darling of more than a few unlikely fans: Mick Jagger and the other Rolling Stones, and a complete entourage of Beautiful People, including Tony Perkins and Berry Berenson. Indeed, she has even made an admirer of New York *Times* music critic John

Rockwell. While praising her "asymmetrical freshness," Rockwell also observed that she is "at the brink of a radical shift that should, if there is any justice in pop-music heaven, make her one of the great stars of American entertainment."

Popular ever since her 1967 teaming with country-music star Porter Wagoner and her solo debut two years later, Dolly's career *really* took off in 1977 with the release of the album *New Harvest, First Gathering,* an album which was, not so coincidentally, the first she'd produced herself.

In quick succession came *Here You Come Again* and her current smash, *Heartbreaker,* both certified million-sellers. Though RCA executives are reluctant to discuss figures, the revenues from Dolly's albums are believed to exceed those of any other country-western songstress. A new Dolly Parton "single" shoots automatically to the number-one spot on the country charts, and even such "classic" hits as "Jolene" and "Love Is Like a Butterfly" continue to sell and sell . . .

Piled almost as high as her earnings are the awards she's amassed. In the past few years, Dolly has lugged away more than 100 trophies, including last year's Songwriter's Hall of Fame "Hitmaker's Award," a tribute given previously to such stars as Frank Sinatra, Barbra Streisand, and Bing Crosby. In 1978 she was the Country Music Association's "Entertainer of the Year." Nor has her enormous popularity been overlooked by Hollywood; 20th Century-Fox has reportedly offered her a three-picture contract.

No question: Dolly's act has been a-changin' and she's getting hotter and hotter. Yet many unanswered questions remain. She has a public image that's harder to crack than Pollyanna's and no one knows much about her private life at all. She's been written up in the tabloids as the wife of a "mystery husband" who has never heard her sing or watched her perform. What kind of relationship does she have with a man who, according to her own press releases, refused to have his picture taken with her?

Hmmmm.

I board her bus, "The Coach of Many Colors," now parked in the Howard Johnson's motel lot outside of Albany. Through the wide windshield, I catch my first glimpse of Dolly: tottering across the asphalt on five-inch wedgies. Dwarfed by her mountain of sprayed platinum hair, she looks like Marie Antoinette in jeans and a plaid shirt.

Motel doors pop open, and vacationing Howard Johnson's guests emerge, clicking Instamatics as Dolly walks toward the bus. It is just sunset, and 100-degree heat practically presses people to the asphalt, yet they keep coming. Children emerge, like dolphins, from the nearby swimming pool, to wave and cry: "Dolly!"

Dolly pivots, as pretty and automated as the Dolly Parton dolls that are licensed by her corporation. (The "Dolly Doll" stands twelve inches tall, has the biggest bosom on any children's toy, and sells for about ten dollars.) Now the real Dolly assumes her public persona: Again and again, her cheeks dimple in a smile. Again and again, she bends, breasts pooching forward, rear-end cleavage equally defined, to sign autographs.

"Thank ya, thank ya," she says, easing up the bus steps. Single red roses (a customary offering from her fans) are clutched in her tiny, bejeweled hands. Her standard remark for the evening, repeated over and over, in reference to the weather, her performance, or whatever, is: "Ain't it amazin'."

She has just returned from a day trip to New York City, and is tuckered out by the record-high, egg-fryin'-on-the-sidewalk temperatures: "Ain't it amazin'."

"You 'n' me will talk sometime," she says, then vanishes into the bowels of the bus. Which leaves me up front—with the cologned members of the Gypsy Fever band.

The Gypsy Fever band—seven male musicians and one "girl" singer—are, themselves, human indications of the new, changed Dolly. All but one or two of the musicians have only recently joined her. The group itself is just two years old—new as such backup groups go—and changes are still being made. Given country-band standards, they are an eclectic crowd. Not for them the cowboy hats and studded belts that mark most Nashville ensembles. The young men wear fresh sport shirts and plain slacks, while the girl looks pretty in a sundress. They could pass for college kids on summer vacation, instead of a country-western band. Gypsy Fever has drawn its talent from places as obvious as Nashville and as *un*country as Los Angeles.

"Dolly is just trying for the right sound," explains Gregg Perry, her piano player, an ascetic fellow who munches sunflower seeds and reads serious literature.

All the band members are young—the eldest, macrobiotic Gregg, is a mere lad of twenty-nine. This, too, is unusual for a country band, which generally will contain several aging cousins of the star. Even the bus looks different from other country buses: "The Coach of Many Colors," despite its name, is subdued and routinely upholstered in gold and black vinyl. Other country stars have let their imagination run riot on the décor: Loretta Lynn's bus is a fantasy of flocked purple velvet and "marbleized" rococo toilet seats. The only "standard" of the tour bus: At the back are six red corduroy sleeping bunks. "We call them 'the coffins,'" jokes Gregg Perry. "We sleep in them if we're doing one-night shows. But this trip's been real easy, so we've been able to stay at motels all the way."

Other sleeping arrangements exist—in case. The very seat I'm sitting on can bunk two more musicians. And the luggage space at the very rear can become a bed for Dolly's thin road manager, Don Warden, who, along with Dolly, is a "rul country" person. In fact, Don Warden, with his giant diamond steer ring, adds Nashville color to the group. (It may help to know that back home Don has an office containing a statue of a nude girl; to keep her glistening, this statue is regularly wetted down with sprays of cooking oil.)

On to the auditorium—a few miles further outside of Albany, in the town of Colonie.

At the Colonie Coliseum, an outdoor hardtop summer theater that seems to be made of fiberglass, we head for the dressing rooms. There, the girl singer fluffs her hair and drinks Tab. Dolly herself remains in the bus, where she keeps her supply of custom chiffon costumes.

Next: Show Time. The Gypsy Fever band literally beats the drums, and *voilà*! Flying in like the Good Witch in Oz, chiffons aflutter, diamond wand waving . . . Dolly Parton!

This is the fantasy I have read about: the extravagant dream in which More is More. Not enough to wear two wigs, in sprayed splendor, but also—a fake rose is pinned in back . . . And then, then, it's not enough:

Glitter! Diamonds! Sausage-tight salmon pants . . . a flowing salmon-pink sheer veiled top . . .

She raises her tiny white hands: a queen's greeting to her subjects. The crowd roars. And everywhere, people cry: "She's so beautiful!"

And, incredibly, she *is*! More *is* more. She must be seen in the flesh. Her look "hardens" in photos, but here in the fiberglass coliseum, she *glows* . . .

Dolly sings buoyantly—her voice rising to the hardtop and floating out to the humid night. "*Higher and higher. . .*" she sings, and nothing could hold her voice in . . . the sweet chime seems propelled, somehow, by the voluptuousness of her breasts. Perhaps the breasts work, like bellows, beneath the hot pink chiffon.

She is working, all right—rotating on a high stool to face alternate sections of the audience. "I apologize to those of you who have to look at mah rear end!"

"That's all right," growls a heavy-necked man next to me.

She intercuts her songs with a repartee with the attentive, sweating listeners. "We've had some nice folks, but yer the best batch yet . . . We have some pretty people here . . . There were some ugly ones last night . . ."

Her stage patter contrasts with her songs: Singing, she soars. Speaking, she goes canned and flat: "I heard some folks brought binoculars to see if they's as big as they heard they wus . . ."

Some laughter.

"Wal . . . I don't know whut yer laughin' at . . . I wus talkin' 'bout mah wigs . . ."

Performing, she's all over the stage: picking up a zither, plucking a banjo. She skips from exuberant rock to dip into sentimental country ballads. Her voice is so pure, she succeeds in making you believe the impossible: that this glittering miniature Mae West is indeed:

"*Sitting on the front porch on a summer afternoon . . .*

Watch the kids a-playin' with June bugs on a string . . ."

But the most incredible transformation comes with a song she has not yet recorded, but sings only in person: "Me and Little Andy." The song recounts the death of a little girl and her puppy. And it's more than a tear-jerker, it's a tear-*yanker*.

Most singers couldn't get away with it, but Dolly does—denying her physical appearance to become, on stage, a six-year-old girl.

"Ain't you got no gingerbread, ain't you got no candy?
Ain't you got no extra bed for me 'n' little Andy . . . ?"

Dolly, as the song's narrator, does have a bed—and the little girl and her puppy lie down and die in it. The song would be to throw up over if Dolly performed it in a cutesy way. But her little girl is not a Shirley Temple moppet. Her voice projects another kind of child—a starved, terrified orphan . . . unwanted and slightly resentful.

Dolly, with her diamonds, her rose, her salmon chiffon, disappears, by some magic in her voice, and is replaced by a ragged, knock-kneed little girl.

All around me, there are sniffles. A few Kleenex come out, and the honk of a nose being blown echoes under the hardtop.

Dolly performs other songs . . . some lilting, others wistful; but the songs that seem to play upon the audience's collective spinal column are those in which Dolly reverts to the plaintive child. Even in "Jolene," the song in which she begs "the other woman" to leave her man alone, she sounds oddly adoring, like a little girl to an admired big sister:

"Your beauty is beyond compare, with flaming locks of auburn hair . . ."

Hearing this, I recall the first time I ever listened to a Dolly Parton album. The occasion: a country-western songfest in the Los Angeles home of actress Susan Anspach. Before such country enthusiasts as Wayne Rogers, Robert Duvall, and Susan Anspach herself began to sing, Susan turned on a record player and said: "I want you all to hear this. This is *it*. The most vulnerable song ever written or sung by any woman. To sing this song, a woman must have no ego. *Listen . . .*"

Vulnerable. That's the word most often applied to Dolly. And, perhaps, an explanation of why women are so drawn to her: How can you resent someone who is so damned *vulnerable*?

Standing in full regalia, she seems to be saying: *Go on, laugh at me, tell me I look ridiculous.* And so, by God, you can't.

The crowd roars—she flies for the stage door, the bus, and then, back to Howard Johnson's.

There, a unique event is shaping up. Tonight is her husband, Carl Dean's, birthday. And we (I now feel like one of the team) are springing a surprise party for "the mystery husband" in the best dining room of the Howard Johnson's Inn. There are two dining rooms, and the better room is to the rear, sealed off by sliding fake-wooden panels.

We—the Gypsy Fever band and I—stand in semidarkened readiness. On our heads: plastic cowboy hats. In our hands: colored paper noisemakers. We anxiously peer through the window to catch sight of Dolly and her man.

This will be a double surprise party—a surprise for Carl Dean and a surprise for me. Having heard that he never travels with Dolly, I never dreamed I'd get to see him in the flesh. All I've ever read about Dolly's husband is that "Carl Dean prefers to stay out of the limelight and tend to his asphalt paving business in Tennessee."

"He never goes with us," concurs Gregg Perry, who is staging this fete, "but this week, he's made a real exception. I guess 'cause we're here for an entire week, and also, 'cause it's his birthday."

"Hey . . . here they come!" the girl singer cries.

I look: Dolly Parton, still a vision in hot pink, floats through the main room of the Howard Johnson's. Diners look open-mouthed, ignoring their frankfurts grilled in butter, as she nods graciously to each in turn. Behind her, a Lincolnesque man walks slowly toward us . . .

The crucial moment is blown: A waitress pulls back the sliding panel, revealing all of us in our cowboy hats—

"Happy Birthday!" we cry, prematurely.

The lanky stranger—is it really He?—turns, enters the room backward, as if making way for yet another person behind him. He makes mock gestures of greeting to some invisible person.

But—there can be no mistake . . . Dolly is hugging him. It's *him*!

"Wal," he laughs, turning around to face the group, "I thank you from the bottom of mah crotch."

He is an unusual fellow, this mystery husband. Tall and good-looking, rather like a young Gregory Peck, he has a way of moving his angular body so that he seems to come toward you in sections. He also makes exaggerated faces, talks to his right shoulder, hangs his head, looks under the table. Still, there's real charm along with this strange series of tics. Carl Dean announces that he is a fan of television and night-club comic Steve Martin, and no doubt that explains a lot. His occasional speeches to our group, as we assemble at the party tables—to be served HoJo drinks and fried clams—all have the style of an impersonation.

"You sure are a rul nice bunch a folks," he announces, several times.

"Wal, yer seein' mah husband," Dolly calls to me across the table. "Did you see that picture *The National Enquirer* sneaked of him last month?"

I had—the photo showed Carl, his mouth hanging open, at the wheel of his asphalt truck.

"The photographer hid in our bushes to git that," Dolly explains. "And when it come out, everybody said, 'So *that's* why she keeps him hid.'" She leans against Carl and giggles. "He was all covered with mud and tar, too."

Carl grins. "No wonder ya got to hide me." Then he notices me, and asks: "Who is this nice young lady?"

Dolly tells him, and he pales (he *does* like his privacy). And immediately, he says, "Fergit whut I said about the bottom of mah crotch."

Never.

The Party goes on. Domestic champagne flows, the fried clams are passed around for sampling in one of the plastic cowboy hats—"You've never had fried clams until you've et 'em from a hat," says Dolly, who didn't et them.

"All I kin eat is this itty-bitty steak," she explains, holding up a fork. "Ah bin fastin' twenty days . . . on Dr. Robert Linn's Last Chance Diet. On special occasions, I kin have a piece a meat."

For the rest of us, there is a HoJo birthday cake, decorated with orange and turquoise roses. "Oh, it looks so good," cries Dolly, slicing up the sections.

A young blonde has joined the group—she is the girlfriend of one of the band members, just here for the night. Dolly passes her an orange frosting rose on a napkin: "Here, I want you to have this."

The girl delicately places the rose in her purse, then turns to me with shining eyes: "She's made me feel so welcome."

The night is young—after the refreshments, we all run out to the back lawn of the Howard Johnson's for a game of volleyball under the stars. Carl Dean hands me the champagne: "I want you to have this," he says. We pass the champagne around for quick swigs between games.

Overhead, constellations sparkle like the rings on Dolly's fingers and the diamonds at her ear lobes. But Dolly herself cannot play—not tonight, or any night. She props herself onto a chair, sits cross-legged. "I cain't play 'cause of mah nails," she tells me, holding up her vermilion-tipped Madame Nhu fingertips.

She has taken off her wig, though, and, in its place, wears a ruffled bedcap. She has exchanged the pink chiffon, too—for a shirt and jeans. As is her habit, she kicks off her five-inch wedgies, and tucks her little white feet under her.

I take part in the volleyball, but am continually aware of her small presence beside the court. The neon lights from the Howard Johnson's sign, and the white streak of nearby Route 87, illumine her ruffled head-dress. As tiny as she is, she looks still smaller with her legs tucked under her. She has sat out countless games this way—and will, doubtless, sit out countless more. I see her as a sort of *totem*, carted from Howard Johnson's to Howard Johnson's, propped up as a Buddha-like symbol of benign rule and ritualized sex appeal.

Dolly's role is to applaud the good serves and high-flying returns. When the volleyball soars up to the starred and neon-lit sky, she calls out: "Aw-*right!*"

The volleyball bounces, and champagne flows . . . until the sky over Howard Johnson's blanches and the stars pale. "The bugs is bitin' me, I'm gonna go to bed . . ." Dolly slips on her high heels and walks tippy-toe to the volleyball teams to kiss Carl good night. He's not ready yet to call it quits.

"Gee, thanks, Da-*dee*," she says in her baby voice, performing a mock curtsy.

Carl, delighted, rolls over and over on the grass. There will be no morning for Dolly. "I wake up at one in the afternoon," she tells me. "So you can come see me after that, and we kin have our talk."

For the band, the morning is Vacation Time: We lounge by the Howard Johnson's pool, sunning and swimming. "Dolly hasn't appeared in a bathing suit in years," the girl singer tells me. "She caused too much of a stir. And she's really very modest about things like that."

She is also determined that no one (except possibly Carl) see her without her wigs and makeup. Of the entire group, only one band member has ever seen her face *au naturel*. "It was strange," confides the young man (who prefers to remain unidentified on this topic). "She looked entirely different—much younger . . . at least ten years younger."

I ask if the musician feels Dolly doesn't want to be seen because she thinks she's less pretty without her makeup and fixings.

"Yeah," he says, and his voice is sad. "I think that's it. And you know, she *is* beautiful."

At around two P.M., a curtain pulls open at Dolly's ground-floor room. I see the bubble of her blond wig, and realize she is ready. Opening the door to a royal-blue curtained dimness, Dolly Parton greets me. She is, as predicted, in full regalia: double-decker wig, pancake makeup, blue eye shadow, mascaraed lashes, pink-creamed lips.

The funny thing is, even with this virtual *mask*, you can see how perfectly symmetrical her features are, how dense and cream-cheesy perfect is her complexion. I'm sure, if her face were scrubbed, she would look like an angel. And her hair, she tells me, "is the same color and length as mah wig–only it's baby fine and just hangs there."

Meanwhile, just in case—I see through the door to the adjoining room that two more perfectly sprayed platinum wigs sit on a bed. The blond headdresses, fixed on their blue Styrofoam forms, look eerily like decapitated heads (Marie Antoinette again). A bed-light aims at them, and the whole time I'm talking to Dolly, I never quite escape this sight of the two more Dolly Parton heads waiting in the wings.

Because Dolly has been wearing two wigs during this record heat wave, I ask her, "Don't you get too warm?"

"Wal," she says, taking her seat in a Danish modern chair by the window, and kicking off her wedgies, "I always wear 'em, so I don't know. It's like mah panty hose . . . I always wear them, too, and people say, 'Don't they get hot?'" She puts her tiny white feet up on the coffee table, which already holds her gallon jug of distilled water, a bottle of predigested liquid protein, and a copy of *The Last Chance Diet*.

"I'll give you a tip," she offers. "If yer hippy lak I am . . . never wear panties. They jest make it look worse . . . the panty line shows. Wear panty hose, and that's *it*."

She takes a swig of the predigested liquid protein. "Tastes lak garbage," she says, "but it rully works. You shoulda seen me before. I was all blowed up. And you cain't afford to get fat, not when yer known for yer hourglass figure. You wouldn't believe the weight I was carryin'. I couldn't get into mah costumes. I don't know whut caused it. I guess turnin' thirty, mah metabolism changed. I went on every diet there wus . . . and din't lose nuthin'. I fasted on water for one week and lost one pound. This Last Chance Diet *wus* the last chance for me."

I compliment her: "You looked very shapely in your costume."

"Yup, I look good in mah costume, and I look good nekkid, too. Jest in regular clothes . . ." She gestures to the "civvies" she has on—tight jersey and jeans. "When I sit down, I kind of double over." She tugs at folds in her belly which, considering the massive ledge of bosom above, doesn't look fat at all.

Tentatively, I bring the subject around to What Is It Really Like to Be in That Body?

Dolly sighs, the breasts bobbing. "They *hurt*." She reached for the back of her neck. "I git aches there, from carryin' the weight."

She goes on, to give me the History: "They come in when I was eight. Yes, I've had titties since I was eight. Got mah period when I wus nine. I jest grew up rul quick. Took after mah father's people, more than mah mamma's. I looked grown-up when I was eleven . . ." Soon after, the boys of Sevierville, Tennessee, pursued her. "I was *purr*fect," she recalls. "Purr-fect for country, that is."

She whips out a brochure which features family and school portraits. "Here I am at seventeen."

I lean over, expecting to see the nymphet Dolly—fresh-scrubbed and natural. Instead: Dolly, much as she looks this very day—complete with six inches of sprayed bouffant blond hair. There is another photo, though . . . Dolly at age eight, with cropped blond hair and wide blue eyes. A tomboy face.

"Yes . . . that surprises people, that I was sort of a tomboy . . . always out in the fields, chasin' butterflies. That's how come I love butterflies so much, and I sing about them all the time."

Talking about her childhood, Dolly's voice tends to go flat, as it did during the canned chatter of her performance. She has told the story so many times, that's only natural, I suppose. But she is monotone as she reports: "I was one of twelve *keeds*. We were poor, but we were so rich in love." She does better when she giggles, remembering: "We all lived in three rooms, we had three beds in a room. We all slept together, jest piled in, din't matter if it wus boys or girls."

But she goes flat again, as she continually characterizes herself: "I am a happy person. I am a positive person. The only thing I hate is negativity."

She takes an angry swallow of her predigested liquid protein. "That's the one thing I won't put up with . . . negativity."

She is used to being on the defense about her appearance: "I don't look this way out of ignorance. I don't look this way because I'm dumb. It's a gimmick. I want people to know it's me when they see me comin' and when they see me leavin' . . . I look extreme anyway . . ." She checks her bosom. "So I figured I might as well look even more extreme."

I agree—saying her look is right for her. And it is. I do ask if turning thirty two years ago made her feel differently about herself.

She stands up to her full five feet. "Sure . . . that's when I decided to git goin'. I had to make a lot of changes. I had to let a lot of people go. I changed my managers."

Two horseflies suddenly zoom toward Dolly. Perhaps they are attracted by her magnolialike perfume. She goes after them with a folded Dolly Parton brochure. *Whack. Whack.* "They seen me comin' . . ."

Returning to the subject of her managers: "I was dreamin' big, and nobody there was dreamin' as big as I wus! I just had to *git*!"

The hardest part of becoming the "New Dolly" was when she had to change her band. Her former group, The Family Band, was just that—Dolly's cousins. "People say I fired mah own family!" Dolly cries. "Wal, it ain't so. When I explained it to them, they were all happy for me. They understood. They had their own things to do, anyhow. Still, I had to go away for a while and think, before I told them. But I knew whut I wanted. I'd jest been spinnin' mah wheels."

The horseflies dive for Dolly's hair. She waves them off again with the glossy publicity flier. The flies buzz off.

"Whut rully hurts me," Dolly confides, "is when people are layin' on that I'm changin' mah music . . . I'm goin' pop . . . Wal, basically, I'm still country. The smart ones saw whut I wus doin' . . . The other ones . . . Wal, *I could kill those people and bust their heads. Mah show will always be me!*" She goes on to explain her new audience—of celebrities and gay people.

"Wal, I love people, so they love me. And the gay people—I guess they're happy, that's why they call 'em gay . . . and I'm happy, too, so they lak me." But, she stresses, "I'm singin' lak I always wus. And I feel more free singin' other kinds of songs. I do it 'cause I want to, not to make more money."

Happily, the money pours in, too. Dolly is reputed to be a million-dollar baby. She owns her own company, Velvet Apple Music, as well as 51 percent of Owepar, which also publishes music, and 50 percent of an operation called Dolly's Doll House, which licenses the Dolly Parton doll. "She has her own little stage costumes. I think she sells so well because she's one of the cutest dolls around." Also in the investment department, Dolly has bought a great deal of real estate. She owns a vast white ante-bellum–style plantation house outside Nashville which Carl built for her, and which she shares with him and her kid sister, Rachel.

Home is where Dolly's heart is, too—"I can't wait to get back next week," she says, dimples creasing. "That's whut I work s'hard for . . . so I can have that."

When she goes home, she will break completely with her professional life. "I block it out. I won't see people from the business at mah home. I won't have parties. Carl is not a party person. And I don't entertain fans. When I go home, I don't lak people comin'. Mah house is built so I kin see them, before they see me. I kin go nekkid in mah yard. I love mah fans, and they know I love 'em, but I spend more 'n half mah time with them. I got to have time to relax, go without no hair, without no makeup. That's how I keep mah sanity. I have never needed a psychiatrist."

Dolly settles back into her chair and sips more predigested liquid protein. "Mah marriage is separate, too. I have mah life on the road and mah life with Carl. He has seen me perform, *once*. But we have our own life at home—without music people."

Dolly stares at me for a moment, "You 'n' me can be friends lak now, here . . . but . . ." She heaves her chest. "I could never invite you to mah home."

I nod. *It's okay.*

"Only way I kin keep mah sanity," she stresses.

The door to the adjoining room flies open, and Carl, bony-legged in trunks, slams through, picking up some gear for the pool. Dolly and I both watch him lope out again . . .

"He's the only man I've ever been in love with," she tells me. "Doesn't he look jest lak [Don Galloway] the guy on 'Ironside'? We're funny together—he's so tall and thin—I call us 'Spaghetti and Meatball.' We fell in love when I was eighteen—on my first day in Nashville."

But now she's on the road, away from him most of the year?

"I think it's healthy for us to spend time apart. And I don't git jealous. It never crosses mah mind. And if he does somethin', I never want to know."

Dolly herself admits, "I'm flirty, I love men, and I'm friendly. But if I ever did somethin', I'd never say. I love Carl and we have a rul happy marriage. He's a gentle man . . combs mah hair . . . in the back. If he died, I couldn't stand it."

Will they ever have children?

"No, I don't think so. We've raised my *keed* sister. I don't miss it, and he doesn't want 'em. Besides . . . ." Dolly brightens, her dimples digging in, and her perfect, even little white teeth flashing, "I'm Carl's *keed*. I even call him "Daddy'. . . I got the idea from the movie *Bonnie and Clyde*, the part where Estelle Parsons's husband is shot and she leans over him and cries, 'Oh, Daddy. . . Daddy.'"

With no plans for a family, then, what does Dolly see in her future?

She recites: "I want to be a better writer . . . a better singer . . . a better entertainer."

The slant of the afternoon sun changes then, and a beam hits Dolly on the face. She shades her eyes with one hand. "This fasting will clear yer head. I was up all last night. Wrote four new songs, and they're gonna be . . . ." She frowns. "Now, *whut* was I thinkin' . . . ? I had a rul sharp thought jest passin' through mah head . . . Oh, wal, it's gone." She shakes her head; her blond hair remains stationary.

"I know one thing, I'm gonna get me a house in Hawaii . . . get away from all this . . . get a place where mah kinfolk can come an' visit . . ."

There's a knock at the door.

Dolly cautiously opens up. Two little flaxen-haired girls stand outside. Each girl holds a ruby-red rose.

Behind the girls, a tall man, bald pate reddening under the summer sun, mimes, while pointing to the head of the littler girl: "*This one loves her!*"

Dolly chats with the children, accepts the roses: "Ain't it amazin' . . ."; the father keeps pointing at his daughter's head, repeating the lip-sync: "*Loves her . . . loves her . . . loves her . . .*"

And the child's eyes are wide and blue, her face upturned . . . just as Dolly Parton's will be, tonight, when she becomes her own little girl again.

DOLLY PARTON: DOIN' WHAT COMES NATURALLY

Gerri Hirshey | January 9, 1979 | *Family Circle*

In her book, *We Gotta Get Out of This Place: The True, Tough Story of Women in Rock*, Gerri Hirshey, former senior editor of *Family Circle*, recalled riding "blue highways in Dolly Parton's pink-lounged bus" during the fall of 1978: "Gracing the pages of *Rolling Stone*—and starring in pneumatic similitude in countless drag clubs—was the seventies' unlikeliest glam crossover. Country queen Dolly Parton arrived as a 40DDD conundrum—a honey-voiced, Bible-quotin' sweetheart with a wicked gleam beneath those heavily Maybellined lashes. . . . Leaping off her tour bus in the deepest Wisconsin, I dashed into a Wal-Mart to fetch her a fresh supply of mascara. After three days with Dolly, I felt like I was carrying the Olympic torch back to her impossibly frou-froued domain."

Just weeks after the *Family Circle* magazine hit newsstands, Porter Wagoner surfaced again, this time filing a lawsuit against Dolly. He claimed she owed him money for breach of a management contract and for other results from their separation. Seeking $3 million, Wagoner argued that he'd given Dolly two cars, rings, and diamond necklaces. His suit asked for a number of items: 15 percent of her net income from June 1974 through June 1979, 15 percent of her outstanding record royalties, 15 percent of future record royalties, and so on. "This is the only way we could get it settled," Wagoner told the press. "I haven't seen or talked to Dolly since 1976. She's made it big, is out on the West Coast and has so many people handling her business it's impossible to get to the bottom." The two eventually settled out of court in 1980 with Wagoner receiving a reported $1 million. —Ed.

She's gone from rags to rhinestones without *a fairy godmother. "Nobody's got to be ordinary," says Dolly, "once you learn to believe in yourself."*

The story is Hans Christian Andersen with a Tennessee twang. The little girl had no shoes, but she had imagination. She had no money, but she had love. She grew up in a two-room mountain shack with 11 brothers and sisters, but her dreams drifted far beyond the Smokies. The bits of quartz that glittered on the tobacco fields she imagined as diamonds; swallowing cold biscuits and lard, she wished for strawberries and cream. The day after high-school graduation she packed a cardboard suitcase and climbed aboard a rattletrap bus to Nashville, determined to become a country music queen.

Now, miraculously, it's all come true. The skinny little girl is a dazzling woman. The bus has become a customized silver coach, upholstered in velvet, curtained in chintz. There are diamond rings on her fingers; her closets are crammed with rainbow fantasies in organdy and sequins. There is a mansion outside Nashville with enough gold records for her own yellow brick road, a movie contract and a million-dollar music publishing company. She has been a Hollywood Square and a Daisy Mae pinup. Barbara Walters has interviewed her, so have Merv, Dinah and Johnny. Everywhere, fans besiege her. At 32, Dolly Parton is a star.

"Sure sounds like Cinderella, don't it?" says Dolly. "'Cept for one thing. You better believe there's no fairy godmother in *this* story."

There is only Dolly, and something she calls her "rightful thinkin'," a concoction of fierce optimism and elbow grease that she applies vigorously to make her dreams sparkle and come true. She has been practicing it since she was five and says she came to it naturally. Basically, its premise is this: All things are possible to them that believeth. And things will go along water-smooth if you believeth in yourself.

But come on now. Doesn't this sound a little too much like one of those instant success ads from the backs of fanzines? Can sheer concentration conjure up a fabulous career, a dream lover, the perfect figure? Can you really *think* your way to whatever you want?

Sure thing, says Dolly. It's a natural process anyone can use. Through her agent, she says she'll be happy to explain it out in Iowa—or is it Missouri? She is on a concert swing through the Midwest, part of a string of engagements that keep her on the road 200 days a year. A schedule is consulted, and it will be Green Bay, Wisconsin.

A skeptic raps on the door of Room 357 in the Midway Motel.

"Well, hi there."

Hello, Dolly! The exotic creature that opens the door is breathtaking: a youthful Mae West who's been lost in Liberace's closet. Beneath a cloud of cotton-candy hair is a pretty, smiling face with china-doll makeup. By the laws of gravity alone, she should not exist. The figure that has left Johnny Carson speechless is poured into a hot pink jumpsuit, swathed in a flowered organdy wrapper and set teetering on a pair of 4" pink platform shoes. Dolly has been doing what she calls "girlie things" before it is time to leave for her show. The room is heady with nail polish and perfume as she kicks off her shoes and settles in on the bed.

It takes a moment to get past the window dressing and focus on the clear green eyes that peer out between layers of thick mink lashes. Dolly's features are quite lovely, with smooth, creamy skin and twin dimples that deepen when she smiles. That is very often.

"I'm just a real positive person," she says in her east Tennessee twang.

This afternoon, she is thinking positively about losing 20 pounds from her 5' frame because she's going to be in the movies. She is going to be in the movies because she thought positively that she'd like to try it, had her new Hollywood agent arrange a screen test and—poof!—a three-picture contract with 20th Century-Fox. Now if she can only train herself to positively resist the French fries and the bread and the rolls and the spaghetti . . .

"I love those starchy things," she says wistfully. "Good thing we never had money for sugar when I was growin' up. If I'd a got a sweet tooth I'd be big as a house."

Rejecting weight loss methods like jogging ("Lord, I'd black out both my eyes") and fasting ("a real torturous thing"), Dolly figures she'll have to rely on the powers of mind. "It worked for everything else," she muses. 'I believe the mind is a mighty force. Most of us just don't know how to use it."

Obviously, Dolly does. She insists it is the powers of mind that have kept her 12-year marriage and her career on a smooth upward track. It is positive thinking that transforms childhood pain into those heartbreaking, chart-busting country songs. Trying to explain it all, she is off like a runaway freight train:

"First it has to do with believin'. I believe that all good things come from God. And after you believe in Him, you got to believe in yourself. You got to believe you're special. I truly, truly believe that ever'body can be somebody special if they learn to develop their positive qualities. Now some people don't know how to do this and they get theirselves trapped into insecurities and complexes and all that. I just don't encourage negative things in me and work at things I do good."

Sounds simple. But this is no simple-minded woman. In the hills they called her Blossom, but along Nashville's Music Row they call her the Iron Butterfly. For her fans she will stand for hours posing for Polaroids, but she will fire a drunk or incompetent musician in a blink. And though her first hit was titled "Dumb Blonde," it was no dizzy peroxided creature that nailed down recording contracts and royalties. It took a clear-thinking businesswoman to cancel her own TV variety show when she decided that it was leading her career in the wrong direction.

"There's nothing more important as how I feel. It's me we're dealing with, the real person behind the wigs and the gaud. I know what I'm after and why I've done the things I have. Aw, I'm not real good at explainin' it all. I just go out and *do*."

Sensing puzzlement, Dolly refers me to a book called *The Magic of Believing*. It is a small, cheery volume of self-help, the kind you find on the racks next to books that tell you how to be your own best friend, make a million and remove stubborn grease stains all at once.

"Hey, that stuff *works!*" Dolly says. "Now I never needed a book, seein' as I come to it naturally. But I was gratified to read this one and find I was plowin' the right furrow."

Does your whole appearance set you apart from many who pass unnoticed in the crowd? . . . Take a tip from the automobile manufacturers and the Hollywood makeup artists who know the value of eye appeal . . . When you have a combination of proper packaging and the highest quality goods, you have an unbeatable combination . . .
—THE MAGIC OF BELIEVING *

"I don't look this way outta ignorance," says Dolly, "It's my gimmick, I've always tried to look as different as I felt. I could have played it safe in jeans and a workshirt, but it left no room for imagination. I figured the way I look would at least hold people's attention long enough to see that there was somethin' that came from within."

Dolly's customized bus has pulled up to the stage entrance at Dane County Arena in Green Bay. While her band sets up, she will stay aboard and rest until showtime. A crowd has begun to collect outside; elderly women in pantsuits, sweaty-palmed teenagers holding 8x10 glossies of her carefully by the edges. They are craning their necks, trying to catch a glimpse through the tinted windows. It is somewhat surprising that most of them are female, considering Dolly's image.

"I'll tell you why I love her," says a red-haired woman with a husband and two children in tow. "Dolly is everything I never dared to be. Sure, she's outrageous looking. But just once, didn't you ever want to do something outlandish—without worrying what everyone will say? She's got the gumption to do whatever she wants."

Funny. I've heard the same thing from the Perrier-and-lemon set in New York and from homemakers in Green Bay. Dolly dares to be Dolly, a gaudy, spangled monument to a woman fulfilled.

I climb back aboard the bus to try this theory out on Dolly and find her wedged into a corner of her tiny pink and red room, trying to decide which costume to wear. Bits of ostrich plume float from the closet as she pulls out a white sequined gown.

"I just do whatever's natural for me," she says. "I'm not tryin' to promote bein' a girl. Oh, I enjoy bein' a woman, it's been an asset for me. I've never, ever felt limited by my sex. As to my fans, yeah, I believe I have mainly little children and women as my fans. I think the children love the fantasy way I look. And women don't feel threatened by me. I'm too bizarre to be sexy. I mean, no woman in her right mind would want to look the way I do. Still, when they look at me it may touch something somewhere. They may think of somethin' they might like to have tried, somethin' different or unusual. Just an unexplored possibility they might have passed up . . ."

Exactly. It's like circling the cosmetic counter in Woolworth's when you're 14, wondering about the possibilities in those gleaming tubes. You'll never use that throbbing purple eyeshadow. But it's fun to imagine . . .

Dolly is laughing. "You picked a real good example," she says. "Now makeup ain't natural, but feelings are. So I let myself be whatever I feel like, whenever. As far as my looks go, some days I'll just pile it on, change my perfume, dress up or down. In life it's the same way. I want to try a little bit of everything, leave myself open to all sorts of changes. I put no limitations on myself. I got dreams so big they'd scare some people."

———————

. . . Desire is the motivating force of life itself. Hunger promotes a desire for food, poverty a desire for riches . . . It's the generating power of all human action . . . It makes the difference between the clerk and the executive, the failure and the success. *

———————

"If you been hungry—and I don't mean bein'-on-a-diet hungry—having money takes gettin' used to," Dolly says. "I mean, I'll buy a set of fake fingernails for $35 and this little voice says, 'Hey, $20 was all Momma had to put clothes on 12 of us. For a year.' Even though I've got the money now, I can't be a crazy spender. That little voice won't leave me be."

It is a hot, dry Midwestern morning, and Dolly is headed downstairs to the $130,000 coach that will carry her, nine band members, her road manager, a dozen costumes and four wigs to the next stop. Last night's concert went well, and Dolly is charging down the hallway, ready for the next round.

"As a tiny child, I dreamed of bein' famous," she says on the run. "Of bein' loved by everybody in the whole world, of havin' money and big houses and cars. I wanted to know what the world was like on the other side of the mountain."

To that end, Dolly chased her dream the way a child would a butterfly, following it from branch to branch, step by step. She sang in church ("My family was always musical and we believed in makin' a joyful noise unto the Lord"). She wrote a trunkful of songs and sang them to her mother and friends. She and her stagestruck Uncle Bill dogged country star Chet Atkins outside Grand Ole Opry stage door until he let Dolly sing there at age 13.

"The whole time, I just knew I was different from most mountain people," says Dolly. "They're a quiet, bashful sort and that wasn't my natural self AT ALL. I was talkative—maybe you noticed—and a fun-lovin' child, real forward. I was an early developer in a lotta ways." She looks down at the straining silk shirt and giggles, "I mean I looked 20 at 13, liked to wear my clothes close fittin' and all. But I never dated the high-school boys. I always felt older, strange and set apart. I guess I wanted more than I was supposed to."

In the hills, where 16 was considered a late marriage and a woman's place was at the back half of a milk cow, wasn't Dolly's undisguised ambition just short of scandalous?

"Oh, it set some tongues to waggin', all right. The other women were sayin', 'That Avie Lee'—that's Momma—'her girls is too free for their own good.' But Momma paid no mind. I owe a lot to her when it comes to independence. Now Momma was the daughter of a Fundamentalist preacher and her people was strict. A woman wasn't allowed to dance, to wear bright clothes. She couldn't even cut her hair. Well, Momma married Daddy at 15—he was 17– and the first thing she did was cut her hair. She was so young, she really grew up with us kids, and as she found her own self, she taught us to be ourselves no matter what. Life was hard, but Momma made it seem beautiful. She didn't have much to work with, but she always encouraged imagination."

Thus Dolly chased her dream, fluttering in the distance over Route 70 to Nashville. "I was tellin' all the kids I was goin' to be a star and they laughed and laughed. Graduation day, people wrote some smart-alecky things in the yearbook, but the next day I was on that bus and gone. I didn't know a soul in Nashville; but funny, as soon as I got there I felt at home, for the very first time.

"You see, I've just always had this thing burnin' in me, about bein' a star and all. At bottom I guess I had a pretty old-timey goal. I wanted to prove somethin' to the world and maybe to myself. I wanted to know, I *had* to know, that you *can* come from nothin'—don't have to be educated, don't have to be rich or sophisticated—and still make somethin' of your life. You just got to want it so hard you can almost reach out and grab it."

———————

Suppose you want a new home. After you've got the first glimpse of the picture, start your affirmations going: "I'm going to have that new home. I'm going to have that new home." And one day the way will be found and the new home will be yours.*

———————

Dolly says she built her home the same way she built her career, starting with a series of vivid mental pictures that would make Cecil B. DeMille tremble.

"My husband Carl and me was dreamin' fools about a house," Dolly says, "Every year we'd drive down to Mississippi for our anniversary with this old camera and we'd take pictures of parts of the Southern mansions we liked. A porch here, a pillar there. Then we'd take 'em home and look at 'em real hard, puttin' it all together in our minds. I knew that house before it was built and I built it long before we could afford it 'cause I knew we'd be able to—someday."

If Dolly is frank about the way she's constructed her home and the façade that is her public image, she has also taken pains to sandbag her private life against the flood of demands her growing celebrity has placed on her.

"There are things about myself I can't reveal right now," she says with a mischievous grin. "Things I feel might shock people. I'm no goody-goody. I'd *hate* bein' a vanilla person with no mystery in my life. I'm naturally curious and I've tried a little bit of everythin' that wouldn't mess up my brain. But I have a responsibility, you know, to my fans and all . . ."

The fans. Already there are women—and some men—who show up at Parton concerts as Dolly look-alikes. And there are the few crazies who force Dolly to change hotel rooms with calls and knocks. "I've only had one death threat," she says, "and the poor man just wanted some attention. I'm not scared, since the boys in the band look out for me. And like a lotta mountain people, I do carry a gun."

A gun? Dolly Parton packing heat? "Aw, I wouldn't use it unless I absolutely had to," she says. "But all along this crazy star trip, I've tried to be prepared for everything."

Just where that trip will land her, only Dolly knows. She describes her ultimate mental picture as "big, real big" but there are others willing to be more specific.

"Dolly wants to be bigger than Elvis," says Don Roth, who used to play in her band and is still a good friend. "It's all there—the huge talent, the glitter, the unbelievable ambition. And now she's added the movie contract and the mansion."

I ask Dolly if she sees that mansion as the next Graceland (Presley's estate-cum-shrine) and the sly grin reappears. "Well, I'll tell you this much," she says, "I scouted all over Tennessee for a piece of land with hills in front and a stream around it. It's got a bitty bridge, and I made sure it's just narrow enough so's no tour bus can git over it. Carl and me can walk around stark naked there and nobody'd see. We have chickens and cows and a vegetable garden. It's a quiet, homey place for me and the special people in my life."

Only one person knows what Dolly Parton looks like without her wig, and that is Carl Dean, the man she met in the Wishy Washy laundromat her first day in Nashville and married soon after. Described by one of the few people who's met him as a rangy, good-looking man who runs an asphalt business, Dean never saw his wife perform until last year when her schedule demands made their separations too long.

"Carl travels some with me now," Dolly says, "But what we have together has nothing to do with careers and such. People are always gossipin' about what a weird arrangement it must be and all but they don't know me like he does. The man gives me what I need, which is freedom. And love. And security. He and my family are the center of my life. We practically raised five of my younger brothers and sisters when they came to live with us, and while I don't have any children of my own, I really feel I've been a parent already."

Cranking up her mental movieola, Dolly says she does see children in her future, but not as a mother. Instead, she'll be playing the role of the favorite, eccentric auntie.

"I can visualize myself real clear as a joyful old person, sittin' around all gussied up, tellin' stories and bakin' gingerbread and all," she says. "And I'm buildin' a fantasy castle on my farm, startin' on it real soon. I'm gonna make it child-size and fill it with trunks of my old costumes and beads and a projector with Walt Disney movies..."

The voice has become waif-like, as though little Dolly Rebecca is reliving her own childhood dreams. "An' I'm gonna have towers and moats and secret passages, and I'm gonna let my nieces and nephews and their friends play and dream and fantasize all they want. And I'll be writin' children's books—I got dozens in my head, and romance stories, and some mysteries. And maybe a play. Maybe . . ."

Dolly is back with us now, laughing at herself. "Maybe I'll even write a book for kids on how to be a success."

---

*Success is a matter of never-ceasing application. You must forever work at it diligently. Otherwise it takes wings.**

"Where are we tonight?" Dolly asks a security man jokingly. She has just arrived backstage at a fairground arena in Madison, Wis. When the man asks if such a delicate-type lady don't get tired out by all the travel, Dolly giggles and shakes her head.

"I've got enough restless gypsy blood in me that I enjoy bein' in a different city every night. And besides, like they say, you got to make hay when the sun shines."

Dolly's Gypsy Fever Band has rumbled into her entry number and she is gunning her engine, stomping the concrete floor with glitter-shot Lucite heels. There is a mighty roar as she sprints into the spotlight, a dazzling white figure with a high-voltage smile.

Dolly's concert is a 50-minute Disneyland tour; back to Frontierland with a dulcet country lament, jet-propelled into the '70's with a disco number that booms from the 10-foot speakers. It's an escapist's joyride, and at the helm, Dolly is a marvel of animation, hopping, swirling, kicking her tiny feet until the lights catch the sequins and rhinestones to send tiny galaxies twinkling across the domed ceiling. And there is the voice, the magical instrument that made it all possible, clear as a mountain stream and just as capricious, whispering one minute, roaring the next, shattering a note so it falls in a rainbow.

"Testify, woman!" yells a man in overalls. "Make the people feel *gooood!*" Dolly winks at him and he swears he'll die happy. Too soon it's over and while fans besiege her bus, Dolly escapes out a side door to a waiting car,

"Remember," she says over her shoulder. "Next time you see me I'll be skinny as a fence post."

Sure thing, Miss Dolly. Positively.

"The Magic of Believing" by Claude M. Bristol — 1948, Prentice-Hall.

DOLLY DIAMOND

On Dolly Parton Jokes

"I make up a lot of Dolly Parton jokes. Why not? Somebody's got to start them. There are a lot of them I didn't make up that I'd rather somebody hadn't, but I can always joke about myself and the way I look. I think when you get to where you can't joke about yourself, you're in serious trouble."

—To David Reed, *Lexington Herald-Leader*, March 9, 1979

DOLLY DIAMOND

On Writing Her Life Story

"I'm writin' it now. But I don't wanna print it yet, not till it's all lived. The real truth would curl your hair. When I'm older, I'll be like all those old haggard ladies that write their life stories, about all the men they slept with, and all . . . not that they shouldn't. But they're right to wait so long, 'cause if you start too soon tellin' about who all you slept with, you're gonna run into a lot of guys that don't want to take a chance on makin' your next book."

—To Roger Ebert, 1980

PART III
City of Schemes

"Along came *The Best Little Whorehouse in Texas*. The wonderful time I had on *9 to 5* had whetted my appetite for another movie. *Whorehouse* was a completely opposite experience. It was as if *9 to 5* had been my first lover, sweetly seductive before and gentle and caring during our lovemaking. *Whorehouse*, then, was a rapist."

—From *Dolly: My Life and Other Unfinished Business*, 1994

THE UNSINKABLE DOLLY PARTON

Chet Flippo | December 11, 1980 | *Rolling Stone*

Sandy Gallin's negotiations with 20th Century Fox resulted in her being cast alongside Jane Fonda and Lily Tomlin in *9 to 5,* a comedy about subjugated working women who take revenge on their chauvinistic boss. Filming began near the end of 1979 and lasted for nine weeks. In anticipation of the release of *9 to 5,* Dolly became a cover girl for numerous publications, but none so prominent as *Rolling Stone*. Announcing "Dolly Parton Bursts into the Movies," the cover of the December 11, 1980, issue flaunted a playful Dolly dressed as Mrs. Claus with a Santa ornament nestled in her cleavage.

Dolly always seemed so at ease when visiting with Chet Flippo. He was one of the most prolific and respected journalists in the country music field, but more of a friend to Dolly by 1980. They had a history and theirs was a special relationship, as evidenced by the candor exhibited in this feature. Years later, Flippo became editorial director of Country Music Television (CMT) and in 2011 championed Dolly for having paved the way for female country stars like Taylor Swift, Carrie Underwood, and Miranda Lambert. "Dolly created a very powerful and realistic role model picture of artist and songwriter for aspiring young female country artists," he told the *Los Angeles Times*. "She showed what could be achieved by challenging the gatekeepers. . . . She helped rip apart the gingham ceiling that had relegated women country singers to secondary status." –Ed.

She's a working girl going from 9 to 5 but she's doing a lot more than staying alive . . . she's a movie star

There are few vistas more majestic than Central Park in autumn from the twenty-sixth floor of a Fifth Avenue apartment. Late-afternoon sunlight softly gilds ocher trees, and stray sunbeams shoot through the canyons between elegant apartment buildings on the far side of the park. My attention drifts to another majestic sight: Dolly Parton silhouetted against the windows of her apartment. Part of her beauty is external—the extraordinary body, alabaster skin and delicate features—but much of it comes from within. She turns, and with a dazzling smile and a little girl's voice asks what she can get me, then pads barefoot past her Claes Oldenburg painting to pour me a drink.

About four years ago, Dolly Parton was a country singer churning out one-nighters on the C & W circuit. Back then, Fifth Avenue was a movie fantasy to her and Oldenburg just a foreign word. In a few short years, she has turned her career around. Now she is hotly pursued by TV; she has a multimillion-dollar contract to play Las Vegas; and she commanded more than a million to be teamed with Burt Reynolds in her second movie, *The Best Little Whorehouse in Texas*, before her first one, *Nine to Five*, had even been released. If ever somebody figured out the American dream and made it work, it's Dolly Parton.

One of the lesser noticed of twelve children in a poor Tennessee family, Dolly began planning her escape to the world of money and glamour as soon as she heard about it. The minute she was out of high school, she was on a Greyhound bus to Nashville to try to be a country star. But girl singers—that's what they called them then—in country music were rare and generally regarded as so much flesh. Parton used her iron will, her incredibly seductive and powerful voice, her ability to write songs and her self-confidence and ambition to knock down the brick walls that stood between her and her goals. She also played up her beauty and her hourglass figure. She started to make secret lists of the fairy-tale futures she sought. She is a fiercely positive thinker, and her private lists worked like voodoo. Nashville never knew what hit it. She became a country star.

Still, Nashville wasn't enough, so she plotted her superstar map and left Nashville for Los Angeles and full blown pop management. Her husband, Carl Dean, a seldom-seen Nashville contractor, approved, and she set out to become superfamous. She deliberately made the kind of pop music she thought would gain her both a new audience and the power to do whatever she wanted. She thinks the strategy is working.

The test should come with her new album, *Nine to Five*. She wrote the title song for her first movie, in which she costars with Jane Fonda and Lily Tomlin. "She was wonderful; she's so quick, so natural, dazzling, down-to-earth, bigger than life," Tomlin said of Parton. "She's just the quintessential . . . whatever it is. She ended up giving me lines. You could have replaced Jane or me in a more satisfactory way, but once you got the idea for Dolly to be in her role, it would have been more of a disappointment to not have her."

It was, in part, Fonda's idea to make a movie about secretaries. Once she decided that it should be a comedy, she knew immediately that Dolly had to be in it. "I had never met her," said Fonda, "but I was really into her music. Anyone who can write 'Coat of Many Colors' and sing it the way she does has got the stuff to do anything. This was not a woman who was a stereotype of a dumb blond. I felt that she could probably do just about anything she wanted, that this was a very smart woman. We developed a character based on who she is and what she seems like. Did we coach her? No. Her persona is so strong, you get somebody mucking about with that and making her self-conscious, and it could be negative. Even though we're from different backgrounds and different classes, we're very alike in many ways. Dolly's not political, but her heart, her instincts—she's just on the side of the angels. Very often someone will wow you, but as you get to know them, the mystery wears off. One of the things that just flabbergasts me about Dolly is the amount of mystery she has. She's a very mysterious person."

Back in Manhattan at sunset, Dolly brings me a drink and sits back on her white cotton sofa in her skintight jeans and ready-to-bust, low-cut sweater. Even though she's only five feet tall—the heels and wig add almost a foot—she can take your breath away real quick. My first question is out before I can even think about it.

Are you ready to give it all up and run away with me now?

If you're ready—but let's wait and see how much money you make from your book!

You told me once you wanted to be a superstar.

Yeah, I did and I still do, and I think I'm on my way. It's not just a selfish thing; I've thought a lot about it, about exactly what makes me want to do it. I've always felt like everybody was born for a reason. Everybody has a purpose. Lots of people don't ever really find it, but I was luckier than a lot of people. I was born the fourth in a family of twelve, so I was kinda independent and really didn't have a lot of things pulling at me. I was always kinda free to think, and I had the opportunity to do more than I realized for a long, long time.

Anyhow, I worked in Nashville, where I did well and was known as one of the big country artists, but I still wasn't really selling any records.

Around 100,000 or something like that?

Yeah, I think *Jolene*, which I think was my biggest record at that time, sold like 200,000. So after takin' all that into consideration and knowing that I had the freedom to do what I wanted, that I had the talent to back it up—and I had more personality and guts than I had talent, I guess—I just tried to figure out what things were workable and usable and tried to combine them to make something special.

I'm certainly not your greatest writer, although I feel one of my strongest talents is songwriting. And as a singer, I'm just different—I don't always hit true notes and all, but I'm a stylist. So I went all out and tried to find good management, which I did, and to record stuff that I don't particularly even like and am not even particularly proud of, other than the fact that it worked.

Well, to be frank, I didn't like your last few albums.

To be even franker, neither did I [*laughs*]! *But,* the thing is, it got me where I wanted to be. Now you will like, you *will* like the next one, because I finally got myself to a point where my personality was strong enough. And I got to the point where I could have a big deal in Vegas;

I didn't want to work Vegas until I could go there as myself with good music, until I could have the power to draw people and also have enough power to say what kinda show I would do.

Movies were another thing I didn't want to do until I felt *I* was ready. Sometimes if you jump into something too quickly, you can screw up something that might have been good two years down the road.

Now, was this on one of your lists? You were telling me before about your lists . . .

I never really had a big desire to be in the movies, although I knew if my career went the way I wanted it to, Vegas and the movies and all that stuff would eventually come.

The main thing is, now I've got the freedom to do my music without havin' to worry about whether I'll make money or not, and because I don't have to worry about money, I will make more from it because it will be good. From here on out, I'll be involved in producing my own records. I wrote about half of the songs on the *Nine to Five* album. I wrote *all* of the songs for the one that will follow that. You know, people thought I had sold out: what's this piece of shit that Dolly's done now? Or what's this and that? I'm very aware of all that stuff. The reviews of the last four or five albums were not good, but I still knew that I was tryin' to accomplish the right thing.

Now I've got their attention; now I have to prove myself. Every day I feel like I'm just startin' my career. But yeah, it's on my list!

What is the price you have to pay to be a superstar?

Well, I'm not really sure, because I doubt that I'll even know it if I am. It's just that I'm tryin' to do everything I'm capable of doin' and have a perfect balance in my life—to be successful at my work, and at bein' a wife and a sister and a friend. I have to have all of those things in their proper place. I don't want to be a star if I have no life. I'm not willing to be like Elvis, who had no personal life. If I want to go out to a movie, I just go out to a movie. If I want to go out to supper, I go out to supper, because I happen to feel that I have no reason to be afraid of the people.

I've observed a whole lot since I've been in the business. I've seen a lot of people who panic at the thought of somebody runnin' after 'em on the street; instead of takin' it as a compliment, they take it as a threat.

If I can't sign autographs, I can always speak and be friendly and say, "I can't right now, I'm late for a plane." Because I *do* appreciate it. I don't believe we owe everything to the public. I think I have a right to my privacy, and I also feel that people have a right to the time I'm in public. That is *their* time; that is not my time.

So I provide for my own personal time a little differently than that: camping trips, traveling cross country in a station wagon, camping out with no wig and no makeup. I mean, there's always a way to do it if you want it bad enough.

I think one of the big mistakes celebrities make is that they think because they are so popular, it sets them apart and makes them like gods instead of just extremely lucky people. I really feel sorry for a whole lot of stars, and I hope and pray I never get that way. I don't really believe I will.

You won't go Hollywood?

I don't know what goin' Hollywood means; if it means goin' to shit, no. It's important to me that I accomplish things as a human being, as it should be to all people to accomplish all that they can without sacrificing other people. I didn't sacrifice the happiness of other people to get where I am. My husband likes the freedom as much as I do. He's got his own work to do, and he's glad when I'm gone a certain amount of time. We're not afraid that one of us is gonna run off with somebody else, because we couldn't find in nobody else what we found in each other.

Do you think you were ever in danger of losing your country base? That's something you should probably keep forever.

It's something I *will* keep forever. I don't jump to conclusions just because everybody else has—any time you make a move, it's gonna make somebody uncomfortable.

There were people in Nashville who hoped you would fail when you went to L.A.

But I would like to think that they cared enough to worry that I would get into trouble. That's what I prefer to believe. I never intended to lose my country audience. I knew that I had to get myself into a position to do what I thought I should be doin' for country music. I think I have now. For what few people I may have lost, I feel like I've gained thousands more.

Everybody can't like ya, and I know that. Everybody will *not* like ya, but I feel I have a lot of good fans, I have a lot of good friends. I think I'm as well liked as most any celebrity.

People take things as different signals, too. When you went back to Nashville to record, a lot of people said, "Well, look, she's learned her lesson."

They can interpret it in different ways, and they have the right to do that. But see, my interpretation was that this was the first time I had everything in order the way I wanted it to be. Anybody with any sense would know that I didn't *have* to go home to record. The sound I was lookin' for was a sound that lives in Nashville.

Was *Nine to Five* the first movie you were offered? Were you seeking scripts, or were they seeking you?

They were seeking me, which made me feel even prouder. This was not the first movie I was offered; it was the first one I accepted. If one I were to do on my own flopped, it would have been Dolly Parton's flop. That was why I was so picky—I hadn't found a script I thought was good enough. I was amazed at how little talent there is among the writers of Hollywood. But *Nine to Five* fascinated me, and I knew instantly that I should do it—I knew that it was a career move. And it fell together really well—just according to my lists.

I heard that Jane specifically wanted you for it.

She wanted me, and she wanted Lily. She said she was drivin' down the freeway, and a song of mine came on the radio, and she knew my personality, and she'd been a fan of my songwriting for a long time. She said she almost wrecked because it just hit her right in the face, to think what a great combination.

So it just seemed like the right thing to do. A lot of people were sayin', "Boy, I would l-o-o-o-v-e to see that. There ain't no way them three bitches are gonna get along! Can you imagine three women like that?!" And you know, we had the greatest time.

I heard that you memorized the entire script.

I did! [*Laughs*] It was so funny, 'cause I didn't know exactly what the movies were all about; I just knew that I would do it as good as anybody else. I just assumed they would start in the front and follow the story to keep up the excitement, so I memorized the whole script: my part, Lily's part, Jane's part, every part. But it really worked out great. I got a kick later when I saw how few lines they do a day and how they shoot out of sequence.

And of course, we got a lot of laughs out of it because—you know me and my tacos and all that I was terrible; I could go in the door skinny and come out fat, all in the same day [*laughs*]!

And it's funny how everybody gets into character. I've never had an acting lesson in my life. A lot of people probably say I should have, but I didn't feel that what I played was phony.

I was lucky in the respect that they had written it according to my personality; I carry a gun, and she carries a gun in the picture. She was really just me as a secretary, so I played it like that. I was playin' her everyday role, knowin' the kind of stuff the girls at the office go through—anytime you work in a big business there's so many demands.

Is this a message movie?

Not really. It's about women, but there's women and men in the office. I'm the executive secretary to the boss, and he's a real turd. He got where he was because Violet [Lily], who had been with the company for twelve years, had trained him, and she had never gotten a promotion because they felt that position should not be held by a woman, that men prefer to deal with men. So actually, a lot of people thought it was just going to be women's lib; I wouldn't have been involved if I'd thought it was gonna be a sermon of some sort. Not that I'm not for rights for everybody, I'm just sayin' I didn't want to get involved in a political thing. It's just a funny, funny show. I think it's very obvious what it's sayin'. It's mostly about this boss and these three women—not bosses in general or the plight of secretaries.

The boss is one of those lyin' kinds of people. He's always tryin' to make out with me and is tellin' everybody that he is, but behind the door—no, no! In fact he makes me sick. At the start the girls don't like me at all. I have to eat by myself in the lunchroom. Then at one point we all become friends, when I'm standing in the office, and Lily says something to him like: "Well, why don't you ask her if she's the one that this-and-this," sounding like I'm sleepin' with him or something. I grab her and say, "You hold on! Just a minute. What's this shit mean?"

He tries to push her out. Then she says, "Everybody knows you're sleepin' with him!" And then I just fly into him. That's my best scene, because I get so mad, and he just keeps on saying "naw, naw . . . ," then I march him around. And there's another time when I throw him on a chair and hogtie him and get my gun. It's really funny.

People weren't sure that you and Jane would mesh.

Yeah, but you see, we knew right up front that if I did the film, that didn't obligate me to make political statements, it didn't obligate me to do benefit shows for different people's causes. If I was goin' into it, it was because somebody thought I was good enough or had something to offer.

I happen to see a side of Jane that I guess most people don't. She is very intelligent but she is also very shy. She is just like a little girl. I tell you, I just fell in love with that side of her. We don't discuss what I believe and what she believes. But our friendship is strong enough now that if we ever did discuss it, I would tell her what I think.

What are all these things I've been hearing about you saying you're going to spice up the love scenes in *Whorehouse* because this is your chance with Burt Reynolds?

Oh, a whole lot of that is just being cute and funny. People make such issues out of everything.

When they started askin' for suggestions, I said I would like to see more of a romance. Wouldn't you feel like you wasted five dollars if you paid to see *Whorehouse* and you didn't see me and Burt kiss? I was makin' a joke, and I stuck to it—I'm not going to miss my chance to kiss Burt Reynolds. There ain't no way I'd do sex scenes. I'm talking about love scenes.

Is being a madam—your role in 'Whorehouse'—anything you've ever fantasized about? There's nobody in the world who would make a more elegant madam than you.

I've never fantasized about being a madam, but some of my best friends have been hussies or called whores because they are usually the most honest and open people. And even if they don't do it as a profession, I just relate to it, and I know myself and my personality, and I've often said—you know I have, even to you—that I honestly do look like a whore or a high-class prostitute, not even so much high-class, with the makeup and the bleached hair and the boobs and the tight-fittin' clothes and the high heels.

I can't wait. She was everything that I am, except that I'm not a whore. But if I hadn't made it in this business, who knows [*laughs*]!

What kind of stuff are you writing now?

I'm writing some awful good stuff. I wrote some of the lines in "Hollywood Potters" while I was doing the movie. I met so many people who were extras. They have big dreams, and they've studied and worked, and some of them are a thousand times more talented than I would ever dream about being. They would tell me different things, so I wrote a song. [. . .]

The title of the movie was *Nine to Five,* and I knew that I could write a song about myself and my dad and my brothers and my sisters and my friends and the people who work nine to five. Working nine to five—what a way to make a living [. . .]

You've worked into the position you said you wanted to be in, where you are free to do just what you want. So what's your next five-year plan?

I guess I'll probably do real well in the movies, writing them and doin' the music for them. I think I'll probably become a huge recording artist because of all this other stuff, mainly because what I'll be doing will be worth buyin'. You know, it's quality stuff. What I've done was good for what it was, but now I'll be doin' the Vegas thing. I still want to do concerts—I don't want to ever just get into Vegas and movies.

That does not take the place of my audience and my records and the concerts.

Will you still do the bus tours, the regular shows?

Yes, I hope so—I really miss the family, the band. I enjoy that, and I enjoy the real people who work all week, who save up money to buy your records and come see you at the show. I miss those people; they're the real thing. It's from them that I draw ideas to write about and creative commercial ideas for movies.

What's the most outrageous thing you've ever done?

The most outrageous thing? [*Laughs*] Boy, that could be a number of things . . . A lot of this stuff I can't hardly tell you about. Sometimes one of the great thrills is just to go ahead and do something nobody would expect me to do.

I have a real stubborn, mischievous streak. And I have a girlfriend, Judy, who thinks she is just as stubborn and as mischievous, but she backs down a little easier than I do.

So this happened while I was doin' *Nine to Five*. Judy and I were coming home one night; we'd been out to Lucy's El Adobe restaurant, and we'd had a couple of Margaritas. Judy and two friends of hers were in one car, and me and Gregg [Perry, her keyboardist-producer] were in his car. Well, Judy started doin' silly little things—they started givin' me the finger or something. Then it got to where we were trying to top each other. Judy thought she was gonna flash me; she started unbuttoning her blouse. Anyhow, I just pulled up my shirt and I flashed them with one of them. Well, they just about wrecked; they just about died because they thought it was so funny. So anyhow, they did something else, and the next time around, I mooned them [*laughs*]!

Judy was tryin' to top this, and I thought, "What *else* can we do?" I thought, "Now I know Judy. She's gonna think she can pull one on me; she's gonna really get one on me." So I thought, "I *must* take off all my clothes." And I thought, "Well, now how can I?" Because this next stop we were gonna make was a stop sign going toward the Bel Air Hotel. So I said, "Gregg, I'm gonna ask you to do something that I don't think anybody should ever ask another person to do. I'm gonna take all my clothes off—I have to—but you can't look. You've got to look straight down the road!"

He thought I was kidding. I said, "Now I ain't kidding!" I was getting upset 'cause I had to get this done real fast. I just had to do this, because I knew that Judy was gonna get out in her panty hose or something.

So I started takin' off my clothes. And I tell you, I had 'em peeled off. I had my clothes layin' on the side and I was just threatening Gregg at all times. All I could think of, mainly, was that stop sign, because I knew Judy was gonna get out in her panty hose or something. I knew she was gonna think she had really done something. When we stopped, I saw the door scramblin' open, and they were letting Judy out. She took off her pants, so she was gonna come out in her panty hose as if that was some big deal. So I waited, then I just casually got out. I opened up the door and I started walkin' around the car in the moonlight. Here I was, just Snow White—you know how fair my skin is. There I was, and I tell you, I thought the girls were absolutely goin' to die. I just did it real casual, and then I just flew back in the car.

And then it was like I was immediately exposed! It was like nothing had mattered until then. Then all of a sudden I realized I was naked. I was so embarrassed, but feelin' so proud that I had done it—that's the kinda stuff I'll do. Is that good enough?

INTERVIEW: DOLLY PARTON

Lawrence Grobel | January 1981| *Playgirl*

Dolly was reunited with Lawrence Grobel for some naughty talk in this feature coinciding with the Christmas 1980 release of *9 to 5*. The film's title song topped both the country and pop charts in 1981 and earned Dolly two Grammys, Best Country Vocal Performance by a Female and Best Country Song. It was also featured on her *9 to 5 and Odd Jobs* album, which netted her the Female Vocalist of the Year Award from the Academy of Country Music. —Ed.

"PEOPLE THINK I DON'T HAVE AS MUCH DEPTH AS I LIKE TO THINK I DO. THEY JUDGE ME BY THE WAY I LOOK, JUST A DUMB HICK. MAYBE THE WAY I LOOK SHOCKS PEOPLE . . . ."

When the Country Music Association nominees were announced in 1980, Dolly Parton's name was not to be seen. She wasn't up for Entertainer of the Year or Best Female Vocalist—both of which she had won a few years back—or for Best Songwriter or Best Album. The conclusion one might draw from this is that Dolly Parton, at age 34, is on the decline.

But it would be a wrong conclusion. This was the year Dolly quite literally went Hollywood. She'd been searching for the right film script for years, but it wasn't until Jane Fonda sent her *Nine to Five*, a wacky comedy with an underlying feminist message about three secretaries who rebel against their stereotypes, kidnap their boss and wind up running the company with no one the wiser, that Dolly's instincts said this was the one. And with Fonda and Lily Tomlin as her co-stars, she figured she'd be in the best of company as a fledgling actress.

It never occurred to her—or to anyone else—that she'd never made a movie before and might want to ease her way in. Dolly has always had the confidence and the natural talent to go for broke and come out in the money.

For years she's been saying she didn't feel right playing Las Vegas, and the longer she held out, the more her value increased. Then last year it was announced that the Riviera Hotel had signed her to a three-year, eighteen-week contract for what is said to be the highest price ever paid an entertainer: $9 million, which breaks down to about $500,000 a week.

Burt Reynolds has also pursued her for years—wanting her to co-star in *W. W. and the Dixie Dancekings* and any of a number of other films. But Dolly waited until the right project came along—and when she went to see the Broadway hit *The Best Little Whorehouse in Texas*, she felt she had found it. Reynolds agreed, and the two will soon begin production on the film version of *Whorehouse*, which might prove to be a 1980s variation on Gable and Lombard.

One of twelve children, Dolly Rebecca Parton didn't know what a toilet was until she was nearly a teenager. Her bathtub was the local river, and her outlet to the rest of the world was a transistor radio. On that radio she heard songs. She also listened to the songs her mother would sing. And when she was five, she began writing her own.

The first in her family to graduate from high school, Dolly left for Nashville alone the day after graduation and never looked back. She met her future husband, Carl Dean, in a Laundromat, and there's never been another man in her private life.

After singing with Porter Wagoner for a number of years, she left to make it on her own with a band consisting mostly of members of her family. But she knew she needed proper management to reach the goals she set for herself, and when she turned thirty she reassessed her position and made the decision to come to Hollywood and find a manager. Mac Davis recommended his manager, Sandy Gallin. The moment Gallin met her he knew she had the potential to be a big star, and together they mapped out a career plan which meant broadening her audience from just country folks to include *all* folks—and her first album under Gallin's guidance, *Dolly* (RCA), was a step in that direction.

Since then, Dolly's popularity has risen dramatically, and there are hopes that the theme song she wrote for *Nine to Five* will garner her an Oscar. With Vegas and now the movies about to be conquered, the horizon seems endless for Dolly. To see if all this activity has turned her head, we sent writer Larry Grobel to spend some time with her. The two talked at her suite in the Bel-Air Hotel in Los Angeles, where flowers and helium balloons kept arriving from distant admirers.

Playgirl: You were reluctant to do this interview, weren't you?

Parton: Yes, I was.

Playgirl: Was it because the magazine offends you or because you're concerned about your image among a certain segment of your fans?

Parton: Well, I know that I'll be plastered on the covers of this and that magazine (when *Nine to Five* is released), and there won't be much I can do about a lot of it, but I don't want to get on the cover of too many sex-oriented things, although I love that stuff myself. I just don't want to do 'em to a point where it looks like, here I am in Hollywood, I start wearin' low-neck clothes, I start doing *Whorehouse*, I start doin' *Playgirl* and *Playboy*, and then my image changes. It means something to me, what my family and my people think and feel. I'm still the same person I was before I ever got to Hollywood.

Playgirl: The low-neck clothing you're referring to, is that the dress you wore for the Academy Awards?

Parton: Yes. I got a lot of comments about the dress. It was very low. It was a little much for me, but it was somethin' I wanted to wear because I wanted to look like Old Hollywood, 'cause it was kind of a thrill and a fantasy for me. I went home to Nashville and somebody made the statement, "Well, hell, I'm real glad to see you; I'm surprised you're talking to us. We figured you got out there with all those people and went crazy with all of them dope heads." It kinda hit me real hard, but it was good that it did.

Playgirl: Are you uncomfortable in Hollywood, or have you adjusted?

Parton: I like bein' here. I like it better than I used to. I've adjusted to it more. There area lot of wonderful people here. It could never be my home, but it's excitin'.

Playgirl: You are on record, though, for calling show business in general a "phony world."

Parton: I'm talking about the surroundings, all the airs people have to put on. Everybody is trying to be different, to have a gimmick. I'm just talking about all the hokey things, all the freaky people like Elton John and myself who try to come up with something to catch your attention. It's kind of a joke, what I said, but there was a great deal of truth in it as well. I take my music extremely seriously, but I'm talking about all the things that go along with it—the parties, the award shows, all the people trying to outdress the others, trying to get into *Time* magazine with their dresses cut below the tailbone or whatever.

Playgirl: And here you are in *Playgirl.* Do you look at magazines like this one or any of the men's magazines?

Parton: I don't usually look at either.

Playgirl: But if someone handed you a copy of *Playgirl* and *Playboy,* which would you thumb through first?

Parton: Well, to be honest—I don't mean it to sound strange, as if I get off on women—but *Playboy,* I think. I enjoy the stuff that's in it . . . I get embarrassed, too, really. I mean, I like naked bodies and all that. I don't have any hang-ups about it, but somehow it embarrasses me more when I see a naked man in pictures, totally naked, than when I see naked women.

Playgirl: Do you think women—or men—are exploited in these publications?

Parton: Not any more than they want to be exploited.

Playgirl: Do you think women and men find different things erotic?

Parton: I don't know. I can't answer for all women. I know a lot of girls who read *Playgirl,* and they look at it mostly in a joking manner, like,

"Hey, look at this one" or, "Hey, did you see that one?" Although the men are beautiful, it's hard for me to take it seriously. It seems natural for women to pose and be pretty, and it just seems a bit clumsy for a man to strike so-called sexy poses. I love men, I love skin, but I can't think of it as serious. Usually, when I look at nude pictures it's with a whole crowd of girls and there's so much jokin' and laughin' going on that you don't really see the person. You just see an *it*.

Playgirl: You're about to become a full-fledged movie star, with *Nine to Five* opening around Christmas and *The Best Little Whorehouse in Texas* to follow. Will there be security guards outside your door the next time you're interviewed?

Parton: It's possible. We don't *know* yet how I'm gonna affect the public. There is certainly a possibility that I'll need bigger gates and security guards at home, but I'm prepared for that. I built my house years ago with the thought in mind that there would come a day when I would need privacy and security, so it's located far enough off the road that I can wander around in the front yard and nobody can see me. I planned my whole life carefully preparing for success.

Playgirl: But can you ever prepare for the kind of isolation that usually follows movie-star success?

Parton: I have not been isolated yet. I think that I'll always be able to find a way out because I love people enough.

Playgirl: What kind of disguise will you use?

Parton: Probably just take it all off—my hair, wash my face, pull my boobs in—I'll just walk right out the gate and they'll think I'm the care-taker's wife. Wouldn't that be somethin'? I'll be curious to see how I deal with it. I'm a real stable person. And I'll always have certain places to go where I can get away. I can always have certain disguises, if I really want to go somewhere and don't want to be bothered. I don't run from the people. I'm not afraid of the public, and they know it. People only run after you when you're runnin'.

Playgirl: Or when you're Barbra Streisand. She's certainly isolated herself. Her life seems so different from yours.

Parton: I sense it. I'm concerned about what people like Streisand must think or what they must feel, if they feel like a prisoner in their own home. But I suppose every personality has her own way of dealin' with it and she has to set up her own set of rules.

Playgirl: Having dedicated fans is, of course, a great compliment. Yet it also seems somewhat sad, these die-hard fans who brave stormy weather just to bask in a star's momentary presence. Can you relate at all to such people?

Parton: I do understand it. I never was a hero-worshipper myself, but there are people I really admire and respect, people who are powerful enough for other people to want to follow. I know how important it is for people to have somebody to look up to. Some people don't really have enough goin'. They have never looked deep enough into themselves, or they never had the intelligence, or haven't cared enough, or didn't have the chance to be satisfied with who they are. So if there's somebody they love, idealize and almost worship, they want to be as close to that person as they can, so they can pattern their own lives after that person. It makes it easier for 'em sometimes.

Playgirl: Do you feel you're changing people's lives?

Parton: I would like to think that I'm helping people in a lot of ways. I'm helping myself in a lot of ways by dealin' with people the way that I do. You know, I try to really get close to 'em and to be aware of what they're thinking and feeling. I would like to think that I can change people for the better.

Playgirl: According to Jane Fonda, you changed an entire movie crew for the better on the *Nine to Five* set. She said that your spirit and your goodness made everybody else come up a bit, and that the film was a little better because of you.

Parton: That's a nice compliment. This movie was a real special project. It was a meant-to-be thing, a blessed thing. It's real important to make people feel good so they don't lose interest in what they're doing. Give 'em something to look forward to the next day. My philosophy, when I'm workin' on a project with other people, is that if I'm at a good level and really feeling good, then I create all sorts of excitement around me, all kinds of energy. Other people feel lazy if they don't try to come up to that energy. It makes everybody try harder to be better.

Playgirl: Were you the least bit intimidated, acting in your first film with such heavyweights?

Parton: Never. I did not have one bad moment on the whole picture. The attitude was great with everybody. If a lot of people are being really nice, it's very hard for someone to come in and show their ass—because they're going to really look like one.

Playgirl: Were you comfortable with your role?

Parton: I was real comfortable with the part I played because it was so *me*. It was just amazing how well (writer/director) Colin Higgins got me down, as far as my character. She's pretty much like me, a believable, likeable person. In *Whorehouse*, I have a chance to be sexy and wear elegant, sexy clothes. But in this, I'm a secretary whose boss has been telling everybody that he's sleeping with me. My best scenes are the ones where I'm really mad at the boss. I play mad real good. It gave me a real chance to do something besides being my own sweet self.

Playgirl: In what ways could you relate to the character you played? How much sexual harassment did you suffer on your way up?

Parton: I was never harassed where I didn't have control of it, really. But it made things hard sometimes, to coin a phrase. It just made it uncomfortable, but it wasn't anything that I didn't grow from. I guess all women are harassed to a degree, but a lot of people bring it on themselves and then want something to bitch about.

Playgirl: But do you understand the depth of the problem? Sexual harassment seems to be a major problem with secretaries who live in constant fear that if they don't give a little they won't get ahead—to coin a phrase.

Parton: I know that it happens. I know that a lot of people just can't go right out and find a job that easily. It puts you in a hard spot. You can't just walk off, you can't just say to hell with it, because you've got to consider everything. But I also know that there are a lot of business women who are sexually aggressive towards people too. I'm seein' both sides. It's an uncomfortable situation no matter who's doin' it.

Playgirl: Who did you feel closer to during the filming, Jane or Lily?

Parton: Actually, I felt a bit closer to Lily during the film because I had a chance to get to know her, and Jane had so much business stuff to do. And Lily and I are both with the same agency now. I spent more time talking to Lily. With Jane, we got to be close, but we really hadn't gotten together enough to totally relax and just be pals. I have such respect and admiration for Jane. I'm not star struck, but I know when a person's great.

Playgirl: Did Jane teach you any tricks of the trade?

Parton: When it came to looks, turns or a certain way to pause, she was real helpful. She was always saying little things like, "Don't talk on the same voice level. Don't get too excited when you've got nowhere to go. Don't start out high. Make a definite look, don't move your eyes around. . . ." Things like that. She also suggested that as a part of my contracts in the future, I might want a coach on the job with me. And she gave me names of directors to think about. A lot of people think she's hard because of her strong beliefs, but I found her very sensitive. She's very firm, very intelligent. She said to me, "I'd like to see you someday do something really serious and dramatic. Not comedy, not funny."

Playgirl: How do you feel about that?

Parton: I think it's good. In fact, from what I saw of myself on the screen, I see now that I could do that. I see that my face and expressions would be able to carry a serious role. If the lines were serious enough, then I'd be able to do it.

Playgirl: What about your looks? Would you be willing to change your appearance?

Parton: If I felt strongly enough about the character I was going to play, I wouldn't mind changing my look. Eventually that will be one of my challenges, to be another personality.

Playgirl: Getting back to Fonda, did you talk politics with her at all?

Parton: That's been a question everybody has asked me. Did Jane talk politics? She did not. Did she ask me to do anything? She did not. Do I think I would have if she had asked me? I don't know. If we were doing something for crippled children, the cancer society, stuff like that, yes, I do it all the time. I do benefit shows year-round. In fact, sometimes I wind up doing more shows for free than I get paid for. But I don't want to get involved in something that stirs up a bunch of controversy. For certain personalities, it's best to just do what you feel and what you believe, but not make it public. If I believe in something strongly, I'd rather donate money and do my bit in another way, because it suits my personality best. 'Cause I don't want to get involved in a whole bunch of shit.

Playgirl: Didn't you and Jane take a trip through the South together after the picture was finished?

Parton: She's doing a story called *The Dollmaker* (for television), about a woman from the Appalachian Mountains during the Depression. I'm gonna write the music for it. It's gonna be a challenge for Jane to play a woman from the South. She figured the best way to research the story would be with the help of somebody who knows the South. So we travelled around together for a week. We just had the best time you could imagine. We totally relaxed. It was like I was a little girl having a great time in the country entertaining a city cousin. In fact, we came up with some great ideas for movies and series and stories. It was really special. It was hard to say good-bye. We became good friends.

Playgirl: One last question about *Nine to Five* before we move on to *Whorehouse*. You wrote the song for the movie—do you think it might become a national anthem for working women?

Parton: I don't think it will for ladies necessarily. I think for working people. It's just about working nine to five [starts singing] . . . *Just to* *stay up on the boss man's ladder, you spend your life puttin' money in his wallet. You want to move ahead but the boss won't seem to let me. I swear sometimes that man's out to get me.* I was writing it for workers, period. I hope it will be a big record. It's got a lot of good stuff in it. I was proud of the way it turned out. I love the part that says [singing], *Tumble out of bed and stumble to the kitchen, pour myself a cup of ambition. And I wonder if I'd a been rich, what it would have been like. I jump in the shower and blood starts pumping, out on the streets the traffic starts jumping. With folks like me, on the job from nine to five.*

Playgirl: How long did it take you to write that song?

Parton: I was writing it on the set, just clicking the rhythm with my nails. I had my guitar there. I figured it out in my head. It all came at once. The rhythm is like the sound of typewriters, when the little bell rings and the telephone's ringing.

Playgirl: Were you a bit nervous about doing *Whorehouse* when you first heard the title?

Parton: A lot of people seem to be offended by it, a lot of religious people and country fans, but they don't know what the story's about. There's really no sex in *Whorehouse*. You don't see anybody going to bed with anybody, and I definitely don't go to bed with anybody. It's just a love story between two people and a musical comedy, so it didn't offend me. I had refused it before, when they first approached me with it, because I thought that way myself. I thought, "Well, I don't want to be playin' a whore or something." Then I went to see the play and I read the script and I thought, "This is really a lot of fun. It's got music and all, too. . . ."

Playgirl: Will you be changing the script at all to accommodate some of your own ideas?

Parton: I'm going to present some of my ideas because I'll be doing some of the music—writin' it and, of course, singin' it. I'll probably be producing my own tracks on the songs that I sing. But I also have some ideas of how to make Mona [her character] more colorful than she is right now.

Playgirl: Does Burt Reynolds play your lover?

Parton: In the story Burt, the sheriff, is my love. But we never touch, we never kiss, we never have a love scene. It's like Miss Kitty and Matt Dillon. I think, to make the movie stronger, with two personalities like mine and Burt's, there should be at least a couple of times . . . where we get drunk together or share a fit of laughter . . . . Of course, everybody knows his laugh, but my laugh is just as crazy; they just don't know it yet. One of the funniest things in the movie could be me and him laughing with our crazy laughs. And hopefully at some point we'll be able to have a love scene.

Playgirl: Did you ever see Burt Reynolds' centerfold in *Cosmopolitan* some years ago?

Parton: Yeah, I did see it, but it didn't show nothin', did it?

Playgirl: He had his hand over his little pecker, so—

Parton: [screeches] I'm not goin' to tell the girls back home that you said it was little! But I remember seeing it; everybody was talkin' about it. He had a lot of nice hair on his body.

Playgirl: Have you ever met Streisand?

Parton: I met her this past year at Sandy Gallin's beach house.

Playgirl: Did you get along?

Parton: We didn't have a fair chance. She's a fantastic talent, and I love her movies. I would love to be able to be as suited for my parts as she is for hers and carry them off with my personality. I didn't feel like she really liked me too much, but there were a lot of people around. It wasn't anything bad, but it wasn't anything good.

Playgirl: You had no chance to be alone?

Parton: I don't know if we would have known what to have said to each other. I'm such a fan, but I'm not a squirrel. They say that she doesn't like people saying "I'm a fan." I don't know what she thought of me. If we got to know each other, I'm sure we could be friends. I know we're going to be together again on occasion because of Sandy and just because of the business. I personally think we would be fantastic in something together.

Playgirl: You mean you and Streisand in a movie together?

Parton: If it's the right thing. A country, Southern girl befriends a strictly big-city, Jewish girl and the problems that would follow. How dumb I would find her in situations I would know how to deal with and relate to with a common touch, and how stupid she would find me with certain matters. Like two friends who fight like hell, but there's this thing that they love about each other. Or even two girls that are single, that are in business, who are friends but don't get along, but who stay together out of a need for love of some sort. Or do it for business reasons. There are all kinds of possibilities. Wouldn't even have to have anything to do with music.

Playgirl: It would certainly be interesting. And there'd be that competitive edge, with your glamorous looks.

Parton: I think she is so glamorous. In the movies, to me, there ain't nobody prettier. She is so different and so sexy-looking. Our looks, that would be another thing totally different. Mine is a made-up look. Hers is not made up. In many of the scenes she would come across as far more glamorous than I would. She has an elegance that I don't have. I just have a look, I know exactly what I look like, exactly what I *can* look like, and when I don't look good.

Playgirl: Now that the movies are expanding your horizons, who are some actors you'd like to work with? How about Woody Allen?

Parton: I'd love to do something with Woody Allen. It would be one extreme to the other. I relate to him for some reason; I feel like I know him. I appreciate his mind, his comedy. I met him once in an airport in Paris or Germany. He came over and said hi. It was a big thrill to me. He was quiet and charming. He's just one of those people whom I like for whatever reasons. It isn't that he should write a property for me, because I could give a shit whether I'm in the movies, whether I further my career or not. But if I do movies, I would like them all to mean something special to me. I'd like to like the people I'm with, not just do them because they're a good property. Like with Burt. Burt Reynolds is the perfect choice for me. Our personalities are very similar. Our fans are very similar. He's the working man's dream. An everyday hero. And I sort of am, too.

Playgirl: Is it true that Sandy will executive produce your movies after *Whorehouse*?

Parton: If I let him. I respect Sandy's feelings, and he respects mine. If at any time he gets out of line without meaning to . . . it's so easy for him to think in terms of big business and money, and I love him for that. He's got great ideas. But in fact, I hope to have a lot of control over my movies in general. I'll be writing any music for the stuff that I do, so it's a great outlet for my songwriting. And I'll be involved in the business wherever necessary. If there's any money to be made off Miss Dolly, I'm gonna get some of it, 'cause that's the way it should be.

Playgirl: Your relationship with Sandy is somewhat of a mystery. He is, actually, the second man in your life, isn't he?

Parton: I love Sandy. We become closer all the time. He was just a God-given person to me. When you know something's right, it never goes wrong. When I feel that confident about a person, it can only get bigger and better. He's amazing. When I'm around people that I feel are psychic or spiritual, like Sandy, it just seems to make life real special. He's a true friend of mine. I have told him things that I ain't told anybody. That's just the way I am with Sandy. There's a certain mischievous side to my personality that he brings to the surface more than anybody else. There's such an energy that floats between us that I tell him some things just for his reaction, because I know that it takes a lot to baffle or floor him, 'cause he's seen and done everything. I am so complex, there are so many sides to me, that somehow I get a thrill out of flooring him, just throwin' him totally off.

Playgirl: When was the last time you did that?

Parton: [laughs] Yesterday. It's the same way with Carl, too. The people whom I'm closest to that way are people who amaze me year after year after year.

Playgirl: Didn't you announce to the guests at Sandy's fortieth birthday party that you had never slept with Sandy, and then break into the song you wrote for him?

Parton: Well, I was so high, I didn't know what I was doing. I'm not used to drinkin' a lot of wine. It's true that I've never slept with Sandy. There's a line in my song that goes, "You've touched me in places no one's ever reached," but anybody who knew him would certainly know I didn't mean *that*! *It* wouldn't reach that far, I don't think! [breaks out in laughter] But seriously, he's really touched my life and he's allowed me, without knowing it, to bring a side of my personality to the surface that otherwise I wouldn't have. It's a good relationship, and it's the kind of love that makes it so much fun to work together.

Playgirl: Now that your career means being out in Hollywood more, have you and your husband, Carl, talked much about how this might affect your own relationship?

Parton: No, we don't talk about it. Sometimes people muster up stuff before it's time. We're in a good place now as far as my career is concerned. It's almost like we've retired in a way. We spend months together out here in the wintertime, then he goes home in the spring when the weather breaks. I don't demand a lot from Carl, therefore he feels free to give a lot. He doesn't demand a lot from me, so it excites me to give. We don't feel obligated, and we never burden each other.

Playgirl: What is Carl's opinion of Hollywood? Has it changed any since he was out while you were making *Nine to Five*? Is he wary or concerned about your being out here?

Parton: No, he feels better about it because he actually did come on the set, and he met a lot of nice people. It's so easy to think that everybody in Hollywood is screwed up. Well, that's not the truth. There are lots of screwed-up people and Hollywood has its share, but there are respectable, family people too. Everybody's not shattered. And Carl trusts my judgment. He knows I ain't gonna get in somethin' I can't get out of, and he knows that I ain't gonna get in somethin' I don't like, 'cause

I won't stay. And he knows I'm too stubborn to put up with other people's stuff.

Playgirl: Did you really meet Carl in a Nashville Laundromat?

Parton: I was at the Laundromat, which was the first one I had ever been to in my life. I brought dirty clothes from home because I left home the day after I graduated from high school. While my clothes were being washed, I just walked around outside thinking how I was in Nashville and what was I going to live on and this and that . . . and Carl just drove by. He saw me; I guess he liked what he saw. He must have, he married me. He just hollered and waved. And I hollered and waved. It was one of those love-at-first-sights. When we went out for the first time, he took me straight over to his mother's.

Playgirl: Would you say your relationship is more passionate or affectionate?

Parton: More affectionate. And as passionate as it needs to be. The more passionate you are, the more apt you are to fight and scratch and disagree. People who have to have each other for sex purposes usually have a tendency to fight the most. Then they have the greatest joy getting back together.

Playgirl: What gives you the greatest joy when you're with Carl?

Parton: I like to sleep with Carl. It's a real comfort. We like to talk together a lot. We like to go up to our bedroom early at night. He takes a bath and piddles around, and I read and talk or just watch television. We do a lot of talkin' in the bedroom because we have a lot of different things to talk about, such as what he's been doing. I like to travel with Carl. We go on vacations or short trips sometimes for three or four days and stop at little cafes in some little country hick town. We went to Yellowstone Park a couple of years ago, and we were gone for four weeks. Camped out. Cooked on the riverbank.

But we don't eat together a lot normally. I eat more with everybody else than I do with Carl 'cause he's not a big eater; he eats three meals a day and that's it. We just spend a lot of good, comfortable times together.

If we're in the middle of a conversation, if I lose interest without real-
izing it, I just get up to go do something else. He doesn't get offended at
that; he just figures we'll pick up the conversation another time. It's the
same with him. I'll be tellin' him something and I'll be really involved,
and he'll realize that he's left the engine runnin' on a truck up in the
woods and he gets up and leaves. I know it's not out of disrespect. We're
not real sensitive. That is, we're very sensitive people, but we're not
supersensitive to silly little things like is he forgets to send me an anniversary card.

Playgirl: Do you argue much?

Parton: Never argue. Sometimes we'll get a little touchy if we're tired
or aggravated, but the worst it ever gets to is "Why don't you get out
and go somewhere? Why don't you get out of my face for a while?" We
never put ourselves in a situation where we bicker back and forth. It's
just too easy to pick up the habit of arguing. Years ago we decided that
if we never started then we'd never have to keep it up. It becomes a
form of recreation, and sometimes it's the only excitement in people's
lives. I'd rather argue with anybody rather than Carl, 'cause I don't want
that stuff between us. It would hurt my feelings too much if he got so
mad that he said somethin' really hard to me. It would just crush me,
and it would be the same with him if I said somethin' really awful to
him like people do when they're really mad. So I try not to let myself
stoop that low.

Playgirl: Have you considered having children?

Parton: I love kids, but it wouldn't be fair to put children through the
kind of life that I lead. Carl doesn't want children either. If he did, I
would have them, I'm sure. We're each other's children. He's like my
little boy. But he's also like my daddy and my brother. And I'm all those
things to him.

Playgirl: Sounds like the ideal relationship.

Parton: Carl was the person who gave my life meaning and a foundation. Somebody to make plans with, to give us both a reason to work,
somebody to build a home with and talk with about bein' old together

Celebrating the opening of Dollywood, 1986.
Author Collection

Performing with Kenny Rogers on the *Kenny, Dolly and Willie: Something Inside So Strong* TV special, 1989.
Globe Photos, Inc.

With costars Sally Field, Olympia Dukakis, Shirley MacLaine, Julia Roberts, and Daryl Hannah at the Ziegfeld Theater in New York City for the *Steel Magnolias* premiere, November 5, 1989. *Adam Scull-PHOTOlink.net*

As Doctor Shirlee in the 1992 film *Straight Talk*. *Hollywood Pictures*

With fellow "Honky Tonk Angels" Loretta Lynn and Tammy Wynette, in rehearsal for the 27th Annual Country Music Association Awards, 1993. *Photo by John Barrett-Globe Photos, Inc.*

Publicity portrait for the 1996 *Treasures* album.
MCA Music Entertainment Group

At the 2007 Songwriters Hall of Fame Awards Induction Ceremony, New York City.
John Krondes-Globe Photos, Inc.

Performing for the NBC *Today Show* Summer Concert Series at Rockefeller Center in New York City, 2002.
Ace Pictures/ImageCollect

With actress Megan Hilty, Broadway's "Doralee," on break from rehearsals for *9 to 5: The Musical*, July 15, 2008.
Henry McGee-Globe Photos, Inc.

With *Joyful Noise* costar Queen Latifah on the set of *The Queen Latifah Show*, 2013.
Courtesy Sony Pictures Television

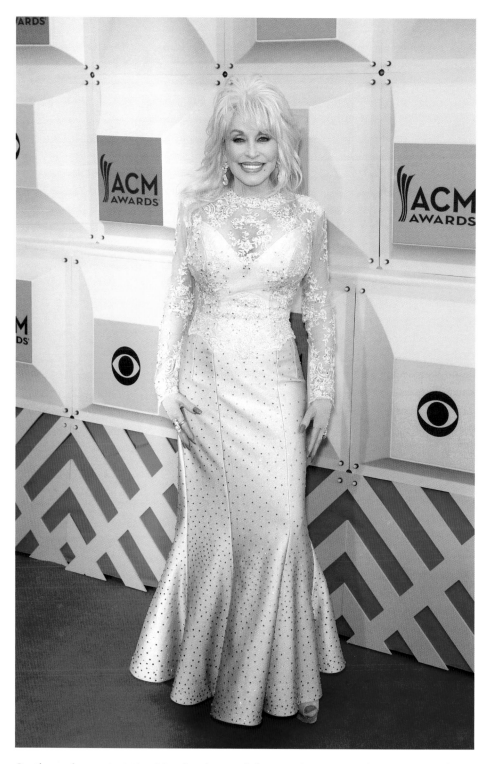

On the red carpet at the 51st Academy of Country Music Awards, MGM Grand, Las Vegas.

MJT/AdMedia

With sister Stella Parton at the cast and crew screening of *Dolly Parton's Coat of Many Colors* in Hollywood, December 2015.
David Longendyke-Globe Photos, Inc.

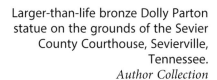

Larger-than-life bronze Dolly Parton statue on the grounds of the Sevier County Courthouse, Sevierville, Tennessee.
Author Collection

Photographed in Nashville for *Southern Living* magazine, 2014. *David McClister*

and where we're goin'. Somebody not to bug me, not to choke me; and for me not to choke him, because he needs his freedom as much as I need mine. Another kind of woman would have choked him to death, and he would not have become the person that he is from lovin' me. And it's the same as far as I'm concerned. Nobody could have brought out of me all the good things that he has and still have been willing or strong enough tolerate the weaknesses.

Playgirl: How do you think you're perceived by people who don't know who you are?

Parton: They probably think I don't have as much depth as I like to think I do, as much intelligence as I like to think I have. They probably judge me by the way I look, and think I'm just a dumb hick . . . a little dense. Somebody who looks like me, maybe it just shocks people.

Playgirl: Let's talk about your looks for a minute. How long does it take you to put on your makeup?

Parton: Ten, fifteen minutes. I like to have an hour to get totally ready. If it's a special evening, I like to have an hour and a half, to take a bath, do the toenails and fingernails, shave my legs, the whole works.

Playgirl: Do you do anything special to keep your skin looking so smooth?

Parton: I've been real lucky as far as my skin. I'm very fair, which makes my skin look like it's actually prettier than it is, because from a slight distance you just see the fair skin. I actually don't take care of myself like I should. I go to bed a lot of times with makeup on, get up the next morning in a hurry and patch it up. I sleep in eyelashes. But I'm thirty-four; I should take better care of my skin.

Playgirl: What about exercise? Do you do it or do you still avoid it?

Parton: I *think* a lot about it. One of these days I will. I have a swimming pool and a sauna house, a tennis court. I live on a farm.

Playgirl: How do you swim in high heels?

Parton: Carefully.

Playgirl: Do you still have to watch your weight all the time?

Parton: No. But I think about it a lot.

Playgirl: What does it hurt the most to give up when you diet?

Parton: Potatoes. I'm a starch freak. I'm not a sweet-eater. Usually I eat so much I don't have room for dessert. I'm a junk-food person, too. I like pizza, potato chips, Fritos.

Playgirl: To change the subject, how are your latest albums selling?

Parton: Not as good, the last three. But I haven't been doing the same type of promotion, either. We've been so involved in the movies and new projects that we haven't devoted as much time to lookin' for material or getting into producing an album. Now with the movies and the Vegas thing, I don't have to worry about money anymore, so I've won my musical freedom. I'm goin' back to record my next album in Nashville, use a lot of Nashville musicians, people I used in the past. Now that I'm where I feel like I want to be as far as my career, I can go back and do what I always tried to do all those years before.

Playgirl: How have your greatest hits sold?

Parton: There have been two albums. We call 'em Dolly's Greatest Tits.

Playgirl: Dolly's Greatest Tits. Nothing sexist about that! [laughter] Of all the things you do, what is it you like to do best?

Parton: Write songs. That's what I love to do best. And what I get the most satisfaction from. I love to perform. I'm really enjoying doing these movies. I like it all. But I get the most satisfaction from writing.

Playgirl: Are you writing anything now?

Parton: It usually comes in a clump. I thought of a line one day, just a thought, "I would die for you and I often do." I wanted to write something around that, and I just couldn't write anything that didn't seem corny. Maybe it is better as a closing line, rather than trying to build an entire story around it.

I have in mind doing an album of working people's songs. I want to do "Detroit City." Do you remember that song? Just about the miners and the truckers.

Playgirl: How do you feel about Bob Dylan becoming a born-again Christian? Dylan is known for being a few steps ahead of the public. Does his going towards religion indicate to you that we're in for a religious revival of sorts?

Parton: Yes, I do think that, whether it's with Dylan or the things that made him start thinking that way. I do think there is definitely goin' to be a big revival as far as religion goes. I know the Bible real well. And the Bible speaks of it in the latter days.

Playgirl: And are we reaching those days?

Parton: Nobody knows, but according to what I read and what's been prophesized, we're certainly living in the autumn of life. I really don't care to talk about religion in an in-depth interview. But if it's gonna come, it's got to come; there's nothin' I can do to stop it. I believe in tryin' to give as much to life as I can, to give as much to people, to take as much as I need to make life more meaningful.

Playgirl: How much do you need?

Parton: I need it all, and I need to give it all. I don't want a little bit of nothin'. I'm an extremist. I should have a group called The Extremists.

Playgirl: You're also a listmaker, aren't you? Don't you make lists of everything you want to see happen in your life and then cross them off as they do?

Parton: You sure are about the nosiest fucker I have ever seen. You pick my brain so much. I've got a lot of things on my lists, but I don't like to talk about them, especially not for magazines. A lot of my things are really personal, and they're written in such a way that they're almost embarrassing to share.

Playgirl: Can you give some generalizations if you don't want to be specific?

Parton: One of the things on the list is that the right projects come as far as the movies are concerned, and that I be successful as an actress. I would like to be an inspiration to everybody on the project, and that in turn it will be an inspiration to me.

Playgirl: These become, then, like pep talks to yourself?

Parton: I guess they are peptalks. My faith is great, but I like seein' things written down. It just reconfirms my faith; it creates an image.

Playgirl: Do you keep the lists after you've accomplished all that's on them, or do you throw them away?

Parton: I kinda hate to throw 'em away. I've got a lot of things that I've had through the years, and it would amaze you to see the ones that I've marked off that have happened just like they were supposed to.

Playgirl: Nothing you could do would surprise us. Unless you said you had limitations.

Parton: I have no limitations. Everything depends on the time, the situation and the mood I'm in.

RADIO INTERVIEW

Ralph Emery | 1981 | *The Ralph Emery Show*

In the mid- to late-1960s, when her uncle Bill Owens was playing guitar and touring with Carl and Pearl Butler, Dolly was appearing on early morning shows such as *The Eddie Hill Show* and *The Ralph Emery Show*. In fact, at the onset of Dolly's career, Emery would pick her up at her Nashville apartment, take her to perform on his early morning show, and then drive her back home. When Dolly married Carl Dean in 1966, she was set to guest on Emery's show the next morning. "I got married . . . in the afternoon, came home, and I had to get up at three that next mornin' 'cause I was on your show," she recalled to him in 1989. "That's when you did that really early mornin' show. I didn't let marriage, love, or nothin' stand in the way of me and you, Ralph!"

Emery has often named Dolly as one of his favorite interview guests, and, as evidenced here, the chemistry between the two is irrefutable. They were lighthearted and playful as Emery quizzed Dolly about her recent *Rolling Stone* feature and what it was like to be on the cover of *Playboy*. In a particularly candid moment, while discussing home and family life, Dolly revealed the marital problems of her parents. —Ed.

Ralph Emery: Hello, everybody. We welcome you again to our show. My name is Ralph Emery, and I'm sitting in RCA's Nashville Studio, Studio B, with one of the hottest stars in the world, Miss Dolly Parton. Dolly, welcome back to our show.

Dolly Parton: Boy, I didn't know I was that big a deal. You was spreadin' that on a little thick, weren't ya? You think I'm that hot, do you?

You wrote it down here . . .

[*Laughs*] You didn't say it exactly like I told you to say.

It says, "one of the hottest stars in the world."

I did not. How are you?

How you doing Miss Dolly?

I'm doing good!

Dolly what? Dolly Marie?

Dolly Rebecca.

Oh, Dolly Rebecca.

Dolly Rebecca Parton. A lot of people ask me if Dolly's my real name. They think it's a show name, but I guess my mama knew I was gonna wanna be a star, so she just named me Dolly to start with.

Well, I wanna ask you about your next movie. You're going to go back to Hollywood and make another picture, aren't you?

Yeah, in fact, I'm really excited about doing this next film. It's with Burt Reynolds, and it's from the Broadway musical comedy of *The Best Little Whorehouse in Texas*. I'm gonna be writin a lot of the music for that. I like working with Lily and Jane, but working with Burt Reynolds, that's just something else!

You gonna do love scenes with Burt?

Oh, I sure hope so! I've asked Carl's permission and I got it in writin'. [*Laughs*] So if I can convince Burt that he should kiss me, I think I'll kiss him for every woman in America that ever wanted to. I'm gonna lay a good'n on him!

Did you have any sort of love scene in *9 to 5*?

A sorta love scene. It wasn't really heavy. I was married to a guy in the movie—that's my movie husband—and he's the real husband of one of my good friends, Diana Thomas. His name is Jeff Thomas. And [Diana's] one of the secretaries at Katz Gallin, my management agency. People didn't know that I knew him, so he got the part strictly on his own talent. But we didn't know we was supposed to [kiss] and this was the very first day of the movie and boy you talk about clumsy and awkward. It's hard enough to kiss somebody else, much less somebody else's husband, much less on the first day of shootin' a film and, on top of that, with all the cameras and the crew and all the people lookin' on. I never felt so embarrassed in my whole life! But it was just sort of a sweet love scene. We were supposed to be married in the film, so it made it OK. Well, me and Burt ain't gonna be married in [*Whorehouse*] so that'll make it juicier. [*Laughs*]

Dolly, I picked up the paper the other day and I read a story about [how] you were runnin' around out there in Beverly Hills in the buff.

You did?

Yes. Did you read the same story?

[*Laughs*] Nah, I didn't hear nothin' about it. I don't know nothin' about it, I ain't talkin' nothin' about it, and I ain't said nothin' about it 'cause I don't know nothin' about it! [*Laughs*]

It stated that there had been a story about you in *Rolling Stone* magazine and you were allegedly running around out in the streets of Beverly Hills with no clothes on.

Well, now we gotta clear that up, Ralph. It wasn't exactly like it sounds. I didn't do it to be ugly. I didn't do it to be dirty. It happened like this. It was when we was doing *9 to 5*, the movie. And you get a little bored being away from home like like three or four months at a time. Well, I was feeling really good this particular night and my girlfriend Judy and me were coming back from a Mexican restaurant. I was riding in the car with Gregg Perry, who also produces a lot of my records and works with me, and Judy was in another car with two of our girlfriends. So Judy got to actin' real smart and cute. And you know how stubborn I am. And I'm pretty mischievous myself. And I can't stand to be dared.

Really?

Or if somebody were to back me in a corner to say, "I dare you to do this," or if I'm in a contest, which is like all in fun, but I'm the kind of person I do whatever I feel like I have to, even if it harelips the devil.

And sometimes it does! But anyhow, we were just doin' things. So finally, we had done everything that a body could do, and I thought, *Now what am I gonna do to top this?* So I just kinda jumped out of the car . . . and I just kinda ran around the car . . . and I didn't have on any clothes. But it didn't last but a minute! And I got back in the car and I won the contest. But she double-dog dared me, so I had to do it.

[*Laughs*] What do you mean, "It didn't last but a minute"? Who saw you?

Well I'm just saying I didn't walk *around* . . .

Who saw you?

It don't make no difference. They'll never forget it, whoever they were! [*Laughs*]

Were you on a busy street?

No, actually I was at a stop sign in Bel Air, in the old sophisticated snooty part of Hollywood. Anyhow, I hope they *did* see it. It might be good for 'em! But actually, I don't think anybody saw me except Judy and the two girls in the car 'cause I threatened Gregg with his life if he looked. He didn't. I don't think. Don't care. It didn't matter at that time. It only mattered after I got my clothes back on. [*Laughs*] Is that bad? A lot of people were real upset with me about that, but I couldn't help myself!

I was gonna ask you if you had received a lot of criticism about that?

I did, some, but I receive a lot of criticism about most things I do, so it didn't really matter.

You say you just hate to be dared?

Yeah, so don't dare me now! [*Laughs*]

I was gonna say . . . I'm gonna dream up a good dare before I get out of here.

I mean, it's got to be something you know that's really bein' played out by the other person, too, and I've got to win if there's any way I can. You know how you hate to be dared.

Tell them who Judy is.

Judy is my best friend and she's worked with me.

You grew up with her didn't you?

Yeah, we've been together since we were seven years old. We grew up just as poor as the other one and we lived close to each other all our life. We went through grammar school, high school, reform school together. We've just been in a lot of meanness together, so she's like the same as a sister.

Now, some people will take you very literally, so don't say reform school.

Oh, are you kiddin'?

They'll say, "Well, I didn't know Dolly was in reform school!"

Well, we should have been!

But Judy has been with you a long time, hasn't she?

Yeah, Judy's really great. She's worked as my personal secretary and personal assistant for years. We travel together. She's a great, great friend.

Did you play baseball or softball?

Yeah, I was pretty good at it, as a matter of fact, when I was littler. Then it got to where I couldn't run without blacking my eyes. I had to give it up. [*Laughs*]

Have you ever been on one of these television shows where the stars have to participate in games?

No, I've been *asked* to be, but you don't *have* to be on them shows if you can't do nothin'. [*Laughs*] But they're always asking me to like to play ball or to play tennis or to be in the runnin' things and all, but I've never participated.

I remember several years ago you used to play tennis.

Yeah, I still do that sometimes, but I don't do it in public. I ain't that good. I like to play golf a little bit, but I ain't that good at that either. I like to just kinda piddle around at stuff like that. I can't stay at it long enough to get good at it.

Can't or don't have the time?

I just won't. I guess I could find the time, but I enjoy doing it the way I do it . . . just kind of hitting at it here or there.

You and Carl ever play golf together or tennis?

No, but we play tennis every once in a while and we swim together now that we got a swimmin' pool. But what we like the most about all these modern things that success has brought . . . we got a hot tub and we just live in that thing in the summertime and up until, like, November. You got one? A hot tub? A Jacuzzi?

No, I don't have one.

Yeah, well they don't cost all that much, Ralph. You cheap thing! You could buy one. [*Laughs*] I know you make enough money off this show. I seen your check!

I have a child who has one. I'll go use his.

Yeah, do that. Do that.

One of my favorite songs by Dolly Parton was not one of her big hit records, but it was a song [*to Dolly*] I used to see you do this in person: "Me and Little Andy."

You know, we never did release the song as a single. I think if we *had* that it could have been a big record. It was on the *Here You Come Again* album, I believe, wasn't it? Or *Heartbreaker*?

I'm not sure. You have so many of them.

Yeah, I think it was on the *Here You Come Again* album. But I get as many requests for that little song as anything I ever wrote. When I used to be with Porter years ago, we used to sing those songs about kids and in that little girl voice. Songs like "Jeannie's Afraid of the Dark" and some of the stuff we used to record. But I wrote this song 'cause I just thought it would be a good thing to do. I still do it on stage and it's one of my special songs.

Is there a story about the character?

Well, I sorta linked it to some kids back home where their mama was pretty wild and their daddy was a drunkard. They're just as poor as we were and as big of family as we had. They used to kinda hang around our house a lot and mama always kinda took 'em in. But it wasn't like the *exact* story, but it was because of that, in the back of my mind, and it's called "Me and Little Andy." [. . .] It's sad, boy. When I do it on stage I look out in the audience and I see 'bout five or six people just a-slinging tears and that other stuff they sling. [*Laughs*] And sometimes when I'm singin' it, I sling some of it myself!

Do you ever get emotional on stage?

Ooh *yeah*! It depends if I've been out on the road for a long time or if I'm kinda feeling bad or real emotional or something. Sometimes a song like "Coat of Many Colors" does it if I ain't seen Mama and Daddy in a long time, or my folks, or if something has just built up in me emotionally. I'm very sensitive and emotional, as most people are, and sometimes, like right in the middle of a song, it's just all I can do . . . I've just had to turn away from the microphone a time or two on songs like "Coat of Many Colors."

There used to be a song about a dog, "Crackerjack"?

"Crackerjack," well, that one didn't make me cry, but I liked that song.

Did you have a dog named Crackerjack?

It was about my sisters little dog and it got killed. It was kinda a sad story and she loved it a lot. Only, its name was something else and I called it "Crackerjack" to protect the innocent. I changed his name.

Dolly, Jim Reeves passed away in '64. You came to Nashville in '65, so you didn't really know Jim Reeves, did you?

Well, I came to Nashville in '64 and I got here just before he died. But I had made trips back and forth to Nashville before I ever moved here, and I remember seeing him once. I never talked to him or nothin', but I always thought he was awful good.

Well RCA still releases his records.

He's still a big star in a lot of places in the world.

Right. The Jim Reeves fan club is very active throughout the world.

You'd be surprised, Ralph. I know this sounds a little bizarre and a little bit unbelievable, but I see people all the time in different parts of the world . . . They don't really realize because of the distance . . . They don't get what [songs] was hits years and years ago. [Certain songs are] just now being big hits in certain places, and it amazed me to find how few people know that some of our bigger stars are dead. A friend of mine from Ireland was sayin' they couldn't wait for Jim Reeves to come to Ireland. They don't even realize that he is dead because his records are so hot. And also, it's the same with Patsy Cline. I had somebody say once somethin' 'bout did I ever see Patsy Cline or somethin'. Don't you find that amazing that they don't even realize that they're dead?

That is strange. There's a revival among the Patsy Cline fans. She's become a cult figure as the result of Loretta's picture [*Coal Miner's Daughter*].

Didn't you love Loretta's picture? By the way, I love Loretta in it *and* Patsy Cline. Two greats.

We were talking about how fans think and feel about stars and about people they don't see often. I would imagine you have a hard time convincing people that your husband exists.

You know, that's beginning to be a bigger deal now than it used to be. In fact, I was at RCA today . . . I spent a couple of days just makin' phone calls and callin' disc jockeys and just checkin' in with people and sayin thanks and all that . . . and I had about four different people in two days say, "Is this something you and your manager dreamed up, this husband thing? We don't believe that there *is* a husband or Carl Dean. We think this is a mystery that you've built up," and this and that. And you'd be surprised at how many people really think that. But there really *is* a Carl Dean. And you know it for a fact, don't you?

Well, I've met Carl.

Yeah, you've met Carl. But, now, you don't know . . . that could have been a "rent-a-husband." [*Laughs*] I wanna get some kids, some "rent-a-kids," you know and make a whole [family]. But now really, Carl don't wanna be in the limelight. He's proud of me and he likes the fact that's what I wanna do. And I don't interfere with what he likes. But he knows if he ever started doing interviews and if people started photographing him and all that, then he wouldn't be able to go to the auto parts store or the ballgames and the places he wants to go without bein' bothered. And he don't wanna be a star. And so it's his choice and I respect that.

Dolly, it's like being on the perimeter of an atom bomb, though. I mean, he's got to work at staying out of the spotlight.

Well, not really. I respect his privacy and he respects mine. We have a gate around our house. It's not that he can't be seen or anything. It's not that pictures of him have not been in certain magazines. It's just that we don't build it up. We try to keep a separation in our private life. I think it's healthy and smart. For everybody else's husband or wife that's involved in the business too, it creates a whole lot of problems, a lot tension and strain. We don't want to be in the same business. So we're happy and our marriage is working.

How long you been married now?

Well, we've been married since 1966.

When's your wedding anniversary?

May the thirtieth.

Where'd you get married?

Ringgold, Georgia.

You just run off one night?

One day. We had plans . . . I'll tell you a funny story here . . . I don't know if I ever told you this or not but I was with Monument Records at the time with Fred Foster, who is a wonderful man, was great to me back then, and is still a good friend of mine today. But I had just started with him and they didn't think I could sell country music, so we started doing some rockabilly or some kind of rock stuff, like "Happy, Happy Birthday, Baby." Those songs are good, and [Fred will] rerelease them one of these days. I won't mind, 'cause they were pretty good. I just wasn't ready for that particular thing at the time, but he was putting a lot of money and a lot of time and effort. I was so in love with Carl I couldn't see straight and I was gonna get married. I wanted to get married in church and have a big wedding, and my folks couldn't afford to pay for a weddin', but Carl's mother and daddy were gonna have a wedding for us at the church. They were gonna pay for my dress and the invitations and all that. So Mama Dean, Carl's mother, was just real excited about it and she'd already got the invitations done and the cake and the whole thing. Well I told Fred Foster that I was gonna get married and he didn't like it at all. He said, "I just don't think you should get married. We're puttin' all this time and this effort," and this and that. He said, "Just promise me you'll wait for a year." And I thought *Wow, I don't want to mess up.* So I told Carl the situation. I said, "We'll go get married anyway, but we just won't have a church weddin' and we just won't get married in Tennessee. So we told our folks what we were gonna do and that we were gonna keep it a secret, pretty much, for a year. We went the same weekend I told Fred we'd wait for a year. We went to Ringgold and got married [in Georgia] so it wouldn't be in the Tennessee papers. Well, then everybody thought that we *had* to get married, and everybody kept waiting for the baby that never did come. [*Laughs*] They didn't realize that we just wanted to do it without everybody knowing it. And so after a year had passed, we were so happy and I was so feeling so good and so content. I had done twice as good of work and all that. So after things were going good, Fred said, "Now, see . . . ain't you glad you waited to get married?" He said, "You still want to get married?" I said, "I got married the same weekend you told me not to!" [*Laughs*] So we always laughed about that. Not that it was funny, Ralph. [*Laughs*]

You open more can-o-worms every time you open your mouth. Your mommy and daddy doing all right now?

Well, they're havin' their trouble. You know the thing with Mama and Daddy . . . They're the best in the world. They were the best parents and they got married so young and started having kids immediately. Mama was fifteen and Daddy was seventeen when they married, had their twelfth kid when Mama was thirty-five, the same age I am right now, and Daddy was thirty-seven . . . with twelve kids! Then, after we all left home, they realized they didn't have that much in common. They just have a hard time keepin' it together, so they're gonna divorce every week but they're so in love, they never do it.

That's cute, that's cute. Dolly, you earlier alluded to the fact that you were not going to play a nude scene in the picture you're gonna make with Burt Reynolds. Have you been asked to do nude scenes?

No, I've never been asked to do that. I think people know that I respect myself, and people usually respect people that respect themselves. But I would never even do any really *heavy*, serious love scenes, like even slobberin' kissin' scenes and all. I certainly wouldn't do anything as outrageous as being naked. It's fine for some people, if that's what they wanna do, but I always think of my Mom and Dad and my people and the way I was brought up. And besides that, I have a great deal of respect for me. I've never really gone through a lot of disrespectful things. People have always treated me nice.

Several years ago, did *Playboy* magazine ask you to pose for them?

They didn't ask me to pose *nude*, they just asked me to do the cover of a *Playboy*, and I wouldn't do that for a good while. I gave that a lot of thought, too. I thought, well, if they're gonna do a *good* story and if I can pick the way that I do the cover, design my own outfit—in keeping with their magazine but in keeping with myself as well—then I'll do it. That's when we picked the little bunny suit. It was like a bathing suit and the little ears. It was certainly a *full* little bathing suit . . .

Yes, it certainly was!

But I didn't think it was vulgar. I got a lot of good reaction from that. I didn't get any criticism from that that I knew of.

It was a cute picture. No, it was a cute picture.

And the story was good. And it was honest. In a magazine like that, of course, you talk about stuff that you don't in *Ladies' Home Journal*.

Have you read *Ladies' Home Journal* lately?

No.

It's getting pretty spicy, I hear.

Well good! Then I've got some stuff to tell them then! [*Laughs*] I'll fix their goat.

We're spending a week here with Dolly Parton. Boy. I can think of guys that would pay a thousand dollars for this.

You can? Well, can I have their numbers? [*Laughs*] I need the money. It goes to a needy family . . . my own!

Dolly, are you gonna write your autobiography?

I couldn't, Ralph, without hanging myself and a whole lot of other people. I am writin' it in a lot of ways. I'm writin' my life story as a musical and it's called *Wildflowers*. It's about me, and a lifestyle, and the way I grew up, and a lot of people combined. But if I told my real life story I would want to tell the truth, the whole truth, and nothing but the truth. And in order to do that, that would be the truth as *I* saw it. It wouldn't necessarily be somebody else's view of it. It's hard when you try to tell your life story and involve other people and you can't just leave chapters out, you know, like certain relationships or certain people, whether it would be Porter or family or whatever. I just think it's kind of tough to do it. And the way I would want to write it, it would be too hard and too sticky to do it.

You afraid of hurting a lot of feelings?

I'm afraid that I *might* hurt a lot of feelings without intendin' to. And besides that, I'm too young to write my life story. I ain't lived my life yet.

OK, all right. Well, we are living in an era of books: Loretta's book, Johnny Cash's book, Tammy Wynette's book. And there was a book out about you, which I heard was not authorized.

Well there's been about three or four books out and most of 'em written by people I never even heard tell of, much less know. Some of them I knew were being put out and we were kind of put out about it, 'cause some of the stuff that was in it kind of hurt the feelings of family and embarrassed a lot of people. That's what I'm sayin'. It's just real touchy.

When you don't cooperate with a writer, where do they get the information they put in the books?

Well, they gather up information from every interview that you've done in the past, things that other reporters have written about you, and then they give their own opinion of what they think about the stuff and the way they see it, which is fine, you know. That's freedom of the press. But all I'm sayin' is the books of mine that have been out have not been authorized. It's always tricky. But when I'm real old, as I may be real soon [*Laughs*], then I may write my life story. But it's too soon. It's just too soon.

Dolly, there is a record and it's in the country charts these days by you and Porter Wagoner. It follows one that was out earlier, called "Making Plans." Why are we hearing records by Porter and Dolly again after a hiatus of some two or three years?

Well, the songs that's in that album, and the "If You Go, I'll Follow You" and "Making Plans," these were songs that we did years and years ago that we had, as they say, "in the can." That means songs that you've recorded at different times during your career that didn't make it into an album, or you just had too many songs and they just kept being put aside. But when we were in the lawsuit together, when we were settlin' that with our business things . . .

Did you and Porter Wagoner sue each other?

No, he sued *me*. It turned out, well, it was just kind of an embarrassing thing that I wish had never happened. In a way, it was kinda good that it did, but that's hindsight. Anyhow, when we were settlin' the lawsuit, that was part of the agreement . . . that he could take those songs we had in the can and redo them, put new music to 'em, and release them as an album. And I thought the album was very good. I was real proud of that album, and it's doing really good. I don't know that there'll be any duets in the future. It's certainly not an impossible thing. I don't feel that we're enemies.

Are you saying you would record with Porter in the future?

It's certainly not impossible. I would if we could come to some sort of an agreement on how we would do it and where we both had control of what we were doing.

Creative control?

Yeah. I wouldn't want to *just* go in and do it again with *just* Porter and get back in the same situations that we had.

I assume that when you made records with him, he had all of the creative control then. He was the boss.

Well, he was the boss, but he didn't have all the creativity. He had control. [*Laughs*] Let's put it that way. But we had some wonderful times. I'll always respect Porter. We went through some bad times. We spent seven of the best and the worst years I ever had in my life. There's a lot to be said about Porter, both ways. [*Laughs*] But I'm sure there's a lot to be said about me, so it was pretty equal. I think that we did a lot of good for each other. I will always be grateful for the good things that I was always grateful for.

Porter gave you a big break, didn't he?

Yes, he did. And I appreciate it.

Dolly, let me ask you something about yourself. You seem to have an awful lot of confidence and you have mentioned that in this interview. You have a lot of confidence in Dolly Parton. I don't detect any insecurities. Is that a fair statement?

Well, I have a lot of confidence in myself. I have a lot of confidence in people. I think that, no matter what we are, we can be more. I think you *have* to be sure of what you can do. I know my limitations. I don't like other people placing limitations on me. [When it comes to] the things that I feel like I want and that I can do, I feel that I should get out and try. As a human being, I feel like I should find out what my purpose and reason is in life. I want to know that I have done everything that I can with all the things that God has given me. Otherwise, I feel like it would be a sin. But I like people, I enjoy life, I like to give more than I take . . . I'm happy! I have all the reason to be. I got a good family, was brought up with good parents, and my personality and all that comes from my background in church and believin' that all things are possible. I just kind of work with that attitude.

Positive thinker.

Yeah, but that's good!

I think it's very good.

But I'm not a person with a lot of emotions or a lot of feelings. People say, "Don't you ever get depressed?" or whatever. I'm very emotional. I don't make a career out of being depressed. I refuse to waller around in it. But yeah, I get hurt deep. You gotta work at being happy, just like you gotta work at being miserable. Some people are pros at that. But I just choose a different way, I guess.

[*Laughs*] I'm glad you said that. I think that's true. Some people are happy being miserable.

You know, that is true. But I'm not happy being miserable. I hurt bad. I hurt deep. And I cry hard at times. But I get it out and get it over with and get back to better things.

Dolly, I've known you a long time and there is a *mean* streak!

Ralph!

And I'm gonna tell you what I'm talking about. I really think, particularly with reporters who don't know you well, or people who interview you who don't know you well, I really think you would take the occasion to put them on. Is that right?

Well, it would depend on . . . If it was something very serious I wouldn't.

You ever just make up stuff to tell reporters?

I might! [*Laughs*] Why, what have you got in mind?

No, I'm just talking about your personality!

Oh, I will pull your leg in a minute, but not if it was somethin' you were sincerely asking me about. Well, it's possible. I would be a great creative liar.

If you thought the story was whimsical, and if it was the type of story that the answer didn't really matter, I suppose you would take that occasion to put people on, wouldn't you?

I suppose I might. You wanna make something out of it, Ralph? [*Laughs*] Are you callin' me a liar?

No!

Well, at least you did say I was creative with it. But no. I pull people's legs. Yeah, I'm full of bull. But if it's something that matters and if it's something serious, then I give you a very honest answer. Sometimes I like to kid people just to see if they'll know or pick up on it. I usually won't let it go all that far either if I see they really fell for it. I'm always doing it to Johnny Carson. When I do Johnny's show, I'm always tellin' him some rigmarole and he really believes me, like some people do. I just let them fall right into it and then I'll usually let them come out of it.

He likes you.

I like him, too.

If what I seen on television is an example, he looks like he likes you.

Well, we like each other, but, you know, I don't know him except on the panel and when they go into commercials. We talk at the panel. I've never seen him otherwise. People think we're like these long, long friends.

What did he say . . . he'd give a year's pay [to peek under your blouse]?

[*Laughs*] Yeah, that was funny!

Well, shoot! We're just about to the end of our visit with Dolly. Miss Parton. Dolly, how many wigs have you got now?

Oh, the same old cheap ones. I don't really know. I just say that I have 365, one for each day of the year. But I don't know.

I saw you when you were on *The Tonight Show*, talking about your wigs, and you refer to them as these "old cheap wigs."

[*Laughs*] Well, they're a dollar a dozen!

I wondered if people really believe that.

Well, they *are* cheap wigs! I ain't kiddin'. They're like the Eva Gabor and all those wigs like that. The way I wear my hair and the look that I've got used to, I could buy whatever I wanted to as far as wigs are concerned right now, but they ain't as convenient. These are just synthetic wigs and I like 'em. They're handy and they're not expensive. The way I get 'em, they're like thirty dollars a wig. Now that's the honest truth. But when you consider the people that wear expensive wigs, they cost like $1,000 for a hand-done wig. Now, I have a few of them, especially for the movies and stuff, but they still look cheap the way I wear 'em.

Are they all blonde?

Yeah, they're all blonde.

Got any dark wigs?

I got a red one and I got a brown wig, but I don't look good in either one of them.

I remember seeing you on the television show *Dolly* one time in pigtails. How long since you have appeared in public without the wigs?

It's been a long time. It's probably been five years . . . six years . . .

This is part of your image, though, isn't it?

Yeah, and it's handy too. My hair don't hold curl a lot, and to tease it the way that my look is gets to be real damaging, especially since I color my hair. My hair's straight and it just don't hold its curl. That's why I like synthetic wigs because they hold their curl whether it's rain or shine.

Well, Dolly, this is where we have to break it off.

This is where we get off?

Yep.

OK, well . . .

By golly, I really enjoyed being with you.

Well, I enjoyed it, too. I always love you. Still got a crush on you, if that's OK. And I'll see you whenever you can grab ahold of me again.

Well, you're kind of hard to grab ahold of.

Yeah, but if anybody can do it, you can! [*Laughs*]

I mean, not that there ain't a whole lot to grab hold of, it's just that I don't see you that often.

Well, that's true, but I'll see you again. We'll have some good stuff to talk about next time. If you saw me too much, we'd get boring. We might have been anyhow, but we thought we was good, didn't we?

Good luck in Hollywood.

Thank you.

I hope to see you in the movies a lot.

Well, you might. We'll see.

Our show featuring Dolly Parton. And we hope you've enjoyed it, my friends. This is Ralph Emery and we thank you for listening.

Bye!

GOLLY, DOLLY!
(WHAT *WILL* SHE SAY NEXT?)

Cliff Jahr | July 1982 | *Ladies' Home Journal*

Dolly and Burt Reynolds graced the cover of *Ladies' Home Journal* to promote the summer release of *The Best Little Whorehouse in Texas* in 1982. She openly discussed with entertainment writer Cliff Jahr the problems that plagued the production and shared her thoughts on volatile costar Reynolds. Labeling Dolly's an "open marriage," Jahr was one of just a handful of journalists to meet her stealthy husband Carl Dean, who just so happened to be lurking around the *Whorehouse* set.

In addition to her movie troubles, Dolly hinted to Jahr about a more personal kind of despair that would soon send her into the worst depression of her life. Apparently, 1981 had started with what Dolly calls here in *LHJ* "an affair of the heart," not with Burt Reynolds, as the tabloids suggested, but with Gregg Perry, her band leader since the late 1970s. "Gregg and I became very close," she wrote in her autobiography. "I had never spent so much time with such a well-educated and knowledgeable man. . . . I let myself get completely wrapped up in him." At one point, Dolly's attention was so focused on Perry that Judy Ogle excused herself from the entourage. Judy saw herself as the third wheel, became resentful, and soon went back to the military. She eventually returned, of course, and remains Dolly's assistant and constant companion.

When it came time to do the music for *Whorehouse*, Dolly arranged for Perry to join her in the task, but the experience turned out as badly for him and it did her. "It was not a fun project for anybody involved," she wrote in 1994. "Gregg quit altogether. He told me he couldn't take the pressure and the B.S. of the business anymore. The joy had gone out of it for him, and I'm sure that I was no picnic to live with at that time. . . . I was crushed when he left." The two were so close, in fact, that Dolly was inspired to write the passionate "What a Heartache" in response to Perry's departure:

> I thought I'd found a safe and lovin' place inside your heart
> And I was warm and willing anytime
> The same soft lips that kissed me sweet were lyin' from the start
> But I swear I thought your love was genuine.

Dolly rarely speaks of the affair or Gregg Perry anymore, but she described the ordeal quite clearly and concisely to *Vanity Fair* in 1991: "It all involved a personal heartbreak—I'm not gonna call names. But it's plain, ain't it? It was a love." –Ed.

Here is Dolly Parton at her most outspoken. In this revealing interview, she tells you what she thinks of the Moral Majority, Burt Reynolds, and her own open marriage. And she even introduces Carl Dean, her reclusive husband.

Mention her name and people smile. They think of a sunny little woman teetering on high heels, the hourglass figure spilling out of her dress, her pretty face framed in a cloud of wiggy blondness made radiant by a smile that sometimes appears sweet, and sometimes sassy.

Dolly Parton at times resembles Mae West, Daisy Mae, Madame Du Barry, two Marilyn Monroes—and every mistress of ceremonies who ever worked in burlesque. Yet, she is an original, and, to intimate friends, the woman inside is even more complex than her evocative image. This complexity was heightened during the recent filming of *The Best Little Whorehouse in Texas*, in which she co-stars with Burt Reynolds. Making the movie, Dolly claims she faced "more problems, sorrows and enlightenment" than ever before in her life.

Nothing about the making of *Whorehouse*, to be released this month, came easy. Two directors were fired, one set was pulled down and rebuilt and in all the movie took three years to complete. Coming on top of personal problems, the film made for Dolly's roughest year ever. "On the movie, we've gone through so much bitterness," she says, "tension, quarrels, hurt feelings. I threatened to quit so many times. Oh, I don't ever want to work that hard again. Or need to. There is a tiny voice in me that keeps saying, 'This is the last movie that you will ever make.'"

Burt Reynolds was finishing his last two days of work on the film when I arrived. Everyone seemed to heave a sigh of relief as he departed, for Reynolds had grown difficult. America's No. 1 male box-office star was under the gun after three of his movies in a row grossed less than expected—and a fourth looked shaky. But also, he knew what people at the studio were saying—that Dolly's irresistible glow would walk off with the picture. She plays Miss Mona, a brothel madam with a heart of gold. When the role was offered to Dolly, she knew she was *born* to play it. Nonetheless, she accepted only after some prayer and soul-searching because of her concern about the film's frankness.

"I am not trying to glorify prostitution," says Dolly, "but if I do, may God forgive me. Not everyone is so lucky as me to get a chance to *portray* a whore instead of having to *be* one. But I kinda wanted to make a statement with this picture. It points a finger at a lot of people, and some of 'em ain't whores. Like people who get fake religion. It's a shame the title sounds so risqué because certain people in the Moral Majority who should see it may be turned off.

"There are many wonderful people in this world," Dolly continues softly, "but there are many more people who just *think* they're wonderful. In fact, they are self-righteous hypocrites, sinners because they commit crimes like judging thy neighbor. The truly religious forgive. I have been judged a bad woman by some of these people just because I am too open and free and honest.

"Prostitutes, I will tell you, are some of the sweetest, most caring people I've known because they've been through *everything*. I've met them at parties, and I've talked with them. Usually they're people with broken dreams who never had a chance in life or were sexually abused or ignored as children. A lot sell themselves to get some kind of feeling of being loved. The movie will show these women have feelings. You're gonna cry your eyes out."

Dolly's own story would make quite a movie as well. A former country music queen, she leaped overnight to national attention some five years ago with a hit recording ("Here You Come Again") and with her television appearances with Johnny Carson on *The Tonight Show*.

Then she scored an enormous hit in her first movie, when she outshone her more experienced co-stars, Jane Fonda and Lily Tomlin, in *Nine to Five*. In fact, she was probably the main reason for the movie's immense $120-million gross.

Her origins recall the Appalachian poverty of another country music queen, Loretta Lynn, of *Coal Miner's Daughter* fame. Dolly was born the fourth of twelve children to a poor, proud farmer and his wife who lived in a two-bedroom log cabin that had no electricity. The house was nestled by the Little Pigeon River near the town of Sevierville in the Great Smoky Mountains of Tennessee.

"In a big country family," she says, "you're just brought up by the hair of the head. You do what you got to. I—believe it or not—was a tomboy. I could climb a tree or wrestle or run as fast as any brother. We faced starvation, but Mama and Daddy taught values you don't learn in schoolrooms—God, nature, how to care for other people and for the land, how to trust people and when not to. In a way, I'm still that little stringy-headed girl who ran around barefoot, sores on her legs, fever blisters, no clothes, who dreamed of being someone special someday."

By guitar picking, she discovered early on her talent for music. At age ten, her singing and songwriting led to local television appearances and, by age twelve, to a debut at the *Grand Ole Opry*. And she proudly admits that the way she looks today owes a lot to prostitutes she first saw as a child. "I always liked the look of our hookers back home. Their big hairdos and makeup made them look *more*. When people say that less is more, I say *more* is more. Less is *less*. I go for more."

Therefore, Dolly built overstatement into what she calls her "gimmick," that is, looking trashily sexy on the surface while being sweet, warm and down-to-earth on the inside. "I look one way and am another," she agrees. "It makes for a good combination. I always think of 'her,' the Dolly image, like a ventriloquist does his dummy. I have fun with it. I think, what will I do with *her* this year to surprise people? What'll *she* wear? What'll *she* say?"

Dolly and I have now settled over a fireside dinner in the living room of her Hollywood-hotel bungalow. Painted birds fly across its vaulted ceiling and a jogging trampoline stands sadly in one corner ("I don't even go near it"). This is her "magic suite" where for three years she has written songs, screenplays, poetry and a novel in progress called *Wild-flowers*. Unseen, her husband, Carl Dean, a man of Howard Hughesian shyness, is by himself in the far bedroom wing downing a steak. "The Doralee role in *Nine to Five* was not great," Dolly continues, "but she was fine for Dolly's first role. She could kinda sneak in as a little old fat secretary, cute and lovable and fun. But Miss Mona in *Whorehouse* is the epitome of everything I've tried to create with this image, so I may not have a need for it after the movie comes out. Maybe I'll totally change Dolly's look to surprise people."

She pushes away dinner and begins to tug at her wig. Some of her own blond strands are peeking out. "You know," she sighs, "I'm careful never to get caught up in the Dolly image, other than to develop and protect it, because if you start believing the public persona *is* you, you get frustrated and mixed up. Like, I suppose I am a sex symbol, but that idea is funny to me because I see Dolly as a cartoon. She's fat, wears a wig and so on. Oh, sure, I *feel* sexy, and to some people I come across as *extremely* sexy, but Dolly's as big a joke to me as she is to others."

And few jokes make her laugh harder. Last October she and three friends joined the outrageous costume parade of street people that gathers on Hollywood's Santa Monica Boulevard each Halloween. In the crowd were several women (and men) in Parton look-alike costumes, but none recognized the Real Thing prancing among them, disguised to look like a pregnant hillbilly. "Lordy, was I ugly!" Dolly gasps. "A pillow in my stomach, teeth blacked out, Sores and bruises and chigger bites painted all over. I'd go up to the others and gasp, 'Are you really Dolly Parton?' and they'd holler 'Oh, honey, of *course*! Who else?' And we'd fall down laughing. I thought to myself, 'God, if they only knew who I was and how ugly I can look!'"

She remembers something and grins slyly. "My husband Carl always said to me, 'Angel Cakes, you know why you are just so beautiful to me? It's the way you make yourself more than what you actually are. Because you just lack about a half-a-inch of being ugly as hell.'" Dolly squeals with laughter.

An explosive Reynolds

Clearly, Dolly doesn't take herself or her image too seriously—unlike her co-star, some say. Insiders moan about Burt Reynolds's odd behavior during *Whorehouse*, complaining that he's starting to believe his image—stepping on people, blowing up and making snarling demands. "The difference between Dolly and Burt," chuckles one executive, "is that when Dolly goes home at night and takes off her wig, she knows she's still just Dolly Parton. But when Burt goes home and takes *his* off, he doesn't know *who* he is."

Dolly won't criticize her co-star, though she admits there were "sensitive times when things were said—not meaning to—that brought tears to his or my eyes. He's had a very hard time," she explains. "His broken heart with Sally Field, broken plans, working too hard, all those things can cause him to overreact in a lot of situations, especially being as sensitive as he is. But I do believe that inside him there's a wonderful, wonderful man. And I think we have screen magic."

What they had off-screen was "even sweeter than a love affair," she declares. But there was talk at one point that their relationship was exactly *that* sweet. Burt reportedly spent several nights with Dolly during her Las Vegas debut. She is not talking. "I ain't saying yea or nay," she drawls, holding back a grin, and repeats, "Just sweeter than a love affair."

However, other stories were clearly over-eager tabloid nonsense, such as the report that Burt sneaked Dolly off by private jet for a cozy weekend at his house in Florida. "What they didn't print," Dolly giggles, "is that Burt also brought along Jim Nabors and several cast members."

But Dolly's life recently hasn't been all weekends with handsome Burt. In fact, she has noticed the pattern of a "major turnaround" in her life every seven years. In 1974, for instance, came the wrenching split from Porter Wagoner, the country star who discovered her; and in 1981—the year she turned 35—she says she "suffered more, experienced more and realized more than ever in my entire life.

"My heart was shattered in the beginning of the year, not by a romance, but by an 'affair of the heart.' And it about killed me."

Dolly won't elaborate. "I do have a right to some secret spots," she counters. "Then also last year my throat was bad, I was trying to write, there were lots of family problems, and this came on top of all the movie's putdowns and dragouts and misunderstandings. Suddenly, six months into the year, everything switched, cleared up and turned into a year of enlightenment. It will happen again, I'm sure, in seven years, when I'm forty-two."

It is sometimes surprising to confront the serious side of Dolly Parton. But she *can* be serious. Last September, for example, during a break in filming, she vanished for five days on an odyssey to nowhere in what proved to be for her a religious experience. Accompanied by Judy Ogle, her longtime aide and confidante (they played snare drums in the Sevierville High School band), the two drove the back-roads north in a rented station wagon, finally ending up in the wine country above San Francisco.

"Dolly didn't come along," she winks. "No wig, no makeup—and only three people recognized me because I smiled or talked. That always gives me away. I planned to hike and write songs, but midway we fell into these heavy conversations and I got caught up in a spiritual awakening that was joyful and real. I felt so close to God that I expected to see a revelation. I thought if I could *just* go around that next bend in the road, there's an answer. Oh, I wanted to keep going, and when I had to come back to work, I cried. I learned more things in those five days because it was like before I got to be a star. And I thought, well, I'm not going to miss this anymore by getting caught up living in a mansion. I'm going to fix me a van—a dream machine—and do more of this. I'm also going to buy some property far away from everything where I can write and read. It'll be my Garden of Eden, closer to God."

The mysterious Carl

Seeming somewhat apart from Dolly's ups and downs is her husband of seventeen years, Carl Dean. Dean has become to her fans an intriguing shadow figure, always the mystery man in the other room. He never speaks to reporters, and has been photographed only once, five years ago, when a spy cameraman caught him speeding away in a truck. Yet, the next day, when I am on the set, I am surprised when Dolly sidles up to me and says, "C'mon, you gotta meet Carl."

Nobody much notices the good-looking guy in plaid shirt and buckskin boots who sits nonchalantly on the set, on the whorehouse's front porch. He has big rough hands and soft brown eyes and no one can miss what Dolly must see in him. His fine features and short chestnut hair combine with about six feet three inches of sinewy muscle to project, at age 38, an image of sexy boyishness. His well-lined skin is a result, no doubt, of so many hours working in the sun. He often visits, unrecognized like this, "just to do nothin'," when Dolly is working away from home for long periods, in this case, a nine-week absence. No longer an asphalt contractor, he still "hoists and hauls," especially in the running of their big house near Nashville.

He prefers anonymity because he has "no ambitions in show business. Soon as you pose for 'just one picture,' well, how do you say no to the next?" Shucks, he wasn't upset by the spy photographer. "The guy was just doing his job," laughs Carl, "and I was doing mine."

He's an easy talker, charming and droll, quick to ask your opinions and ready to share his, among them a fondness for certain rock groups, James Michener's *Centennial* ("The greatest book I've ever read") and Mick Jagger ("Now he's something *else* again"). Carl also has an eye for handsome women. As one leggy showgirl sways by, he remarks, "*That* could make a person nervous."

It is clear that he loves "Mama" (meaning Dolly), and vice versa, despite what is often rumored in the tabloids about the "openness" of their marriage. Among friends and associates, they are even open about the openness. Carl doesn't hide his half-serious flirting with showgirls, while Dolly lightly kids about it, even eggs him on. Anyway, she likes to mimic Daisy Mae flirtations with the guys herself—mostly for laughs. After all these years of a two-career marriage they seem a happy example of the adage that the tightest hold on someone is with an open hand.

A new man in Dolly's life

For years the press has printed divorce rumors, most recently in February of this year after Carl did not join her on an Australian Christmas trip. She was accompanied instead by her manager Sandy Gallin, who shares a New York Fifth Avenue apartment with Dolly. Their relationship, while close, is strictly business-platonic, no matter what you may read.

On the Christmas trip, star and manager were shopping for real estate by viewing land from an airplane. Dolly wanted waterfront acreage for a Down Under hideaway, but she was mobbed everywhere by friendly Aussies, and has switched her hideaway plans to Hawaii. In fact, she cut the Australian trip short, due in part to a gynecological problem that required emergency surgery in Los Angeles and an indefinite delay of her appearance in Las Vegas. (She earns that town's top wage, $350,000 a week.)

"Carl 'n' I are *good* friends," explains Dolly. "We have a real special relationship, and they'll have to wait a long, long time for our divorce. We're so totally open and free that whatever happens, happens. Carl was the wittiest boy in school. He's a fool like Steve Martin, yet there's that depth. He's so brilliant and sensitive and good. We've never had a serious argument. Oh, we get a little aggravated like any couple. The hardest time was when we built our house: *Carl, I don't like that faucet. Well, then why don't you do it yourself?*"

She covers her mouth and grimaces. "It makes him fee-urious when I call him Carl. I always call him Daddy and he calls me Mama or Little Kid or Angel Cakes. Sometimes he calls me Dotty to be silly: 'Okay, Li'l Dotty.' Maybe once a year I call him Carl and it seems so cold that it really upsets him. Then he gets back by calling me Dolly, which cuts me to the quick." She waves away the thought.

"Built the way I am, I've always been fascinated with tall, skinny men; no big muscles, no hair on their chest. Carl has the smoothest skin and not an ounce of fat on his body. When we first got married, I always tried to get him into those sexy little see-through, mesh underpants. But he wouldn't wear them. Finally my feelings got hurt, so he put 'em on. By pure coincidence, there's a scene in *Whorehouse* like that. Burt wears boxer shorts, and I go buy him sexy briefs, and he don't want to wear 'em. You can see why I was really good in that scene.

"Carl also buys me sexy underwear, and for some reason, he loves me in hot pants, especially when I lose weight. He'll say, 'Now go put on them hot pants, cuz you probably ain't going to lose any more weight.' I'll say, 'Daddy, I don't think I'll look so *hot* in those hot pants, but okay.'"

Though they may be "Daddy" and "Mama" to each other, the Deans decided against having children, partly because they helped raise so many relations to whom they are known as Aunt Granny and Uncle Pee Paw. They have a big, white-columned plantation house, an exact copy of Tara in *Gone with the Wind*, which stands unseen behind high gates on sixty-five wooded acres. Furnished "real gorgeous" by a top Los Angeles decorator, their work areas are in separate wings, with a decor accent on durability. His rustic den has hardwood floors to repel an outdoorsman's muddy boots, and Dolly's blue and gold music room is finished in washable fabrics because, "When I write songs, I *live* over there, and I want to be able to spill Kool-Aid or Jell-O or peanut butter. It's real plush, though. When you pull the curtains up, they're all puffy. Of course," she adds, "our bedroom belongs to both of us." Preferring privacy, they mostly do their own housework, being thereby free to run naked between hot tub, swimming pool and a small private lake. That's about the extent of Dolly's exercising, though she will briefly fast or occasionally diet to get her weight down. "I look better fat, though, don't you think? Skinny, my face looks too long. I'm just very hefty. People are always telling me to lose weight, but being overweight has certainly never made me less money or hurt my career. And doctors always say I got the best blood they ever seen. Besides, everybody loves a fat girl."

A smile lights up her face. "See, I know I'm not a natural beauty. I got short legs, short hands and a tiny frame, but I like the way I am. I am me. I am real. I am Dolly Rebecca Parton Dean."

DOLLY DIAMOND

On Dollywood

"I have an idea that I've had for years that's beginning to become a reality. There's a place in East Tennessee called Gatlinburg, in the Great Smoky Mountain National Park, which is one of the biggest tourist areas in the United States, and I happened to have been born and raised in that part of the country. And there will be a new park—a new city, actually—called Dollywood USA, and it's like a mountain fantasy, like Disneyland, only it will be in the Smoky Mountains. I would say that within three to five years that it will be a big, big park. We'll have a golf course, I'm gonna have a race track, we'll have all the fantasy things. It's a major dream of mine . . . very similar in nature to Disneyland, only there will be many, many other things: canoeing, horseback ridin', campin' out, and actually, sort of a southern way of life, a combination of all the wonderful things of this world that people look for."

—To Terry Wogan, March 1983

PART IV
Toast of Dollywood

"A few years back, when I first started seeing the Hollywood sign, I kept thinking how cute it would be if I could change the H to a D and see how long it would take anybody to notice. It just popped into my mind that it would be a good name for a park."

—To Scot Haller, *People*, May 5, 1986

DOLLY'S DAZZLING COMEBACK

Cindy Adams | March 1984 | *Ladies' Home Journal*

In this interview with Cindy Adams, longtime gossip columnist for the *New York Post*, Dolly detailed the health problems that plagued her for nearly two years and explained that she was undergoing a revitalization in terms of health and well being. She also revealed plans to get tattoos to conceal scars from the recent medical procedures. Dolly's body art went unnoticed for many years, but in 1996, Jay Leno spotted one during an interview on *The Tonight Show*. "Is that a tattoo?" he asked, tugging at Dolly's off-the-shoulder getup. "Yeah, I have a little tattoo, but don't start pullin' my clothes down!" she laughed. "That's an angel, as a matter of fact. I have a little butterfly and a little angel. My guardian angel."

Comedian Rosanne Barr revealed on the *Late Late Show with Craig Ferguson* in 2011 that she'd seen Dolly's tattoos with her own eyes. "She's got all these awesome tattoos all over her body," she explained. "No black or no blue lines. All pastel. Gorgeous bows all over everything." The Leno discovery, Barr's comments, and some odd press photos led to rumors that Dolly might be covered in "secret tattoos" under her clothing. "Do you have tattoos?" Anderson Cooper asked her in 2012. "I might," Dolly responded. "But I'm not going to show 'em 'til they catch me at it."

Two years later, Savannah Guthrie of *The TODAY Show* asked her the same question. Dolly laughed and said she heard a story that she always wore sleeves because her arms were covered with snake tattoos. That wasn't true, she told Guthrie. "I do have a few little tattoos, but they were mostly done to cover scars because I'm so fair. I do have a few but they're not where you can see them . . . they are mostly for my husband." —Ed.

Move over Jane Fonda. Now that she's recovered from her recent illnesses, Dolly Parton is fitter—and slimmer—than ever. And she's ready to share her own very special health regimen with the rest of the country.

"The day I knew I was going for surgery, I recall thinking, 'Well, if I come out of this okay, I'm really going to get myself together. If He gives me another chance, I'm going to make sure I give myself another chance. I will shape up, and I will wise up.'"

It's been three long years for Dolly Parton, but she has conquered the illnesses that plagued her and has earned her second chance. Newly slimmed down, she is wearing skintight white cord pants and a red scoop-neck sweater (size small), which show off her recent weight loss, and she looks vibrant. But the health that she now finds so precious was not easy to regain. The last few years are a chronicle of missed performances and hospital visits, brought on by bleeding ulcers, gynecological problems and a digestive system totally out of whack.

"I went to the very bottom as far as my emotions and my health are concerned," admits Dolly, as she talks for the first time about her illness and her recovery. "See, I was thirty-five when I first got sick. And I was getting away with murder. I wasn't watching what I ate, wasn't conscious of nutrition, wasn't taking care of myself. I was working hard, and underneath I was a pile of personal and emotional problems.

"All at once I fell apart. It was stomach problems and female problems—allover health problems actually. It was God's way of telling me to get myself straight . . . I'm grateful it happened when I was still young enough to bounce back."

Caught in a downward spiral, Dolly believes she actually pushed herself to the bottom. It happened when she was making *The Best Little Whorehouse in Texas* and was feeling pretty shaky emotionally. "I had problems, and they just got me off the track. Some of it was brought on by work. *Best Little Whorehouse* near killed me. That was a tough picture to do. There was constant bickering, and I tried to please everyone. *Whorehouse* was a bloodbath.

"Then some members of my family were suffering with their own illnesses. They depended on me to make decisions. I'm always the one who's up, the one who carries the ball. They came to me in time of need. But I was in need myself. It was bad timing.

"I was also having some heartache about the people around me—some shaky experiences with people I'd been in partnership with for a long time and dearly loved. That's what really knocked me over. As those personal relationships deteriorated, so did I."

How much these disappointments contributed to her ill health, Dolly doesn't know. But her frame of mind certainly kept her from taking proper care of herself. "I was taking medications for all kinds of things," she explains. "I took one bunch for nerves. For my gynecological problems I took pills and hormones and Provera. That stuff makes you retain fluids, and I was bloating up. For my stomach, I had another variety of medications plus antibiotics for the infections.

"I got sicker and sicker. I canceled shows. Having to disappoint promoters who'd been good to me through the years added to everything else. They got mad and sued me, which caused me to get sicker. I became more tense. My stomach tightened, and my throat dried up. The hoarseness was nerves. That's where it just hit me and gripped me. Problems always get you in your weakest point. Then, the cortisone I had to take for my throat made me blow up even more."

On top of all her other problems, Dolly admits she was overeating. Although she confesses, "I'm a natural-born hog . . . I also eat when I'm happy," the protracted illness added more pounds on an already overloaded five-foot frame. "See, I'd always had this eating problem. I'd gain twenty pounds, lose it, gain it back the next week. In ten days, I'd put on ten pounds. On top of being sick and being medicated, Dietin' Dolly would go on liquid protein, Scarsdale, Atkins, the water diet; then I'd binge, diet, gain, start all over again. Eventually my system wouldn't work anymore. My body couldn't hold up under that strain.

"My doctors would tell me, 'Okay, you have about twenty pounds to lose, but you can do that easily. Just eat right." Well, that's easy to say. I just love those beautiful people who tell you, 'I *cahn't* see how anybody could let themselves get in that awful shape. Oh, my dear. That's gross,'" says Dolly, aping a fancy society voice. "Hell, that's ridiculous. Overeatin' is as much a sickness as drugs or alcoholism. But you don't have to drink to live. You can stop drinking alcohol. You can stop all your habits. But you cannot stop eating. You have to eat to live."

The lowest point during this dismal period in Dolly's life came at an open-air concert in Indianapolis, where she very nearly collapsed. Warned by doctors not to perform (she had begun hemorrhaging a week before), she had nonetheless gone onstage in the driving rain. But after the concert, it was clear that she needed medical help fast. The remaining thirty stops of her thirty-five-stop tour were canceled, and Dolly immediately flew to New York for surgery.

"When I was going under the knife, I didn't know what they would have to do. But I didn't need a hysterectomy. I'm grateful I'm still left with most of my parts."

Looking back, Dolly says, "A lot of my physical problems stemmed from my emotional ones. I felt the good Lord would give me strength to let my body eventually heal itself and that I'd be okay if I could get that positive attitude going, get my mind straight, draw from the energy God has given me. Some doctors were saying we should just go ahead and take this out . . . take that out . . . and I said no. I can now understand why people commit suicide or become drug addicts. I mean, if I had to spend my life in bed, become an invalid . . ."

It wasn't that she was frightened of death, Dolly insists. As the grandchild of a [Pentecostal] preacher, she has "a close companionship with the Lord," is a student of the Bible and devours spiritual treatises. "I'm not afraid of death," she insists. "Lots of people are afraid that what's beyond is something weird, full of spaceships or whatever. Not me. I can't wait to see what's on the other side. I figure it must be something even greater."

Today, up close, Dolly is a knockout. Facing me in the suite of a New York hotel, she is bursting with vitality—fresh from working on a new movie, *Rhinestone*, with Sylvester Stallone, and on a new album, *The Great Pretender*. She is professionally happy and looks buoyant. Her skin is flawless; her waist is twenty-one inches going for twenty (in her salad days it was eighteen), and when we order lunch (hers is soup), it's clear that she is committed to a new and disciplined approach to eating.

The revitalization of Dolly Parton began the day she woke up in the recovery room. And an important part of it is attitude. At last ready to "shape up and wise up," she began to formulate a whole new lifestyle— new patterns and habits that would work for her and her personality. Put simply, the plan is: Eat less. Eat better-quality food. Be conscious of nutrition. Eat slower. Chew each mouthful longer. *Think* about it.

"Before, I consumed steak, potato, salad and dessert purely because it always went together. Today, I try to *think* what I'm hungry for. I'll sit and look at it and think about the flavors. I'll think, 'I'm really craving steak sauce. And potato. I don't really want meat or salad." So I'll put steak sauce on the potato and eat that. I call it 'The Individual Awareness Method.' If what I really want is dessert, I'll tell the waiter, 'I'm dieting and would like to take this food home and eat it for lunch,' which is my big meal. Then I'll order chocolate mousse while the others eat dinner. While they're on dessert I'll have black Sanka. It used to be coffee with cream and sugar."

Lest anyone think the old, fat Dolly, who loves the very smell of food, who still loves french fries, popcorn, peanuts and McDonald's, is gone forever—forget it. She lives inside the new, thin Dolly. She's always struggling to get out. "I cannot deprive myself of what I like," she says. "I just try to calm myself down. If it's junk food, I'll still eat it. I try not to go off my diet too often, but I can't live on fruit and vegetables. Hell, I gotta have gooey stuff, gotta go crazy occasionally with ice cream and candy bars.

"Suppose I want Mexican food. I'll order a tableful. But I'll pick. And by taking little bits of five, six things, I won't make anybody with me feel bad. They'll see I'm busy; there's stuff on my plate. On those old diets I'd be eating nothing while everyone else would be tasting everything, and I'd feel sorry for myself, so I'd fall off.

"I don't even *want* to eat so much anymore. I'm not hungry. I could be if I thought about it, but I already know what it's like to eat every bit. I've been there. So I've changed my *attitude* toward food.

"People make excuses. They say, 'I can't diet because I have to cook for my family, and they like pasta and potatoes.' Lord, I'm a cookin' fool. Carl, too. He's so into food that when I get home he's thought up something new. These days he don't put a lot on my plate. He leaves it on the stove and says, 'If you want more, then just you get up and get it.'"

Outdoorsy Carl, who's in the construction business, stands six-three, weighs 165, looks "like a model," eats everything and never gains an ounce. Carl loves his woman fat, thin, any way. "He doesn't care if I'm fat. He was never turned off. He's fool enough to think I'm the sexiest, prettiest woman in the world."

With her strength and stamina increasing, Dolly plans to jump into the next phase of her health program: serious exercising. As she tailored a food program to suit her, so she intends to personalize an exercise regimen.

Bodybuilder Michael Romanelli, who builds some of Hollywood's best-looking bodies, gave Dolly two weeks of private classes at home. Designed to decrease weight, increase firmness and—as he put it—"tighten her hips and bum," they were general overall exercises: warm-ups, toe touches, side twists, knee-bends, thrusts, bouncing in place. From the all-fours position, it was leg-scissors, knee-raises. Lying flat, there were abdominals, like bicycles and elbows-to-knees. His new client, avowedly nonathletic, had never worked out, so sessions began with twenty minutes of stretching.

Dolly admits: "I hate doing anything physical. I don't even walk much. I'm short, so I wear high heels, and I won't put on tennis shoes, because we all have our complexes. And I can't do those Jane Fonda things. They're too hard for me.

"Whether it's thighs or whatever, I'm trying to figure out my problem areas and think up fun things such as yoga, dancing and karate. With this Individual Awareness Method, I'll create routines that fit *me*. I'll even design new equipment as it becomes necessary. I plan to work really hard.

"I'm starting to work out with weights. Look, I have a three-month basic-training plan in mind. I'm checking with doctors about vitamins. I'm working with bodybuilders because I don't want to pull muscles or hurt my legs or screw up anything. Sly Stallone says you have to work with professionals. I'm meeting with nutritionists about what foods go together, what I should and shouldn't eat, what are the proper nutritional balances."

Dolly also has big plans for turning her hundred-acre Nashville farm—called Tara—into a training ground. "I'm going to make my place like a military camp where there's no choice. You *have* to learn. After I determine how long it takes to put a body into shape, I'll organize a follow-up maintenance program.

"If this works for me, I'm going to set up Dolly Parton Basic Training Centers around the country. People who live in the area can go there from nine to five. My centers will teach the spiritual part of fitness, including meditation. The method will be mind-body-soul discipline.

"Then I'm putting this entire thing into book form along with my whole mental and spiritual attitude. See, I sympathize with folks who have a bad weight problem. There has to be something done to help all people like me.

"And when I'm into this three-month basic training project fully for myself, I'm taking off the false nails, the wigs, the shoes. I'm cuttin' my hair. I'll get this short little body hammered into shape. If it means mountain-climbing, then I'll mountain-climb. I'm really going to do it."

Her goal is 40-20-36, and she's within a hot-fudge sundae of it. And suppose she loses too much and notices sags or bags? Practical Parton says, "I don't mind to say I'll get a face-lift."

And suppose, just suppose, with the loss of poundage evenly distributed that maybe, just maybe, her bosom might need a little lift? "Well, I'll think about that, too, although I don't think so . . . but maybe."

Dolly already has plans for a first bit of cosmetic "surgery." "I have keloid scars from my operation, and the doctors can't do anything about it . . ." Dolly's face suddenly lights up in a pixieish smile, "So I'm going to get tattooed right over my stomach incision. I don't mean mermaids. I mean, from the left side of my navel down, I'll make what looks like a tiny ribbon of eyelet lace in very light colors.

"I'll make it baby pink. Baby lavender. With faint, tiny roses. I'll make a sweet, delicate bow with what looks to be a little end that falls over like a piece of string. Like a little streamer. With the big scar down the front of my abdomen, I'm going to tattoo cross-stitches from one side to another. Like a bodice. It'll be very delicate. All the bows and ribbons will be matching. Isn't that precious? I sketched my design and already had a consultation with someone in New York who's going to do it for me . . . my doctor can't wait to see my tattoos."

And how does husband Carl feel about it? "He's proud of me. He trusts my judgment. He's just happy to see me looking good. He told me the other day, 'I haven't seen you looking so terrific since we got married.'"

As our afternoon winds to a close, Dolly straightens up, perches on her chair a moment and grows reflective. She's come a long way and she knows it. "I can never allow that evil to get hold of me, never again let the bad overtake the good. I believe I have a mission in life. If I am a shining light and people look up to me, I'm very humble and grateful God has let me be a vehicle. It's a big responsibility."

Does she feel secure that there won't be any giving in to depression again? "Oh, I'll get into moods, Depression is part of life. If you *never* get depressed, you're never ever getting down deep enough to think about things. Nobody's up all the time unless they're liars, phonies, hypocrites, or unless something in their brain ain't working.

"But I won't stay depressed. I won't allow myself to be depressed more than three days in a row. When it happens, I say, 'Now, look here, you just set down with a piece of paper and write down all the good things you have to be grateful for.

"'*Then*, you get your butt up and get the hell out of here. Fix yourself up. Talk to someone. Better still, do something nice for someone else.'"

DOLLY PARTON

Maura Moynihan and Andy Warhol | July 1984 | *Interview*

Dolly met iconic pop artist Andy Warhol in May 1977 after one of her shows at the Bottom Line in Greenwich Village. "We used to go to Studio 54 together many years ago," she told *Interview* in 2001. "He was the only person I've ever met who's weirder than me, that dressed worse and looked stranger—and didn't care: just like me. I would always ask him: 'What do you look like under that wig?' and he'd reply: 'What do you look like under that one?' I'd say: 'Well you'll never know,' and he'd say: 'Well you'll never know either.'"

Sandy Gallin once commissioned Warhol to create a series of five paintings of Dolly to hang over his mantel at home. He wasn't pleased with the finished product, though. Apparently it wasn't Warholian enough. "They'd thought it would be more colorful, more Pop," Warhol remarked in his diaries. In 1985, he phoned Gallin after not hearing from him about the finished portraits. "The secretary got on and said, 'Ohhh, Sandy's soooo embarrassed' and saying that it just doesn't look like my art."

In her autobiography, Dolly recalled the Warhol episode as one of her most awkward and embarrassing incidents. "We had expected them to look something like the ones of Marilyn Monroe, but these were in a different style and looked harsh and severe. These looked more like Bill Monroe! Sandy didn't want the paintings. More important, he didn't want to pay for them. Sandy is cheap. Sandy thought that Andy Warhol would be more sympathetic to me, so he sent me to try to finagle a way out of paying for them. I hate that kind of thing. I would rather shoot myself in the foot than confront somebody over a thing like that. I didn't know what to do, so I finally just said to Mr. Warhol, 'Look, Sandy's too cheap to pay for these pictures and they're not exactly what he had in mind. So could you take them back?' He did. The laugh was on Sandy. After Warhol died [in 1987], each one of the five paintings sold for many times what Sandy would have paid for them. He would have made a million dollars on them if he had kept them."

This cover feature for Warhol's *Interview* magazine was timed to coincide with the premiere of Dolly's next film, *Rhinestone*, costarring Sylvester Stallone. —Ed.

The life story, like the woman herself, is almost too extraordinary to be true. The fourth of twelve children raised in the Smoky Mountains of Tennessee, Dolly began composing songs at the age of seven, singing on radio three years later and—by twelve—performing at the Grand Ole Opry. The first person in her family to graduate from high school, she hightailed it to Nashville the day she received her diploma, and in 1967, joined Porter Wagoner's television variety show. Firmly established as a country and western star, Dolly was earning $60,000 a year at 21, and rising fast.

Breaking away from Wagoner, she formed "The Travelin' Band" with some of her kin, but the enterprise was a failure. Dissolving the group, Dolly hired a manager and another band—this time, professional musicians—and headed full stream into her solo career.

The C&W world welcomed its newest and most outrageous star without hesitation, and her albums were big news—here and across the Atlantic: "Heartbreaker," "Here You Come Again," "9 to 5." The latter was the theme for Dolly's movie debut with Jane Fonda and Lily Tomlin, and earned her an Oscar nomination for Best Song. "I'm not leaving the country, I'm just taking it with me," Dolly said to the Tennessee eyebrow raisers, and continued on her way.

Her second film outing, co-starring with Burt Reynolds in "The Best Little Whorehouse in Texas," wasn't such a happy one. Though she escaped from the turkey unscathed by the critics, the grueling films schedule as well as a personal anxiety brought on a serious illness which kept her bedridden for 18 months.

Bouncing back last year, Dolly tackled her biggest acting job yet with "Rhinestone," a project she developed for herself and co-star Sylvester Stallone (who gets in a country number or two). Concurrently working on other movie projects, books, albums and a television special with Kenny Rogers, Dolly remains driven by success. "I'm still not the star I'm going to be," she says with characteristic candor.

Be that as it may, the woman is a phenomenon. Her theatrical appearance and inflated style have excited public interest from the beginning, and the press has showered as much attention on her platinum wigs and staggering proportions as it has on her music. In the flesh, she stands a mere five feet tall, and the effect of her golden white wig and vermilion nails and lips—combined with irrepressible wit—is an unusual kind of beauty; effervescent as champagne. Dolly visited our Union Square office and joined Andy Warhol and Maura Moynihan for lunch on St. Patrick's Day, looking trim and squeezable in white jeans, a red sweater and slick red boots with perilously high heels.

ANDY WARHOL: Where is Maura? Maybe she got caught in the parade.

DOLLY PARTON: Maybe she got hooked up with a horny leprechaun somewhere, dressed in green with no pants on.

WARHOL: Do you want some lunch?

PARTON: I'd love a glass of white wine.

WARHOL: How did you like working with Sylvester Stallone?

PARTON: I think he's beautiful. I'd never seen him in person before I started on *Rhinestone*. I was surprised when I first saw him because I thought he would be gigantic. When I had my surgery I decided I had to get myself in better shape, eat better, because I just turned 38. I lost all of my weight before I even met Sly. He's a great inspiration to be around, though. He was more than happy to help me. I loved working with him, he's a great person.

WARHOL: (*doorbell rings*) Oh, maybe that's the magic person. Oh there she is. You're late, Maura.

MAURA MOYNIHAN: Hi, it's nice to meet you.

PARTON: You're Irish and we forgive you.

MOYNIHAN: You look wonderful. When did you finish *Rhinestone*?

PARTON: We finished filming about three and a half weeks ago. I'm the musical supervisor. I'm still working because I wrote all the music, and so I'll be working with it till it comes out June 22nd. I had the best time doing the movie.

MOYNIHAN: *Whorehouse* wasn't as fun?

PARTON: Well, *Whorehouse* was *not* fun. I loved Burt Reynolds and Jim Nabors and all those people, but at that particular time I was ill, and coming from a Broadway play, we already had everything against us.

MOYNIHAN: You got great reviews.

PARTON: I was happy with the success of it; it was just a hard one to do.

MOYNIHAN: How many wigs do you have?

PARTON: I don't know, I've got better things to do than count them. But I wear one every day of the week, so probably 365.

MOYNIHAN: You have all these different ones so you can completely change your hairstyle any time you please.

WARHOL: How long were you sick?

PARTON: I'd never really been sick in my life until a couple of years ago, and then I was sick for 18 months to two years. It was brought on by a lot of emotional problems that I was having. I had to make a lot of decisions with a lot of people I had been with for years and years, and we were not helping each other emotionally. We did great business together, but it was just very hard. I just had to shuffle a lot of things around in my life and make some decisions that were very painful, and I'm a very sensitive person.

MOYNIHAN: Did you have to fire some people?

PARTON: Yes, but I've always done my own hiring and firing. But in this particular case, I was going through a lot of problems with family and stuff.

MOYNIHAN: With [your husband] Carl?

PARTON: No, me and Carl are fine. We have no problems at all. We've been together for 20 years, and we've been married for 18. First time for him and first time for me.

MOYNIHAN: How did you meet?

PARTON: I met him the first day I got to Nashville, in 1964. I graduated on a Friday night, went to Nashville on a Saturday morning with dirty clothes and I went to a Laundromat looking for *anything* but love. I had just left two boyfriends back home and I wasn't looking to get involved because I had gone to Nashville to really get started in the business. I met him at the W[is]hy Washy and he's been wishy washy ever since. We dated for two years before we got married. I often get myself in love trouble because I'm so passionate; I love so much and so deep. But Carl's a special guy, I didn't have any problems with him.

MOYNIHAN: Do you get lonely on the road?

PARTON: Yes, but I can fix that shit. Though it causes me trouble. At the time I was making some decisions, making myself go way, way back to muddy waters. When you spend your whole life working . . . In fact, out of this came a book I'm writing called *Life After Success*. To me, that's when you should be the happiest. I had to make some decisions that I needed to make for years, but I kept holding on because I loved these people so much, a person in particular, but we were just destroying each other emotionally because we loved each other so much.

MOYNIHAN: Was this a personal affair and somebody you were working with?

PARTON: Yes, it was a personal business affair. It was just very painful. I have a tendency to be awfully big-hearted and it's very hard for me to say no, even when I need to. I can handle the business—the bigger they are the better I like dealing with them—but when it gets into business where I'm very attached to the people, it's hard. I was going through a period of time that the nerves and the tension and the stress were actually what got me sick. So then it was like, which came first, the chicken or the egg? I just kept getting worse and worse and then I started having stomach problems, ulcers and intestinal problems. But it was the best thing that ever happened to me. It made me really smart. When I was flat on my back I realized that I could never retire, that I hated it, that I would never get myself in that place again.

WARHOL: You could be a great preacher.

PARTON: What do you mean? I *am* a great preacher.

MOYNIHAN: Your grandfather was a preacher.

PARTON: Yes, he was with the Church of God.

MOYNIHAN: Do you go to church regularly?

PARTON: No, I don't.

MOYNIHAN: Do you pray?

PARTON: Yes, all the time. As a child I was scared to death of hellfire and brimstone, but I loved to sing. Out of that I started to remember the things that really stuck in my mind, and I think that's followed me through the years, things like "Through God, all things are possible." I just remember the positive. I just thought, "I can't deal with this shit. There cannot be a God that is that mean and cruel, and if there is then I'm too afraid to deal with Him anyway." So I had to decide who I was, and what God meant to me. I feel that sin and evil are the negative part of you, and I think it's like a battery: you've got to have the negative and the positive in order to be a complete person. I used to punish myself a lot for things I felt, and then I'd just say, "Well, if it's wrong for me to feel this why do I feel it?" I used to have a lot of problems with all the stuff I felt. [*The following section is slightly edited from the original due to a misinterpretation in that piece in the process of going from tape to print. —Ed.*] One of the songs in *Rhinestone* ["God Won't Get You"] has the line, "'Torn Between Two Lovers' on the jukebox . . . I'm thinking how I could have wrote that song." See, to me it's how *you* deal with it yourself.

MOYNIHAN: Do you work out?

PARTON: Not much, but I do, some.

WARHOL: What did you stop eating?

PARTON: It's not *what* I stopped eating as much as *how* I stopped eating. I was always just a hog, I still am. I'm short and I have a big appetite. I can't do nothing *just a little*. It's the same with anything I do. It's very hard for me to love a little, have sex a little, to eat a little. I like to do everything, and I like to do it all the way that I want to do it. I was always a junk food person, still am. I didn't stop anything. I just try to eat less and I try to think of my diet now like a job, five days a week. I try to eat fish and vegetables, things that are better for me, but on the weekends . . . If I get crazy, if it's three pizzas I want, that's what I'll go out and eat. I gained a lot of weight when I was sick. I was taking a lot of hormones for female problems I was having. I'm only five feet tall.

MOYNIHAN: You don't look it.

PARTON: I walk tall, I got a tall attitude. But I'm just a little bitty person. When people see me in airports they stop me and say, "Gee, I thought you were a big person." When I was doing "Whorehouse" was when I got so sick. It was right after that diet that I gained so much more back. That was my second film, and it was so close to my personality as far as me getting to say what I wanted to say, dress the way that I like to dress, that I was real comfortable in the part. Like *9 to 5*, I always joke about playing a secretary. That was good, but that was not really my true nature.

WARHOL: You were great in that.

PARTON: I make a better whore than a secretary.

WARHOL: No. You made *9 to 5* a big hit.

PARTON: That was a special thing. I was real proud of that. I'd never even seen a movie made when I walked into that one. I always laugh at myself. I learned everybody's part, which was great because I didn't have to study at night. It's easy for me to memorize because I write. I knew that script back and forth in two weeks.

MOYNIHAN: Does acting come naturally to you?

PARTON: If it's acting that I do, it does. I don't think I'm a great actress. I think I can act or I can *react*. Coming from a musical background and being a dramatic singer and writer, when I write stuff I *really* feel it. So I sing it like it comes from *here*. That's how I do the acting. I've done three movies now and I think I could do some good acting. I think I did some good things in *Rhinestone*, but I think now I could do a dramatic part, something real serious where I'm not a comedian or a country singer.

MOYNIHAN: What are your favorite movies?

PARTON: My favorite movies of all times is *Doctor Zhivago*, and I love *Gone With the Wind*. I'd love to play some Southern belle or something where I owned a plantation.

MOYNIHAN: Isn't your Tennessee farm called Tara?

PARTON: No, I don't know how that ever got started. They say that in all the magazines, but we don't call it anything. It's just a big old house with 23 rooms that we're about to sell. We built it, but it's just too big for us. Back when I had the kids, my brothers and sisters, it made more sense, but it's just too much for us now. It's got 65 acres and me and Carl are both at the age where we don't want to be tied down to it, so we're going to find a smaller place in Nashville. We just bought a house in Hawaii where we'll spend a lot of time now. We don't have kids, and we're free, and he's independent as he can be. We don't like to be together *all* the time. Nobody likes somebody to be stuck in their face all the time—that's why we get along so good, because when we are together we have a good time.

MOYNIHAN: Did you have a happy childhood?

PARTON: I think I did. At that time I wanted more. I lived in fairy tales and storybooks, and I knew that we were missing a lot that I saw in books, but we were real happy. You see, Mom and Dad stayed together. We had our problems. Daddy, he often ran around and he had some children outside of us, but he was a good father and a good husband. He always came home. He was just a little wild, and I can certainly understand that, because I'm a combination of both of them. But he always loved Mama and always treated us good. It was hard times. Mama was sick a lot and there were a lot of depressing times. What was good about it was we lived out in the country. We were very close to nature and free to grow up the way we did. We didn't have cars to get hit by, we didn't have neighbors to get raped by, we just lived way out in the woods. We lived close to God and close to nature. I think coming out of that gate gave us a real good solid foundation, a good wholesome attitude.

WARHOL: Did you ever think of leaving?

PARTON: Yes, I did. I was probably a real pain in the ass when I was little because I had such dreams. And I needed a lot of attention that I didn't get. My folks loved us, they loved us all the same, but I had a sister and two brothers older than me. My older sister, of course, being the first, was more responsible and got more attention. My older brothers, being boys were just stronger and bigger, and me, I was born in an odd spot and was a very sensitive kid. My feelings could get hurt so easily because I always wanted to be loved, I wanted to be touched, I wanted to touch somebody. I wanted everybody to love me, so I think I was louder than I should have been. I was just trying to get attention. I always felt like I was somebody special, maybe it's because I *needed* to be somebody special. I just always knew I was going to be a star. I was always going to be rich so I could buy things for Mommy and Daddy, so that I could buy them a big house and we could have things.

MOYNIHAN: Did you have a lot of confidence?

PARTON: Oh yes, I'd sing for anybody.

MOYNIHAN: Do you still have a lot of confidence?

PARTON: Yes. You couldn't scare me as a kid because we lived hard and we worked the fields. We were strong little kids. I was always a tomboy. And I can't even believe now that I'm so fragile, so to speak. I have little short hands so I like long nails, and I'm short so I like high heels. I never could get my hair to do what I wanted it to do, so I started wearing the wigs. It all came from a very serious place. I wanted to look a certain way.

MOYNIHAN: How did you survive when you first went to Nashville?

PARTON: Real well, although I didn't have a radio, or car, or friend, or phone. When I first moved to Nashville I stayed with my Uncle Bill. He was the one who saw so much in me. I'd beg anybody to take me around, take me to sing. I was first on the radio when I was ten years old on a local station in Knoxville. I was scared to death, but my desire to do it was greater than my fear. I didn't even know what the hell I was doing. I didn't even know what a microphone was. I just played my guitar and sang the songs I wrote. Then when the crowd loved me, that gave me that confidence that I was always going to need. I know now it wasn't because I was good, it was just because I had the nerve to do it.

MOYNIHAN: What do you want to do now?

PARTON: I just want to be free to work. I want to think, I want to write better songs, I want to write different styles of music; I want to write Broadway plays, which I am; I want to write books, which I will. I'm going to write a lot of positive thinking books. I'm writing a book now called *I Am*, which is an individual awareness method.

MOYNIHAN: I read somewhere that you were going to set up awareness centers around the country.

PARTON: Yes, and I will do that. People need help and I can help.

MOYNIHAN: Do you think pop stars are like spiritual vehicles for a lot of people?

PARTON: Being brought up very religious, I have a fear of people that look to idol gods. But we are idols and we're all gods, so to speak, and I think that celebrities should acknowledge their responsibility, because we are in a position to help. That's why it hurts me so bad to see what happened to people like Elvis. So many people need you so much. Just look at people like Jim Jones. See, you have to be responsible. I understand how people can commit suicide, how people can get on drugs and alcohol. It would be wrong of me to try and give anybody advice, and I won't do it unless people ask. I love everybody, and I go right through the bullshit and I go right to the core of every person because we are all one, we are all the same. A lot of people say to me, "There are so few worthwhile people in the world," and I say "That's the biggest crock of shit I ever heard." I don't ever meet a freak. The biggest freaks in the world for me are my favorite people, like *you*, like *me*.

MOYNIHAN: Do you think you could ever lose your following or fans?

PARTON: I think about it, but I don't worry about it. I think this could all end tomorrow. That's all the more reason that I'm grateful, but I would be a star wherever I was. Being a star just means that you just find your own special place and that you shine where you are. To me that's what being a star means. It's just that I wanted to be a bigger star, I wanted to do bigger and greater things. If I was a waitress I'd be Flo. I would own my own club. If I was a barmaid I'd be Miss Kitty. I would tell the worst jokes, I would make everybody happy, I would loan everybody money, I would have a good time. If I worked in a factory I'd be the one making cookies for everybody at Christmas. I would always make a living. I don't have children, and I've done the best I can by my people.

WARHOL: Why didn't you have children?

PARTON: I couldn't have children, I tried to for years. I've never been pregnant in my life. When I was a girl and fooling around I was scared to death I'd get pregnant, and then when I got married and wanted to have children I couldn't have any. But I don't miss it. I did for a while, but I realize that I am everybody's mother. I've raised five of my younger brothers and sisters and now their kids call me Aunt Grannie. I'm like the grandma and the aunt.

MOYNIHAN: Where do you go in New York?

PARTON: Everywhere. I go to eat, I go to the clubs, I love to get out and have fun. I'll never let myself get trapped. I think that one of the bad things that stars do, that deprives them of a real life of their very own, is they won't get out. They're scared to death somebody is going to kill them, to kidnap them. I think you have to be aware and alert, that's only smart, but I think when you close yourself off . . . When I was sick those 18 months I got to where I didn't want to go out because I didn't feel like I looked great, but then I thought, I've got to stop this because I love people. I want to be out there. I'd rather take a chance. If they couldn't protect the president of the U.S. and the great leaders of the world that have been shot and killed, how do I think they're going to protect me.

MOYNIHAN: Do you carry a gun?

PARTON: I do, because I'm a mountain person. We grew up in the mountains where you just have guns around. If an animal comes up to your porch at night or the kids are out in the yard and you've got to kill a snake . . . So guns were not foreign to me, and being a young woman in the world by myself I know how to shoot one and I know how to handle it. It's not that I'm really into weapons, it's mostly just for protection. But then the press made such a to-do that I really don't say anymore whether I do or don't. I just say, don't mess with me.

MOYNIHAN: What do you do for yourself, for your own pleasure?

PARTON: I go out with friends. I love to dance, I love to laugh a lot, I love to go to parties, I love to camp out. My husband and I love to travel by car, we love to go for two or three weeks. We went to Yellowstone Park once and stayed two weeks. We had a great time. We camp out and I unravel all the wigs, and the high heels and the makeup.

MOYNIHAN: Would you ever appear in public without your wig?

PARTON: No, not in public. Well, I might without my wigs, but not without being dressed up, because people expect it of me as much as I expect it of myself. Anybody can be tacky. In fact, I've often thought that some spring, in some great magazine, that I might do a layout on the new spring fashions and not wear the wigs. I'm not a bad-looking person and I've got fairly good features. I have baby-fine hair, but I have plenty of it.

MOYNIHAN: Do you spend a lot of money on clothes?

PARTON: Well, yes, but they're not expensive clothes. I spend a lot of money on cheap clothes. I don't go buy just one or two things. I can thank the Lord I can do whatever I want. I wear the same things over and over and over. I look a certain way and I like it because I'm comfortable with it. I was impressed with kings and queens and velvet and jewelry when I was young. When I was a freshman in high school hair teasing came out. I'd already bleached my hair and got in big trouble. I have blonde hair, but it just wasn't radiant, it's sandy blonde. It wasn't yellow and white and bright. When teasing came out I just thought I had died and gone to heaven. Being creative with my hands, I started teasing. I fixed everybody's hair. I had the biggest hair in school. I had lots of teachers that had a hard time dealing with me because I felt sexy.

WARHOL: You have the smallest waistline.

PARTON: That was always one of my best assets. I loved wearing tight things around the waist. My dad used to think I was making myself sick because he thought I was pulling myself that tight. I had a real pretty body when I was a girl, though it's kind of gone downhill since then. When I went to Nashville they liked my personality, and I never sold myself out. I never went to bed with anybody unless I wanted to, never for business reasons.

MOYNIHAN: Is the country music business hard for a woman to break into?

PARTON: Back then it was. I don't think it is now. I think anybody who can sell records for any businessman or any company—if you got something special they'll grab you. I don't think it makes any difference whether you're male, female, gay, Boy George or whatever. I don't think it matters any more, business is that open. The first record I made was when I was ten-and-a-half, eleven years old. The first record I ever made . . . was on Gold Band Records, and it was called "Puppy Love." On the back was this real tender love song, me ten years old singing, "I'm a girl left alone, there's no hope for me." It was a song that me and my uncle had wrote.

WARHOL: Did you have the same kind of voice you have now?

PARTON: It was little and a lot of trill. I've worked hard through the years, but it was always something I loved. I was not a great singer. I'm still not a great singer, but I got a style, I like that part. But anyhow, that was my first encounter.

WARHOL: What happened to the record?

PARTON: Nothing. It played in my hometown and became a collector's item. Gold Band records still sells it; many people have it now.

WARHOL: Did you do a lot of records before that?

PARTON: Well, I did that song on Gold Band when I was ten or eleven, and then I did a record when I was fifteen on Mercury. I was walking down the streets saying, "Look, you got to record me because I'm going to be a star, I'll make us a lot of money." I recorded a song called, "It May Not Kill Me, But It Sure Gonna Hurt." It only got played in my hometown, too. But I had made some other tapes. When I moved to Nashville I got real lucky. I'd already started to record for Monument Records just when I moved to Nashville. I got a contract immediately. Then I recorded "Dumb Blonde," which was like one of the top ten country records. So that was my first big chart record. Then came a song called "There's Something Fishy Goin' On." That was when I was still on my own. Then I started working with the Porter Wagoner Show in 1967.

MOYNIHAN: How many songs have you written?

PARTON: I've published 3,000. Since I was five years old I've been writing songs. I started playing guitar when I was seven, I started making up stuff before I could write. I don't have to work now, but I like to. I like to give it all away so that I have reason to work.

MOYNIHAN: Do you have good investments?

PARTON: Yes.

MOYNIHAN: How many businesses do you own?

PARTON: Many. First of all I have a lot of money in my publishing company, that's a very stable thing. I have a lot of property. I invest in property, like farms, cows, hardware stores, hogs, and macadamia trees. You'd be surprised. I make more money on my outside heartfelt investments like farm equipment, garden centers, than I do even from record royalties. The thing that I am proudest of is my publishing company, because you not only write songs you get your royalties from, but you own your publishing—you have it all. Like with *Rhinestone*, I've written 20 songs for this. I get paid a large amount of money for the use of the songs plus I publish them. I don't have to do it—they want me, they come to me.

MOYNIHAN: Do you make all your own business decisions?

PARTON: Yes, I have good management and good accountants, but I go outside of all of them to make my own decisions. I need them mostly for advice in certain areas and to negotiate certain things. So I don't *have* to work, I *love* to work. But I think everybody has to work. What's a million dollars or three or ten or fifteen if you're not happy doing what you're doing? At least it's good to know if you want to take off for a year you can. But if I took off and didn't feel creative I'd just get stale. I can't even go on vacation. I do know how to have a good time, and I do, but when I'm on vacation I can just have the best time doing whatever. Right in the middle of some great time something will hit my mind, and I'll make myself stop and write it down.

WARHOL: Are you working on another movie now?

PARTON: I have written a movie for me and Jane [Fonda] and Lily [Tomlin] I'm going to produce. One of the things I'm real proud of is I just made a deal with 20th Century Fox, and I've got my own production company now. I'm developing some television and movies for other people because I have a lot of fresh new ideas. To write is what I love the most. I'm starting some movies of the week and some TV series and writing my own movies.

MOYNIHAN: What do you think of the women's movement?

PARTON: The women's movement has a great respect for people in general. I'm not really a political-type person, meaning that I don't really make great stands or whatever, but if you ask me a direct question I say it shouldn't matter who you are, whether you're black, white, green, gay, male, female. If you can do a job and do it well you should be paid for it, you should be respected for it, and you have to be responsible. I think sometimes people can go too far trying to make a point. I think they should just make their point and go on about.

MOYNIHAN: Do you have groupies? Do you have men following you?

PARTON: Of course, I do, and women. I got a huge gay following and some really macho-looking women. To me people are people, but I always say, you like me because you want to look like me? I can tell you where I get my stuff. So many of my friends are gay, male and female. I don't judge people. I don't care what people do in their bedrooms and people shouldn't care what I do in mine, but yes, I do have a lot of groupies.

WARHOL: You have groupies who actually just follow you around?

PARTON: I don't think there's an artist on the road that doesn't have groupies. I have a huge group of people who follow me from town to town. They know your show and they sit out there and sing every word you sing. They know what you're going to do before you get it done.

WARHOL: You should buy Monument Records.

PARTON: You'd be surprised how close you are. I am trying.

MOYNIHAN: Do you think success has changed you much or not?

PARTON: To the better.

MOYNIHAN: Do you think it's been a burden?

PARTON: No, it never was. I had hard times, I've been burdened, but overall it has not been a burden.

MOYNIHAN: Do you think the sexual revolution went too far?

PARTON: I'm just not going to say, because I cannot do that and not be a hypocrite. My fantasies carried me to where I wanted to go. My imagination is greater than the reality. I really get into whatever I get into, and I do it my own way. I like to think that somewhere down inside me there's still a Garden of Eden. I'm still innocent and sweet in a wonderful way.

DOLLY PARTON: "HOW I CAME CLOSE TO SUICIDE"

Cliff Jahr | June 1986 | *Ladies' Home Journal*

When Dolly announced her "big dream" for a "fantasy city" called Dollywood USA during an interview with Barbara Walters in 1982, there was already a Silver Dollar City theme park in Pigeon Forge, Tennessee. Jack Herschend, one of Silver Dollar City's owners, realized their park would never be able to compete for business with a new park bearing Dolly's name and likeness, and what happened next was a classic case of "if you can't beat 'em, join 'em." Silver Dollar City joined forces with Dolly Parton, agreeing to manage and operate the park, which would soon be "Dolly-ized" and expanded as Dollywood.

The gates to Dollywood, "the friendliest town in the Smokies," swung open for the first time on May 3, 1986. Everyone but Dolly seemed apprehensive about the joint venture; however, fears were calmed when attendance jumped from 750,000 to nearly 1.4 million the first year. Dollywood was the fastest growing theme park in America. A comprehensive media campaign surrounding the opening of Dollywood had its namesake busier than ever, and Dolly's celebrity guaranteed her a spot on virtually any media outlet she desired. She was interviewed by Johnny Carson and Phil Donahue, profiled on "Fame, Fortune, and Romance," appeared on *Entertainment Tonight*, and even made stops at the morning shows on all three major television networks.

Features in nearly all the major women's interest magazines were arranged to coincide with the opening of Dollywood. While this *Ladies' Home Journal* piece touched on the news of the theme park's opening, interviewer Cliff Jahr was focused on Dolly's personal turmoil. Candid and forthcoming with details of her issues with depression, Dolly explains just how close she came to ending her own life and how that dark moment changed her future for the better. —Ed.

Health problems and death threats drove her to despair. This month, she launches a comeback.

"Turning forty this past January," says Dolly Parton brightly, "gave me a whole new lease on life. It was like a switch clicked on. Suddenly I felt younger than at twenty-five, when I was working so hard and fighting to get ahead. I've always known what I wanted, but now I know what to do with it."

Until very recently, though, the country-music superstar was conspicuously absent from recording studios and concert halls. For three years, she put her career on hold as she struggled to get her private life in order. It was a time of ups and downs—mostly downs. During one tough period, she even considered suicide.

"I've been through just about everything—tragedy, heartache, disappointment," she says. "But now I'm smarter about things, about family and friends and business, and I don't think there's anything I can't do. I'm ready to *live*!"

This is her first sit-down interview in well over a year, and she seems as sunny and fun loving as ever. Yet there's a hint of greater self-assurance in Dolly's voice. She talks confidently about the Las Vegas shows, the scheduled release of a new album this fall, and the filming of another movie with her *9 to 5* co-stars, Jane Fonda and Lily Tomlin. In May, she opened Dollywood, her own theme park, in Tennessee.

"Oh, I've got *lots* of things on the burner—you'll be surprised," she says, tugging at her upswept yellow wig. "I've kept a low profile lately, and that's on purpose, because when I come back I want to come back strong. I told myself I'd make my return when I was forty, because at this age you can't sit on the fence any longer. Who knows how much time you've got?"

She is lunching today at a Los Angeles restaurant she adores for its famous green-corn tamales. Daintily, she dips a tamale in hot sauce, being careful not to spill any down the deep neckline of her black angora sweater. She recently lost twenty pounds without sacrificing her famous curves, and as a bonus, Dolly's lovely high cheekbones, one of her best features, have reappeared. It's nice to see her smiling again after so many years of heartache.

Dolly's troubled period began back in 1982. At the time, she was at the height of her career, following the worldwide success of her first movie, *9 to 5*, and then *The Best Little Whorehouse in Texas*, which is the third-biggest movie musical in box-office history. Then, one September night, during a performance in Indianapolis, she was suddenly stricken by internal abdominal bleeding. Gynecological surgery was successful and stopped short of a hysterectomy, but it left Dolly weak for months.

When she returned to work, telephoned death threats from a man in Kentucky forced her to cancel her tour. "I still don't know whether he was a killer or just a crank," she remarks. "But, of course, you always have to be prepared for that kind of stuff."

To compound matters, she was still trying to get over the unpleasant experience she had shooting *Whorehouse*. There had been endless production delays, fights and firings, as well as struggles with temperamental Burt Reynolds. His black moods, which swung between sulks and tantrums, sometimes brought Dolly to tears. "Making that picture was a nightmare," she confides.

She was also feeling downhearted because of snarled relations with some of her relatives. "It's very hard to be the family of a celebrity," she notes gently.

At the same time, she faced the disloyalty of "a special friend, an affair of the heart, which just about killed me. Oh, I cried an ocean. But I ain't gonna talk about it anymore," she says playfully. "I've got to keep *some* mystery."

Whether a romance or not, the friendship did not threaten her seemingly open marriage to Carl Dean, a union that has flourished for twenty years. "There's no way Carl and I are ever going to break up," she insists. "We have a happy marriage, a great marriage." Has she ever been tempted by other men? "Of course I've been tempted," she says with a laugh. "I'm married—I'm not dead."

Going downhill

As her problems worsened, Dolly began to fall apart. Binge eating made her overweight. Hoarseness and fragile health led her to cancel concerts, which resulted in lawsuits and more unhappiness. Finally, she became so depressed, she dropped from sight. For the next two years, Dolly accepted only a few carefully chosen projects, such as a Christmas TV special and the hit single "Islands in the Stream," both with Kenny Rogers, and one solo album, *Real Love.*

How blue did she get? "It was bad," she replies. "It was devastating to be in that depressed state of mind. For about six months there I woke up every morning feeling dead."

Did she ever think of suicide? Dolly looks off into the distance. "I got close once," she says softly. "I was sitting upstairs in my bedroom one afternoon when I noticed in the nightstand drawer my gun that I keep for burglars. I looked at it a long time, wondering and saying to myself, 'Well now, this is where people get the idea of suicide, isn't it? Guns around the house and people sorrowing and all.' Then, just as I picked it up, just to hold it and look at it for a moment, our little dog, Popeye, came running up the stairs. The tap-tap-tap of his paws jolted me back to reality. I suddenly froze. I put the gun down. Then I prayed. I kinda believe Popeye was a spiritual messenger from God, y'know?

"I don't think I'd have done it, killed myself," she explains, "but I can't say for sure. I always thought I was absolutely not the suicidal type because I'm too well anchored with roots and family and friends. But now that I've gone through that terrible moment, I can certainly understand the possibilities even for someone solid like me if the pain gets bad enough.

"After that, my life changed in a positive way," she says, brightening. "I have greater wisdom now, more tolerance and patience for people who are struggling with liquor or drugs or suicide or being in prison. That frightening moment with the gun was very, very humbling. I kind of think it was God's way to bring me to my knees long enough to pray."

The experience also made Dolly more appreciative of her close friendship with Judy Ogle, her aide and companion since high school days.

"Y'know, you often hear that stars who died sadly, like Elvis and Marilyn Monroe, had all kinds of people around them, but you never hear that they had a best friend, someone who really knew them and loved them. Well, I have Judy. I can talk to her about anything, especially on our long trips in the camper. She knows about me, and anything's okay with her. I think friends can literally save your life."

During much of the tumultuous period, Dolly retreated to the love of her big family in Tennessee, lying low with Carl at Willow Lake, their eighty-acre estate outside Nashville. When she was on the West Coast, she'd often hop into a camper with Judy or by herself, wearing no wig or makeup, and drive southeast from Los Angeles to her hideaway in Hemet, California, an old cottage with a swimming pool, hot tub and total privacy. For weeks on end, she swam, soaked, strummed a guitar, wrote songs and read everything from self-help to poetry.

All that glitters

As 1984 approached, Dolly felt restored enough to take on her third movie, *Rhinestone*, a romantic comedy filled with country songs she wrote herself. Everyone expected Dolly and leading man Sylvester Stallone to make a dream duo, but the result was a standoff between curves and muscles. At the box office, *Rhinestone* didn't sparkle.

"Which *devastated* Stallone," recalls Dolly. "Sly probably thinks I nearly wrecked his career with that movie, but to me, I was the one taking the chance. I've done two musicals with men who can't sing—Sly and Burt Reynolds—and here I am a singer. Both were bad casting, of course, but I have only myself to blame."

Though she was less than impressed with her co-star's singing voice, Dolly found Stallone to be intelligent and humorous. "He was so funny that he'd make me laugh until I'd lose my breath and beg him to stop," she recalls. "He's really fun to work with—he's nuts, sick, crazy, a scream! He's pretty to look at, too, and I know that when Sasha, his last wife, was getting her divorce, she said we were having an affair. Not true at all. Sly and I are just not each other's type.

"Both he and Burt are egomaniacs," she continues, "but Sly is the perfect balance of total ego and total insecurity. I see how his mind works. If you were in love with him, he'd pick out all your weaknesses and either use them to help you or use them against you. I told him right up front, 'Sly, please, please, *please* don't get on me like you do other people. I know what I am, who I am, and I happen to be happy with me.' So he never bothered me, but when he was in a bad mood I couldn't wait to see who he was going to fire or curse out next. I always told him he was spectacular but that he had a blind spot where compassion and spirituality ought to be. He was amused by me, I think, but he couldn't deal with me on a day-to-day basis because I'm too raw and honest."

Just as Dolly was beginning to gain back her old confidence, she was forced to confront another obstacle. A songwriting team claimed that she had used their music to create her Oscar-nominated title song for the movie *9 to 5*, and they sued for plagiarism. Last December's trial in Santa Monica, California, which put Dolly and Jane Fonda on the witness stand, dragged on for twelve days and made unsavory headlines.

"So degrading," Dolly says with a wince. "One of the most painful things I've ever gone through. It damaged my reputation, I think, because there'll always be some people out there who think I would stoop so low as to steal from working people. Hell, I know how hard it is to get a break in this business. Besides, there were only five musical notes in question, and they have been used in a hundred songs."

Dolly picks up a taco chip and examines it for a moment. "Well"—she smiles, snapping it in two—"the jury was out for twenty minutes, and we won. The court awarded me attorney's fees, which is a lot of money. Then the couple who sued me tried to get a retrial, claiming I charmed the jury because I played songs on the witness stand. The retrial was denied, and then they actually started trying to get me to record some of their songs."

A birthday present

The trial ended shortly before Dolly turned forty. By the time her birthday rolled around, she was ready to take back control of her life. "Y'know what I did?" she drawls, smiling broadly. "I got up early that morning and went straight to a list of names I'd made. I wrote letters to four people, some family, some business, who I had let mess with my head. They're people who'd had the upper hand on me for years. When I saw them comin', I'd cringe. When they called, I wasn't in.

"The letters were very blunt. They said, I'm not going to put up with your B.S. anymore. You have no control over me and little control of yourself, so you should examine things very carefully. Then I made some phone calls, too. I decided to get all the grief and worries over irresponsible people out of my life. And it worked—it really cleared the air. I'm perfectly comfortable with those people now."

With her life straightened out, Dolly pressed on with plans for her comeback, timed to follow her new theme park's grand opening on May 3. Dollywood is a mini-Disneyland nestled on 140 acres in the Great Smoky Mountains. Its unique attraction is a rags-to-riches museum that displays Dolly's humble birthplace, the two-room tar-paper shack in which she spent her childhood with eleven brothers and sisters. Actually, it's an exact copy of the original house, which still stands nearby but was not moved to Dollywood, because it has sprouted a fancy price tag since her rise to fame.

Dolly is still devoted to her family, especially to her mother, Avie Lee Parton, a hardworking backwoods homemaker who was determined that her dozen children not grow up stigmatized by poverty. Explains Dolly, "Mama always said, 'We're rich people because we know we got love and we got each other.' But then again, there were hungry times when the crops were down, and that's when Mama made stone soup."

To make stone soup, Avie Lee sent her children outdoors to fetch the smoothest stone each could find. She then selected one to drop in the pot with whatever potatoes and onions she had.

"She made such a big to-do about picking the right one," relates Dolly with a laugh. "She'd say, 'Oh, I feel some *magic* in this one.' It was Mama's wonderful imagination that distracted us from the hunger. Maybe it didn't work on a few of my brothers and sisters, who still resented being poor, but for others, like me, it was the best thing that ever happened."

Dolly's parents don't have to worry about crop failures anymore. They now live in a hilltop mansion ("like a Hallmark Christmas card," she notes), but the family is as close as ever. "Daddy saw *9 to 5* so often"—she laughs—"that I think it was his way of getting to know which kid I was. He just lived in that drab theater, and it touches me to think of it. Y'see, he and Mama had so many kids that none of us got special attention. What's more, I was so busy working on my music that I had just about left home by the time I was ten.

"Mama and Daddy don't cater to me any more than the other kids," she adds. "I'm still just their li'l Dolly. I'm so much like my mother, who always sees to it that she's the center of attention. Mama's attitude is, Why, of course Dolly's a star—she's just like me."

Home sweet homes

These days, Dolly softens childhood memories of the tar-paper shack by indulging her love of buying houses. To the list of places she keeps in Manhattan, Nashville, California and Hawaii, she is adding a big, glamorous "dollhouse" in Beverly Hills. Despite rumors she would sell Willow Lake, she is actually spreading out in the Nashville area. She recently bought a weekend house on a nearby lake, partly as a way of accommodating Carl's passion for privacy. "He doesn't like a lot of people around him," Dolly explains. "So I'm limited in using that big, fine house. But now when I want to have some people over for a cookout or a swimming party, Carl can take Popeye and go down to the lake house. Or vice versa. We're doing it up just like an old sea shanty, and it's on water that connects all the way to New Orleans. It's so private that you could run around naked—and we probably will."

Dolly's blue eyes shine merrily. Does she consider herself happy now? "More than I've ever been," she says firmly. "But I think you have to work at being happy, just like you have to work at being miserable. I'm going to grasp every happy moment I can find. It would be a great sin for me not to enjoy my success. Oh, I still sometimes feel pain and sadness, and I get emotional and cry, but I don't think there's anything missing from my life now. Of course, I do have my little shortcomings. I know I will always be short, for instance, and that's okay. What is not okay is when I'm short and *fat*. But I like me. I just hope everybody else likes me as much as I do."

Does she think she'll still be happy with herself when she's sixty? "I'll be a great old lady," she affirms. "Just a little older than I am now, but lots of fun and busy and smarter, full of life and still foolin' around a little. If it's God's will that I'm healthy and I keep my mind, I can always sing, write for other people, manage, produce, do a talk show, a variety show, a TV series. I get these incredible offers all the time, but during this part of my career, I'm going for the bigger stuff, the movies, Dollywood, books I'm going to write, and helping to run my new film and TV production companies with my manager.

"I don't know what the big deal is about old age," she continues. "I'm writing a book about old people right now called *Old Dogs, New Tricks*, and I think people give age too much importance. Old people who shine from inside look ten to twenty years younger. I swear that some of them shine so bright that they're still sexy."

She sits back and delicately dabs a napkin at the corner of her mouth.

"Of course," she drawls, "I'm gonna be one of 'em."

DOLLY DIAMOND

On Her TV Series

"I want it to be really uplifting, spiritually uplifting, at a time when people need to feel more confident about themselves. At the end of that hour, I want people to feel so good that they'll want to see it again. The human spirit could use a good shot of what I hope this show is going to have. . . . Everyone says variety is dead. Well, I say, 'If variety is dead, what are we doing here? If variety is dead, we're all in deep s--t!' . . . I'm gonna go at this as if it were the last show I was ever going to do. I will lay everything on the line. I will show the people who I am, good and bad. If they want to see me without wigs and makeup, that will happen."

—To Susan Cheever, *TV Guide*, October 17, 1987

DOLLY DIAMOND

On Her TV Series

"If the show fails, it won't be the end of my life—I'll move on. I'm not afraid to try anything, and I'm certainly not afraid to fail."

—To Mary-Ann Bendel, *Ladies' Home Journal*, November 1987

"I AIN'T DOWN YET!"

Lawrence Grobel | July 1988 | *Redbook*

In this third and final of Lawrence Grobel's interviews with Dolly, the two seem to have lost the rapport and lightheartedness that permeated their previous dialogues. They were still simpatico enough that it's mostly enjoyable, but it's a little awkward and uncomfortable at times, too.

As explained in this feature for *Redbook* (and written about in greater detail in Grobel's book *You, Talking to Me*), when Dolly called Grobel one night, the subject turned to an assignment he was contemplating for *Playboy*. When Dolly learned it was an interview with Charles Manson from prison, she became so upset with the notion that she told Grobel that him even considering such an assignment made her wary of him.

"I thought Dolly's friendship was valuable enough to turn down the assignment," he later explained. "That was too bad. I lost the assignment, and I lost Dolly as well. At least, the closeness that we had. But, as that song of hers goes, I will always love her." —Ed.

Why wasn't Dolly's TV show a mega-hit? "I was just one little country hillbilly and nobody would listen to me," she explains. What does she say about those rumors that she's become anorexic? "I'm the healthiest I've ever been!" Here, in an exclusive interview, Dolly send the world a message: "Don't mess with me!"

"How ya doin'?" she squealed, giving me a huge hug, an all-embracing squeeze that made me squirm self-consciously. "Boy, it's good to see you. Sure been a long time."

Sure had. In fact, just a few nights before I had wondered to my wife if I'd ever see Dolly Parton again. And here I was, my arms around her, actually *feeling* the new slender body. The last time we'd embraced, there had been more of her to hold. Her waist has since shrunk to 17 inches, her chest looked firmer, her eyes larger, her face more sharply angled. She looked and felt like a whole new Dolly.

I first met Dolly Parton ten years ago, when I was on assignment for *Playboy* magazine. I spent a week traveling with her to concert appearances in West Virginia and Virginia. We traveled together on her bus, stayed in adjoining motel rooms and often talked late into the night after her performance. One night, in particular, we talked until three o'clock in the morning, mostly about ghosts and spirits and things that go bump in the night. Having been raised one of 12 children in a sleepy back-roads hollow in the Smoky Mountains of Tennessee, Dolly's head was filled with stories of the supernatural. And since I had spent three years in the Peace Corps living in Africa, I too had my share of stories to contribute.

Sometime around two that morning Dolly called room service and ordered a plate of fruit and cheese. It arrived a few minutes later. Sitting cross-legged on the bed, Dolly patted the mattress and said, "Come sit over here and have some of this." It was, I'm sure, a perfectly natural and innocent invitation to sample the fruits by her side, but it made me feel awkward. I remained in my chair. I was actually *afraid* to sit next to Dolly Parton on the bed in that West Virginia motel at two in the morning—afraid of committing a faux pas I might never live down.

Of the many celebrities I have spent time with over the years, Dolly is the only one who's capable of taking my breath away. It isn't just her exaggerated hair and clothes and makeup. It's almost as if she is more than human. Her intelligence is obvious and overwhelming. Her sense of things—of *knowing* things about people—is uncanny. She has a certain strength and confidence that is deeply spiritual. She's just so damn *different* from anybody else—a self-created creature with an enormous talent and a heart just as big.

A few years after I first met Dolly, I saw her again in Los Angeles, on the set of her first movie, *Nine to Five*. I was writing a magazine story about the film, and when she had finished that day's scenes, we got into my Fiat and drove to the beach. We stopped at a diner for something to eat. While waiting for our food, she tapped her long fingernails against a water glass in time to the title song she was in the midst of composing. She sang a few verses and asked me what I thought. It hadn't all come to her yet, but she was close. "Workin' nine to five, what a way to make a livin' . . . ."

After eating we decided to take a walk along the beach. Dolly didn't want to take off her high heels, so we stayed on the bike path. The beach was empty that day, except for one large man who was sitting on a bench as we walked by. He was more than six feet tall and weighed perhaps 230 pounds. He spotted Dolly and muttered a few coarse words. Dolly gripped my arm and said, "Oh shit! And I left my gun in my purse in your car."

Her *gun*? I had never been with a woman who packed a pistol before. Suddenly, I started to worry about what might happen if the man decided to follow us. Would I have to defend Dolly against this behemoth? Or would *she* have to defend me? And what if she *had* taken her gun with her? Would she have pulled it out, just to be safe? I couldn't help wondering how far she might go if push came to shove. Fortunately, it didn't.

"Once, in New York," Dolly then told me, "I was walking with a girlfriend when some man came on to us. He thought we was hookers, I guess, and he propositioned us. Well, I stuck my hand in my bag, pulled out my gun, pointed it at him and told him if he didn't take a hike, I'd turn him into a soprano. He left us alone right quickly after that."

A few years after that walk on the beach, I received a call from my *Playboy* editor asking me if I would be interested in interviewing Charles Manson, the notorious ringleader of "The Family," the cult that had gone on a killing spree in California, taking the lives of seven people, including film director Roman Polanski's wife, actress Sharon Tate. Manson had put the fear of death into many of Hollywood's biggest stars, until he was finally apprehended.

My editor knew that I lived in the Hollywood Hills, not far from where Manson had once lived, and he wanted me to think seriously about whether I should do the interview. "There are still a lot of his followers out there," he warned me, "and if word gets out that you're seeing him, you might be subjected to various attempts to get to him through you."

Since I was married and had a small child, I had more than myself to worry about. I told my editor that I would let him know my answer in a few days. I then called friends and associates who had written about Manson to see what they thought about the assignment. Most of the men I spoke to thought it was a great journalistic opportunity and I should do it. Most of the women thought I should pass.

The more I thought about it, the more I was drawn to the assignment—even after I found out that a producer I knew who had been in touch with Manson had had his mailbox blown up by one of Manson's followers. I think I wanted the thrill of coming face-to-face with such an evil figure, and trying to get to his very core. After all, I am a writer, and that is my job. Interviewing Charles Manson would be an ultimate test of my journalistic skills.

I was leaning toward accepting the assignment when the phone rang late one Saturday night. "Hi, guy, howya doin'? I was just thinkin' about you and thought I'd call." It was Dolly. I hadn't talked to her for a long time, and suddenly, out of the blue, she was checking in. I started to tell her about the possible Manson assignment and the decision I was wrestling with when she very abruptly and very curtly cut me off.

"I don't know what this is worth to you," she said coldly, "but I want to tell you what I think about it. The man is pure evil. He's the devil. His kind rubs off on anybody who meets him. If you see him, if you even talk to him, if . . . have you talked to him yet?"

"Not yet," I said. "I'm not even sure he's going to do it. My editor just asked me to consider it."

"Well, consider this then," she said. "If you so much as talk to him—*even on the phone*—then I will never see you or talk with you again. I feel that strongly about it. I've kept my life as pure as I can make it—I've kept away from evil and the bad vibrations that come from being around evil—and I truly believe that man is the devil. If you ever had anything to do with Charlie Manson, I wouldn't want the vibes you would pick up to get around me. Now I know that may not be fair to tell you this, but I'm telling you from my heart. That's the way I am. It's your decision to make, but if you value my friendship at all, you better stay clear of that one."

Others had given me advice, but Dolly was giving me an ultimatum. Say yes to Manson, and kiss her friendship goodbye. As a professional journalist, her words shouldn't have had any effect on me. It was my decision to make. Yet I heard myself say, "Well, Dolly, I guess you've decided for me, I won't do it."

"Now don't say you won't just because I don't want you to," she told me. "You shouldn't do it because *you* shouldn't want to. Why let that evil come anywhere near you?"

"You're right Dolly. I won't even think about it anymore. And besides, your friendship is too important."

I never interviewed Manson . . . and I stopped hearing from Dolly. Oh, she continued to send her annual Christmas baskets of jellies, candies, polished glass and herb-scented balls, but the phone calls ceased. So did her letters, which she had occasionally written until the Manson incident came up. Last Christmas, I sent Dolly a note, thanking her for her basket of goodies and inviting her to lunch. Weeks later, I received a large envelope from the "Dollywood Ambassadors" in Pigeon Forge, Tennessee. Inside was a letter that began, "Dear Fan, Thank-you for your letter to Dolly Parton. Because of her hectic schedule, we are answering mail for her. The Dolly Parton Fan Club is now Dollywood Ambassadors, and we have added you as a member." Included in the envelope was a picture of Dolly and some brochures about Dollywood and about gifts I might want to purchase, most of them variations of the Christmas basket she had sent.

Dolly, I had to assume, had changed. She had gone through some hard times, been ill for a while, had an operation and been told she could never have children. She had signed a two-year deal with ABC—worth $44 million—for her own variety show. The show was having problems. Its timeslot was moved from Sunday night to Saturday night. But the ratings were still disappointing, and I had heard that Dolly decided to take more control over the show, changing its format to one that was more "country." Dolly had just gotten too big, even bigger than she had been when I first met her ten years ago. So when I met her for this interview—our first meeting in about four years—I assumed that any time we had together would be strictly professional.

We met in the corridor of her office in Los Angeles. Dolly was dressed in skintight jeans, a white tank-top and a faded denim jacket. She looked skinny, but more beautiful than ever.

We went out to lunch—only this time, instead of going in my Fiat, we went in her white stretch limo. We talked about how she looked; how she felt; the problems her show was having; her plans to tour this summer; her new record deal with CBS; her long-distance relationship with Carl, her husband of 22 years; her ability to juggle the many projects in her life. It was like old times—we just picked up where we left off years ago, before she had gone through her difficulties.

She started to tell me about those times, when everything seemed to have gone wrong with her, when her weight ballooned up to 157 pounds, when her body was giving her "female problems," when people she loved and trusted were betraying her, when she had to get rid of certain people in her life because they were not healthy for her, when she started having questions about her life and career. It had been a gloomy, depressing time—a time for self-reflection and for testing her belief in God.

"For the first time in my life, I understood how people commit suicide. I understood how people get hooked on drugs and alcohol," Dolly said. "I was that hurt. I was so unhappy for about eighteen months. I just couldn't get myself together. I couldn't think my positive thoughts because I was so sick. It was the worst time ever in my life. I couldn't even watch TV because I couldn't stand to see the human suffering on the news. I couldn't hear sad stories and sad songs. I was that sensitive. It was hard when I found out I could never have children—*knowing* that I couldn't, whether I had wanted them or not. But I've come to terms with that. I pray every day that God's will will be done, and that He'll direct me and lead me and I'll live my life according to the way I'm supposed to. So I just assumed that it was not in His plan for me to have kids, or I would be having them."

I asked Dolly how supportive Carl had been during the time when she was so sick. "He didn't even know it," she answered. "He knew I was sick but he had no idea I was in the shape I was in 'cause I wasn't gonna worry him with the shit that I should have more control over. It was something between me and the Lord. Only Sandy Gallin, my manager, and Judy Ogle, my best friend, really knew just how sick I was. Judy has been with me for thirty-five years—ever since we were little kids—and she makes it possible for me not to need a psychiatrist. During those eighteen months Sandy and Judy were the ones I depended on most. My sickness forced me to make all the decisions that have made my life so much richer, better, more meaningful. It's helped me to weed out the bullshit and take better care of myself."

Dolly talked about her recent weight loss. "When I was fat, people would say, 'You have such a pretty face. If you'd lose twenty or thirty pounds, you'd be beautiful.' Well, I lost the weight and now they say, 'You're too skinny.' So there's no way to please people. I'm not trying to gain weight, although I did recently put on a few pounds because my weight loss has been worrying my parents. They think I'm sick. People say I'm anorexic, but I'm *not*—I'm the healthiest I've ever been! I really worked hard to get my mind tuned to losing this weight. People crucify me now for being thin, but they don't know what a difficult thing I've done. Being a foodaholic is like being an alcoholic or a drug addict—believe me, it was easier becoming a star than losing that weight! When somebody tells me, 'You've got to gain weight,' I think, 'Don't say that! This is a fight to the finish.' I'm afraid that if I don't stay where I am, I'll lose control and go back to my old habits. And I'd rather be dead than be that miserable again."

I wondered how Dolly's personality might have changed now that she's down to about 105 pounds. As usual, she had an answer. "When I was fat, I ate all the time. I ate everything I wanted, and I had more personality. But I've noticed that since I've been skinny, I *don't* have the same tolerance that I used to have. When you're fat, you're eating everything you want and you're getting all the vitamins and minerals your body needs. Fat burns, so you got lots of extra energy. And I use up every bit of what I eat. I eat everything I want—I just don't eat a lot of it. So, in three hours I'm hungry again. My blood sugar gets low. And if you get in my face about something you ain't got no business being in my face for, if I'm hungry, watch out! Sometimes I will snap and bite somebody's head off. Then, after I've done it, I won't believe it. I'll think, 'Did *I* do that?' I put forth a great effort to be nice, but there are some people who just insist on trying your patience. A lot of people think that I'm more short-tempered than I used to be because I'm arrogant and vain. They think that I act like that now because I look so much better—at least, I do to me—but they totally misunderstand me. I may not have the exact tolerance level that I used to have, but other than that, I have *not* changed at all.

"For the most part," said Dolly, "I do better than most people, with the demands that are on me. But people don't even think I work—they think it's all glamour and smiles—because nobody ever sees me working, I work before I go to sleep or when I get up in the morning. I'm an early bird. I work for two or three hours in the morning before anybody else has even gotten up, Ninety-five percent of the time I enjoy my work, but when it comes to the other five percent, buddy, you don't want to mess with me!"

By now, we had reached La Toque, a restaurant in Los Angeles. Dolly and I sat across from each other at a corner table and she proceeded to order lunch for the both of us—soup, potatoes with caviar, chicken salad and seafood pasta. "I don't want to get back into my old habits," Dolly said as we waited for our food to arrive. "I have to think about what I'm eating. When I'm halfway through a piece of pie, I have to tell myself, 'That's enough!' I get irritated that I have to be that disciplined. I'm such a free and natural spirit. But there comes a time in your life when you learn that there's a price to pay."

"You sure weren't tolerant with me the last time we talked," I said, easing into the Manson episode. "I've often thought that was why I hadn't heard from you. Just the fact that I was even considering doing the interview turned you off."

"Yes, it did," Dolly said. "I just had the worst feeling about that. I really think you'd have suffered for that—to see him that close, all that bitterness and insanity. I didn't even want nothing to do with you if you were going to have something to do with him."

When the food arrived, I asked Dolly about her show, which has not been the success everyone thought it would be. "I wasn't as involved in the beginning because I had hoped I could just trust all the people who kept saying 'Trust me.' I was just one little country hillbilly, and nobody would listen to me much. They'd say, 'You've never done a variety pro-gram. How would you know what works?' I say, 'Hell, you don't have to have done one to know what's working and what ain't.'

"What was missing in the early stages of the show was that nobody had a real, true vision of me—who I am, what I am, what I'm capable of doing, what I should and shouldn't be doing. Considering all the things that I've been up against, I've done pretty good. I took on a show that was going to be ABC's big comeback, so there was all the hype and publicity to overcome. When the show was on Sunday nights, I had to contend with the movies and specials on the other channels. These people who program them don't give a shit what Dolly Parton's dreams and feelings are. They're in business—they're going to give you the stiffest competition. In addition to that, I got preempted a few times, and that was confusing to the public. And a lot of people were put off that I lost so much weight—it was like they were trying to get used to a different person. And there was all that hype about the money I was paid. People resent that. They think I gotta show something. Then we changed time slots and I got preempted *again* for three weeks. I knew it was gonna be hard; I didn't know it was gonna be *this* hard. It's a challenge and I ain't down yet! My show is now about as good a variety show as I can do. If it's still not what the people want, then it's really true that variety television is dead."

The question of personal failure and rejection had to be brought up. At press time, ABC still had not officially renewed the show. And yet it seemed strange that someone who was being watched weekly by nearly 18 million people could be considered a failure.

"I won't feel like a failure," she insisted. "I learned enough on this show to last me a lifetime, and I will apply that knowledge to other things I'm doing. I have decided that I *do* want to do television, whether it's on ABC or another network. I *will* do television. It has given me an outlet for all the different kinds of things I love to do. It's an outlet for my songwriting and my acting, and I love to be a host, to do concerts. So if something should happen and this variety show doesn't work, I'll keep going."

Of course! When you're Dolly Parton, hosting a prime-time variety show is only one of the things you could be doing with your time. Dolly has songs to write and record concerts to give, a theme park to visit, a book about her life to write . . . even an autobiographical Broadway musical which she is currently working on.

How does Dolly do it? How does she juggle all these things and still maintain a personal life? "First of all," she said, "I'm not your average woman. I don't have children. I don't have a husband who depends on me being home at a certain time. My time is pretty much my own. I choose to do the work that I do. And I've always enjoyed what I'm doing, and I'm always healthy when I'm happy. It's when I'm not enjoying it that my energy runs down."

The dessert tray is brought, and Dolly selects two for us. She then tells me how easy her life has become now that she's more disciplined. "It's not hard work," she insisted, outlining her work schedule which leaves her free four nights a week. She said that her husband Carl hadn't been out to see her in several months because he had been suffering from back problems, but she goes back home to Tennessee as often as she can. "It's hard for Carl to drive, and he won't fly," Dolly said, although he once flew to Hawaii with her. "But I've never been able to get him to do it again. He says he's not afraid of flying, he just doesn't see the need to do it. Anyway, we got a little Boston terrier, and he uses that as an excuse for staying home."

Besides all the projects in which she's involved, Dolly is also producing a country bluegrass album with country singer Ricky Skaggs. She's aware of the mistakes she has made with previous albums, and has concluded that, "Rock people don't want me to do country, and country people don't want me to do rock. So whenever I would do country *and* rock it turned out to be 'crock!' I'm sick of it, so I'm doing pure country as part of my deal with CBS."

Three quarters of the way through her slice of lemon meringue pie, Dolly gently placed her fork on the plate. She licked her lips and looked at what remained of the pie. "You want the rest of this?" she asked. I shook my head sadly. I weigh a lot more than Dolly does, and if she could resist the extra calories, so could I. That's what being around Dolly is like. No matter how long it's been, once you're back in her positive energy field, some of it rubs off.

PART V
Steel Magnolia

"A lot of men thought I was as silly as I looked, I guess. I look like a woman, but I think like a man. And in this world of business, that has helped me a lot. By the time they think that I don't know what's goin' on, I done got the money and gone!"

—To Morely Safer, *60 Minutes*,
April 5, 2009

DAISY MAE IN HOLLYWOOD

William Stadiem | July 1989 | *Interview*

In her second cover story for *Interview*, Dolly gave readers a behind-the-scenes look into her upcoming film, *Steel Magnolias*. She also discussed in detail and at great length her newly released *White Limozeen* album, which spawned two Number 1 country singles, "Why'd You Come in Here Lookin' Like That" and "Yellow Roses." Also included here is one of Dolly's earliest accounts of having said no to Elvis Presley when he sought to record "I Will Always Love You." —Ed.

Between cutting her hit album *White Limozeen*, appearing at Dollywood in the Smoky Mountains, and acting with the all-star cast of *Steel Magnolias*, Dolly Parton has been keeping on the move. William Stadiem caught the platinum-blonde powerhouse at the Beverly Hills Hotel before she hit the road again.

If the South is going to rise again, there is no one better equipped to lead the resurrection than Dolly Parton. A legendary singer-songwriter and movie star, a mogul with a powerful production company, a philanthropist, and the owner of her own theme park, Dolly is the closest thing America has to a Renaissance woman. And she did it all on her own. Born, like Davy Crockett, on a mountaintop in Tennessee, in a cabin with no plumbing or electricity, she rose, as she puts it in the autobiographical title song of her new album, White Limozeen, *"from the breadlines to the headlines" to become the toast of Hollywood.*

The Parton odyssey began in 1946 in the backwoods of east Tennessee. A farmer's daughter and the fourth of twelve children, she was writing songs and singing on the radio at ten, and appeared at the Grand Ole Opry at twelve. Graduating from high school (the first in her family) at eighteen, she left directly for Nashville, met her husband, Carl Dean, an asphalt contractor (they're still married), and became the lead female on the Porter Wagoner road show. She became a giant country star with such platinum hits as "Here You Come Again" and "Islands in the Stream," and soon Hollywood came courting.

Dolly stole her first movie, 9 to 5, from co-stars Jane Fonda and Lily Tomlin, and received an Oscar nomination for Best Song. She went on to steal The Best Little Whorehouse in Texas *from Burt Reynolds, but neither she nor co-star Sylvester Stallone could give away her third effort,* Rhinestone. *Undaunted and determined to take control of her celluloid future, she teamed up with her personal manager, Sandy Gallin, to form Sandollar Productions, which just produced* Jacknife, *starring Robert De Niro, and is one of the hottest shops in Hollywood, with development deals all over town. Turning to the small screen, Gallin negotiated for Dolly the largest deal in television history—$44 million over two years for a weekly variety show, which, alas, became a victim of too great expectations and was not renewed. A greater success is Dollywood, in Pigeon Forge, Tennessee, a multimillion-dollar entertainment park, which has hosted over five million visitors since opening in 1986. This fall Dolly will be back on the big screen, with Shirley MacLaine, Sally Field, and Olympia Dukakis, in* Steel Magnolias, *Herbert Ross's version of the Off Broadway play about small-town southern womanhood.*

I met Dolly at the Beverly Hills Hotel and was surprised to find that she was barely five feet tall, yet larger than life at the same time. The big, teased platinum hair, the heroic cleavage erupting above a wasp waist, and the five-inch stiletto heels matching stiletto magenta nails combine to create an overwhelming effect. Yet Dolly's southern drawl and her southern charm put me instantly at ease. Having grown up in the Tobacco Road environs of eastern North Carolina, I had met lots of girls like Dolly, albeit never as accomplished—sweet country girls who had gone to the shopping mall and gotten themselves all made up, dressed up, and tarted up because that's what they thought the big-city girls looked. Not Scarlett O'Hara, but Harlot Mascara. They were the sort of girls you'd take to the big dance at the country club, not only to épater la bourgeoisie *but also because you'd have a thousand times more fun with them than with the stuck-up debutantes your parents were pushing.*

Escaping the bedlam of press agents, photographers, and makeup and hair people, Dolly took me into her bedroom and locked the door. What southern boy could ask for more?

WILLIAM STADIEM: They never get the South right in movies, do they?

DOLLY PARTON: Hardly ever. The Hollywood version of the country and mountain people has always bothered me. They usually make us look a lot more stupid and dumb than we really are. It's a very distorted view. But I guess the met that they even notice us at all is something.

WS: Did you see Mississippi Burning?

DP: No, I didn't.

WS: It made us all look like a bunch of cavemen down there.

DP: *[laughs]* I guess there're parts of that area of the country where folks can be pretty backwoodsy. There're some parts that are as bad as *Deliverance.* But the majority of people are very sweet, very religious, very kind, very giving. It's only when you get into those rural areas, the very mountainous areas, that they don't know how to protect themselves other than with crude behavior and violence.

WS: You grew up in the Smoky Mountains.

DP: I grew up at the foot of the Smoky Mountains—the actual area is called Mountainview. Some called it Locust Ridge; we called it Over in the Holler. It was up in the mountains, but there were some valleys and our little ol' house in between the mountains. I was born in a one-room cabin on the banks of the Little Pigeon River, on January 19, 1946.

WS: It must have been a cold day.

DP: *[laughs]* It was. I was born at home, and it was snowin', they say. There's twelve of us kids, and six were born at home. I was one of the first six. I have a sister and two brothers who are older than me, and eight are younger than me.

WS: *All your family is still back in Tennessee?*

DP: Yes, all of my people live in Tennessee.

WS: *Where is your home now?*

DP: Well, my main home is Tennessee, always will be—that's my home, that's my heart. I moved to Nashville in 1964—my husband, Carl, is from Nashville, born and raised in that area—so that's where my big house is, my dream house, so to speak. My roots are in the Smokies, so I bought the old Tennessee mountain home and fixed that up for a retreat for myself. But I spend a lot of time in L.A. and have an apartment in New York, so it's kind of like my home is where my work is—but my real home I would definitely have to say is Tennessee.

WS: *Did they get the South right in* Steel Magnolias?

DP: I think they did. That was written by a southern boy, Bobby Harling. It's a true story, centered in Natchitoches, Louisiana. We did it all there on location. In the movie it's called Chinquapin—they changed the names of some of the places to protect the guilty, I guess. *[laughs]* Natchitoches is a beautiful old southern town; the people are very sweet—they used a lot of the local people for atmosphere. I definitely was a country girl, and my part was Truvy the beautician. Olympia Dukakis plays the mayor's wife; Shirley MacLaine plays Ouiser, the eccentric old rich lady; Julia Roberts plays the young girl; Sally Field plays the mother; and Daryl Hannah plays the assistant in the beauty shop. Sam Shepard plays my husband, and Tom Skerritt is Sally Field's husband. All those people have a great deal of love and respect for the South, and they studied the dialogue; they depended on me and Bobby Harling a great deal to show them how the people really speak. They tried very hard, and I think Herbert Ross did a great job of directing it. They've done as good a job of capturing the South as I've ever seen.

WS: *Shirley MacLaine is sort of a southern girl—she's from Richmond.*

DP: Yeah, she is. And I bet Julia Roberts is from Georgia or Alabama—a southern town, that's for sure.

WS: *And they got their accents right?*

DP: Yeah, they were good, I thought. It wasn't hard for me, because that's the way I talk. I think that movie's very special: it's a comedy—it makes you laugh a lot—but it's got some parts where you'll cry your heart out. It's just about this town and its people, and the love, and how everybody knows everybody's business but sticks together anyway. It's a story about this young girl who dies from complications from diabetes because she's very headstrong—she's not supposed to have a baby, and that's what kills her. That's the sad part of the movie, but it's a comedy. It's the people, really, the characters and personalities that make the movie.

WS: *Did you see the play Off Broadway before you agreed to do it?*

DP: Yes, they asked me about doing it and I read the script, but I couldn't get much out of it, so they sent me to New York to see it. I went there and met Bobby Harling. I liked the play and thought I could play that part. And it was the chance of a lifetime to work with all those people— 'cause I was hearing about who they were trying to get to be in the movie and that they were definitely interested in doing it. I took it and I'm glad I did. I'm real curious to see what the outcome will be.

WS: *Do you get to sing in it?*

DP: No, I'm just a country girl who owns a beauty shop. My contract called for me to write the theme song, and I could have pushed that on through, but after we saw the movie, my character was so different from just Dolly Parton that I didn't really have a chance to do it. The movies I've been in before were more personality pieces; they were very much Dolly Parton. I think if I did the song up front it would take away from my character, because you'd be thinkin' Dolly Parton too much.

WS: *You said once that if you hadn't become a star you probably would have been a beautician.*

DP: If I hadn't been in the business I would have been a missionary or a beautician. I love being with people, and I love working with them and being out with them. I think that in a beauty shop, when you make people feel pretty or feel good about themselves, that's great. That's why this part was really good for me—I really related to it. I love to play with hair and makeup, andI love gaudy things—it's true.

WS: *Now, speaking of missionary, what was it like working with Shirley MacLaine? Did she try to get you out on a limb with her?*

DP: *[laughs]* I think we had a mutual respect for each other. I'm very definite about my faith and my religious beliefs—and I really like Shirley a lot. We became good friends, and it was not based on whether or not I believed in her faith. We didn't have any conversations about anything of a spiritual nature. I wasn't that curious about what she's into.

WS: *She wasn't trying to convert the cast?*

DP: No, not at all. People asked her a lot of questions, and she was always talking about her beliefs, but I wasn't one of the ones who were curious. I know all that sort of thing; I've studied all kinds of religions and faiths. And that's all fine—it works for her, and it's good. It's not to say that I believe or don't believe—I'm open for everything.

WS: *You grew up in the Pentecostal church. Are you still active in it?*

DP: I never go to church. I believe faith is in the heart. I'm not a religious person, but I'm very spiritual. I believe that God is love, and I've always been a firm believer in that thing that is greater than us, that great energy, that great love, and I've used that all my life. I think a lot of my achievements have come from the strength that came from my faith in God.

WS: *Have you seen the Madonna video "Like a Prayer"?*

DP: No, I've heard a lot about it. But I would have no comment about it anyway. I don't judge other people's work. I believe we do the best we can, and do what we think is the best for us at the time. But I know there was a lot of controversy about it. I think Madonna is very talented, and I'm sorry for the public and for her that things didn't turn out better.

WS: *I love the title song of your new album, "White Limozeen," in which you talk about Daisy Mae in Hollywood, who is rising "from the breadlines to the headlines." How autobiographical is that song?*

DP: Oh, totally. It's not everything I've ever done or all that I've ever felt, but it's all Dolly, totally based on who I am and my trips to Hollywood, and just the whole idea of a country girl trying to make it big in show biz, concerts, etc. I've had equally hard times in Nashville, trying to make it big, walking the streets from the breadlines to the headlines, trying to become a star. That's a song I wrote with Mac Davis, a good friend of mine, one of the great songwriters. We co-wrote two songs in one night, and they're both on this album.

WS: *In one night? They're so great. You want to get up and dance to them.*

DP: I enjoyed working with Mac. He's been very good to me since my early days. He was responsible for getting me together with Sandy Gallin, my business manager, when back in the '70s I was looking to move from Nashville, trying to expand my horizons and looking for management. He helped me. Then Mac was very kind and let me open some of his shows in those early days. We had often talked about writing together. So when I got ready to do this album, I called Mac and said, "Why don't you put your golf clubs in the closet and get your guitar out?" 'Cause Mac's very well-to-do now and he doesn't have to work if he doesn't want to. He plays a lot of golf. I said that I missed his writing, and why didn't he come do this with me. And he did.

I told him I wanted to write like we were hungry again. I had a white limousine when I had the Dolly show, and I had a person to drive me back and forth to work. I got hysterical in the back of the car, thinkin', Here I am, in the back of a white limousine being driven up to Mac's mansion in Beverly Hills, and we're gonna write like we're hungry again . . . yeah, right. It just hit me real funny. So I was laughin', and when I got out of the car I told him how tickled I was, so he said, "Let's just write that." So we did. His beautiful wife, Lisa, came into the room just as we finished "White Limozeen" and I said, "Why don't we write about your beautiful wife?" They were kissing and acting just like newlyweds, very much in love. So that's how we came to write "Wait 'Til I Git You Home." That's how good we write together, how right it was.

I think the time is perfect for me to do country music again. It's kind of come back around to that traditional sound that it had when I could make a living at it years ago and wanted to get out and expand. The time's perfect for that, so I got Ricky Skaggs to produce the album. He had a better understanding of who I am, because he grew up in eastern Kentucky, very similar to the way we did, and his people are like my people. He knows that Appalachian music, the Irish-English-Dutch influence that came there to the Appalachian mountains. And I felt that if I was gonna do a true country album in a big way again, it was important to have somebody who has an understanding of my roots, all of them—bluegrass, country, the mountains, the gospel—not just country music as we've come to know it. I just felt we'd be right for each other. He played a lot of instruments on the album, did a lot of background singing, and I think he did a wonderful job.

WS: I think the album transcends country. I think anybody would like it.

DP: That's what I'm hopin'. I've hoped and wished that I could be accepted with the music that I do best—not only by the country fans but by a broader audience. And I'm hopin', with all the groundwork I've laid through the years and all the fans I've acquired through the movies and television and the many things I've done, that once I have that good music there they'll accept that as just Dolly's music instead of saying it's country or pop or whatever.

WS: Did you do a video for any of the songs?

DP: I just did a video of the first single, which is "Why'd You Come in Here Lookin' Like That?"

WS: There's one line that I just loved—

DP: "Big ideas and a little behind"?

WS: Yeah, that's right: "A wanderin' eye and a travelin' mind/Big ideas and a little behind." Is that your type of guy?

DP: Yeah. But I like those with little ideas and big behinds too. *[laughs]*

WS: The love songs on the album are very touching—they're songs about heartbreak. And yet you've been married ever since you were a little girl, and I know all of your music comes from the heart. How do you get into that?

DP: But that doesn't mean that I've been dead . . . that I've been blind . . . that I haven't suffered. My life's very colorful. Yeah, I've been married for twenty-three years, and I have a great husband and he's also a great friend. But I've done a whole lot of things, and as a writer I draw not only from things I've experienced but from things that I see people go through, people that I know and love. So it's certainly easy for me to write sad things; I grew up with that. It's like some kind of a chord struck in me every time I take a guitar in my hand—I want to write sad songs. I guess it's just those songs that've been embedded in my body, those old songs Mama used to sing, those Appalachian songs, songs of tragedy, and story songs that I grew up with. And I love them. Country music's famous for that. There *are* some good love songs on this album.

WS: *Tell me about the song about Jesus, "He's Alive."*

DP: It's a beautiful song. I found it years ago. My husband and I were drivin' back to Nashville from California, out in the middle of nowhere, and we couldn't get a big radio station. We were just punching around, and on this local station in the desert we heard this song. We pulled into the next gas station and called them up to see who it was. It was Don Francisco, and they gave us the information off the back of the album, and when we got back to Nashville we looked the record up. I've been wanting to record that song for years. It's the story of the Crucifixion through Peter's eyes—Peter was the one who betrayed Jesus. It's so emotional. Bein' very spiritual, I like to say something about God somewhere in my albums.

WS: *You're about to go on tour, aren't you?*

DP: I haven't had a full band together in almost seven years. I took off ill and I lost my band. I've had pickup bands, and I've done shows, but not a full show with a theme. I've put together a new group called the Mighty Fine Band. What I want to do is record with my group and perform on the road. I have a show put together that's the story of my life—just tellin' about the early days, the hit songs, my first record, through the Porter Wagoner days, the comedy, the talk, puppy love, and all that—and so I think I have a real special show. I have leased buses for goin' on tour out into the rural areas. I'm gonna be on the road for a lot of years now with this show, and I'm very excited about that. I *will* take off to do movies and special projects, but I'm taking my music a lot more seriously than I've been able to do in a lot of years.

WS: Did you ever meet Roy Orbison?

DP: Oh yeah. I knew Roy. He was the sweetest person. I hadn't seen or talked to Roy in many years. He was someone I've been with on different occasions, a very warm person. Yes, I'll miss him. He was so gentle.

WS: You never met The King, Elvis?

DP: I'm not sorry that I didn't—because there was something about him that I held sacred within myself. On many occasions I had a chance to meet him. He wanted to record "I Will Always Love You." He loved the song and was gonna record it. I had my own publishin' company, and as the writer I wouldn't give Colonel Tom Parker the song, because I didn't want to start doin' that—you know, leavin' myself open—because then everybody would record it. So Elvis didn't do it and I'm sorry. I would have loved to have had somethin' of mine recorded by him. He also liked "Coat of Many Colors," and he tried for a few years to find a way he could do it and make sense of it, but I wouldn't have given up the publishing rights on that either.

WS: The Colonel had to have the publishing?

DP: Yeah. It was heartbreaking.

WS: You've become a Hollywood mogul through your Sandollar Productions. It's one of the most powerful production companies in Hollywood.

DP: Yes, I think there's gonna be a lot of wonderful things coming out of it. I like being involved in the business. One of the things I'm real proud of, in addition to the production company, the Hollywood end of it, is Dollywood. That's one of the dreams of my life—to be able to go back home to do something great for that part of the country.

WS: How far is it from Pigeon Forge?

DP: It's in Pigeon Forge. It's about ten miles from where I grew up. It's a theme park, not an amusement park, though we do have an amusement area. We have a couple of hundred acres of beautiful land there. We add a couple of new things each year—it's kind of a culture thing, arts and crafts—and it's a way to preserve the Smoky Mountain heritage.

WS: How many people do you employ?

DP: A few thousand. It's provided lots of jobs not only in the park but in the area—hotels, motels, restaurants, new shops.

WS: So it's becoming an important tourist attraction?

DP: Yes, it is. The Smoky Mountains National Park is the most visited national park in the U.S. Most people don't know that 10 million people come through there every year. They have the biggest assortment of trees. It's a great thing to have up there.

We do a lot of work not only for that—we also have what we call the Dollywood Foundation, a foundation set up for the education and health care of the people in Sevier County. We focus mostly on the education of the kids. We have the highest dropout rate of any place in the U.S., and that's sad.

We work very hard to give scholarships to those kids. We have what we call the Buddy Plan to get these kids to stay in school. It started out with seventh and eighth graders, potential dropouts. If they help each other stay in school, they get $1,000 when they graduate. It's not much money, but that's for them. We have a hotline to the Dollywood Foundation in case they get in trouble. The reason we have such a high dropout rate is that we have a lot of poor people there. Kids don't have clothes to go to school, and they're ashamed. A lot of their parents didn't go to school, so it's not a high priority with them. We have to show them the importance of staying in school. We get them clothes and things they need. And now we're getting a lot of colleges involved. They've offered to match what we put out from the Dollywood Foundation—scholarships, grants, student loans, jobs for students. We're gettin' all those people involved. I do a lot of work around the country for different charities, but mostly I try to help in my part of the country. They say charity begins at home, and I believe that.

WS: Have you ever thought of getting into politics?

DP: *[laughs]* No. If I ever ran in east Tennessee, I'd probably win. I'm just jokin', but I *have* been asked to run, to be involved. But I don't want to get into that. Too much pressure.

WS: *Did you ever get involved in fundraising for politicians?*

DP: No. I don't get involved in politics. I just have my own views, and I usually don't tell people my opinions; I keep them to myself.

WS: *You've been writing songs since you were five. When you came to Hollywood you were already a big star. Can you compare Hollywood and Nashville?*

DP: The people in Nashville are simple country people. Everybody is like family. It's not cutthroat and high-pressure, but it's never easy anywhere. I love the energy and the high power of the city.

WS: *When you came out to Hollywood, how did you get into* 9 to 5?

DP: Jane Fonda produced that movie, and she had a definite idea of getting a country girl with a lot of strength and power. So she approached me with it. I had never seen a movie being made, so even if I do something that wins an award, nothing will ever be as special as that.

That was fun. *Whorehouse* I wasn't sure about. I wanted to do it and I didn't want to do it. I told my manager I didn't want to do it, I didn't feel right about it, it was gonna be a heartache for me. That movie turned out to be nothin' but a bloodbath. It was the hardest project I've done in my life. So much fightin', so much trouble. It made a lot of money, but it was a disaster as far as the critics were concerned.

WS: *Had you seen the Broadway play?*

DP: Yeah. I wish we could have captured all that. It was very good, very colorful. I loved working with Burt [*Reynolds*], with Dom DeLuise and Charles Durning; they were just precious. But it was very hard for me. I wasn't in good health, I was on medication, I was having surgery, I was going through a broken heart during that whole time—that was as hard for me as *9 to 5* was a joy. When I was doing that I thought, Boy, this is fun, this is just great. I got spoiled. Then I found out in the second movie how hard it is. I realized how important it was for me to have some sort of control over the projects that I did from then on.

WS: But on Rhinestone *you didn't have any control.*

DP: No, I had no control over the movie, but it was the first project I did after I was ill and had been out of work for eighteen months, and it was a hit with me. Being around Stallone was fun—I really enjoyed doing it. It was a disaster—but fun, cute.

WS: The writer, Phil Robinson, complained that he had written a wonderful script but that Stallone decided he knew better and rewrote it.

DP: Well, Sylvester Stallone does get very involved in writing and rewriting.

WS: He didn't sing in that, did he?

DP: He tried.

WS: [laughs] He did?

DP: *[laughs]* It's a matter of opinion. I've done two movies with people who can't sing. Burt Reynolds and Stallone both knew they couldn't sing. They were good sports about it—it's not like they were trying to prove they could.

WS: There's always been talk, since 9 to 5, *of you and Jane Fonda and Lily Tomlin doing another movie together.*

DP: We've talked about it. We've had some scripts. I even came up with a few ideas of my own. But I'm not sure that's meant to be. When you do something great, you don't know if it's wise to go back. I've never liked sequels, and I've often said I don't like to chew my tobacco more than once. To do it again you've got to be twice as good as you were the first time—and the chances of us being that good again are slim. Like the *Trio* album with Linda Ronstadt and Emmylou Harris. Lord, it took us ten years before we tried it, and it was a hit—it was such a wonderful thing; it was *so* good. Now everybody's talking about us doing another one. But the chances of that are also slim. Could we ever find the time again? Should we? But the trio opened up the way for me to decide that the people had really missed hearing me sing country, and a lot of people had wanted me to do an album on my own that was similar in nature and simple. So that was really a turning point in my music career.

I really don't know if I'll ever do another thing with Linda and Emmylou, or if I'll ever do anything again with Lily and Jane. But I loved doing both those things the first time. I work great with women; my greatest successes have been with women; and now here we are with *Steel Magnolias*. I'm hopin' that one is charmed and blessed too. I think I work well with women because I like women. I have all these sisters, all these aunts that I love, my mother, good girlfriends. I enjoy the men, but I just don't have the same success—except with Kenny Rogers, who is a magical man, and I love workin' with him.

WS: *Is there any star you're dying to work with?*

DP: I've always—I don't know why—wanted to work with Dudley Moore. I think he's just eternally cute, and we'd maybe be able to do something great if it was the right thing, but neither of our movie careers is on the upswing at the moment.

WS: *A lot of people compare you to Marilyn Monroe. You're both very blonde and pretty; you're both voluptuous, sweet, and likable. Do you see any parallels? You both came from adverse backgrounds and became stars.*

DP: Well, I don't see any similarities. We're very different kinds of people. I don't relate to her. I would relate more to somebody like Mae West— I'm little and overexaggerated, very outgoing and ballsy. I've had more people compare me to her. I'm very complimented either way, but I've never patterned myself after either of them. I was grown before I even saw their movies.

WS: *You didn't have any movies or TV where you grew up, did you?*

DP: No, I was a big girl before I saw movies. I think it's good, because that way I wasn't musically influenced by anybody. Most of the people I was influenced by were my family—my mother's family are musical. I grew up singin' in the church, hearin' my uncles and aunts sittin' around pickin' guitars and banjos and mountain instruments and singin'—that, more than the big stars, was my introduction to music. I was pretty much established and on the radio before I paid that much attention to other people.

WS: *You once said that you got your style from the Bible.*

DP: From the Bible?

WS: *Yes. I read somewhere that you got your ideas from the kings and queens . . .*

DP: Oh, yes, from the fairy tales and from Bible stories—witches and kings and queens from the fairy-tale books. That's how I knew there was a world beyond the Smoky Mountains. I thought you were saying that was where I got my look, the way I dress, the image I have, with the clothes and the makeup and the hair. I've always said—and it's the truth—that it came from a serious place: a country girl's idea of what glamour is. I was impressed with what they called "the trash" in my hometown. I don't know how trashy these women were, but they were said to be trashy because they had blond hair and wore nail polish and tight clothes. I thought they were beautiful.

WS: *How old were these girls you were noticing? High-school girls or—*

DP: No, these were streetwalking women, not schoolgirls. These were like "strollops," as my mother called them—strumpets and trollops. [*laughs*]

WS: *You've always said, "I have bad taste." It's almost as if you revel in it, as if you're wearing a costume.*

DP: Oh yeah. I don't care what the style is. I like to look a certain way, and I'm happy when I look a certain way, the way I feel most comfortable. And like I say, I've made the most of it. When I first started being even more outrageous than I really am was when people started payin' a lot of attention to me and tellin' me how I should change my hair and the way I dress. And I just thought to myself, Not only will I not change it, I'll make it even more exaggerated. But it's worked for me. It's fun. I'm like a kid playin' with crayons. I love hair, makeup, shoes—as I say, it's born out of my idea of what glamour is. I wear long nails because I have short little fat hands, I wear high-heeled shoes because I'm short, and I wear my hair real big because my hair won't do everything I want it to. I love the makeup because it makes me feel radiant. I just feel that part of the magic that I may have is that I look totally artificial but I'm totally real.

WS: How does it feel being so skinny? You're as thin as a fashion model now.

DP: I love it. I never was a fat person. I always had a nice body, always weighed about 110 to 115 pounds. I'm five-one, or five-two if I stretch. It was when I was about twenty-eight that I started to gain weight, when I started to be able to go out to finer restaurants and wasn't so active anymore. Then I started having a lot of health problems. But I was eatin' like a hog. I love to eat.

WS: Well, southerners like to eat everything fried.

DP: All the time I grew up eating that stuff, it didn't pile up on me, but from the time I was thirty until I was forty I gained. I love being slim. Everybody says I'm too thin, but I've found the place where I'm comfortable, and everybody'll just have to get used to it—if I'm lucky enough to stay there.

WS: You probably have the smallest waist I've ever seen on a woman. It looks like an eighteen-inch waist.

DP: Well, it's small. Even when I was heavy, though, I had a small waist. It runs in my family. That's the one thing that kept me from being the same size all over.

WS: Have you started to change your wardrobe now?

DP: Oh yes. I used to have three or four sizes in my closet, 'cause I never knew what I was going to fit into. But I've pretty much maintained my weight for about a year and a half now, within five to ten pounds.

WS: Do you stay on a diet, or do you just eat small amounts of things?

DP: I eat what I want; I just don't eat a lot of it. I eat a lot of small meals: I eat the sweet things, the pizza. I cook my own stuff. I don't have maids or servants. People come and clean my house once a week.

WS: What do you do for exercise? Do you do Jane Fonda's workout?

DP: Oh no. I hate to exercise. I don't do it. I'm trying to get myself used to it, but I'm particular about who I sweat with, so I don't go to these sweatshops. I've always been real self-conscious about that. Even in high school, I would make every excuse in the world not to have to exercise with the rest of the kids. I was embarrassed. I just don't like to work out with other people.

WS: *How do you like to spend your time when you're in Hollywood? Are there any places you like to go to when you're here, or is it always work?*

DP: No, it's not always work. I like to go out to restaurants. One thing I love about Hollywood is the great restaurants.

WS: *Do you have a big fan club here? Are people always coming up to you?*

DP: You know, it's really amazin'—I go everywhere I want to, I do everything I want; people are very nice, in general. I guess it depends on who you are, the type of personality you have. When somebody speaks to me, or a few people want an autograph, I don't consider that being bothered. Now, that drives some people crazy. I speak to everybody, and smile and am friendly. A lot of times that's all people expect of you. But then because I'm nice and friendly and sweet, lots of people come up who wouldn't normally go up to someone. But it's just a matter of "Hi, how ya doin'? Will you sign this?" To me it's much easier to be nice.

WS: *That's because you're from the South.*

DP: I love people. I guess some people might think I'm squirrelly and odd, but I don't mind that kind of thing. I *do* have fans here. Thank goodness.

WS: *Have you performed all over the world—in Europe, Japan?*

DP: All over the world.

WS: *Are you popular in Japan?*

DP: I guess they like short blonde women with big boobs. They really do. I'm little, so they relate to me. The men really love women with big boobs. I guess I'm intriguing to them.

WS: *I think you brought big breasts back into style. Here in Southern California these plastic surgeons are doing land-office business. What do you think of that?*

DP: Whatever makes somebody feel good about herself . . . If you've got the money and you've got the nerve, if you've got the desire, whatever makes you feel good, I think you should do. I'm certainly not one to condemn anybody for anything like that. I think that if you feel better about yourself you work better. If it makes you a better person for everybody, I say more power to you. I'm for anything that makes your life richer and fuller and better.

WS: *Do you have a favorite designer?*

DP: I have a great designer who's the best for me: Tony Chase. He's from New York. He does things for a lot of people, but he does a lot for me—all the stuff on my TV show, the things I'm gonna wear today for *Interview*. He sure has made me look better than anybody else has. He knows how to coordinate things. He's the only person I would let touch me anymore.

WS: *Does your family come out here to L.A. and spend much time with you? Or do they stay back in Tennessee?*

DP: My family's welcome wherever I am. I'm crazy about my family. Some of my best friends are in my family.

WS: *Do they like Hollywood?*

DP: Well, they love it the way they come here, because I show them the best times.

WS: *You give them the "White Limozeen" treatment?*

DP: Yes, I do. That's no joke. I love for my family to come and visit. It's a treat for them, and it's a treat for me. I love to take them around and show them the things I enjoy.

WS: *Do any of your brothers or sisters want to be stars?*

DP: Lots of them are involved in the business—they write and sing. A lot of my family works at Dollywood, performing there on the grounds, singing.

Years ago I had a whole show with my family. That was very difficult for them and for me. I was like the mother; I felt extremely responsible. And then, of course, they were growin', and they had girlfriends and boyfriends and were gettin' married—it was hard to keep them all together.

I had a wonderful time while it was happening. I wouldn't take nothin' for the experience, and neither would they. It was fun, but it *was* hard, because it's hard when it's family. You worry about them if they're sick, you worry about them if things aren't right, or whatever. But it was not the best situation for any of us.

WS: *Your husband, Carl, doesn't like to fly, does he?*

DP: Carl's flown only one time in his life, years ago. That was when I threatened to kill him if he didn't go with me to Hawaii. See, I love to travel; I love to go all around the world. So I have all these great friends, all these male friends, and that's why I always get accused of cheatin' and all that, because some of my best friends are men. Carl would prefer that I be with men if I'm gonna go out and do things. For the safety, if for nothing else. So he doesn't mind the escorts that I have, and I have many good friends. I've traveled with other people much more than I have with Carl.

WS: *You said it was very easy for you to communicate with the woman, Liz Landrum, on whom your part in* Steel Magnolias *was based, because you're a southern girl and not some Hollywood actress. When I was growing up in the South, those southern girls were pretty good actresses too. The southern women were always very calculating, wanting to get that rich man. There was a lot of that, and I see many of the same things here in Hollywood. What would you say is the difference between the ambitious southern girl and the actress who comes to Hollywood?*

DP: I don't think that's just southern women. There are those types of women who are just out to get whatever. But that's why I've always been so proud that I've had my own success—that I've never had to depend on a man for it. Never wanted a man for his money; I always wanted a man for his body. [*laughs*]

Liz is very special. I got to meet her, and she's just a real down-home girl. There isn't a pretentious bone in her whole body. I related to her character because she's just a real outgoing, sweet, friendly, warm, wonderful person, and she related to me because, being a southern girl, she knew me from the Porter Wagoner days. She loves country music—that's her style—so she was happy that I was playin' her part, instead of some-body that she didn't relate to. She knew that I had a heart. She knew that I grew up poor. She knew that I was so much of who she was. So that is what I meant about my playing the part rather than having Meryl Streep come in to play a country girl.

WS: *You were one of the girls.*

DP: Exactly.

WS: *Were the low ratings of your television show a big disappointment for you? Everybody thought that it was going to be the biggest show since Ed Sullivan's.*

DP: Well, that was one of the reasons that it wasn't. Too much was expected. Too much publicity and promotion. It put all of the pressure on me, really. It was not so much my doing. I would have preferred just to build the show into what it should have been and let people grow into lovin' it. But anytime you talk about all the money and the stuff that's up-front, people resent you. It's like if you're gonna make that much money, and you're gonna brag about it that much, then they just throw up their arms, sit back, and say, Show me. Right out of the chute I had problems. I saw in the first three months that the show wasn't gonna work, 'cause I didn't have the right staff; I didn't have the right people with me. That's another thing about havin' city people with me—Hol-lywood versus Nashville, city versus country. I had a totally different idea of what the show should have been and could have been. I knew right away it wasn't gonna make it; I knew it was impossible for me to put it the way it ought to go—it was too far-gone. Too much attention, and there wasn't anything to talk about . . . and I'm easy to write and talk about.

I take full responsibility for it. I'm not blamin' anybody for it. The people involved did their best; it just wasn't good enough. I managed to enjoy it, though. I decided to do the most with the parts that were workin' and enjoy that, and not to let it drive me crazy. I loved the clothes, I loved the guests that we had, I loved to get the chance to meet the people, I loved the chance just to do it. And I learned a lot—what to do and what not to do. I don't think the show hurt my career. If I'd continued with the show for another season, it could have done great damage to my career, because people would not have respected me for going on with it.

WS: *But you had a commitment. You could have continued if you had wanted to.*

DP: Well, it was mutual. I didn't want to continue. They felt that it was best not to. It was just not coming together. It didn't sour me on TV. I will do specials, of course, and movies of the week, and produce other things for people, and I still would like to do a great variety show, but more like behind the scenes, bein' out with real people, performin' onstage. So I'm tryin' to develop a sitcom for myself, about the real life of a person, very much like the Dolly Parton story. Very much like what you go through, the battles you have to fight with the network, the family that you have comin' to see you, the problems you have traveling—the real thing. I think there's a magical way to do it, and I'm tryin' very hard to develop that, and I have people workin' on it. And when the time comes I will stick my neck right back out again and try. I may not even do it in Hollywood.

Now, don't get me wrong–I'm not down on Hollywood. I have a lot of great friends here who've helped me do a lot of great things, and they've made me rich—you know, with things that I might never have made money with at all. I'm not sayin' that this is a bad town—this has been a good town to me. I'm specifically talkin' about the TV show now. But let's put it this way: I don't regret it. I'm only sorry it didn't do all it could have. I apologize to the public for that. I'll never apologize for tryin'.

WS: *You were writing a book at one point, weren't you?*

DP: There are so many things I want to do, and some things take priority over others. There will come a time—especially when I'm older—when I will publish a lot of the things that I'm writing. I had a deal with Simon and Schuster. I said, I don't want any pressure, and I'll get the book out when I'm done with it, in the next two years. But then they started pullin' and tuggin', and they put other writers on it, but I didn't want to do it like that, so I pulled out of the whole deal. But I'm still writin'.

I still hope to do *my* story. A lot of people are writing the Dolly Parton story, though I don't know how anybody could write the Dolly story like me—I tell everything; they just get their information out of magazines and make up the rest. Anyhow, someday I hope to do a Broadway musical, the story of my life through music. So that's one of the things I'm interested in. But there's no book comin' out. Everybody on earth has a book right now, and I don't want mine to be one of them.

WS: Are there any people in Hollywood whom you're dying to meet and have never met?

DP: No, 'cause if there were people I wanted to meet, I'm here so much that I would just make a point of meeting them. I just take every day as it comes; I just live life easy. If there's something I want to do in life, I'll find a way to do it.

WS: You said the two keys to your life were luck and love. You still think that's true?

DP: Oh yeah. And I like to think that talent is a plus, because I think I do have talent. But I've had good luck, I've had a lot of great people surrounding me, and I am full of love. I love what I do and I love people. And that's why I don't take myself so serious or take the work so serious that I can't enjoy it. I'm not a perfectionist. You know, I like things done properly, but not at the risk of not gettin' to enjoy the work period, where everything is like a big to-do. It ain't fun for me to sit and do an interview. Why can't we have lunch, and why can't we have a glass of wine, rather than just sit and say, Let's get this over with? I like to make the most of each person I meet. I was curious about your name and I couldn't wait to meet you. I was thinkin', Now where does "Stadiem" come from? I wondered if it was a show name or what.

WS: It sounds like a show name, doesn't it?

DP: So, you see, I even enjoy the simplest parts of me.

WS: Because southerners are naturally friendly—

DP: And curious.

WS: *And naturally curious. One last question: where do you see yourself in ten years? Can you think that far down the road?*

DP: Well, I think that I'm not a superstar yet. I would like to see my music really take hold, and to make really great records and keep goin' and have it be a continuous thing rather than a record here and there, a hit album now and then. I'd like to do another TV show, of the right kind. I'd like to make children's albums, do a day show for kids or something. And I'm gonna have a line of cosmetics. I'm gonna publish a lot of the things I've written. I wanna see this production company do great. I would like to make some more great movies. And the Broadway show is something I'd like to have done within this ten-year period. I want to make the most of what I'm doin' so far, and wake up tomorrow with a new dream and get to work on that.

DOLLY DIAMOND

On Gay Rumors

"Some folks think Carl and me cut us a deal years ago for him to be my husband and keep his mouth shut and for that I give him 50 percent of my money. [Is it true?] I'm not gonna say! As for Judy and me, we've been together since we were both seven years old. I call her Sis and she calls me Sissy. That sums up our relationship. She's not my lover; she has never been my lover. But we are so close and we live so close that I am closer to Judy than I am to Carl. If we were lovers I would not be ashamed of it, I'd just say there's a great love between us—so there. . . . Oh, I get hit on all the time by gay women. I'm flattered that they like me and that the gay men like me, too. But I am not gay. I have a gay following because I love and understand gay people. My dearest friends are gay men. . . . What people do behind their closed doors is certainly not my concern unless I'm behind there with 'em and wantin' to do whatever. I grew up around macho men and have had my lovers that are that macho type. I'm kinda drawn to that for my lovers for the most part."

—To Kevin Sessums, *Vanity Fair*, June 1991

DOLLY DIAMOND

On Cosmetic Surgery

"All my life I've heard people say, 'If God had wanted us to be like this he would have made us this way,' and so on. Well, God made us naked too. I can't see what's wrong in doing a little something to make yourself look better so you can feel better about yourself. . . . I've had my breasts lifted. And I had myself a few little nips and tucks here and there, but I'm not frightened about the work I had done. Everything you do in life carries a risk to some degree, and you just have to decide if it's worth it. Life's a gamble, isn't it?"

—To Joyce Maynard, *McCall's*, May 1992

DOLLY DIAMOND

On the Cancellation of Her TV Series

"Well, it hurt my feelings—hurt my pride—more than it hurt my career. Even though it was canceled, it turned out to be a huge success for me financially. Three months into the show, I knew it wasn't going to work and I knew I didn't want it to. I wanted to do a country-music show, a more simple kind of show. Everybody was tryin' to re-create those old variety shows. I'm no Ed Sullivan. I'm a country girl. So nobody would listen to me. I just didn't fight hard enough."

—To Mary Murphy, *TV Guide*, November 27, 1993

DOLLY DIAMOND

On Cosmetic Surgery

"I don't appreciate people asking me about that. But I'm going to try and be honest. I've had nips and tucks. And I would advise people if they are going to do it: Find the best doctors. So many people can get maimed and screwed up. For instance, I have a bad tendency to scar, so I have to be very careful any time I get anything done. But I've never had anything drastic done. I'd rather have it done every two years than wait too long, when all of a sudden everybody knows you've had a face lift. And you look so tight, like a banjo head! I am not delighted to be discussing this."

—To Mary Murphy, *TV Guide* , November 27, 1993

DOLLY DIAMOND

On Her Measurements

"I'm 40-20-36. I used to never tell anyone my measurements, but the older I get the more proud I am."

—To Charles Gandee, *Vogue*, January 1994

ONE TOUGH DOLLY

Jim Jerome | July 1995 | *Ladies' Home Journal*

Dolly returned to the movie screen in 1992 with *Straight Talk*, a film in which she portrayed a woman mistaken for a clinical psychologist who is given her own self-help talk radio show. "The movie gave me a chance to use other parts of myself," she explained in her autobiography. "I was able to contribute to it as an actress (or at least a personality), as a songwriter, and as a singer. The character was one that was very close to me. I was able to inject a considerable amount of what might be called 'homespun wit' into the script."

The standout story from this *Ladies' Home Journal* feature is one of the squabbles and tantrums surrounding the project that would eventually become *Trio II*, Dolly's second album with Linda Ronstadt and Emmylou Harris. Dolly didn't hold anything back in expressing her frustrations over the delays in recording and releasing of the songs the trio recorded a year earlier. Unfortunately, the conflicts and disputes exposed here persisted long after this interview, leaving the album shelved until 1999. —Ed.

When she recently appeared on *Late Show* to chat with host David Letterman and sing a recut version of "Jolene" from her upcoming album, Dolly Parton also used her segment to plug Jukebox Junction, the seven-acre fifties-motif addition to her theme park, Dollywood, in east Tennessee. Letterman, who delights in scrambling his guests' agendas, headed Parton off at the pass. "So," he asked with an impish grin, "you have rides, too, like Space Mountain?"

The imperturbable Parton thrust out the one piece of her franchise she never tires of promoting and shot back, "Space Mountain? I got Twin Peaks."

As Parton powers into her fourth decade in show business, those proud "peaks" and campy zingers continue to resist erosion from the winds of nineties political correctness. But make no mistake: Behind her fastidiously groomed facade, the superstar is a proud, shrewd hard-edged business woman who knows what she wants and how to get it. Yet Parton seems driven not by a world-beating ego, but rather a practical knack for survival in an industry where the young devour their elders.

"I'm competitive in the business world," she says, "trying to beat my own records. I know my strengths and weaknesses, what I will and won't tolerate and sacrifice. I don't put up with as much bull as I used to, and I don't have to kiss nobody's ass to get along in this world."

And why should she? Parton's fabled journey has transformed a dirt-poor "backwoods Barbie" from east Tennessee into an eye-popping showbiz icon: Her success in music, film, song and book publishing, the theme park and ventures ranging from wigs and cosmetics to kids' books have pushed the worth of "Dolly, Inc." to a reported $100 million.

Yet by all appearances, she remains just Dolly. The day after her *Late Show* appearance, Parton relaxes in a suite at The Pierre Hotel, picking at a crème brûlée and berries. Forty-nine looks fabulous on her. Who else would dare wear a getup best described as Frederick's of Dollywood: A skintight bodysuit with a low-cut top and steep heels?

Parton's bubbly, informal style masks her inner steeliness. But clearly, that's what's helped her cope with recent career setbacks and frustrations like her proposed TV sitcom, which has been "reincarnated" several times. The problem: Parton decided the material wasn't quite right. Having endured a late-eighties variety show she once admitted "sucked," she'd rather hold out than settle for an iffy concept.

With a mixed Hollywood movie scorecard (*9 to 5* and *Steel Magnolias* were hits; *Rhinestone* and *Straight Talk* were bombs), Parton frankly says there are "no big [film] offers." And as for her music, she has quit the grueling bus-tour grind of younger days, but because she is now considered Old Guard by country radio stations focusing on attracting young listeners, she "can't get singles played on the radio. I keep thinking they're going to start playing me again. I'm still a dreamer."

Or schemer: Parton displayed keen survival skills with "Romeo," her 1993 single/video with then-hot Billy Ray Cyrus. "I'm commercial-minded. If I can't get my own hit, I'm not too proud to hang onto somebody else's coattails."

Wielding cat-o'-nine-tails was more like it when Parton, Linda Ronstadt and Emmylou Harris teamed up for a sequel to *Trio*, their 1987 platinum treasure. What should have been a major event last fall backfired amid acrimonious bickering.

To hear Parton tell it, the sessions could have been titled "The Three Tempers": Parton, who can nail a song "just as good the first time as the hundredth"; Harris, the "sweet" country purist who painstakingly researched material; and Ronstadt, the perfectionist diva who "loves to live in the studio and works so slow, it drives me nuts. I wanted to get a cattle prod and say, 'Wake up, bitch, I got stuff to do.'"

True, she says, their glorious harmonies were "like a creative, emotional orgasm." But the thrill was gone once Parton's ever-shifting schedule of business, sitcom and book projects left her unavailable to tour and help promote what would have been a fall release. She "cried and begged" her partners to delay release until this spring, when she promised to promote the record. "They pitched a fit and dumped the greatest project ever. It was a sin and a shame—and a stupid decision—to give that album an abortion. It got into a power play. I was made to feel hurt, insulted, burdened with guilt. I would have lived up to my word, but my word wasn't good enough for them. Finally, I just said, 'The hell with it, sue me.'"

"Linda never sounded bitter," an Elektra Records insider says cautiously. "It seems like it's being made into too big of a drama."

Indeed, when Parton demanded her vocals be mixed out of the tracks so Ronstadt couldn't use them on another album, she settled financially. Did [*Trio II*] also cost her in friendship? Parton offers a pouty shrug. "We were never all that close—just girlfriends in the business." Then, picking up with more Dolly-like sass and animation: "I realized we're now just a bunch of old crotchety, cranky women, set in our ways and getting up there 'round fifty, goin' through change-of-life mood swings.

You never know a true feeling from a hot flash. I thought, I don't need this. I ain't that old yet."

In general, Parton does not obsess about aging. She thrives on "staying busy, making something happen. If I get bored, I get depressed." That seems unlikely, given her energy level and work ethic. When Parton arrived for a recent photo session forty-five minutes early, for instance, she grew impatient with the leisurely pace of the photographer and her crew.

She has business on both coasts, so she has an L.A. bungalow *and* a Fifth Avenue apartment, but she spends close to three quarters of her time in Nashville. And though Parton will forge on with the development of her sitcom, she is excited to finally have time to focus on the mammoth catalog of three thousand songs she's written. She'll make demo tapes and "tailor" her pop, gospel and country compositions so she can pitch to "certain people" to record her songs. After all, Whitney Houston's version of Parton's song "I Will Always Love You" was a record-setting No. 1 hit for fourteen weeks, dwarfing the success that Parton had with it. "I make more money from publishing and songwriting than almost anything else I do," she says. "I've never really even worked at it, never pitched a song myself. Now I'm going to see how well I do if *I* push my stuff."

Parton's one career regret is "never being the consistent recording artist I dreamed of being"—meaning, the sustained platinum-album sales of, say, Kenny Rogers, Houston or Elton John. But, if, as she agrees, spreading herself thin with film and other projects has "absolutely" compromised her in the record business, it has saved her in the piggy bank.

"I have had a half-assed so-called crossover-pop career. But lots of [aging country] people now are starving to death. Most of them are what we call hick rich—get rich quick, spend it quick. Being broke and famous is a sad, hard place to be. Sure, I had a lot of irons in the fire, and it burned people's asses back then. Had I not done all these other things, *I'd* be broke now."

She struck literary gold, too, with her best-selling memoir, *Dolly: My Life and Other Unfinished Business*. The book, Parton admits, raised more questions than it answered about her reclusive husband of nearly thirty years, Carl Dean, and lifelong confidante Judy Ogle, who was in the adjoining bedroom at The Pierre and who shadows Parton on the road as a constant companion.

In *Dolly*, Parton described Dean as loyal and loving but "not strong when it comes to my having problems"; she related often sharing a bed with Ogle ("Why scream across the room when you don't have to?") and a bond "closer than husband and wife."

Such titillation, she says, was "deliberate. I can't tell everything about me without hurting someone else. I prayed that I could satisfy people's curiosity in a kind, Christian manner. But I should have called it *My Life and It's Nobody's Business*. Hell, they only paid what, twelve dollars, at bargain prices?" (They'll pay even less for the paperback version, released last month.)

Bottom line on Dean: "What I meant to [write] is, I loved him too much to put him through a lot of the stuff I brought on myself. I share what I want to with Carl, and he knows the rest. Our relationship is like mine and Judy's. It is pure, it is sacred and it is real."

As for Ogle: "We've never been lovers, nor will we ever be lovers. Judy's never been married. She's an old maid [laughing]. She'd probably rather be called a lesbian than an old maid. I don't care who she sleeps with or when she sleeps with them."

Parton needed all the help she could get from both Dean and Ogle during a medical crisis in the early eighties, ultimately undergoing "female surgery" to stem internal hemorrhaging. ("I had a couple of D&C's to control [bleeding]. I was all nerves. I even started to drink to ease my pain," she wrote.) Parton also had her "tubes tied" so she could go off birth control pills. It was a time of career stress, not to mention personal woes: There was turbulence and "betrayal" within her inner circle (she believed confidants were leaking stories to the press), in addition to a fifty-pound weight gain followed by drastic weight loss ("I was a hog, but then I got too skinny") and depression. Her decision not to have children triggered reactions in loved ones (not Dean) that only added to her anguish: "I was feeling guilty about not having kids, about having a career, that I'm not the woman I should be because I don't have a desire to have them, that I was selfish."

Parton's greatest gift, perhaps, is turning such hardships into song. "I cry, I pray, I kick, I piss and moan and cuss and write and sing my songs and it goes away. I almost feel God puts me through heartaches so I will have more to write about. I don't need a psychiatrist. I blurt out everything that I feel."

And after trying "every crazy diet," she has finally made a comfortable, lasting peace with food and her body image. Parton maintains her figure by simply controlling what she eats with light but constant snacks—and cosmetic nips and tucks for good measure. She makes no apologies for liposuction ("If you got those little [hip] pouches that no amount of exercise or diet's gonna get, well, you just go in for a sucking"); breast enhancements ("I had them little soldiers lifted to attention so I don't have to wear a bra"); or tiny tucks under the chin or eyes ("If it makes you feel your best self—and as long as you don't get your plastic surgeon from the Yellow Pages—what's wrong with it?").

Parton's built herself a dream house as well as a dream body. Her home, situated on seventy-five acres, is a few miles from Music Row in Brentwood, a Nashville suburb. And though the house was once surrounded by lush farmland when she and Dean settled there in the seventies, Parton likes that it's now highly developed, with a mall only minutes away. She loves hiking on local trails and playing with her three Nashville-area sisters' kids in their treehouses. She and Dean can fish and picnic at their cabin and houseboat on Old Hickory Lake a half hour away. Dean, fifty-two, who's retired from his asphalt paving business, buys, improves and sells properties. Parton loves dining out, but Elvis is about as likely to be sighted in town as Dean. "Oh, I get him out once in a while, but he don't like to get cleaned up in a suit and tie that much."

Fortunately, Dean tinkers on farm equipment in the barn, leaving Parton free to channel-surf from Court TV to CNN for her daily O.J. trial fix. Two recent high points, she says, were pulling alongside prosecutor Marcia Clark in L.A. freeway traffic, then spotting F. Lee Bailey dining at Mortons. "I told him, 'I'm trying to get a TV show off the ground, [but] you're having a lot more luck than me. I wish to God I had your ratings.' The trial's just the dangedest thing."

Not really. The "dangedest thing" may just be growing up with twelve kids in a two-room mountain shack with no plumbing, using corncobs for dolls and newspaper on the walls for insulation—and becoming Dolly Parton. Small wonder after three decades that it's an identity she's not likely to surrender.

"I'll be this way when I'm eighty, like Mae West," she boasts. "I may be on crutches, in a wheelchair or propped up on some old slantboard, but I'll have my high heels, my nails and makeup on, my hair'll be all poufed up and my boob'll still be hangin' out. It's not a big job being Dolly. It's just my life."

WELCOME TO THE DOLLY HOUSE

Frank DeCaro | July 1997 | *Out*

Along with Barbra, Bette, Cher, Judy, and Madonna, Dolly has long been a gay icon on a first-name basis with much of the LGBT community. As early as 1977, the press took notice of the fabulous and flamboyant crowds she attracted at hip nightclubs like the Boarding House in San Francisco. The August 1977 issue of *High Times* observed that Dolly's audience there "was mostly kinky gays in black leather and chains." As she told the reporter, "I guess a lot of my popularity with gays is my gaudy, flashy appearance. They like to have a good time—I guess that's why they call them gay."

For many years, Dolly has balanced her popularity between two very disparate groups—right-wing Evangelicals and LGBT fans—and somehow found a way to keep everybody happy (most of the time). This feature for *Out* magazine was most likely Dolly's first major interview for a gay-oriented publication. Her latest music release, a collection of dance club remixes, was the impetus for the talk, but Dolly also touched on the subjects of habitual gay rumors and her close friendships with gay friends. Several years later, Frank DeCaro interviewed Dolly again for his popular radio show. —Ed

Dolly Parton sets her sights on gay dance-club audiences. Frank DeCaro chats about her music, image, and who she sleeps next to.

Dolly Parton is ready for dinner. All five-foot-one of her bodacious curves and Dynel blondness is perched on Frederick's of Hollywood–style mules as she moves through the lobby of the posh Pierre hotel overlooking New York's Central Park. Hers is a Southern manner both gracious and "oh my gracious."

Patsy Cline in Jessica Rabbit's body, she offers a friendly hello to anyone who cranes his neck to glimpse her—which is everyone. As she descends the stairs and settles into a corner banquette in the hotel café, the waiters stand in awe, each wearing a grin that says, It's so nice to have you back where you belong. One thing certain: She *is* looking swell, this Dolly. A triumph of style over fashion in "an Azzedine shirt and a K Mart skirt," she is a star and then some. An icon, I call her. "An icon or an eyesore?" Parton shoots back.

This is definitely going to be fun.

"I can't even begin to imagine dressing up in a nice business suit and coming down to dinner," she says, after ordering seared foie gras and mashed potatoes. "I would much rather have the shock value of walking down the steps with my tits hanging out but knowing that I've still got the same brain and the same talent. What kind of fun would I have doing it if I have to be ordinary?"

Over the past 40 years, Parton has made a career of being extraordinary. By her own larger-than-life design—"It costs a lot of money to look this cheap!"—this backwoods babe has reinvented herself as a devilish cartoon with an angel's voice, a slyly campy comedian who has penned some of pop's most enduring songs, and an entertainer whose fans include punk rockers and Bible-thumpers, cross-dressers and conservatives, Calvin Klein and your mother. As Parton's friend, humorist and social-critic-at-large Fran Lebowitz says, "Even people who hate each other love Dolly Parton."

Worth an estimated $100 million—the royalties from Whitney Houston's megahit version of Parton's "I Will Always Love You" weren't exactly chump change—she has been to Hollywood, built a Great Smoky Mountains theme park called Dollywood, survived more than a few savagings by supermarket tabloids, and conquered a weight problem brought on because, as she says, "I'm a true hog by nature." With her classic country songs ("Jolene," "Coat of Many Colors"), her movie appearances (*Best Little Whorehouse in Texas*, *Steel Magnolias*), and her TV specials, she has garnered four Grammys, seven Country Music Association Awards, and even an Oscar nomination (for the title song to *9 to 5*).

Parton's rags-to-riches story has always had particular resonance for gay and lesbian fans. After all, she was RuPaul before RuPaul was born, a paragon of self-reinvention outlined in lip-liner and raised to the heavens by an industrial-strength push-up bra. Born dirt poor and raised on a farm in Sevier County, Tennessee, Parton came from "a family of dreamers"—people with musical ability and a great sense of humor. But no matter how musical, they weren't exactly ready for a daughter as colorful as Dolly. "I used to fight with my daddy and my mama about the stuff I wore," she says. "I wasn't doing it to be trashy. I was doing it 'cause I didn't feel right just being ordinary. It was almost like being gay. It's a good thing I was born a woman, 'cause I'da damn sure been a drag queen if I hadn't. I can't get flamboyant enough."

Young Dolly found her soon-to-be signature look on a trip into town when she spotted a woman with "yellow blond hair all done up and bright red nails and high heels and this real tight skirt. I was a child, and I thought she was beautiful. Someone said, 'Oh, she's just a tramp.' And I thought, That's what I'm going to be when I grow up. So I patterned myself after the town tramp. I still have that look, and I still love it." As many of us struggle to do, the grown-up Parton merges citified sophistication with the human decency that comes from having the humblest of backgrounds. As Lebowitz says, "She would have been a star in any era."

Now, at 51, the singer, songwriter, author, actress, businesswoman, and theme park operator is reaching out to a new audience—circuit queens and club kids. She's doing it with a house version of "Peace Train," her cover of the 1971 Cat Stevens song. Remixed by DJ Junior Vasquez, among others, and featuring backup by the South African a cappella group Ladysmith Black Mambazo, the track originally came from her 1996 album, *Treasures* (Rising Tide). Released to disappointing sales, the eclectic, all-covers CD included Parton's versions of various country tunes plus Neil Young's "After the Gold Rush" and Katrina and the Waves' 1980s hit "Walking on Sunshine" (the song scheduled to be her second dance remix, due out later this year).

"I was looking for something to do that might be accepted in the 'new country' field," Parton says. "I'd tried a few other things that hadn't worked, and I thought, Well, maybe this'll work, and I did *Treasures,* and sure enough, that didn't work either." She laughs, then turns serious. "It's very hard anymore for some of us older artists to know what to do. You really can't sell yourself completely out and do something that's really not you, if you've always been trying to do quality stuff."

This is not Parton's first time at the disco—her 1978 "Baby, I'm Burnin'" and 1979's "Great Balls of Fire" were dance-oriented too—but Dolly as a full-fledged house diva is a new concept, courtesy of Kyle Utley, president of Flip-It Records, which is releasing the remixes. He thought *Treasures* was "brilliantly produced" (by Steve Buckingham) and that "Peace Train" was a natural for the dance floor. "Dolly sang her ass off on that album," say Utley. "I knew that if this woman would do a house track, the reaction would be volcanic." Judging from the initial reaction in clubs like Arena, the New York hot spot where Vasquez spins, Utley is convinced it'll be a "monster hit."

Parton is pleased by Utley's enthusiasm, but her predictions are more reserved. "They think they can sell it," she says. "I'm always tickled to be in any new place they put me." Those new places include on RuPaul's radio show on New York's disco station WKTU—"RuPaul is beautiful," Parton says—and her picture on the cover of OUT.

These are unusual gigs for someone whose core audience includes members of the religious Right. In fact, at risk of reaching perhaps *too* wide an audience with her gay-friendly image, some of Parton's Southern "businesspeople" advised her to turn down RuPaul's VH1 show. But Parton has no fear of potential repercussions from her conservative fans. "They could probably pitch a fit, but what am I supposed to do? This is what I do for a living," she says. "Gay people are fans of mine. It's two different worlds, and I live in both and I love them both, and I understand and accept both."

Parton has always been good at building bridges. When she first made the crossover to pop—with hits like "Here You Come Again" in 1977 and "9 to 5" in 1980—she said, "I'm not leaving country, I'm just taking it with me." And in her private life, some of her closest friends are light-years from Nashville. Parton's best buddy since the early 1970s is her manager, Sandy Gallin, the openly gay super–power broker who has advised Michael Jackson, Cher, Whoopi Goldberg, and Barbra Streisand, among others, and whose intimate include David Geffen and other members of Hollywood's so-called Velvet Mafia. "He's everything you would think that I wouldn't be compatible with," Parton says, "but Sandy and I fell in love instantly. He's the only person who ever saw my dreams the way I see them and believed it when I said I was going to be a big star." For his part, Gallin calls Parton his "soul mate" and says the two are "as close as two people can be who aren't having sex."

Parton's friendship with writer Lebowitz, the curmudgeon's curmudgeon, isn't exactly expected either. "Now you talk about an off-the-wall person and an unlikely friend of mine. She is such a hoot," Parton says. The twosome's nights out in New York's bohemian East Village—the inspiration for one awestruck lesbian short film—are legendary among the city's dykes.

Fueled by such allegiances, rumors that she's gay have surrounded Parton for years. "Everything that could be said about anyone has been said about Dolly," Gallin says. Parton is glad to talk about the rumors and anything else. "That's half the fun for magazines like this," she says. "I don't care what you ask me. And if it's the truth, I'll tell you that, too." Some of her gay fans—and probably some of her detractors—cling to the belief that there's a bull dyke with a crew cut under all that gussy. At the very least, they want to know what the deal is with her constant companion, Judy Ogle. Parton wrote about their friendship in her 1994 autobiography, *Dolly: My Life and Other Unfinished Business*, and makes no secret of the fact that she's sharing a suite upstairs with Ogle the night we meet at the Pierre. But in divulging everything, Parton can leave you more confused than you were when you started.

"We've been best friends since we were in the third grade," she says. "A lot of people have tried to link us, but I'm not the least bit gay. Like I say, I'm not gay but my girlfriend is. That's like something I saw on a shirt. But anyway, Judy's just an old maid. People think because she's never married that she must be a lesbian, and because we've been together, that we must be lovers. But the fact is, I think Judy would rather be called a lesbian than an old maid. . . . She's had boyfriends over the years. She just never met anybody she loved enough to leave what she loved doing. But we're not lovers. If I *was* gay, I'd certainly never find a finer person than Judy as a mate. I'm as close to her just about as I am with husband."

Parton has been married to Carl Dean for 33 years. Although rumor-mongers say she never sees her husband, Parton says she's with him more than ever, now that she's not touring. "They don't see me see my husband because he hates being in the limelight. But I see him all the time," she says. The secret to their marriage? "We just make a point to enjoy the stuff we enjoy and stay out of each other's faces. I don't get in his shit, and he don't get in mine. And we get along great."

So *does* she have short black hair under her wig, as some have suggested? "Oh, I do not. I keep it bleached, and it's the same length that I keep my wigs. I don't always wear a wig. I do when I'm working because I can't stand to sit under a hair dryer or wait around with people pulling on my head. A lot of my early star days, I wasn't wearing wigs. We teased that hair up there and bleached it till it was just like a haystack." But nowadays, she says, "It's like one of my favorite jokes: How long does it take to do your hair? I say 'Hell, I never know, I'm never there!'"

Parton has always been able to toss off a good zinger. While she may not call herself a feminist, she has use her cartoonish femininity to her advantage. "Being a woman always served me well. Somebody said, 'Well, you know, it's always going to be a man's world.' I said, 'Well, you know what? I don't mind that it's a man's world, as long as they don't mind if we run it!'" Parton even stood up to The King. Elvis Presley wanted to record "I Will Always Love You"—which Parton wrote in 1972 as a heartfelt adieu to her longtime singing partner, Porter Wagoner. Parton was thrilled with the prospect until she was told that as part of the deal Presley wanted half the publishing rights. "I said, 'Well, in that case, I don't guess Elvis is going to be recording "I Will Always Love You."' Everybody said, 'You've got to be out of your damn mind,'" Parton remembers. But she prevailed. She always has.

Still, no matter how rich or how successful she has become, Parton never shuns her fans. "It isn't that she's nice for a star, she's nice for anyone," says Fran Lebowitz. "Dolly talks to everyone who talks to her.

If you're out to dinner with her, it ends up where you have the waiter sitting at the table." At the Pierre, the waiter hovers over Parton's table without ever pulling up a chair. But he would be as welcome as the crème brûlee put down before the guest of honor. "We're all exactly the same," Parton says, savoring the sweetness of her dessert. "Some of us just can express it better."

DOLLY PARTON—THE SMARTEST WORKING WOMAN IN SHOW BUSINESS

Linda Ray | November / December 1999 | *No Depression*

The Grass Is Blue, Dolly's first all-bluegrass album, was released in 1999 to critical acclaim. Although the material wasn't quite suited for airplay on mainstream country radio stations, the album sold well and its success helped to rejuvenate and thrust her career into the new millennium. Linda Ray interviewed Dolly about *The Grass Is Blue* for *No Depression*, a magazine dedicated to the importance of Americana and roots music on the national stage. The album went on to win the Grammy for Best Bluegrass Album in 2001 and paved the way for another successful bluegrass effort from Dolly entitled *Little Sparrow*. —Ed

In this era of celebrity, Dolly Parton could be one if she never sang a note. A sign in her Dollywood museum exhorts, "You're only as big as your biggest dream," and Parton has always dreamed of being somewhat larger than life.

Yet the heart of Parton's identity remains her music. If the raging flame of fame begins to flicker—and eventually, invariably, it does—she'll still have her singing, her writing, her natural inclination toward a good country song. It's home, sweet home, and she'll always find her way back to that place.

Her place in the tabloids will inevitably be assured by her challenge to gravity alone, both metaphorical and physical. A 5-foot-1 bundle of giggly fun, Parton devastates with her exuberant, impossibly energetic stage presence and her Minnie Pearl-meets-Mae West wisecracks. (Once asked why her waist is so small, she answered that it was the same reason her feet are so small: "Nothing grows in the shade.") Her acrophobia-inducing spike heels, eight-inch-high hair and monstrous breasts scoff at the demands of physics, not to mention aging, and she revels in being the global equivalent of her childhood idol, the town tramp. As writer Frank DeCaro said of her in *Out* magazine, Dolly "was RuPaul before RuPaul was even born."

Then there's the TV/movie-star aspect. Parton's had her own network television show, plus roles in six TV movies and as many feature length films. She's also written music for several movies, including *9 To 5,* in which she co-starred with Jane Fonda and Lily Tomlin, and for which her theme song was nominated for an Oscar in 1980.

Finally, there's the tycoon thing. Parton owns her own record label, Blue Eye; her own film production company, Southern Lights; and her own theme park, Dollywood, in which her partners are the developers of Branson, Missouri, the Midwest's wildly successful answer to Las Vegas. She also oversees the Dollywood Foundation [and Dolly Parton's Imagination Library], which promotes reading by mailing a book a month to 2,500 children under age 5 in Sevier County, Tennessee, where she was born. (At her behest, the program starts with *The Little Engine That Could,* given at birth.)

Parton's current projects include a made-for-TV movie, *Blue Valley Songbird,* airing on the Lifetime cable network starting November 1; a gospel musical, *Heavens To Betsy,* scheduled for release on CBS sometime next year; a children's TV series still in the planning stages; and development of a catalog sales company, Parton's Dailies and Nighties, selling a full line of cosmetics, undies, nightclothes, day wear, and books and other resources for building confidence and success.

She'll be the first to tell you, though, that what drives all of this is her music. It's been just over a year since her last release, the return-to-roots, all-originals album *Hungry Again,* climbed onto the country and pop charts without a net, as its label crumbled right out from under it.

February saw the release of *Trio II*, her second collaborative album with Emmylou Harris and Linda Ronstadt. In August, she rebounded with "Walking On Sunshine" [from *Treasures*], a disc featuring dance remixes of that mid-'80s Katrina & the Waves hit, plus Cat Stevens' early-'70s staple "Peace Train" and her own late-'70s crossover smash "Two Doors Down". There's also a new dance remix of her 1974 country megahit "Jolene", and even a dance-single duet with Boy George titled "Your Kisses Are Charity."

But the real news here is *The Grass Is Blue*, Parton's first all-bluegrass album, which came out Oct. 26 on Sugar Hill Records and features an all-star band of the genre, including Sam Bush, Stuart Duncan and Jerry Douglas, plus harmony vocals from the likes of Alison Krauss and Patty Loveless.

From poverty that has crushed many a mortal, Parton hustled herself into the hearts of millions worldwide, many of whom probably couldn't name more than two or three of her songs. Shania Twain made it clear, in her acceptance speech for CMA Entertainer of the Year, that meeting Parton was the first thing on her mind.

Did she? Parton answers with a laugh that opens the windows. "Oh no! I left as soon as I finished the song with Vince [Gill] because I wasn't one of the last ones. I was tryin' to get out of the traffic so as soon as I finished the song we just got right in the car and left and so it was only when I got home I was watchin' the news coverage—my husband [of 33 years, Carl Dean] had the TV on—and they had her on and her speech where she'd won Entertainer of the Year and I saw her say that and I thought AWWW!

"Cuz I could kill myself because if I'd have known she wanted to meet me I would have definitely [stayed behind], but I did send her a telegram the next day and congratulate her and I told her I was so sorry and flattered that she had mentioned my name and not only did I hope that we'd meet but we'd get a chance to visit and be friends and maybe even write or sing something together. I just think she's precious and I think she's just absolutely beautiful and I was so honored. I watched it here on the local news here and I thought, 'Wow!' I couldn't believe she's talkin' about me at a time when she's just won her big award. I thought, 'Wow!' What a nice compliment!"

Parton—a 1999 Country Music Association Hall of Fame inductee and past winner of ten CMA awards herself, including Entertainer of the Year in 1978, talks, well chirps, actually, a mile a minute, a chapter a sentence, italicizing every other word and ending fully half her sentences with an exclamation point. She means every word, every inflection; by her own admission, she can't act.

With a nod to the 1999 Vocal Group of the Year, she laughs, "I thought, 'We had all those Dixie Chicks and one old southern hen!'" Well, hardly. Parton was arguably the most sensational-looking woman on the 1999 CMA Awards show—glamorous, bespangled in blue wherever just-barely-respectable flesh didn't do a better job of eye-catching, glittering from the inside out with energy and showmanship. Ever the professional, she picked the shortest song from *The Grass Is Blue*, "Train, Train", to perform for her induction segment. "They needed the shortest song I could get and they wanted an uptempo one and so that was the one we picked, because it moved and you know they wanted to keep the show moving." In fact the song nearly ran off with it.

"Train, Train" was an inspired choice for the CMA show, but no more so than for the album. Parton had picked the song from one of her husband's old records, the Southern rock band Blackfoot's platinum *Strikes*, released in 1979. The band coalesced in the early '70s around singer and guitarist Rickey Medlocke, who had recently left Lynyrd Skynyrd.

Parton remembered having thought Blackfoot's hit single, "Train, Train", would make a great bluegrass number. It was one of several Parton picks that threw a curve to her producer, Steve Buckingham, and later the copyright birddogs charged with hunting down a credit. As of a week before the CMA awards show, Buckingham said they'd found not a single Blackfoot member, let alone the song's author, Shorty Medlock (grandfather of Blackfoot leader Rickey), to give them the name of their publishing company.

A modicum of internet savvy might have solved that problem, but the CMA performance did the trick. "I just thought Shorty Medlock was just somebody from the Blackfoot group or something," says Parton, "but I got a letter from this boy named Michael Herring and he's the grandson of Shorty Medlock and he proceeded to tell me that he and his family were so excited, they had been so thrilled when they were watching CMAs the other night and I did his grandpa's song. His grandpa's been dead for years and he was telling me all the history about Shorty Medlock and he was evidently a famous old bluegrasser. . . . Until that moment I didn't even know that it was written by a true bluegrasser. So ain't that cool!"

Serendipity struck another seemingly offbeat selection when Parton learned that in recording her bluegrass version of Billy Joel's minor 1973 hit "Travellin' Prayer", she had inadvertently followed the lead of the Earl Scruggs Revue, which had included the song on their 1974 album *Rockin' Cross The Country*. (It turned up again last year on the Scruggs Revue collection *Artist's Choice: The Best Tracks 1970–1980*.)

"I think Billy Joel is one of the greatest writers of all time and I just love his records," Parton says. "I have always loved that song. When I sent some of these songs over to Steve Buckingham, I think he just about had a heart attack. 'We're gonna do this? Blah blah blah blah blah'—but he loved them!"

Parton can perhaps be forgiven if her understanding of bluegrass is less than academic. Born January 19, 1946, the fourth of twelve children, in a sharecropper's shack in the Smoky Mountains of Tennessee, Parton grew up surrounded by the traditional music from which Bill Monroe built the genre. Her mother's family, the Owenses, all have music talent, she says, and it was her Uncle Bill Owens who gave her her first guitar.

If Parton knows a good bluegrass song when she hears it, regardless of the context, it's likely because she's heard them, sung them and recorded them all her life. Many of the tracks on *The Grass Is Blue* are songs she remembers from growing up, including the traditional "Silver Dagger", for which she says she sought family consensus on the lyrics. Among other tracks are fellow Tennessee hillbilly Hazel Dickens' "A Few Old Memories"; The Louvin Brothers' "Cash On The Barrelhead" ("Girls can get picked up for loitering on the streets and girls get locked up," she says, so she changed "son" to "hon"); and Lester Flatt's "I'm Gonna Sleep With One Eye Open".

Parton remembers fondly how Flatt, Scruggs and Monroe looked out for her when she began performing on the Grand Ole Opry at age 13. A Monroe signature song was her second top ten hit as a solo artist. Her first, in 1967, was her own "Dumb Blonde", which attracted the attention of Porter Wagoner and inspired him to include her on his weekly television show. [*"Dumb Blonde" was by Curly Putman —Ed.*] The pairing yielded ten years of top-selling, award-winning duets and, ultimately, an acrimonious split and lawsuit, but in 1970 he produced her recording of Jimmie Rodgers' "Muleskinner Blues", also known as "Blue Yodel #8". The song had been among those Monroe and his Blue Grass Boys had played on their first radio show in 1939. About the only thing Parton's instrumentation had in common with Monroe's was a banjo, but that was a crucial instrument to have on hand, as she tells it.

"That one, we were just kiddin' around in the studio one day when we were recordin' and you know how musicians will just sit around and jam and they always do that inbetween and then I started just singin' on it because I knew the song and it started sounding good and [Wagoner] said 'Hell let's just record that!' Buck Trent, who was an electric banjo player, was in the Wagonmasters and was recordin' [with us], and Buck was sayin', 'Man this is good! Ain't no girl ever sung this song! You should sing that, you should!'

"So right from the studio Porter had somebody go out and get a whip, so we turned out spending like four hours recordin' this song [because] we were trying to figure out who could crack the whip the best and who could whistle the best and I wound up doin' the best whistle, because I was the country girl, you know, I had that whistle thing!" Parton says she believed for years that Monroe had written the song. Her version reached #8 on the country charts.

Parton's fluency in bluegrass and traditional music idioms is apparent throughout *The Grass Is Blue*—in her treatment of tunes by fellow 1999 CMA Hall of Fame inductee Johnny Bond ("I Wonder Where You Are Tonight") and the Johnny Cash standard "I Still Miss Someone", as well as in her own compositions, including "Steady as The Rain", which she wrote on banjo. Her command of the form is made obvious by the fact she wrote the title track on a movie-set lunch break. It's a song made for pretty mandolin and fiddle breaks.

"When I was doing *Blue Valley Songbird*, I had a 30-minute lunch break cuz we don't have an hour because it's a Movie of the Week and we only had three weeks so breaks are short, so I went in on one of my lunch breaks and wrote 'The Grass Is Blue' and it just came so inspired and I wrote it and put it down on a tape and when lunch break was over I had [someone] come down from my office and pick up the tape and take it to Steve and I said, 'Here's our title song.'" She giggles.

The album was made quickly. Parton launched the project in June over dinner with Buckingham, her producer of nine years and original partner in Blue Eye Records. Still a friend and collaborator, Buckingham now works for Vanguard, which is owned by the Welk Music Group. He mentioned to Parton that the Welk Group had recently acquired the bluegrass-heavy label Sugar Hill and, by the way, there was considerable interest on the part of the label and fans in having Parton make a bluegrass record.

"We just went, 'Hahahahaha, really?!' I sez, 'Well ain't that something!'," Parton laughs, "and I sez, 'Well why don't we just do one,' and he said, 'Are you serious?' And I said, 'Well, yeah! I got a movie that I'm doing . . . for the next month or three weeks. After that I've got a couple of weeks, if you think we can get something prepared, we'll just do it!' . . . And he said, 'I'll put together the best band that we can get,' and he did."

Buckingham says he put Sugar Hill honcho Barry Poss and his staff in charge of that commitment. Practically every band member on the record is an accomplished solo artist. There's Sam Bush, founder of New Grass Revival and generally considered one of the top three bluegrass mandolin players in the world. Fiddler Stuart Duncan, who used a 100-year-old instrument for the sessions, has recorded bluegrass tracks with nearly every major Nashville artist since 1981. Dobro player Jerry Douglas, currently with Alison Krauss' band, is "acknowledged to be the best in the world," Buckingham says. Bassist Barry Bales, also of Krauss' band, counts the Cox Family among his credits as well.

Guitarist Bryan Sutton is well-known in gospel circles and left Ricky Skaggs' band to pursue a solo career. Banjo player Jim Mills, who used a vintage 1934 instrument for the sessions, played on Ricky Skaggs' 1999 release *Soldier Of The Cross* and released his first solo record last year, backed by Bales on bass.

"They all knew each other and all have played together, and they all knew this idiom so well," Buckingham says. "The contracts and paperwork were done in two weeks. That's unheard of. I told everyone I had two days to cut 12 tracks, August 3 and 4. We couldn't do that much in two days if it weren't the cream of the crop. Every cut would be one or two takes."

Says Parton, "I just think they're all great. I'm just proud and honored to be part of their group. I just felt like the girl singer in this wonderful band!"

The feeling was apparently mutual. "These days," Buckingham explains, "most artists record their vocals with the band knowing they'll come back and re-record. Dolly does her vocals with the musicians. She sings them like, 'This is it.' The musicians respond differently. When you hear a vocalist like her singing the tracks with the players, nailin' it, she inspires them. They raise their playing to another level and they inspire her.

"Most producers will tell you a singer may spend hours and days on a vocal for one song. There are so many things you can do now to fix vocals. You can tune them electronically, you can comp a vocal from all the different times they sing the song. It's so easy with Dolly because she really does it. Can you imagine what it's like playing in there and hearing her voice coming through the headphones?"

Four of the "scratch" vocals she recorded with the musicians went straight to the disc: "The Grass Is Blue", "A Few Old Memories", "Cash On The Barrelhead", and "Sleep With One Eye Open".

Parton says, "There was like this perfect magic between these great musicians and me singin' and they seemed to be really enjoying what I was doin'; I was certainly enjoyin' what they were doin'. It sort of created this very magical moment at times that I think that this brought us all sometimes to tears, and my booth was right near the engineering booth where Steve was and I would often look in there and Steve would have tears on his face, and he'd be liftin' his glasses up and wipin' his eyes. We did this album together and that's why there's so much magic on these tracks I think."

After their two days of sessions, the musicians left and the harmony singers recorded their parts. Given her choice of songs, Alison Krauss picked "Travellin' Prayer", "I Still Miss Someone" and "The Grass Is Blue" to sing with her bandmate Dan Tyminski. Country star Patty Loveless and bluegrass songbird Rhonda Vincent sang background on "A Few Old Memories"; Vincent's husband Darrin sang with her on "Endless Stream Of Tears". Nashville session stalwart and former Jordanaire Louis Nunley joined the pair for the bass part on the record's closing gospel tune, the a cappella "I Am Ready," written by Parton's sister Rachel Parton Dennison. Claire Lynch and Keith Little added harmony on other songs; Dolly re-recorded all 12 vocals, just in case, in six hours; and recording was complete in seven days.

Richie Owens sighs bemusedly when he hears about Parton and Buckingham being captivated by the energy and excitement of the live sessions. Owens helped Parton, his cousin, produce her 1998 *Hungry Again* album, recording it in the basement studio of his Nashville home and using musicians from his roots-rock band, then named Shinola, and his acoustic band, Richie Owens & the Farm Bureau.

In the liner notes for *Hungry Again*, Parton says she retreated to where she came from, her Smoky Mountain home, to fast and pray for guidance about her life and her music career. The 12 songs on *Hungry Again* were among 37 that resulted from Parton's sabbatical. In recording them, Owens felt she responded to the fact that the musicians "had the vibe of a band. There was a spirit there. She just wanted to be a bit more grass-roots about some stuff."

Owens thinks that in some ways *Hungry Again* may have laid conceptual groundwork for *The Grass Is Blue*. (Parton says she didn't intend for that record to lead up to the new one, but she agrees the latter is "a nice follow-up to that one.") Says Owens: "Because of my dad running her publishing company for years, I grew up listening to all these great Dolly Parton songs, sittin' there watching her write songs. She's at her greatest just singing her songs and just ripping heartstings out because . . . there's such sincerity in what she's singing. You know? She's real.

"A lot of records she's done have been great records with great production, but that's the thing—it's all great production instead of Dolly Parton. It was so much it overwhelmed this beautiful Appalachian voice and this really sweet, strong song. I'm glad if maybe the different mindset [of *Hungry Again*] maybe helped pave the way for the bluegrass record, because that is the best way to record her. It's not to overkill it. Back off. Let her do her thing."

Hungry Again wound up getting caught in the undertow of record industry reorganization. No sooner had Sony launched Parton's Blue Eye label than it was moved to Universal, which linked its distribution to another new Universal affiliate in Nashville, Rising Tide. Parton's 1996 tribute to songwriters of the '70s, *Treasures*, inaugurated that relationship. But before *Hungry Again* was released, Universal suddenly sunk Rising Tide. Parton, Blue Eye, and what was originally called *Blue Valley Songbird* moved to Decca, which had its own ideas about the project.

Owens says that even though she had recorded three dozen songs of her own, Decca tried to persuade her to include new material from other writers. Additional production, red tape and a name change later, the record was finally released, in August 1998. Shortly thereafter, Universal shut down Decca and left more than 200 artists without a label, including Parton. *Hungry Again* became an orphan adrift, owned by a record company that wouldn't lift a finger to keep it afloat, let alone put wind in its sails.

Regardless of whether or not it could have been a hit record, or even had a hit song, *Hungry Again* is one of the best records of Parton's career. The consistency of quality songwriting surpasses every Parton studio recording since 1980's *9 To 5 And Odd Jobs*. Of the last decade, Parton admits, "I did, like all people I think in business, try to keep up with what was current and tried to stay in the flow of things and did commercialize myself—I'd rather use the word commercialize rather than prostitute myself!—you know, to try to stay in the mainstream. So somewhere inbetween there, at different times, by being willing and having the guts to try different things, I would fall somewhere in the cracks of it not being country, not being pop, and not gettin' played.

"There are a lot of wonderful new country acts and those of us that are older, we don't begrudge the success of the new country artists. Some of us just wish we could get our records played ourselves. It's changed! It's called progress! I understand progress . . . me of all people because I'm always out hustlin' . . . tryin' to always stay up with the times." This is, after all, the girl who, taking stock of her life and career at age 10, decided she could topple Brenda Lee by mustering her sisters to sing backup vocals in pig latin.

Parton wasn't much older than 10 when she met Bobby Denton. In fact, he volunteers, he dated her in high school. Now he's vice president and general manager at WIVK in Knoxville, the station on which at age 10, it so happens, Parton began appearing regularly on Cas Walker's weekly bluegrass show.

Denton points out that WIVK and many other country stations do play Dolly Parton classics such as "Coat Of Many Colors" and "I Will Always Love You". "When an older artist says they're not getting played on country radio, what they're saying is every release that they release is not getting played. If the song is there, then people are gonna request it, people are gonna buy it and we're gonna play it. That's true for everyone."

Denton says the *Hungry Again* single "Salt Of My Tears" did not research high in the local market, a predictable result of lack of promotion, but he also says, "I don't think people are tired of Dolly Parton. I think when people say she's too pop—her new record [*The Grass Is Blue*] is as country as anything she's done. If country stations want to play Dolly then they can surely find something off that CD to play." But he adds, "Your new country fan, 90 percent of them don't like bluegrass. Some people have tried to go back and do country. The demographics are much older in that, like 45 plus and even 55 plus.

"Face it, the country radio stations have had available to them what the major labels and producers are sending to them out of L.A. or Nashville. A lot of stuff they're putting out is not what you classify as country music. They're just in hopes that country music stations will play it, but they're aiming a lot of those songs at the pop market where they can sell more records. I call it the Garth Brooks syndrome. Everybody's trying to find . . . somebody that can sell records like Garth Brooks. The closest to that right now is Shania Twain.

"Okay listen, I'll give you a good example: the Dixie Chicks. Country stations were playing those records. They're not country, they're not pop. It's obvious the reason the Dixie Chicks are so big is that they're very talented. They're a lot like Dolly if you think about it—their mannerisms onstage and what they say. They shoot from the hip like Dolly does. But they're gettin' a lot of airplay because country stations are looking for something different to play and not so much pop stuff.

"I think Dolly is so creative that sometimes she hurts herself. She writes pretty deep. As you know, you have to listen to the lyrics. I think you'll see her getting some extended airplay off [*The Grass Is Blue*] because it's more bluegrass/country like the Dixie Chicks in a way, because they're using dobros, banjos and everything in their music, and people are playing them."

The more things change, the more they stay the same. What Parton calls "progress" may be the most constant element of country music. The current "Garth Brooks syndrome," and its backlash, are merely the latest incarnation of an almost perpetual tension between traditionalists and crossover advocates in the genre.

Bill Malone's *Country Music USA*, an essential resource on country music history, revisits the theme repeatedly, beginning in the 1920s, when, Malone says, "The social context . . . encouraged both the exploitation and the rejection of rural culture." Ironically, much of that context was driven, as it were, by the invention of the automobile by a traditional country music fan, Henry Ford.

Malone refers to songwriters who "began moving country music away from its traditional moorings in the twenties," a natural response to an environment that increasingly included phonographs and radios. The latter technology afforded the world the WLS National Barn Dance and the Grand Ole Opry, of which Malone says: "Barn dance shows presaged country music's coming commercial success—and its incorporation into the American popular cultural mainstream." Later, in the '50s and '60s, producer and promoter Owen Bradley ushered in an era of silken-voiced country singers routinely recording pop songs that crossed over to become mainstream hits.

George McCormick, who played guitar with Grandpa Jones for the last 22 years of Jones' career, spent most of the previous decade in Porter Wagoner's Wagonmasters. He was playing guitar and singing baritone harmonies with them when Parton joined the show.

McCormick confirms stories that Parton was not well received at first by Wagoner fans, who were devoted to her predecessor, Norma Jean. She won them over quickly, he says, but, "At that time everybody kinda thought maybe she was ahead of her time . . . She added a lot of stuff. That's when I think things started changing." McCormick left Wagoner's band to escape "pressure" he declined to specify, then played for a time with Charlie Louvin and the house band at the Opry before joining Grandpa Jones' band.

As for country music in general, he says, "It's done. It's not real country music, now." Asked for specifics, he responds, "It's all become mechanic! When we recorded back in those days, you probably wouldn't have but one or two microphones. Even guitar players, they don't tune by their ear like they did back in those days . . . they got a machine. And another thing is it all sounds alike to me. When you hear one singer, he may have one hit record and you never hear of him again. They're not established like an Ernest Tubb or a Porter Wagoner.

"I live in the country, but you talk to these people here and they'll say they won't even listen to this music now. But yet they can't hear the music that they loved, you know, because these disc jockeys won't play it, just except certain times.

"They're losing everything, I think. Even the Opry's goin' under. They sold out Opryland. You go to the Opry, it's not a full house any more. They've lost all the older fans, and the new fans are not gonna come in there. You see what's happened? They took it all away from the old people. I go back to visit to the Opry now and it's sad [his voice breaks slightly], since Mr. Acuff died."

Parton makes the point that even after she crossed over with her 1977 blockbuster "Here You Come Again", she continued to have country hits. At the time, she declared: "I'm not leaving country music. I'm taking it with me!" She survived the slings and arrows of the naysayers, and, characteristically, she talks sometimes as if the other side of the coin is just as bright. She believes her label-free status is resulting in some of the best work she's ever done.

"I don't have to answer to record labels, heads of companies," she says. "I don't have to discuss it with a bunch of managers that head the record labels. I manage myself, I have my own record label, I have total freedom to do exactly what I want to do."

But, she also says, "I still have not given up. I will do more things, different things, and I will keep pumpin' it out and if I can get a record that's worthy of bein' played, I bet they'll play it. I hope the bluegrass album does good and I'm ready to do another one if it does and who knows, I'll be out there humpin' and a-doin' business, doin' somethin'."

Parton's new made-for-TV movie, *Blue Valley Songbird*, is based on a song she recorded for *Hungry Again*. It's the story of a young mountain girl who "sings like a bird and writes like a poet." Abused by her father, she's urged by her mother to run away at age 15. She packs up her guitar and heads for the city, where she forms a band that tours tirelessly in quest of a big break. She never finds it.

"I have seen so many people with twice the talent that I'll ever have work just as hard, been in this town just as long and still have never made it," Parton says. "One never knows why one gets singled out and another doesn't. I've thought a lot about that through the years. . . . I often think that so much of my good luck, I owe to just freedom to be there. I had no children of my own so I was able to go and be where I needed to be, and I've had a husband that was just as independent in his own way and didn't resent or try to stop me.

"And I have a great work ethic . . . I'm like my dad. I get up; I work. I'm up early every day thinkin' what I'd like to do. I organize my stuff, get my things in order, and I do more work between 3 a.m. and 7 a.m. than most people do in a day. So I'm ready and prepared, so I think there's a whole lot to be said just about bein' willin' to work.

"This [movie] is about a girl who'd been abused by her father and all that. Certainly that was not my father. He didn't whup our ass nearly as much as he should've. When I got into the song, though, I just remembered how it probably would have been for me had I not made it. Because I used to travel around in these cars, pullin' the trailer and that's what's in this movie about this girl with a small band. I did that for years before I made it, singin' around in little honky-tonks and stuff, and I used to think about, 'Well, what would happen if I don't make it?' I'd think, 'You know what? I'd be singin' anyway.' I'd sing. If I just made enough money to take me from one gig to another, had enough money for groceries and to keep an old car on the road, I'm sure that had I not made it, I'd still be singin' somewhere.

"I'm very humbled by the fact that I have been able to do so many other things," Parton says, "and it's because of stickin' my neck out that I've got good businesses to fall back on. . . . So it's not about the money, but I love the music and want to record.

"The music is still my first love. What brought me out of the Smoky Mountains was the fact that I loved to write songs and wanted to sing, and it was because of that that all this other stuff has really happened. . . . That's why I will always have an outlet for it, I will always find an outlet for it. I will always sing, I will always write.

"But—I already know, now, that country music does not want me anymore, as far as an artist. Because I've tried very very hard for several years now to be true to what I thought people thought I should be true to, and that didn't work either. So I've found that as always in my own life, I'd best to do what I feel right about at the time. That always works best for me. At least I will find true personal happiness and true personal and creative fulfillment if I just do what I do and have the freedom to do it."

DOLLY DIAMOND

On Cosmetic Surgery

"Plastic surgery? Sure I've had plastic surgery, but that sounds so bizarre. It's really cosmetic, there's very little plastic to it. It's more nips and tucks, things like getting rid of bags under your eyes. It's scary when you first get it done, but I do it because I'm a show person. You are on camera all the time and people expect you to look a certain way. If you've got the money, the desire and the guts, what's the big deal? Of course I'm scared it might go wrong, but I don't go to extremes. I don't have the top of my head took off to pull anything up. A lot of what I have done is just cosmetic procedure, but it all comes under the heading of plastic surgery for a lot of people. But I'm not made out of plastic—though I had my boobs lifted when they started dragging on the floor. Who'd want to look at them if they were like that? I've had implants too, but only years after I had lost all the weight and had surgery done for the tissue that was left behind. At that stage, in order for them to stand up like little soldiers, you put something in there to help them. So what else do you want to know? No, before you ask, I didn't have a penis implant as well."

—To Gavin Martin, *London Mirror*, October 9, 2002

PART VI
CEO of Dreams

"I'm the CEO of Dreams. It's just like a tree. You have great roots, and then you get your tree, then you get a lot of limbs. Then, if you're lucky, there's a lot of leaves. So it's like one thing just kind of adds to something else. One dream adds to another."

—To Peter Marks, *Washington Post*,
July 16, 2016

DOLLY PARTON: "I'VE LIVED SO MANY LIFETIMES"

Jeremy Rush | December 27, 2002 | *Goldmine*

Dolly continued her experimentation of blended folk and bluegrass styles with *Halos & Horns*, released in 2002. In support of the new album, she embarked on a sold-out concert tour of the United States and the United Kingdom, her first outing in ten years. Dolly went into great detail about the *Halos & Horns* album during this interview with Jeremy Rush. She also provided updates relating to her ongoing business and philanthropic ventures. —Ed

Dolly Parton is one of the most recognizable entertainers in the world, especially in country music. While her larger-than-life image and down-home persona are immediately identifiable, Parton's real genius lies in her considerable artistic strengths as a vocalist and songwriter.

Over the last four years, she has released two bluegrass albums with some of the best musicians in the business—way before traditional music was resurrected by the *O Brother Where Art Thou?* soundtrack. On those two critically acclaimed Sugar Hill albums, *The Grass Is Blue* and *Little Sparrow*, Parton has created two durable collections of beautifully articulated roots music that showcase her amble artistic strengths.

Our interview was held in a small house at Parton's private office complex in midtown Nashville. Once given the OK from her assistant Theresa, I was led through a lush courtyard to a welcoming Parton standing at the screen door waving me in as if we were old friends. Her hospitality was overwhelming, and she seemed to bounce around from room to room as she took me on a tour. The Southwestern-styled dwelling is more of a house than an office, with a mirrored dressing and makeup room adjacent to a homey living area and a kitchen.

At the time of the interview, her new album on Sugar Hill, *Halos & Horns*, had just been completed, and she was beaming with excitement. Once settled in, Dolly played me an unmastered work CD on a small boombox as she sat cross-legged on the floor. At times, while guiding me through the album, her enthusiasm would overtake her and she would belt out a line or even sing along to a chorus. The new record features her new band, The Blue-Niques, and a slew of original compositions, as well as two classic covers: Bread's "If" and Led Zeppelin's "Stairway To Heaven."

Whether they are conscious of it or not, artists who endure always offer a tangible personality that people can relate to. Parton's ability to translate her experiences growing up in the East Tennessee mountains have connected with millions of devoted listeners over the years. As readers will see in the following interview, Parton is a fearless person who abides by the belief that one should be connected to emotional and spiritual truth-telling instinct. She wants her fans to laugh and cry with her. She's also a woman who demands passion and intelligently guides her own career the only way she sees fit—her own way.

As a result, Parton has spent years contributing enormous amounts of time and capital investing in the well-being and development of those in need around her. In a music business that's become more image and presentation over art and heart, an individual voice like Parton's is priceless.

Goldmine: First off, thanks for having us over to do this interview. This is a nice little set-up with your office and this house.

I fixed this little house up when I bought the place next door. It's worked out just great, so we could bring people like you over here to do interviews. Do you want some breakfast?

No, thank you.

I can make you some toast and eggs, if you need it.

No, I appreciate it. I'm fine thank you.

Did you get a chance to hear an advance of the album yet?

No. Not yet.

Oh, you haven't? Well, that's a shame. I got just my work tape, but I'll be happy to play it for you.

[We take time out to listen to *Halos & Horns*, being played out of a boombox.]

How did the new album, Halos & Horns, *evolve?*

I went to East Tennessee to try and find as many musicians back home as I could. I had written a bunch of this stuff at my Tennessee Mountain Home, which is my old place that I bought years ago and fixed up like a retreat. I go there and write all the time. Gary Davis, who helped me pull all of this together, put the band together too.

All the people on this album are part of my new band—they're called The Blue-Niques. Unique bluegrass is why I picked the name.

Originally I thought, "What a great way for me to audition these musicians." I was really just trying to find a band. I thought, "I'm just going to go in and demo these songs through my publishing company and just pay for this and find a good studio up home." Well, we got in there and they just all sounded great from the start. It was a great studio—Southern Sounds Studio in Knoxville. Danny Brown, he's the engineer and he's one of the owners of the studio, did a whole bunch of songs—25 over the course of several weeks.

While we were doing this, I told Steve Buckingham, who's my friend and my producer and coproducer for 12 or 13 years now, "This stuff is turning out really good. It sounds like it could be a record." He said, "Well just go on with it. Just let what happens happen." So I did.

Steve was real proud of this and supportive. I didn't want anybody thinking that me and Steve had any problems because he's been really behind me all the way with this. He said, "This is great as an artist—for you writing all these songs and for people to know that you can do it all. Because you do anyway." I missed working with him on it, but I was so excited about my new band.

"Halos & Horns" is the album's title track and also the album's opener. It really seems to set an uplifting, spiritual tone that resonates throughout the record.

That song is just about how we try to do good and we fall down and make our mistakes and ask God to forgive us and take off our horns and put on our halos again for a while. Then we slip and we slide just the same old thing like we always do. I really like it.

I tried to expand on this album like we have the last two because I don't ever want to get pigeonholed, or "Pidgeon Forged" I should say, into people thinking I'm just going to do one thing. I thought the whole title of *Halos & Horns* fit what I was doing because of the last two albums. The first one [*The Grass Is Blue*] was bluegrass. The second one [*Little Sparrow*] added a little more mountain music and a little bit of Irish flavor. In this one, I wanted to add a little more gospel along with some harder country-type things like the old days of country. But it's just solid, more bluegrass country. And, yes, I wrote all the songs on this except "If," the David Gates song, and "Stairway To Heaven," which I did in a very unusual way.

When I first heard that you were doing "Stairway To Heaven," I thought, "That's a bold choice." But from just hearing your version just now, it is very clear that you made it your own song.

Well, they'll either love my version of "Stairway" or they'll hate me for it. I just love the song. I just interpreted it my way. I was trying to make my part come out of my soul too, you know—to Dolly-ize it. I always thought it sounded like a spiritual song, and that's why I wanted to put the choir on it and do it a little different. In fact, [Led Zeppelin's] Robert Plant said that he had always thought of this as a spiritual song, and he was thrilled that I had put the choir on it 'cause he had always heard it like that. Everybody said, "You can't do that. That's a classic." I said, "I know it's a classic, but nobody's ever done it. Everybody's afraid to do it, and these people wrote this great song." But, I really felt it. I really got into the spirit of the song. But, it just goes to show you, a good song can be done any way if you really mean it.

I've always loved the group Bread, and "If" is a great song. There's a certain element of sweetness in that song that seems to be missing in a lot of current popular music.

I agree. I thought they were so great. I was just thrilled to get to do this. I did "If" uptempo—sort of like how Ray Stevens did with "Misty." It also kind of reminds me of the [Harry] Nilsson song "Everybody's Talkin'." It's kind of got that rolling feel. When you get a song like "If" that has touched the lives of so many people, you have to handle it with delicate care. You just don't go and put anything on it. You think, "What can I do with this great song that will not be a gimmick but make it my own and still make it something a little bit different?"

But anyhow, there are a lot of songs on the album. There are some gospel things—one is talking about swimming naked in a pond and the next one is like, "Hello, God, are you out there?" [laughs] It's really just life stories. It goes from heartache to heaven, spirituality to sexuality. [laughs]

It's all part of creation.

Yeah, it's true. That's how I look at life. See, I take this stuff so seriously. These things are sacred to me. When I decided I was going to do "Stairway To Heaven," I truly felt like I was walking on sacred ground. But you still have to take a chance. If you don't take some chances, what are you going to do that's quality?

One thing that has always marked my perception of your career and your persona has been this certain devotion to fearlessness.

Well, I'm not afraid to do things. Of course, we're all full of different kinds of fear for different kinds of reasons, but I have never been afraid of myself. My desire to do things was always greater than my fear of it. I'm a singer. I'm a writer. I'm a person that's just out in this world to have as much fun as I can and put as much into the world as I can—and get as much out of it. If I make five mistakes and do one great thing, well I'm not going to worry about the five mistakes I made. I'm going to waller in the glory of the one great thing I did in hopes that it brought some joy to somebody else.

You didn't tour behind your previous two albums.

No. We couldn't. Jerry Douglas and all them, The Blue Boys I call them, they are all such big stars that we never could pull it together where we could tour. They were all committed to do stuff. Jerry's with Alison [Krauss], and most of them have their own groups. But me and The Blue-Niques are going to be doing some concerts. We are going to go out there and promote this and see how it feels out there. If it feels good, I'm going to do some touring. Not a lot—not like I used to. I'm 56 years old, and I've been doing this since I was a kid. I'm like—up there.

You would never know by the way you plunked yourself down on the floor when we were listening to the album. I don't think I could sit down like that, and I'm in my mid-20s.

Well that's because you got legs. I got no legs. [laughs]

It was almost like a lotus position. I was going, "I bet she's done some kind of yoga."

No. If there's any yoga being done around here, it's in my head. I'm a very flexible person. I'm small, and I'm very energetic. My husband just gets floored sometimes. I'll be painting my toenails and I'll be standing in the kitchen and I'll have my leg completely up on the sink and he'll say, "I can't f-ing believe that you're standing there with your leg hiked up like that. That would break my back!" And I say, "Well I ain't big enough—it ain't that far." But I'm just a little person. I'm not very physical. I'm basically lazy when it comes to that. But my mind is always so open. I never age because I never have time. I don't think about the fact that I'm supposed to be getting older. It's like, "I don't see why, your Honor." So I guess if my mind ain't old, my body ain't either.

That's a good way of looking at it.

Well, the good thing is, if I live a long time and I think I might, I'll always sing. My voice ain't going at all. I can sing as good as I did—If I ever could. I would imagine that, people like me, what they call semi-legends or legends, will be singing from now on like Mother Maybelle. So I'll be doing records from now on, and I'm going to do a lot of surprises through the years. I've got some big thoughts in mind. I'm just trying to get my foot planted solid onto something to know that people will accept it.

Nobody plays artists like me on country radio anymore, because they assume that people my age are over. But artists like me hopefully never are. Because I've lived so many lifetimes and I grew up and spent most of my young life with no electricity or nothing. To come from that, back there in the mountains to this high-tech world where now I'm doing CDs and stuff I don't even understand. By the time I was 10 years old, I was on the radio and television, and we didn't have either one. We didn't even have electricity. But I've lived that life, and its just in my psyche. That's just my Smokey Mountain DNA, and these kind of songs and these kind of feelings and this kind of hurt . . . my own hurt as well as the hurts that you take on of your family and the people that you know and love . . . is real to me. And when I open my mouth, you know it's real if I'm singing about that kind of stuff. Once I start to sing, it just gets in me. That kind of music just hollers at me all the time and says, "You get back in here. This is what you do. This is what you do best."

I want everything to be real from now on. I'm not trying to be commercial. I want everything to have heart and soul. I have had to be commercial through the years, and I don't regret anything I've ever done because it's took all of that to make me who I am.

You know, music is the voice of the soul, but there's just a thing that comes out of certain voices and certain people. You don't know what it is you're feeling, but it stirs you. People have not been stirred emotionally in so long. We just get too comfortable, and a thing like Sept. 11 happens and jolts you back into reality. That whole event really just shook everybody's confidence. You just saw how little life is and how fragile and small and fearful we all are. You just realize that there must be something greater than you, otherwise you'd totally fall apart.

Think about all those people in other countries. There are whole cities that are torn down, and hundreds of thousands of people die all the time. It makes you really think about your own life and the things you take for granted and what you could do to make your own life as well as the lives of other people around you a little better.

I would imagine that "Hello God," which is off your new album, is meant to be a rather poignant reflection of the current times.

Yes, it is, as a matter of fact. I wrote several songs after Sept. 11, like we all did. Everybody just lives their own life and then, when you get in trouble, you think, "Oh, God, help me now." This idea just came to me and it just started rolling out and I just wrote that song in no time. But it was very inspired. I have very strong feelings about that song.

I do have a lot of faith in God, as I perceive him. Everybody thinks of God as a different thing. To me, God is that greater, higher energy— that greater, wiser wisdom. It's that thing in all of us that we have to draw from. I've always trusted God and trusted myself. It's like, if I got those two things, faith in God and faith in myself, which to me are intertwined, I'm fine.

I just always kind of drug from that God thing. My grandpa was a preacher, and I believed that through God I could do everything. That's still where I get my strength, and that's why so many of my songs have an inspirational feeling. It's not just me giving it back to God, it's me trying to give it to other people. To give from God, through me, to somebody else that might not have that kind of confidence. So, it works, and it's fun for me. It enriches my life. Hopefully, I can enlighten and enrich somebody else in whatever way I might. If nothing else, just for somebody to say, "Well, she had the balls to do that? Well, I got the balls to listen!" And at least not crucify me. And so what? What are they going to do—kick my ass?

Well you've managed, somehow or another, to protect yourself enough to be able to stay in touch with what you really feel.

Yeah, that's because money don't mean anything to me. I love having money and what money can do, but money has never been the thing that motivated me. It was always the art. I always figured, if I did well with my music, that the money would always come. It always has. The fact that I never wanted money meant that it was always there. I just always assumed I'd have money. When I was poor, I figured I couldn't get no poorer.

If somebody said, "You're going to have to do one or the other. You're going to have to give up your music or you're going to go back to being poor," I would go poor, totally broke, and start over again and do my music. That's how much I love it. They say a rich man can't sing the blues, but I don't think that's true. I think if you stay true to your roots and home is always in your heart and in your head, you'll succeed. Don't dwell on just the material things. I know this sounds like a joke because I look like the phoniest person in the world when you look at me. But a lot of my look came out of a little country girl's idea of what glamour should be. Then it got to be comfortable, and I liked it, just like how people like to dress up. I always wanted to be pretty and look good, but just poor ragged-ass-looking kids—you look the way you look. You do with what you have and you always think, "Well, when I get money I'll have this and I'll have that." And it didn't buy me any class. [laughs]

But I like looking the way I look, and I'm comfortable with who I am. I like looking like trash, but I know in my heart that I'm not. I am so much inside to just have a plain surface. I feel so many things and my heart and soul is so real. Just to be a plain old person on the outside just don't get it for me. Like Minnie Pearl used to say, "Any old barn looks better with a little red paint on it." That's sort of how I feel. People always say, "Less is more," but I say, "Oh, that's bullshit! More is more—and I can't get enough of more." Everybody's different, and I understand what they're saying, but I just love stuff. I love playing in paints and crayons and I love the way things feel on my body. I dress up even when I'm by myself. I can't stand to walk around slouchy all day. Everybody's comfort is their own, and that all depends. But to me I'm more comfortable when I got on makeup and look the way I want to look. I've always said that if I hadn't have been a woman then I damn sure would've been a drag queen. That may be a funny thing to say, but I mean that in all sincerity. Yeah. I love it.

It is amazing how hard it is for many of us to express our uniqueness.

It's awful how some people have crippled so many wonderful people who would have been so many things, but they had to spend all their time worrying about how to get by because of somebody else's perception of them. I just think that's terrible. Those crippling people are truly unhappy, because they live in a real shaded world. People that aren't willing to open their heart or minds to anything other than what they understand and know. . . . I think those people are missing out on everything, really. That's why it's a great thing to be able to write songs too. I like to write for everybody else, and I write a lot of songs about being somebody or being yourself. Be who you are, have confidence. It's about your attitude. I write a lot of stuff like that. I've often said, "People don't come to see me be me, they come to see me be them." I have written something that they relate to. I'm going to sing something and make them feel something. I'm up there doing something that they might have wanted to do, and whether they wanted to do that or not, they can sense that freedom. People appreciate it. Especially those closed people that don't get to have that self-expression from either a husband, a parent or a wife.

Or themselves.

Or themselves. You're right. But they love it when somebody can just not have fear about who they are. Sometimes things pop out of my mouth that almost scare me, and I think, "Oh my, you ought to keep your big mouth shut!" I'm like an innocent child in that respect. I think, "Why *can't* I say what's on my mind? Why can't I say that, if that's what I think?" Of course, they say it's better to choose what you say than to say what you choose. But, I still think that there's a certain honesty in saying what you choose.

The movie Nine to Five *is a good example of standing up and saying what you choose.*

That little movie has become like a classic, but at that time, that's when women were speaking out for their rights. But I just did it because Jane Fonda called me and told me what it was about and asked me if I was interested in doing it. I thought, "Well I'm going to be in a movie with Jane Fonda and Lily Tomlin. If it's a hit, I can take credit, and if it's a flop then it's their fault. [laughs] It's not like they're going to go punish me. They don't even know who I am." I thought it was a good subject matter. I wouldn't have done it had I not believed in what I was doing. I'd been asked to do stuff before, but that was the first movie I did. Now Jane had heard that I was a pretty big country artist at the time and people seemed to like me, and she heard different people talking about me. Her statement to somebody was, "Dolly will get us the South." I thought, "Well, Dolly might just get you some North and East too!" [laughs] I was like, "What the hell does that mean?" Really, I knew what she meant. She meant the *country* people, country music—the "South"—I guess. But boy, I never let her forget that. I said, "Little did you know that I was going to get some of the others too." Of course that was her business way of thinking and that's what she meant, and that was fine. She was right. She was right in picking a country person.

It's like picking a candidate.

Exactly. Get her, she's got a good personality and she's got big tits and big hair and people like her—she's a "character." I just always thought if something comes to me that feels right, I'll do it. The worst that can happen is it won't be successful. I've tried lots of things that didn't work out. But if I felt really strong about something, I'll take the idea and put it on the back burner. That way I can pull from it later on. A good idea is like a good song—It's always good. It's just the timing may not be right. Either the people that you're with at the time may not see what you see or there are too many egos involved. Some of my best stuff is things I've done years and years ago. A good example is "I Will Always Love You." Look at what that song has done, and I wrote that song in '71 or '72.

What inspired that?

I wrote that song about my relationship with Porter Wagoner, the guy I used to sing with. We had been together for seven years, and we were really big as a duet. When I started with Porter I said that I would stay five years, because I wasn't looking to be part of anyone else's show. I wanted to have my own band and I wanted to be my own show. But he didn't want me to go. Porter was very stubborn and very set in his ways, and rightfully so—it was his show. We fought all the time anyway—especially about my songs, because I'd write them and he'd produce them. I had to try so hard to get my ideas in there. It was kind of like one of those love/hate relationships. I was afraid of Porter. He was very powerful, and he used that too. He scared the shit out of me all the time.

It's codependent after a while.

Yeah, I couldn't handle it anymore. Both my personal life and my emotional and creative self—I just wasn't being everything I knew I should be. But anyway, Porter would just not listen to me. I said, "Let me get some other producers and some outside management and I'll work within the show." That wouldn't do it. He wasn't going to allow nobody to do nothing but him. After so much time, I was like, "I got to go." He was terrible upset about it, so he sued me for a million dollars and took every dime I had. Luckily, my husband was smart with money, so we had saved up enough to get by. Later he said he was sorry about it, and that's OK. It was worth it to me if that's what I had to do.

But anyhow, I was really heartbroken and sick of just trying to figure out how to make the move easy because I wasn't out to hurt anybody. It wasn't that I didn't appreciate him, it's just that I had to go on. He was never going to listen to a word I have to say. He wouldn't even talk without screaming at me or jumping down my throat every time I open my mouth. So, one night, I wrote this song: "If I should stay, truly I'd just be in your way" . . . and he definitely was in mine at that time. "So I'll go but I know I'll think of you each step of the way/and I'll always appreciate you/and I'll always love you/and I hope life treats you kind. I hope you have all you ever dreamed of/Bittersweet memories, that's all I'm taking with me/Goodbye, don't cry because we both know I'm not what you need."

It was one of those relationships that had just got so twisted around your heart and soul and your creativity and work. It was a big mess to where you couldn't move one way without it affecting something else. It was hard. So that song came from a very very real and sincere place of trying to be kind. I just took it in to him one day and said, "If you ain't going to listen to me talk, will you listen to this song?" And I sang him the song. And he loved the song—of course he wanted to produce it. So I let him. But it was still my leaving song. That song is like 30-something years ago. I had a hit on it in '72—I think. Every 10 years since I wrote it, it's been #1. I'm the first artist that's ever had a #1 song on the same song twice. I had one in '72 with it when it first came out and in '82 when I did *The Best Little Whorehouse in Texas*.

Was it re-recorded for that?

Yeah, I re-recorded it and it became #1 again. Then me and Vince [Gill] had a Top 10 record. And then Whitney [Houston]. Now I've got to do it bluegrass. We do a bluegrass, up-tempo version of it as a playoff at the end of my show. It works really good.

Dollywood is one of the most successful theme parks in the country. What inspired that project?

It came from me just wanting to do something to make my people proud of me. I just thought it would be great to have something to leave for my family. You know, you always want your people to be proud of you. I need to have something up home. People don't know it, but the Smokey Mountains is the most visited national park in the United States. We get 10 million people through there a year. We got almost three million people through Dollywood last year, and we're only open six full months. But it's really provided a lot of jobs for the area. It's not only helped me, but it's also helped a lot of people.

Dollywood has also done a considerable amount of charity work, too.

Yeah. We have a huge thing that the United Way is in on now. It's all over the country—we're actually going to be worldwide later—but it's the Imagination Library. For years now, we've given scholarships to people and helped kids with their medical needs and their school needs and still do. We even have a hotline for kids. We also decided we should help the little kids when they are most susceptible. So every kid in Sevier County [Tenn.] gets a book a month from the day it's born until the day it starts kindergarten. We give out thousands and thousands of books all over the country now. They call me The Book Lady. It's important to me because my dad couldn't read or write, and many of my relatives didn't get an education. So not only is Dollywood a theme park, but it also does a lot of good things and a lot of stuff comes out of that.

These days, I'm having to speak to all these educators and all these teachers—and I hated school. I've done more homework in the last five years than I did in 12 years, just working on these projects. But anyways, somebody said, "Well, now that you're The Book Lady and you're involved with these kids and this education, are you going to tone down your look?" And I said, "Why should I? It was all of that that made all of this that put me in this position. Don't you get it?" I might look like a phony to you now, but if I start changing things, then I would *really* be a phony. This is who I am. I see no reason to think that I have to look like a school teacher. I'd rather look like a whore. I'm getting the same job done. It doesn't matter. But people are funny about changing. Like I say, no matter how phony I look or how much shit I've done that people would criticize, I know that when I get into that God place and I start to sing a certain kind of song, whether it's a gospel or a mountain song, there are just certain things that I mean to tell you. . . . It just does everything inside of me. That's why it comes out like that. I ain't making no money doing this kind of stuff. Bluegrass and mountain music ain't never made no money. It's like I said before, I had to get rich in able to sing like I was poor again. I just open my mouth and thank God I can deliver.

DOLLY DIAMOND

On Dollywood

"It gave [the fans] somewhere to go, that they didn't have to hang on to me so much. Almost like a mama. I can't entertain 'em all the time. I can send 'em to the playground, though, with fun people that I trust. You know: 'Go. Go, go, go play. Go swing. Go get on the seesaw.' 'Cause they feel like it's all me. It's under that Dolly umbrella. And I feel good that I've been able to give them something. An extension of myself, so to speak."

—To Michael Joseph Gross, *New York Times*, January 26, 2003

DOLLY DIAMOND

On Her Fans

"I've often wondered if it's healthy for some of these people to depend on me that much, to where people live through you and don't live their own lives. It's like when people say, 'I'm in love,' when they're really in lust. They call so many things love. I spend a lot of time thinking about stuff like that in the wee hours. But I think it's healthier for those people to have something to look forward to than to not. If they've got a show to look forward to or a record to look forward to, it might keep them from doing something bad to themselves or to somebody else. Or give 'em something more to do than just dwelling on themselves so much. I don't know. I just know I love the fans. I appreciate 'em. I love what I do. So I guess we'll all be at it for a long time to come."

—To Michael Joseph Gross, *New York Times*, January 26, 2003

DOLLY DIAMOND

On Dolly Parton Parkway

"In order to get to my house, I have to ride on that road. I see that sign, and I know that's 'Dolly Parton' the celebrity, but the girl that's riding up and down the road looks like hell! When I don't have my makeup or my fancy clothes on, I think, 'Oh my Lord, I hope nobody don't see Dolly Parton on Dolly Parton Parkway!' I wonder what my neighbors or my folks think when they have to ride down through there. And I wonder how many people that don't like me would like to shoot the hell out of them signs!"

—To Chris Neal, *Country Weekly*, February 3, 2004

DOLLY DIAMOND

On Radio Airplay

"I think of radio like a great lover. You were good to me. You bought me nice things. And then you dumped my ass for a younger woman. Seriously folks, I'm still singing. Play my records."

—To Country Radio Broadcasters Inc., February 2005

DOLLY PARTON TALKS ABOUT DAYS FUTURE AND PAST

Lawrence Ferber | 2006 | *Q-Notes*

In 2005, Dolly embarked upon her Vintage Tour, and in October released *Those Were the Days*, an album featuring cover versions of 1960s and 1970s folk and pop songs. She spent much of 2006 composing the score to the Broadway musical adaptation of *9 to 5*, as discussed here in this interview with the spirited Lawrence Ferber. Dolly also shared her opinions on gay marriage, explained how she juggles her divergent followings, and revisited the subject of the long-lingering lesbian rumors. Of special interest here is Dolly's recollection of racism and cross burnings in her yard during the early years of her career. -Ed.

Country music legend and gay icon has a new CD and is hard at work on a musical version of 9 to 5

On her latest CD, "Those Were the Days" (Sugar Hill Records), Dolly Parton freshly interprets a handful of beloved protest/antiwar songs from the '60s and '70s, including "Where Have All The Flowers Gone," "The Cruel War" and "Imagine." These ditties certainly strike a fresh nerve today, as we suffer more and more casualties overseas in a war that seems increasingly abstract. Yet for all of "Those Were the Days" political relevance, the lady insists that she doth not protest too much.

"I wasn't protesting anything," Parton says. "Truth is I'm not a political person but I am extremely patriotic and I purposely chose songs that reflected the times. We're at war and we can't just ignore that. Songs like 'Imagine' still give you hope there's a better place and better way. I would love for us all to live happily ever after but the least I can do is sing about and speak of [what's going on] and that's what I was doing."

With a posse of talented guests including Norah Jones, Keith Urban, Kris Kristofferson, Alison Kraus, Mary Hopkin, Yusuf Islam (aka Cat Stevens) and members of the Grand Ole Opry, Parton injects rich blue-grass flavor and some of her finest vocal performances into additional classics like "Crimson and Clover," "Blowin' In The Wind," and "Me and Bobby McGee." While touring the 12-track album and some of her greatest hits, Parton is also composing her first stage musical, "Nine to Five," which is set to debut on Broadway in 2007 (Parton is collaborating with the film's original screenwriter, Patricia Resnick).

Parton was raised in the deep conservative south of Tennessee's Great Smoky Mountains. In 1964 she moved to Nashville, recorded a single, and the rest is history. While driving through Kansas City on her tour bus, Parton gave me a call to discuss her current album, gay marriage, the lesbian rumors about her and best friend/assistant Judy Ogle, and her nearly 40-year marriage to Carl Dean.

Q. So did you set out to make a political album, Dolly?

A. No. In fact, I don't think a lot of these songs are political. I recorded twenty-five songs, including "The Games People Play," which is about how people won't tell you the truth and all that sort of stuff, and "Joy to the World." If [this album] does good I have enough recordings left over for another album.

Q. Some of your guest stars are politically aware and outspoken. When Bush first called for a constitutional amendment against gay marriage, Kris Kristofferson, who's recognized as an activist, spoke out against it. What are your thoughts on gay marriage, Dolly?

A. Well, I say it in a joking way, because so many people are down my neck about everything. Of course I believe in gay marriage—why shouldn't they have to suffer just like us straight couples do? (laughs) But I am for everybody. I believe everybody has the right to be who they are, do what they do, and have all the rights that they can have.

If you're going to live as a family and be a family you should have the same rights as everybody else.

Q. Let's talk about your dichotomous fan base for a moment. If I may use a breast analogy, on one teat you have the gays suckling, and on the other teat, the right-wing rednecks.

A. Yes, and don't think I don't pay for that! In fact, sometimes because I love all people I do get a lot of flack from the Bible Belt. So be it. I have many, many gay and lesbian friends, many people I've worked with through the years, many people in my own family. So I'm certainly not going to sit in a seat of judgment, nor am I the kind of person who's not going to say what I think and feel. I'll pay the consequences.

Q. Have any rednecks learned anything or become accepting of gays and lesbians because they've met under your umbrella?

A. I don't think people are going to learn anything they don't want to learn. The people who are totally against it are totally against it. But they're also against many other things. Years and years ago I had some [concert] bookings all around the South. There was a CMA awards show where I had won either the female or entertainer of the year and Charlie Pride, the black singer, presented it to me. When I went up on stage he kissed my cheek to congratulate me. And I got crosses burned in my yard and the biggest part of my dates canceled in the South, people calling me "nigger lover!" I thought, "How can people be so blind and stupid and cruel?"

Q. In 2004, the organizers of Gay Day at Dollywood were asked to remove "Dollywood" from the name of the event. And on the big day the KKK protested outside the park. What are your feelings on Gay Day at Dollywood?

A. I think it's fine. We're a place of business and all people are welcome. But the gays need to help me, too, because you have no idea what I put up with by accepting and loving everybody. In fact, I have rounds with my business people as well at the park. I say, "What would you have me do? Am I going to say they're not welcome here?" Of course not, because they are. It's just one of those things, damned if you do and damned if you don't. Just know that any of those things that happen like that are not my doing. I have to try and balance and do whatever I can because it's very possible I could even lose the park over things like that. But if that's the way it should go down I would give up the park before I would say anybody's not welcome—certainly not because of sexual orientation or color or any of that. You'll always be welcome in my heart and home.

Q. So what's going on with "Nine to Five" the musical?

A. Well, I'm sitting on my bus right now with a lap full of songs. I've written probably 20 songs already, there will probably be 13 to 15 pieces of music in the play.

Q. Who would you like to see play Doralee Rhodes, your part from the movie?

A. I don't know yet. She's going to have big ol' titties and big hair, though! I talk about that in some of the songs! One is called "Backwoods Barbie," and in it she's talking about "I'm a Backwoods Barbie, too much makeup too much hair a push up bra and heels, it might look artificial but where it counts I'm real."

Q. You were on Larry King recently and discussed scandals and gossip. What's the most outrageous rumor you've heard about yourself?

A. Oh hell, I don't know. Half of the articles will talk about how many lovers I have, male and female, and all the affairs I'm having and then in the same article they'll say I'm crippled-up and my back is broken and I can't get up. I'm like, buddy, I sure get around for a woman all crippled-up from them big ol' boobs!

Q. What about those Judy rumors?

A. Oh, Judy's my best friend since we were little bitty girls and we've never had any kind of sexual relationship. Because Judy's not married they've got to tag us together. And I'll joke with her—"They think you're a lesbian because you're not married." And she says, "Hell, I'd rather they say I'm a lesbian than call me an old maid!" We are very close and together all the time. She takes care of all my wardrobe and scheduling and because she doesn't have a family she's free to travel and she loves to travel. It's not like I'm carrying around this lover to accommodate me. We work our asses off!

Q. If you were to have a female lover or lesbian experience with someone, whom would you choose?

A. Oh, I don't think in those terms. I told you—I'm trash! When I'm thinking of having an affair I think in terms of all the good-looking guys. But I've never really had a desire to be with a woman and that's the honest truth. I love them all. I think women are beautiful. I have five sisters. I'm close to women and know them inside out, but I'm a guy's gal.

Q. You played the host of a radio advice show in 1992's "Straight Talk." Did a lot of people ask you for advice after that?

A. They did and they still do! They call the Dolly Mama! I've got something to say about everything—whether it's right or whether it's wrong you ask me I'll tell you what I think.

Q. Let's say a queen came to you with this one: "Oh Dolly, I met a guy in the bar last night and he said he loved me and I woke up and my watch was gone but I think he really loves me."

A. (Laughs) I get a lot of that kind of shit! I don't think I can help you there. Love is not only blind but it's also stupid! If that's what you're calling love I think you're looking for love in all the wrong places!

Q. There's one more bit of advice or knowledge I'd like to ask you for, Dolly, to coin a phrase from a song—when will we ever learn, when will we evvverrr learn?

A. I think that will have to be when God comes back to slap us upside the head and says "What are you people thinking?" It looks like we're never going to learn because it seems like we would rather fuss, fight and kill one another than try to put our arms around, accept and love each other. But there are those of us like John Lennon, myself and [others] that at least can imagine what that world will be like.

GOOD GOLLY, MISS DOLLY

Gerri Hirshey | March 2008 | *Ladies' Home Journal*

Gerri Hirshey first interviewed Dolly from a Green Bay, Wisconsin, motel room for *Family Circle* readers some thirty years before this *Ladies' Home Journal* cover story. Their reunion produced one of the more substantial and thorough interviews given by Dolly during a period in which most of her responses to questioners were essentially variations on her trademark Dollyisms. Amidst the wide-ranging topics here, Dolly poignantly recalls the last hours of Porter Wagoner, whose death occurred on October 28, 2007.

At the time of this feature, Dolly's *Backwoods Barbie* album was flying up the country charts, ultimately reaching Number 2, after having made an impressive debut at Number 17 on the all-encompassing *Billboard* 200 chart. The title track, "Backwoods Barbie," was written as part of the score for *9 to 5: The Musical*, which had been in development for several years. The musical adaptation of the 1980 film was unveiled in Los Angeles in the fall of 2008 and opened on Broadway the following year. —Ed.

In a rare exclusive interview, Dolly Parton opens up about the power of prayer, her battle with depression, and how she took control of her destiny

Up since 4 A.M., Dolly Parton is several hours into a workday that would set a lesser mortal whimpering. "I'm a workhorse dressed up as a show horse," she says as personal assistants, managers and techies bustle through the hallways of her Nashville business compound.

Click, clicky-click, Parton's high-heel boots rap a crisp flamenco beat on the Mexican-style tile. Despite the *va-va-voom* iconography—big hair, major makeup and that famous frontage—she is a finely cast porcelain miniature. At "5 foot nothing," barely 100 pounds tucked into tight, crisply tailored knee pants and Western shirt set, I doubt she could arm-wrestle an Olsen twin. Her waist size would turn Scarlett O'Hara emerald with envy. She is sporting a spiky, punkish wig du jour—a little startling this early in the morning.

Neatly she sidesteps a large live cactus, one of many spined and gnarly specimens here that are hardly native to Music City. "I bought this corner," she says of her business quarters, "and I built it up from scratch."

And how. Tucked away in an absolutely unfabulous part of town between car part joints and convenience stores, Parton's block-wide fortress is a mirage as extravagant and singular as the star herself. Built in Southwestern adobe style, replete with a Spanish mission bell tower, the gated complex is suffused with the complex bouquet of Nashville celebrity: strong coffee, breakfast biscuits and gravy, scented candles and nail varnish. In Parton's airy dressing room, a quartet of platinum wigs, in styles that range from Marie Antoinette to intergalactic space vamp, sits on their stands like backup singers.

"I call the whole complex Seven Angels Mission," she says. Ask why and she grins. "Right this way. I'll explain." This stuccoed labyrinth serves as the nerve center for Parton's booming enterprises: her new independent label, Dolly Records, which has just released her first mainstream country album in 17 years, *Backwoods Barbie*; Dollywood, her Tennessee theme park; four Dixie Stampede dinner theaters (think thundering buffalo between courses); a water park and her Imagination Library, a children's literacy charity so expansive it helped earn her a Living Legend award from the Library of Congress.

At 62 Parton is the iron butterfly of country music: most honored, most prolific (she's published more than 3,000 songs) and easily the most business savvy. Reported estimates of her worth hover at $300 million. The European leg of her tour is nearly sold out; Dollywood draws about 2 million visitors annually—more than three times the number who pay their respects at Elvis's Graceland. Nashville disk jockey Ralph Emery summed her up most succinctly: "She has the brains of a computer, the heart of an artist and the spirit of a minister."

Not bad for the fourth of 12 children born in a one-room cabin in Sevier County, Tennessee. The doctor who delivered Dolly Rebecca was paid with a sack of cornmeal by her tobacco-farming father, who supplemented the farm's table with whatever protein he could shoot, trap or net: squirrels, groundhogs, frogs, turtles. These days more than 1,000 hosts and waitstaff dish up a tonnage of barbecue and roast chicken at her dinner theaters.

"People think I'm always so happy," she says. "I'm not. But I always *try* to be happy. I have a lot to be grateful for." And lest she forget, there is a custom-built chapel here for attitude adjustment. "I go in there and pray all the time," she says. "Or I go in there because it's real quiet. And I just sit. And think. And breathe. I have a little church like this on all my properties. And in my house I have a little prie-dieu, just a place to kneel and say hey—to remember it's not about me, that I need to bend my knees and be humble." She laughs. "Now and then."

This chapel, with its murmuring fountain, holds the key to whatever happiness she's found—those mysterious seven angels. "There are seven people—whom I will not name—key people in my life that I feel God appointed to help me. Some you know—my husband, Carl [Dean], and Judy [Ogle, her pal since third grade]."

As to the rest, she's offering no hints. Nobody knows better when to hold her cards and when to flash them. Amid endless cycles of separation rumors, Parton has stayed married for 41 years—"but together for 43," she corrects. And despite her red-carpet life, nary a fan could pick the handsome, very private Carl Dean out of a checkout line at a Nashville Piggly Wiggly. Parton even had the artist stylize the faces of her personal angels in the etched-glass art piece she commissioned for the chapel— the better to keep their identities private. Though Parton has been the target of the tabloids' most creative and persistent ambushes since her early years as the bodaciously endowed protégé of the spangle-suited '60s country star Porter Wagoner, she is protective of those closest to her.

"The thing that bothers me the most about the tabloids is that sometimes they hurt members of my family. It's embarrassing. They don't know how to deal with it. I just say, 'Hey, you think I like this? I am truly, truly sorry. This is what you get for being my buddy. So please accept my apologies. There's not a thing I can do about it."

Musically, Parton takes it all on—image, sex, spirituality, friendship and m-e-n—in *Backwoods Barbie*. "It takes me around my whole life," she says. In the first single, "Better Get to Livin'" she confesses, "I'm not the Dalai Lama." Yet among family and friends she is considered so wise and centered they call her the Dolly Mama: confessor, confidante, platinum-hearted girlfriend.

Parton confesses she's feeling a little bit tender herself, owing to the recent death of Wagoner, who first showcased her, sang with her, cannily encouraged rumors of a romantic liaison, then sued her when she left to go solo. Their painful break was the inspiration for "I Will Always Love You," which she wrote and recorded divinely.

She says there was never any longtime feud. "I was with Porter the day he died," she says. He had lost consciousness and she joined his grown children in the hospital. "We sang and we cried and I sat and held Porter's hand. I had my hand on his heart 'cause it was just flyin'. I knew it wasn't long. He died at 8 that night. It was like losin' a piece of me, like losin' your daddy."

Her time with Wagoner was not the only charged relationship in her Nashville career. For years country music was run by a provincial male-dominated cadre of record execs. "When I came in," she recalls, "it was always that the men were better than us. We were second-class citizens." In 1968 Parton's frank, sassy "Just Because I'm a Woman" was not played by some U.S. radio stations. And Parton took plenty of heat from Nashville purists for '70s pop crossovers like "Here You Come Again."

By her 40s, "they stopped programming me on the radio because of my age," she says. In 2006 her musical achievements won her the coveted Kennedy Center Honors award. But back in Music City, it garnered her little r-e-s-p-e-c-t at the conference table. "Even with major labels I couldn't get a real good contract," she recalls. "They'd say, 'Hey now, let's get real, Dolly. It's not like you're as young as you used to be and you've had your day.'" Some of what she told them is inappropriate for a family magazine. But she was not about to be shown the pasture gate. "I still kept going," she says of those quiet days. "I kept saying, I'm going to make my records even if I have to sell them out of the back of my car."

The solution to her Nashville freeze-out was hardly that low-tech: A new Web site, DollyPartonMusic.net, dispenses information from her label and links to sites for Dollywood, her charity cookbook, *Dolly's Dixie Fixin's,* and a lively fan club that keeps the faithful updated on her latest career: Broadway lyricist and composer. "Backwoods Barbie," her CD's title cut, is from the score and lyrics she just completed for a stage musical of *9 to 5,* the 1980 movie she starred in alongside Jane Fonda and Lily Tomlin. The musical is set to open in Los Angeles this September, starring Megan Hilty (late of the Broadway smash *Wicked*) as Parton's stacked heart-of-gold secretary, Doralee Rhodes.

Parton feels that "Backwoods Barbie" is as autobiographical as "Coat of Many Colors," that '70s heartbreak plaint about her lean but loving childhood. "It's Doralee's story but it's really mine. Her statement is 'don't judge me by the cover 'cause I'm a real good book.' I know my style has been a joke to a lot of people and still is. I've used this line often but by now I hope people see that there's a brain beneath the wigs. And a heart beneath the boobs."

Ah, yes. Them. I wonder—don't we all?—just what Parton's relationship is with those storied breasts. Not long ago she playfully named them "shock" and "awe." "They do seem like public property in a way," she says. "They served me well—I don't know if I'm supporting them or they're supporting me. I've always had nice ones but of course I've had 'em jacked up a bit. And they're part of the persona—it almost takes a little pressure off me."

Given her philosophy that the best defense is a good offense, Parton has armed herself with a quiver of bristling zingers on cosmetic surgery. To wit: "I'll never graduate from collagen," and a quip she attributes to her husband: "Why should I cheat on her when I get a new woman every six months?"

Parton refused to have 50th- or 60th-birthday bashes; instead she marked the occasions, as she does each year, by writing a song on her birthday. "The numbers don't fit my mind," she says. "Ain't nothing I can do about the numbers but there's plenty I can do about how I look. And how I act."

The girl who sneakily surgically clipped the shoulder pads out of her grandma's coat to fashion a pair of falsies at 13 is not shy about most of her beauty secrets: "If somebody asks me point-blank, 'Have you had plastic surgery?' it's like, well, *duh*. I never talk about it unless someone asks me. But I don't want to lie about it."

The scent of temptation has begun to drift down the Seven Angels corridors, past the chapel and into Parton's pastel office: fajitas, nachos, burritos—an entire Tex-Mex lunch is being laid out. The boss seems immune to its seductions, making do with a sour candy. Parton gives no quarter to recent tabloid charges of eating disorders but she does listen to those closest to her. "My weight is in line for someone my size, but people are telling me I'm too skinny now so I'm going to gain 10 or 12 pounds. People worry about me but I'm healthy."

Somebody always has her back, she says. "I think there's nothing in the world like girlfriends. I have five sisters and every single one I could tell anything on earth—just like they can with me." I ask her to describe a perfect girls' night: "For me it's to be with friends where you can be your perfect self. Or your imperfect self. Whether you eat too much, drink too much, talk too much and get pissed off. Where you can feel like any emotion you have is okay. To cook, to laugh, to eat. To gossip, try to solve problems. Just being able to vent can be the best healing and therapy."

She doesn't know what she might have done without the girls when her hormones blindsided her with depression and weight gain in the early '80s, the only time she can recall her writing tablets filling with thoughts of self-pity and suicide. "It was just a big depression. Everybody goes through it, some more severe, some for longer periods of time. Having trouble with the hormones, I just didn't feel good."

She says it lasted 18 months and scared her witless: "Man, I saw how it is when people get depressed, get to drinking and drugs. I've never done that. And that's another reason I think I've lasted. Because I've had to kick my own behind. And if I don't kick my behind, somebody that loves me dearly would. A good friend or family member would say, Well, that's enough of that.""

She would not describe her husband as a confidant: "I don't like to trouble him," she says. "I always lean on my sisters or Judy." She insists she is still crazy about the skinny, gentle but hard-to-fathom young man she met at the Wishy-Washy Laundromat her first day in Nashville. She says that when he was courting her, Carl Dean never told her he loved her—never even proposed outright before they tied the knot on Memorial Day, 1966. His taciturn emotional style, she wrote in her 1994 autobiography, left her "as mixed up as a road lizard in a spin dryer."

That's also an apt description for those who have tried to dissect their unconventional union in the years since. "They have me and my husband divorcing every three years or so. We've never even talked about it. We've never had a big argument in our whole marriage, other than just smart off a little bit." Not many outsiders are invited to the farm they've long shared outside Nashville, nor is there a sighting of Dean at any performance or public event. "My husband and I are great friends," Parton says. "We were together before I became a star so we don't have that between us. I knew he loved me because of me."

They don't give a hoot what anyone else thinks of a lifestyle that requires long periods of separation and veers from Broadway to the barnyard. Ask about a typical day at home and she says, "I cook, he lays around in his La-Z-Boy. He goes over to the barn, mows a bit. We have an RV. We take it and go out to fast-food restaurants, stop at the supermarket, go out and picnic. It's private for us, we don't have to go into a restaurant. Our life is very simple and very peaceful."

She and Carl never had children but they more or less raised some of her younger siblings, who came to live with them over the years. She reasons, "I'm childlike enough that being with kids gives me an outlet, too. I love my nieces and nephews and though I don't have children of my own I realize that's probably good. Now everybody's kids can be mine. And I do love it."

Parton's voice is still strong and supple; even in sprawling arenas and cow palaces, the notes fall soft as mountain rain. Musically, her good girlfriends include Emmylou Harris and the much younger Alison

Krauss, who burst into awed tears the first three times they met until Parton begged her, "Knock it off, I'm not that special."

Ask her about what's ahead and she insists that she plans to do what mountain folk have traditionally done—go out singing. "I just think I'm going to do this for the rest of my life. I like what I do. I like who I am and I know who I am. I was a country girl. Grew up with real strong values. I felt like what talent I had God gave me. He wasn't going to hand me everything, he was just going to guide and help me."

She is on the move again, striding past a rack of sequined gowns, blowing away a pesky shock of wig that's been worrying her lipstick. *Clickety-click*, just try and keep up with the Dolly Mama, who is talking—again—about the brush of angel wings on her cheeks. "Every day I pray that God brings the right things and right people in, and takes the wrong out. I have such a good spiritual life."

DOLLY DIAMOND

On Death

"I want to be like one of those little fainting goats that get scared and then just fall over. I want to go and go and then drop dead in the middle of something I'm loving to do. And if that doesn't happen, if I wind up sitting in a wheelchair, at least I'll have my high heels on. It's not like this is a job that I hope I do good at. It's a joy, and it's just my nature. And I've made it into something I can make money doing. And thank God for that. Because nobody can ever make enough money for as many poor relatives as I've got. Somebody's got a sick kid, or somebody needs an operation, somebody ain't got this, somebody ain't got that. Or to give the kids all a car when they graduate. Let them shine, let them do what they want to. And not just family—it's for a lot of other people to have their dreams, too. Going into a new business, you make a certain amount of money, build your name, build your brand, and it's prestigious, but it gives other people opportunities, too, even if it's not something I particularly want to do myself. I'm creating jobs. I'm like Obama! O-Dolly and Obama!"

—To Jesse Green, *New York*, April 27, 2009

DOLLY DIAMOND

On Her Musical Life

"I don't want to wait until I'm dead for my music to become important. I want it to happen while I'm living because I'm living it every day."

—To Alison Moore, *Maverick*, September 2011

DOLLY DIAMOND

On *Joyful Noise*

"Many times, people tend to think you don't do anything because you're not on the big screen. But, the truth is, I just hadn't had any good scripts come along. I've had a lot of junk come my way. Right after I did the movie *Straight Talk*, I was in one of those periods where a lot of women find themselves—being told I was too old to play young parts and too young to play the older parts. Until something good like this movie came along, where I could basically play my age and still be young in spirit, I felt this was a perfect script for me. I thought this character was all the things that I believe myself to be. She's got a big heart, big hopes and big hair. . . . This was one of those scripts that when I read it, I thought it was not only a great movie, it's great for the times we're in: it's about family; it's about hope; it's about the music, so I thought was great. So many wonderful people worked on this film. I think it's going to appeal to all kinds of people. It was a joy to do and it has the perfect name. We did make a joyful noise and had a joyful time."

—To Sandra Varner, *Talk2SV.com*, January 2012

DOLLY DIAMOND

On Songwriting and Her Career

"Songwriting is just as natural as breathing to me. It was a song that brought me out of the Smoky Mountains and sent me everywhere around the world. Everywhere I've been it's because of the songs that I love to write. Now that I get older I get even more humble about it and I'm so grateful and thankful that I've had a chance to see my dreams come true unlike so many people in this world that never can say that. [This career]'s had its hard times for sure, and [is] not as glamorous as it looks, but I wouldn't trade it and I wouldn't change it and I'm grateful for it."

—To Jonathan Sanders, *Pop Matters*, May 20, 2014

Q&A: DOLLY PARTON ON LESBIAN WEDDING RUMORS & BOOB ADVICE, SAYS DRAG NAME IS "P. TITTY"

Chris Azzopardi | May 6, 2014 | *Between the Lines*

One of the more captivating interviews in support of Dolly's 2014 *Blue Smoke* album and world tour, this feature for the Michigan-based LGBT newspaper *Between the Lines* certainly wins the prize for longest and most attention-grabbing headline. The playful and teasing interrogator, Chris Azzopardi, quizzed Dolly on a number of gay-oriented topics, and the two bantered and chatted about the age-old lesbian rumors, her judgment-free stance on LGBT rights, and advice for drag queens.

Dolly has long embraced her role as a gay icon and news that she was recording an album aimed for her dance floor disciples surfaced as early as 2007. She confirmed the rumors during a press conference in 2014, revealing that she'd written a song called "Just a Wee Bit Gay." "It's a great little dance tune," she said. "It's funny, and it's got a lot of comic in it. . . . I do write a lot of songs along those lines with people that are different and are just themselves."

Understandably, many of Dolly's LGBT followers have made the pilgrimage to her Dollywood theme park in East Tennessee. The flocking of fans was detailed in a 2014 piece in the *New York Times* entitled "Dollywood: A Little Bit Country, a Little Bit Gay," with reporter Kim Severson observing: "There were large groups of Southern Baptists who showed up in matching T-shirts that proclaimed their church affiliations. There were exhausted families from North Carolina trying to get grandma out of the wilting heat. There were rowdy college students from Ohio on a summer road trip, and a single mom from Georgia looking to entertain her young son. And then there was us, a middle-aged lesbian couple in expensive yet practical footwear who traveled from Atlanta to see if we could find the campy gay undercurrent that runs through Dollywood, arguably the most culturally conservative amusement park in the country." Severson concluded that "at Dollywood, the place on a Venn diagram where gay camp and Southern camp overlap, cinnamon rolls might be the great equalizer."

Although the contrasting factions of Dollywood-goers do their best to coexist, there are several noteworthy bits of gay-related history concerning the park. In the mid-2000s, fans organized an annual "Gay Day" (à la Disneyland), however the gathering was never endorsed by the park. In fact, organizers were asked to stop using the Dollywood name. The event ceased after threats were made by members of the area Ku Klux Klan. And in 2011, international headlines were made when a lesbian visitor to Splash Country, Dollywood's water park, was asked to turn her "Marriage Is So Gay" T-shirt inside out. At the time, park officials explained that they often asked people with shirts that could be deemed offensive to cover them or turn them inside out. Dolly issued a statement reiterating the park's dress code, but also making a public apology to the embarrassed guest. "We're in the business for all families," she later told the New York Times. "A family is a family whether you're a gay family or a straight family. If that's your family you should be treated with the utmost respect, and we do that no matter what. I say a good Christian wouldn't be judging anyway. We're supposed to love and accept each other." —Ed.

When Dolly Parton calls you, greeting you by name with her unmistakable Tennessee twang, it's a good idea to immediately establish that the lady on the line is the actual legend herself.

"Am I talking to the real Dolly or is this an impersonator?" I ask, just to be sure.

Proving she's as sharp as the icon she's become over the last six decades—easily the most honored female country music artist of all time, inspiring drag queens galore—Parton is quick with her comeback: "Oh, there's no such thing as a real Dolly. I'm as real as you're gonna get!"

Very real, as it turns out. Currently promoting her 42nd studio album, "Blue Smoke," Parton talked about the country music community evolving beyond labeling gay people "perverse," addressed rumors of her recent lesbian wedding and dished tit tips to drag queens (more stuffing, girls).

Outside of the rhinestones and big platinum hair, why do gay people identify and empathize with you?

Did you say empathize or sympathize? (Laughs) I think there's some of both! Actually, I've been around so long people just kind of feel like they know me. They've seen me enough. I'm more like a favorite aunt or an older sister or somethin', so I just think people know so much about me they just feel like I'm part of them. I hope that's what they think. That's what it seems like!

I see you as our fairy godmother.

(Laughs) Yeah, I do look like the fairy godmother!

You've acknowledged that you felt like an outsider since you were a kid. "Coat of Many Colors" really is about feeling different. What role has that feeling of being an outsider played in the relationship that you have with the gay community?

Well, I do believe that I have a lot of gay fans because I think they do accept me as I am—the differences in me—and I think they know that I see that and love that in everybody else. I am not a judgmental person. I'm a very loving and accepting person. I try to see the good in everybody and I don't care who people are as long as they're themselves, whatever that is. That old saying "to thine own self be true"—no truer words were ever spoken, and I'm just honored and proud to be accepted.

It's more than just you being non-judgmental. You said growing up you felt different, something many gay people can empathize with. Do you sense that relationship?

Yes, I do. I've always felt that. I've always felt that's one of the things that's drawn my gay fans to me. They do know that I do feel different, and all of my life I *will* be different. I always have been. But I enjoy and appreciate and respect that difference in myself just like I do in other people. God made me the way that I am and it's my business to be true to that.

If everyone was free of judgment like you are, what might the world be like?

It'd be a lot better, I can tell you that. But people love to hate, and it's just unfortunate but that's the way it is. People like to judge, they like to condemn, they won't accept anything they don't understand—that's just too bad. We have to work at those things anyway, but most people are not willing to. A lot of people are just blind and they're not seeing through the spiritual eye, and we need to look that way and then we would be more forgiving, more loving and more accepting.

You were one of the first major country artists to advocate for gay rights. Why did you decide to take that step and stand up for LGBT equality?

Why wouldn't I stand up for everybody, for all people? In the country field, we're brought up in spiritual homes, we're taught to "judge not lest you be judged," and it's always been a mystery to me how people jump all over things just to criticize, condemn and judge other people when that is so un-Christian—and they claim to be good Christians! We're supposed to love one another. We're supposed to accept and love one another. Whether we do or not, that's a different story. But that's what we're supposed to do.

What are your thoughts on the progress the country music community has been making as a whole when it comes to embracing its gay listeners?

In defense of a lot of people, they didn't have as true of an understanding as they do now. Now people really see that this is real, these are real people with real feelings, that this is who they really are. I think a lot of people, anytime you talked about gay people, thought "perverse."

Now, they're being more educated that this is who people really are. There's just been so much made of (gay rights) in the last two or three years and it's been brought to the front so people can really see it and be like, "Yeah, I guess there are a lot more gay people than we ever knew! I have a better understanding of it now. I know that these people are for real." I think they're getting that now.

I think it was just a lack of knowledge. And when you're with someone, of course you should have your rights. You're gonna be with who you're gonna be with even if you starve to death and have no privileges and no rights. I think people understand that more now.

You've been such a wonderful ally to us . . . so much so that people have actually mistaken you as a lesbian yourself.

(Laughs) Well, you know what, it's true. In fact, there was some story recently (in the National Enquirer) where I was supposedly marrying my longtime friend Judy (Ogle) and that my husband was OK with it! I thought, "Where did they come up with all this?" I am not gay, but if I were I would be the first one running out of the closet.

And right into Judy's arms?

Yeah, who knows! I might've said, "Judy, you wanna get something going with me?" (Laughs) But our friendship is just a precious friendship.

What do you say to "From Here to the Moon and Back," your love duet with Willie Nelson on "Blue Smoke," being used for the first dance at a gay wedding?

I would be honored. That would be a beautiful wedding song, "From Here to the Moon and Back"—wow! People often use "I Will Always Love You"—I wrote "I Will Always Love You" as a wedding song too— and it really kind of speaks to that, but yeah, "From Here to the Moon and Back" would be a beautiful wedding song. If you get married, you can play it!

What is something about your life that people would be most surprised by?

I can't imagine a thing that people don't already know about me. I think people would be surprised at how really at-home I am. I look like a party doll but I'm very home-lovin'. I'm a homebody, and I'm family-oriented. I don't get out much unless it's a special occasion. So I guess people might be surprised at just how calm I really am.

When you look at yourself in the mirror, what do you see?

I see ways to improve myself. I've never been a true beauty and I'm always thinking, "I need to do this, or I could look better than that," but I guess we all have that.

You've said that drag queens do you better than you. Have you learned anything about yourself from watching people impersonate you?

Most of the drag queens are about six feet tall already . . . and then they put on those high heels! I ain't big as a minute, so I always think, what I've learned about myself is, I'm not tall. I'm definitely even shorter than I knew I was!

But actually, I am very honored when the drag queens all do their thing because I think it's a big compliment. I get a big kick out of some of them. Some of them are really good! Some of them are . . . comical.

Some of them are so good you once lost a look-alike contest that you were in.

(Laughs) I entered one of the Dolly look-alike contests down on Santa Monica at one of the gay clubs down there—I lived right up the street— so I just kind of over exaggerated myself and went and joined the party and walked across the stage. I got less applause than anybody. It's pretty bad when I lose a Dolly Parton look-alike contest!

If you were a drag queen, what would be your drag name?

P. Titty . . . like P. Diddy!

What tips do you have for drag queens who want to get your bust size just right?

Oh heavens . . . I'm so little is why my boobs look so big. But (drag queens) are already big! They're gonna need to really do some paddin'! I'm larger than life, so just get them boobs the way that they fit into proportion to your body. Put it out there, whatever your imagination is of me.

THE INTERVIEW: THE INDUSTRY OF DOLLY PARTON

Elio Iannacci | May 11, 2014 | *Maclean's*

Dolly's *Blue Smoke* album was released May 13, 2014, and entered the *Billboard* country charts at Number 2, the pop charts at Number 6. It was also Dolly's first Top 10 album on the *Billboard* 200 and was her highest debuting solo album on that chart to date. Several notable duets appeared on the album, including "From Here to the Moon and Back" with Willie Nelson, and "You Can't Make Old Friends," her long-overdue reunion with Kenny Rogers, which garnered a Grammy nomination for the duo. In this feature from the popular Canadian weekly news magazine *Maclean's*, Dolly delved into the stories of the songs from the new album, shared memories of Andy Warhol and Studio 54, and discussed plans for a vow renewal with Carl Dean on their upcoming fiftieth anniversary. —Ed

The legendary singer speaks on Miley Cyrus, feminism, and her secret to a successful 50-year marriage

Andy Warhol once described Dolly Parton as "a walking monologue." Over a career that spans more than five decades, the 68-year-old singer, actress and highly regarded songwriter (she's written thousands, including megahits such as "I Will Always Love You") has worked with everyone from Willie Nelson to Queen Latifah to Norah Jones. On her soon-to-be-launched album, *Blue Smoke*, her 42nd, the Grammy-winning, Oscar-, Tony- and Emmy-nominated performer brazenly rearranges hits by Bon Jovi and Bob Dylan alongside her own country tracks. They recall her time toughing it out as the fourth of 12 children raised with no electricity or running water in the foothills of the Appalachian Mountains in Tennessee.

Q: *Fans claim your upbeat songs about cheaters and dead-in-the-water relationships are cheaper than therapy. The way you approach Bob Dylan's* Don't Think Twice *makes me think you and Dylan had a fling. Did you?*

A: It does sound like I dated and dumped him! I'm gonna use that in my next stage show! No, me and Bob didn't date, but I always say I'm going to do a whole album of Bob Dylan songs called *Dolly Does Dylan*.

Q: *On* Blue Smoke, *you sing from the perspective of a child coming from a broken family in* Miss You, *a gospel singer in* He's Everything *and a man who murders his wife in* Banks of the Ohio. *How do you get into character?*

A: I sing as an actress, so it's natural for me. Whatever I'm singing about, I just become the story. I always loved that old song *Banks of the Ohio*—it was always such a man's song, so I've always wanted to record it. To change it up, I wrote a [spoken-word] front piece to it that presented myself as a journalist going into jail and doing an interview with this person who has committed this crime. Years ago, before they had newspapers, news was carried through song.

Q: *The track sounds like a Flannery O'Connor short story. She had a way with making villains likable in her fiction. Where did that curiosity to explore these sinister themes come from?*

A: My childhood. We grew up with mama singing all these morbid old songs but they were beautiful. Oh, she'd cry and we'd cry. It would make your heart heavy, but it kind of instilled a type of emotion in my psyche.

Q: *Websites like* Jezebel *have lengthy debates on whether or not you are a feminist icon. Is that a crown you're proud to wear?*

A: Yes, it is. I don't think of myself as a feminist, but if they call me a feminist icon, that's fine. I've always stood up for women and myself in general. I have a great love and respect, because I have had all these beautiful sisters, aunts and my grandmas, but I love men. I totally understand the nature of men.

Q: You were on the Today Show a couple of weeks ago and you were talking about a 9 to 5 reunion. Is this still going to happen?

A: On Netflix, Jane [Fonda] and Lily [Tomlin] have a new show together, and I'm going to probably visit that now and then, but I don't know that we're ever going to get to do a reunion of *9 to 5*. If we do, we're going to have to call it "95."

Q: Why do you think that film still gets written about today?

A: There are certainly a lot of things that still need to change, when it comes to women in the workforce. That little movie definitely had its message and it really started a lot of balls rolling, where women were concerned. People enjoyed the three personalities stringin' up their boss because everybody wants to kill their boss—male or female. It definitely touched a nerve. I admire Jane Fonda for coming up with that whole idea.

Q: Songs like Just Because I'm a Woman and Dumb Blonde also talk about some serious double standards women face. At the time you released those songs, a lot of people didn't want to hear what you had to say.

A: There were people who wouldn't play my stuff on the radio! *Just Because I'm a Woman* stayed on, like, number 1 for seven years in South Africa, but there were times in the States when people thought it was a little too much. I wasn't even thinking in terms of being a feminist; I was just writing my feelings. That song was written by me because of a situation with my husband. He'd never asked me if I'd ever been with anybody else in bed. After we married, he did. I didn't feel like I should be lying to my new husband, so I told him the truth and it just crushed him. I thought, "Well, look, my mistakes are no worse than yours." I did get some bad letters.

Q: How did you respond to that negativity?

A: My attitude was, "Well, to hell with you!" I write what I write, say what I say, 'cause I feel what I feel, and if I did it different, it would make me a liar! So I'd rather be an honest person than a good liar.

Q: In two years, you'll celebrate your 50th anniversary with your husband. How do you make it work with so much touring? Skype?

A: We don't do Skype. He's glad to get me gone when I'm gone. I'm glad to be gone when I'm gone, because we're both very independent. He's such a homebody, and I'm a total gypsy. That's one of the things that's worked out well. We call each other. We talk for a long, long time on Sundays. One of the reasons I think I've done so well is because I've had the freedom to work. I never had children and I never had a husband who's wanted to bitch about everything I did.

Q: *What plans do you have for your anniversary?*

A: We may have a big old wedding again out at our home place in Brentwood.

Q: *I had to cross the border to interview your goddaughter, Miley Cyrus, a few months back, and a U.S. customs officer found out that's who I was interviewing and almost didn't let me into the U.S. Why do you think so many people are afraid of her brand of sexuality?*

A: The reason she had to be so drastic is to try to get out of that Hannah Montana [phase]. She's very proud of that role, but it's Shirley Temple for the older folks. Nobody wanted her to grow up, either. I think people just think of Miley as their little daughter or granddaughter, so they take it personally. I tell you, I understood why she had to go to such extremes to really make her point. She's so talented. She's so smart.

Q: *Could you relate to Miley?*

A: Yes, I could. First of all, I wouldn't have had the legs and the beauty to have pulled that off. Miley knows what she's doing; I hope she does. If she plays her cards right, she can have a long and good career. She did it like a shock jock. She had to go that way.

Q: *Isabella Rossellini recently said she feels more beautiful as an older woman than she ever did as a model. Do you think you've grown into a version of yourself you're happy with?*

A: Well, I never have thought I was beautiful and I never can get beautiful enough. I'm always doing whatever I can to look as good as I can, nipping and tucking if necessary. When you're older, you probably look more bizarre to people. But I don't care. I'm just totally convinced that it's more important that I be happy with me.

Q: *I was reading Andy Warhol's diaries and he mentioned you guys hung out quite a bit in New York. What kind of impact did that time have? Did you feel like an outsider looking in?*

A: You want to know what I really think? When I was with Andy Warhol, I thought, "God, his wig looks cheaper than mine!" I never felt like a fish out of water. I always felt like I belonged where I was. It was quite amazing when we used to all go to Studio 54. I couldn't believe what I was seeing, but I enjoyed it. I loved the music, but it was just fascinating to me to meet all these famous people, the Calvin Kleins and Diane von Fürstenbergs and the Barry Dillers of the world.

Q: *You read a lot while you're on the road.*

A: I read all the time, at least 50 or 52 books a year. I read a book just recently by a new writer, Peace Like a River [by Leif Enger]—I really enjoyed that. Now I'm reading The Signature of All Things [by Elizabeth Gilbert].

Q: *When it comes to how you view your work—the musicals, the theme park, the clothing line, the perfumes, etc.—do you consider yourself more of an industry than an artist?*

A: I do think that. I've got to be responsible for everything. That's why I still have to work so hard. I wanted all these things and now I've got them. I guess you could say I dreamed myself into a corner. I'm going to come out fighting. I got new dreams to dream. I don't have anything else to do. I don't have children. My husband doesn't care if I'm home or not!

Q: *With so many fingers in so many pies, do you ever feel your work is compromised?*

A: When I think somebody's acting more like a pimp than a manager, and I'm more of a prostitute than an artist, I always tell them where to put it. People will use you as long as you let them. So I just say, "Hey, enough's enough," and things get cleared up.

Q: *What's next for you?*

A: I'm writing my life story as a musical and I want to see my life story onscreen, as well.

Q: *Who would you love to play you? Taylor Swift?*

A: Oh, she's too tall for me, Lord have mercy. Maybe Reese Witherspoon! She's little. We'll just have to get her a big old boob job. No, Taylor's way too classy! Hopefully, it will be done in a year and a half. After that, I am going to [release] a dance album.

DOLLY DIAMOND

On Whitney Houston

"It was only when Whitney Houston took ["I Will Always Love You"] all over the world with *The Bodyguard* that it really became what it is today. So I always think of it as our song. It just killed me when they lifted her coffin up at the funeral and when they started into that song. Man, it was like you could stab me into the heart with a dagger. It just, and that's when I broke down over her I mean I really was, like everybody else, upset and hated it, but it was just then that I just started boohoo'n. I thought, those are my words, that's my song—it's her song. And I was thinking I bet you that won't be the only coffin lifted up for that song to play. And when I'm dead it will probably be the same thing. It's just overwhelming to me. But, I will always be grateful and thankful to her for making that song all the things that it is."

—To Skip Matheny, *American Songwriter*, June 23, 2014

DOLLY DIAMOND

On Dreams

"Yes, I have always been a dreamer, and yes, I have always tried. And dreams are special things. But dreams are of no value if they're not equipped with wings and feet and hands and all that. If you're gonna make a dream come true, you gotta work it. You can't just sit around. That's a wish. That's not a dream."

—To Lisa Butterworth, *Bust*, June/July 2014

DOLLY DIAMOND

On Her Music and Stories

"Everything there is to know about me is in my music. My ups, my downs, my good- and my not-so-good times are all there in the stories I write. Every song I sing reveals a little more about my heart and what guides me through this life. I hope that if folks find it important or helpful it is because it gives them a voice and a knowledge that other people have the same feelings that they have, and that they're not alone."

—To Deborah Evans Price, *Live Happy*, December 2015

ABOUT THE CONTRIBUTORS

Cindy Adams is a longtime columnist for the *New York Post*, a pop culture/entertainment writer, and a former ABC News correspondent. She is the author of *The Gift of Jazzy* and *Living a Dog's Life: Jazzy, Juicy, and Me*.

Chris Azzopardi is the editor of Q Syndicate, the international LGBT wire service. He's a contributor to *Entertainment Tonight*'s ETonline. com, and his interviews have appeared in *Cosmopolitan*, *E! Online*, *Us Weekly*, *USA Today*, and *Vanity Fair*.

Jerry Bailey was a music reporter for the *Tennessean* in the early 1970s and later worked in media and corporate relations with various record labels, including ABC Records, MCA Universal, and BMI. He spent more than a dozen years with Country Music Television and The Nashville Network, and after nearly forty years in the business, retired in 2011.

A prolific songwriter, **Everett Corbin** spent much of his life as a journalist and served as the editor of *Music City News* in 1966 and 1967. His book *Storm Over Nashville: A Case Against Modern Country Music* was published in 1980 and chronicled a battle between "traditionalist-purists" and "modern" country musicians during the 1970s. Corbin died in 2012 at the age of eighty.

As a journalist, **Laura Cunningham** has written many columns for the *New York Times*, the *New York Observer*, and the *London Times*, as well as magazine articles for *Cosmopolitan*, *Esquire*, *Ladies' Home Journal*, and other periodicals. She is a playwright, journalist, and the author of nine books.

Writer, performer, talk radio host, and comedian **Frank DeCaro** is the author of several pop culture–oriented books, including *The Dead Celebrity Cookbook: A Resurrection of Recipes from More than 145 Stars of Stage and Screen.* From 2004 to 2016 he hosted *The Frank DeCaro Show*, a popular daily live radio show on SiriusXM's OutQ.

Ralph Emery, a 2007 Country Music Hall of Fame inductee, is the industry's most celebrated radio and television host. Called "Country's Carson" by *People* magazine, his long-running radio show became the most popular in America and was broadcast in thirty-eight states for more than fifteen years. Emery also hosted the *Nashville Now* TV series for ten years on The Nashville Network.

Born and raised in New York, **Lawrence Ferber** is an arts and travel journalist whose writing has appeared in the *New York Post*, the *Advocate*, *Time Out New York*, *Passport Magazine*, *National Geographic Traveler*, and many other magazines and newspapers. He also cowrote the award-winning 2010 LGBT rom-com *BearCity* and authored its 2013 novelization.

Veteran music journalist **Chet Flippo** joined the staff of *Rolling Stone* as a contributing editor and later became a senior editor in 1977. He also wrote articles for the *New York Times*, *TV Guide*, and *New York*. Flippo served as the Nashville bureau chief for *Billboard* (1995 to 2000) and was editorial director of Country Music Television and CMT.com until his death in 2013.

Best known for his *Playboy* interviews, **Lawrence Grobel** has been called "the Mozart of interviewers." He has written hundreds of articles for magazines and newspapers, including the *New York Times*, *Rolling Stone*, *Redbook*, and *Cosmopolitan*. His most recent book (his twenty-fifth) is *You, Talking to Me: What I Learned Along the Celebrity Trail.*

Active in the antiwar, civil rights, and labor movements of the 1960s and 1970s, **Gene Guerrero** was a founder of Atlanta's underground newspaper, *The Great Speckled Bird* (1968–1976), where he wrote about country and bluegrass music. Since then, Guerrero has worked to support various human rights issues and criminal justice reform.

Gerri Hirshey has been a features writer, columnist, reporter, and essayist for the *Washington Post*, the *New York Times Magazine, Vanity Fair, GQ, Esquire*, and *New York*. Beginning in the 1980s, Hirshey became *Rolling Stone*'s first female contributing editor. Her most recent book, *Not Pretty Enough: The Unlikely Triumph of Helen Gurley Brown*, was published in 2016.

Jack Hurst is a historian and acclaimed journalist who covered the country music industry for over forty years. He has written for newspapers including the *Chicago Tribune, Philadelphia Inquirer*, and the *Tennessean*. Hurst has also authored a number of well-received books on the Civil War, including *Nathan Bedford Forrest: A Biography* and *Men of Fire*.

Fashion and pop culture expert **Elio Iannacci** is an award-winning journalist and writer whose work has appeared in publications such as *Maclean's*, the *Globe and Mail*, the *National Post, UR Chicago*, and *Flare*. He has been featured on a number of television shows, including *CNN Showbiz Tonight, MTVCanada, Fashion Television, Much Music*, and *Entertainment Tonight*.

Cliff Jahr's written work appeared in *Cosmopolitan, Ladies' Home Journal*, the *New York Times, People, Playboy, Rolling Stone*, and the *Village Voice*. He also collaborated with Cheryl Crane, daughter of Lana Turner, to write the best selling *Detour: A Hollywood Story*. Jahr died in 1991 at the age of fifty-four.

Jim Jerome was an associate editor at *People* magazine and has written for *GQ, Playboy*, and the *New York Times Magazine*. He has also cowritten several books, including *Papa John: An Autobiography by John Phillips of the Mamas and the Papas*, and *By All Means Keep Moving* by Marilu Henner.

A former *New York Times*' "Hers" columnist, **Joyce Maynard** is a contributor to NPR's *All Things Considered*, as well as *O, the Oprah magazine, Ladies' Home Journal, More, Redbook*, and other magazines. She the author of the bestselling *At Home in the World*, as well as many novels, including *To Die For*, *The Usual Rules*, and her most recent, *Under the Influence*.

Maura Moynihan is an author, fashion designer, actress, and singer. Her musical career was launched by Andy Warhol, who placed her on the coveted cover of his *Interview* magazine. She has worked as a reporter for the *New York Post*, and is also the author of several books, including *Yoga Hotel* and *Cover Girl*.

Linda Ray is a freelance writer and a former contributing editor for *No Depression*, the magazine. She has also contributed to the *Chicago Tribune*, the *Chicago Reader*, *Option*, *Magnet*, *Illinois Entertainer*, *Phoenix New Times*, *Tucson Weekly*, and the *San Francisco Bay Guardian*'s first online music venture, *Earshot*.

Jeremy Rush worked for a number of years as a freelance writer in Nashville, Tennessee, and spent nearly six years as media relations manager at the Country Music Hall of Fame and Museum. Rush received a bachelor's degree in journalism from Middle Tennessee State University. He's contributed to WPLN Nashville Public Radio, the *Nashville Scene*, and various Vanderbilt University publications, as well as print publications in Kenya and Uganda.

William Stadiem was a columnist for Andy Warhol's *Interview* magazine and a restaurant critic for *Los Angeles* magazine. He is the author of twelve books, including the bestselling *Marilyn Monroe Confidential*, *Dear Senator*, and *Mr. S: My Life with Frank Sinatra*.

Pop art icon **Andy Warhol** was a visual artist, filmmaker, author, art collector, and founder of *Interview* magazine. Warhol died in in 1987 at the age of fifty-eight. The Andy Warhol Museum in his hometown of Pittsburgh, Pennsylvania, features an extensive collection of his art and archives, and is the largest museum in the United States dedicated to a single artist.

CREDITS

Every effort has been made to contact copyright holders, and I gratefully acknowledge the help of all who gave permission for material to appear in this book. If an error or omission has been made, please bring it to the attention of the publisher.

"Interview: *Music City News*" by Everett Corbin, transcribed and used in cooperation with the Center for Popular Music, Middle Tennessee State University Special Collections.

"Miss Dolly Parton: Blonde Bombshell of Great Smokies" by Jack Hurst. From *The Tennessean*, September 27, 1970, © 1970 Gannett-Community Publishing. All rights reserved. Used by permission and protected by the Copyright Laws of the United States. The printing, copying, redistribution, or retransmission of this Content without express written permission is prohibited.

"Porter Wagoner and Dolly Parton" by Gene Guerrero, reprinted by permission of the author, with special thanks to *The Great Speckled Bird* digital archive at Georgia State University.

"Say Hello to the Real Miss Dolly" by Jerry Bailey. From *The Tennessean*, October 20, 1974, © 1974 Gannett-Community Publishing. All rights reserved. Used by permission and protected by the Copyright Laws of the United States. The printing, copying, redistribution, or retransmission of this Content without express written permission is prohibited.

"Interview: Dolly Parton" by Chet Flippo, reprinted by permission of the estate of Chet Flippo. "*PLAYBOY* INTERVIEW: DOLLY PARTON: A Candid Conversation with the Curvaceous Queen of Country Music" by Lawrence Grobel. Archival material from *Playboy* magazine. Copyright © 1978 by Playboy. Reprinted with permission. All rights reserved.

"Dolly Parton: The Sexy Superstar of Country Pop" by Laura Cunningham, reprinted by permission of Hearst Communications, Inc.

"Q&A: Dolly Parton on Lesbian Wedding Rumors & Boob Advice, Says Drag Name Is 'P. Titty'" by Chris Azzopardi, reprinted by permission of the author.

"The Interview: The Industry of Dolly Parton" by Elio Iannacci, reprinted by permission of the author.

INDEX